DON'T TOY WITH ME, MISS NAGATORO

⑮

NANASHI

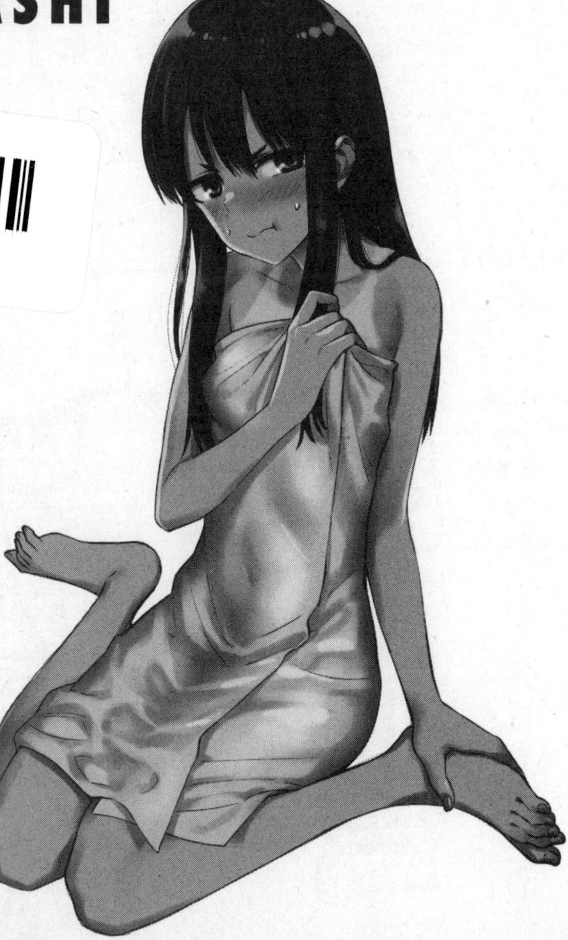

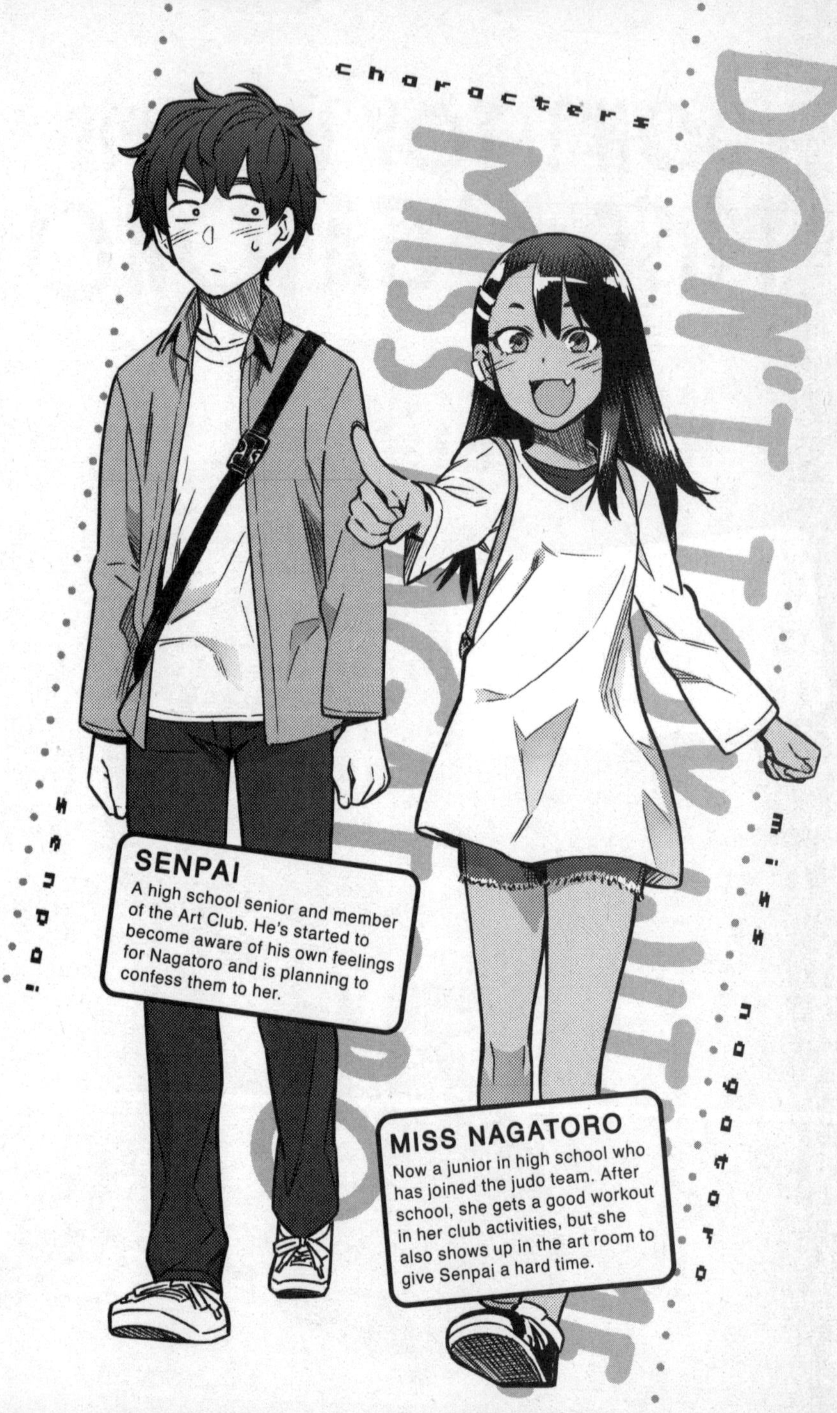
characters
miss nagatoro
senpai
SENPAI
A high school senior and member of the Art Club. He's started to become aware of his own feelings for Nagatoro and is planning to confess them to her.
MISS NAGATORO
Now a junior in high school who has joined the judo team. After school, she gets a good workout in her club activities, but she also shows up in the art room to give Senpai a hard time.

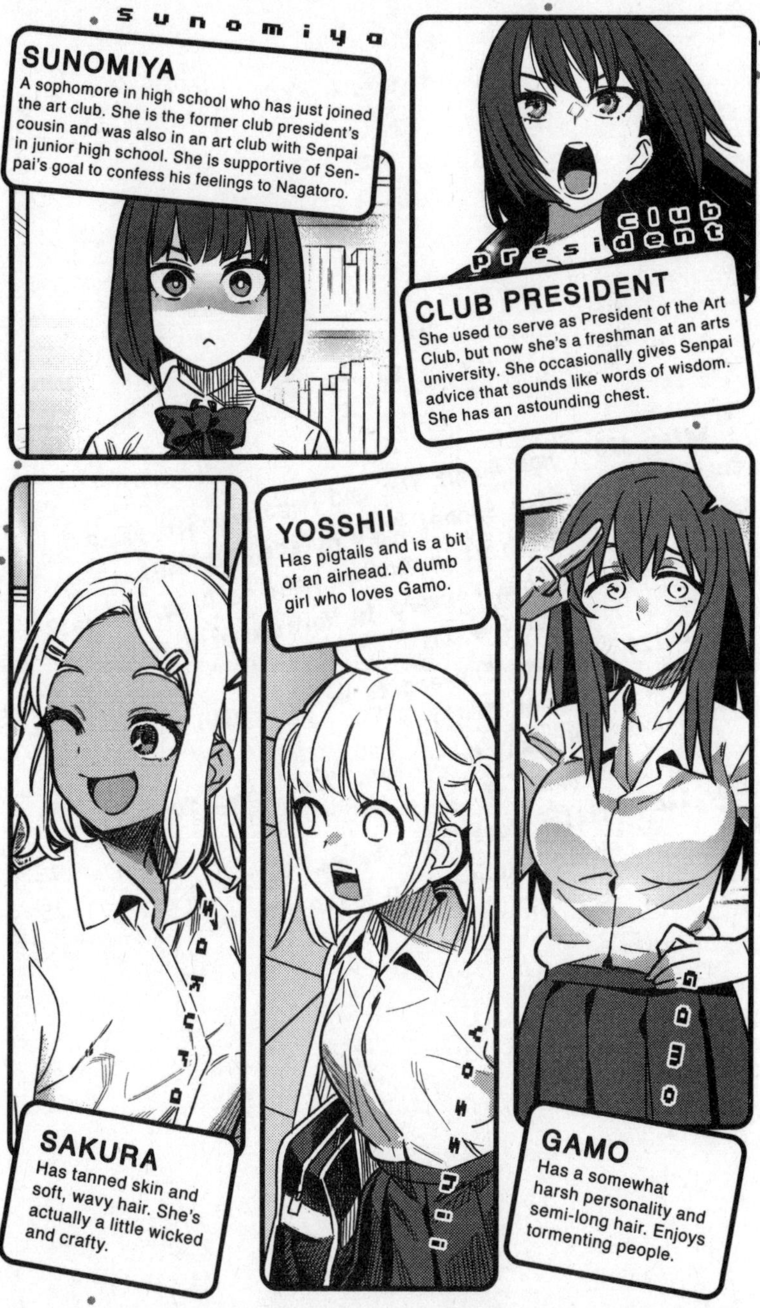
club president
CLUB PRESIDENT
She used to serve as President of the Art Club, but now she's a freshman at an arts university. She occasionally gives Senpai advice that sounds like words of wisdom. She has an astounding chest.
sunomiya
SUNOMIYA
A sophomore in high school who has just joined the art club. She is the former club president's cousin and was also in an art club with Senpai in junior high school. She is supportive of Senpai's goal to confess his feelings to Nagatoro.
gamo
GAMO
Has a somewhat harsh personality and semi-long hair. Enjoys tormenting people.
yosshii
YOSSHII
Has pigtails and is a bit of an airhead. A dumb girl who loves Gamo.
sakura
SAKURA
Has tanned skin and soft, wavy hair. She's actually a little wicked and crafty.

CONTENTS

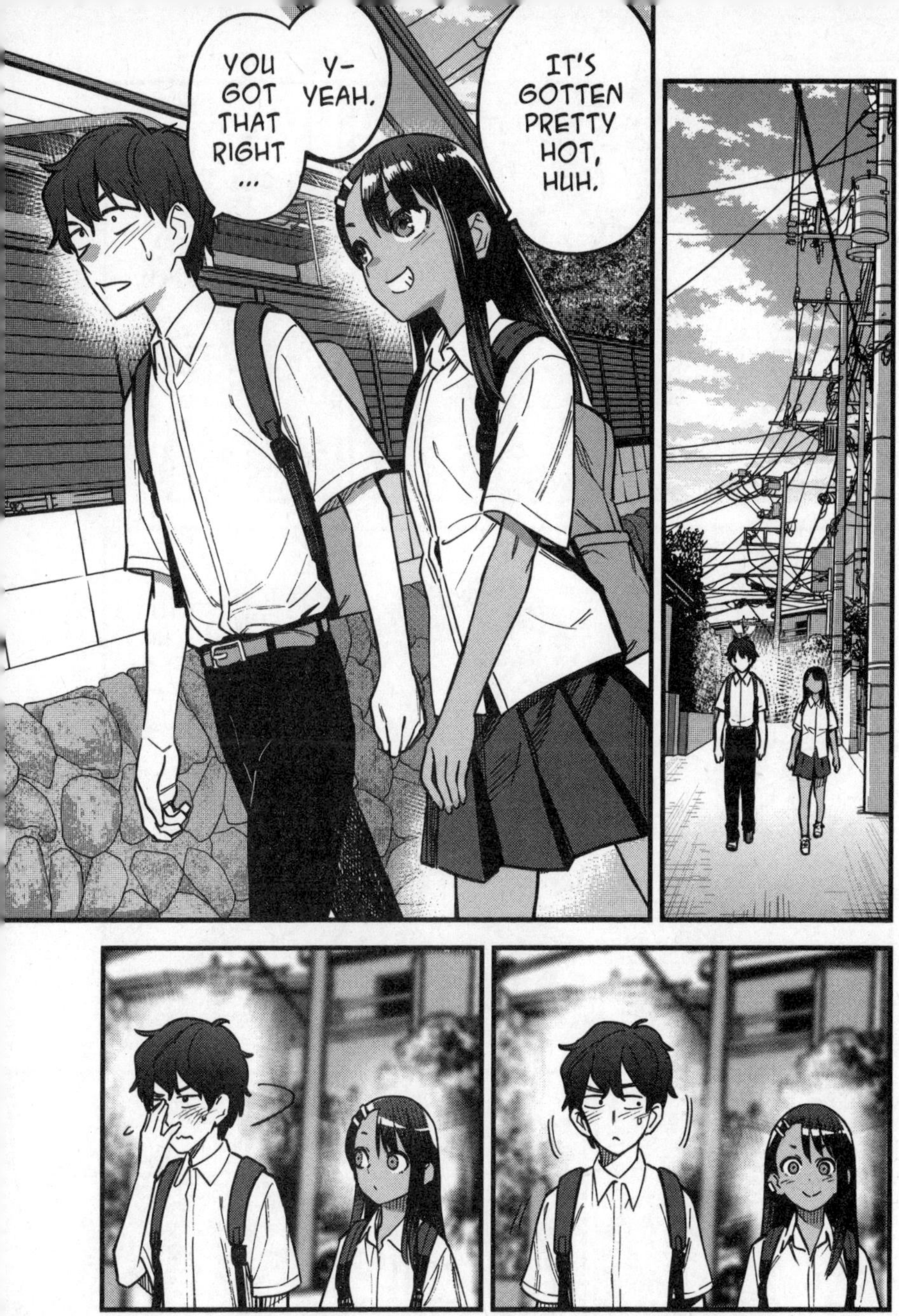
IT'S GOTTEN PRETTY HOT, HUH.
Y-YEAH.
YOU GOT THAT RIGHT ...

CHAPTER 110: HOW ABOUT YOU AND NAGATORO-SENPAI...?

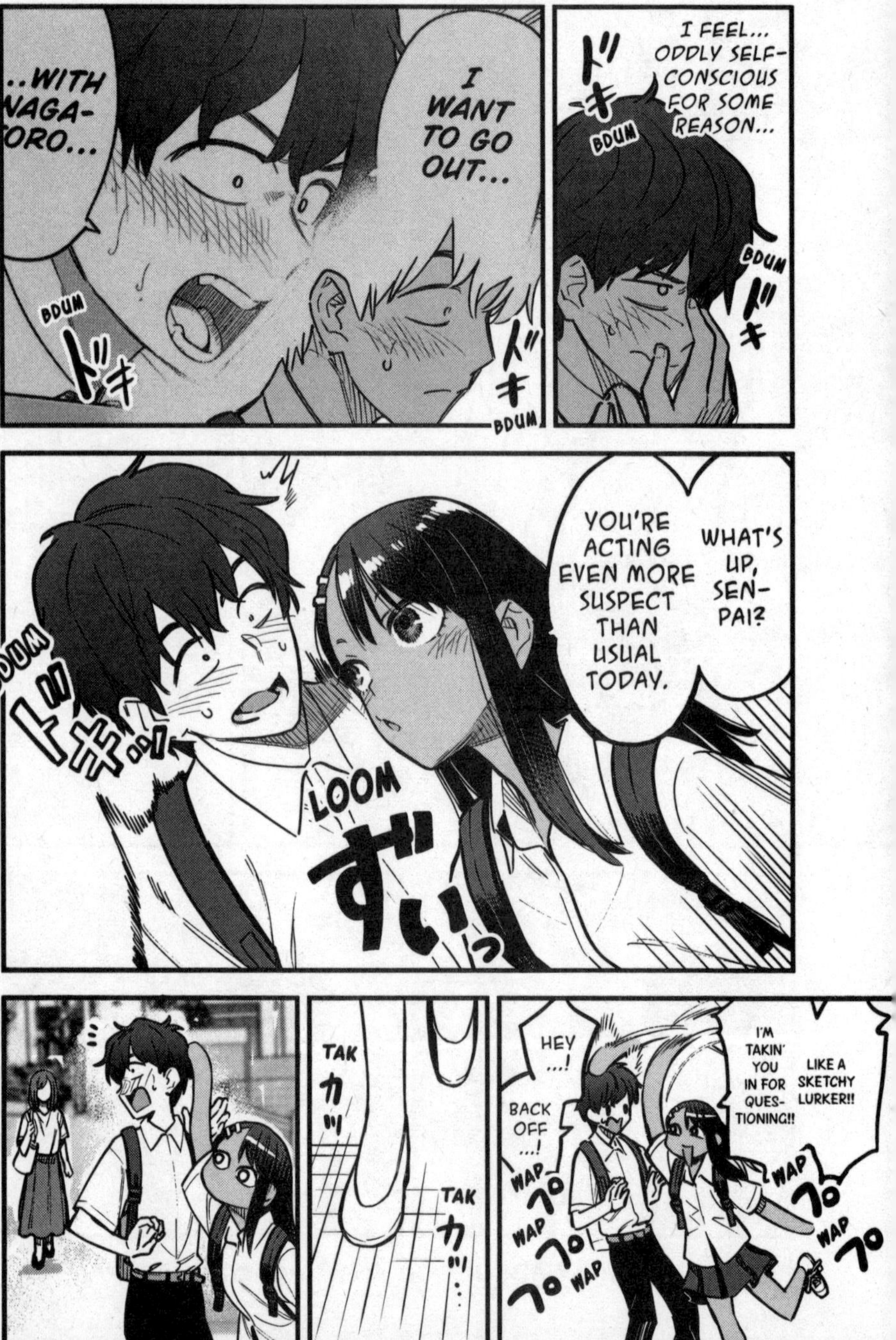
I FEEL... ODDLY SELF-CONSCIOUS FOR SOME REASON...
BDUM
BDUM
I WANT TO GO OUT...
...WITH NAGATORO...
BDUM
BDUM
WHAT'S UP, SEN-PAI?
YOU'RE ACTING EVEN MORE SUSPECT THAN USUAL TODAY.
BDUM
LOOM
I'M TAKIN' YOU IN FOR QUES-TIONING!!
LIKE A SKETCHY LURKER!!
HEY ...!
BACK OFF ...!
WAP
WAP
WAP
WAP
WAP
TAK
TAK

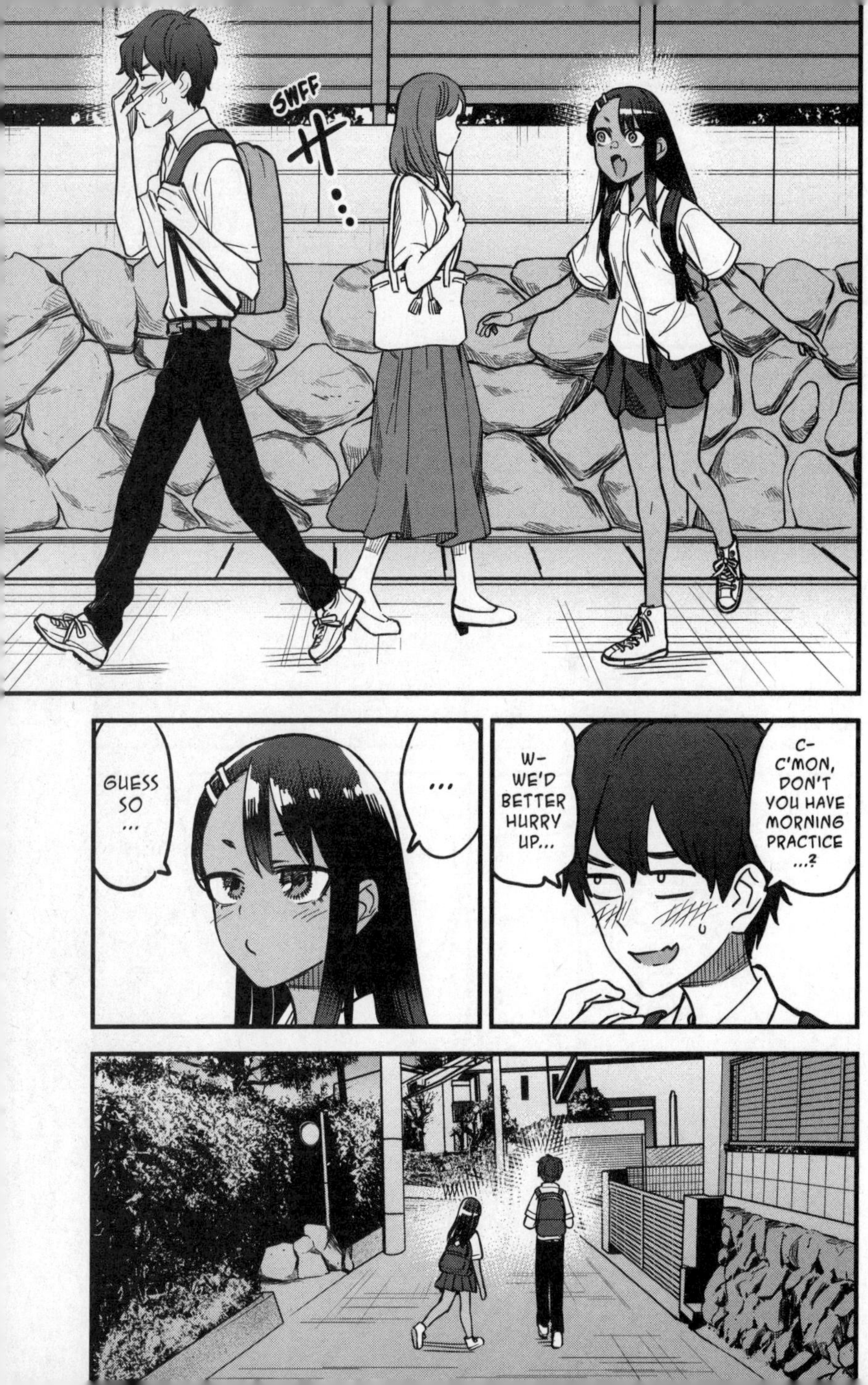
SWFF
C-
C'MON, DON'T YOU HAVE MORNING PRACTICE ...?
W-
WE'D BETTER HURRY UP...
...
GUESS SO ...

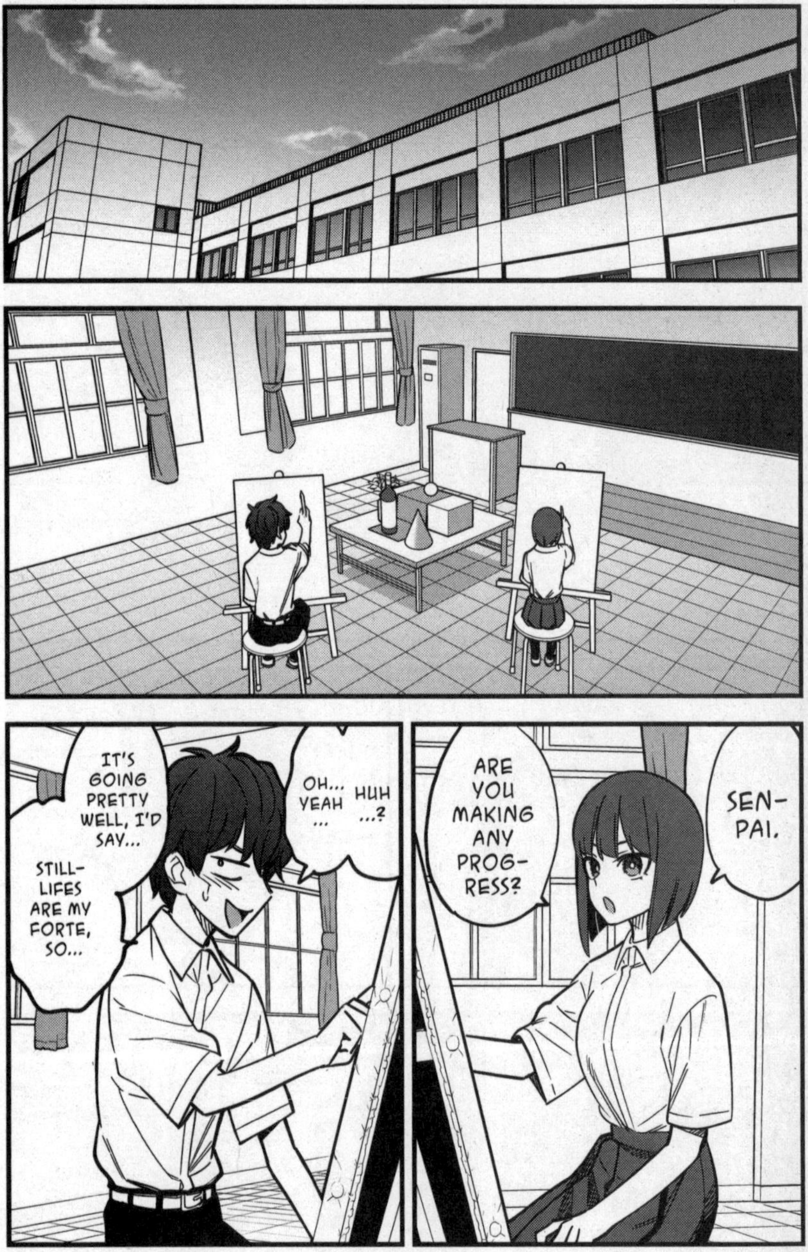
SEN-PAI.
ARE YOU MAKING ANY PROG-RESS?
HUH ...?
OH... YEAH ...
IT'S GOING PRETTY WELL, I'D SAY...
STILL-LIFES ARE MY FORTE, SO...

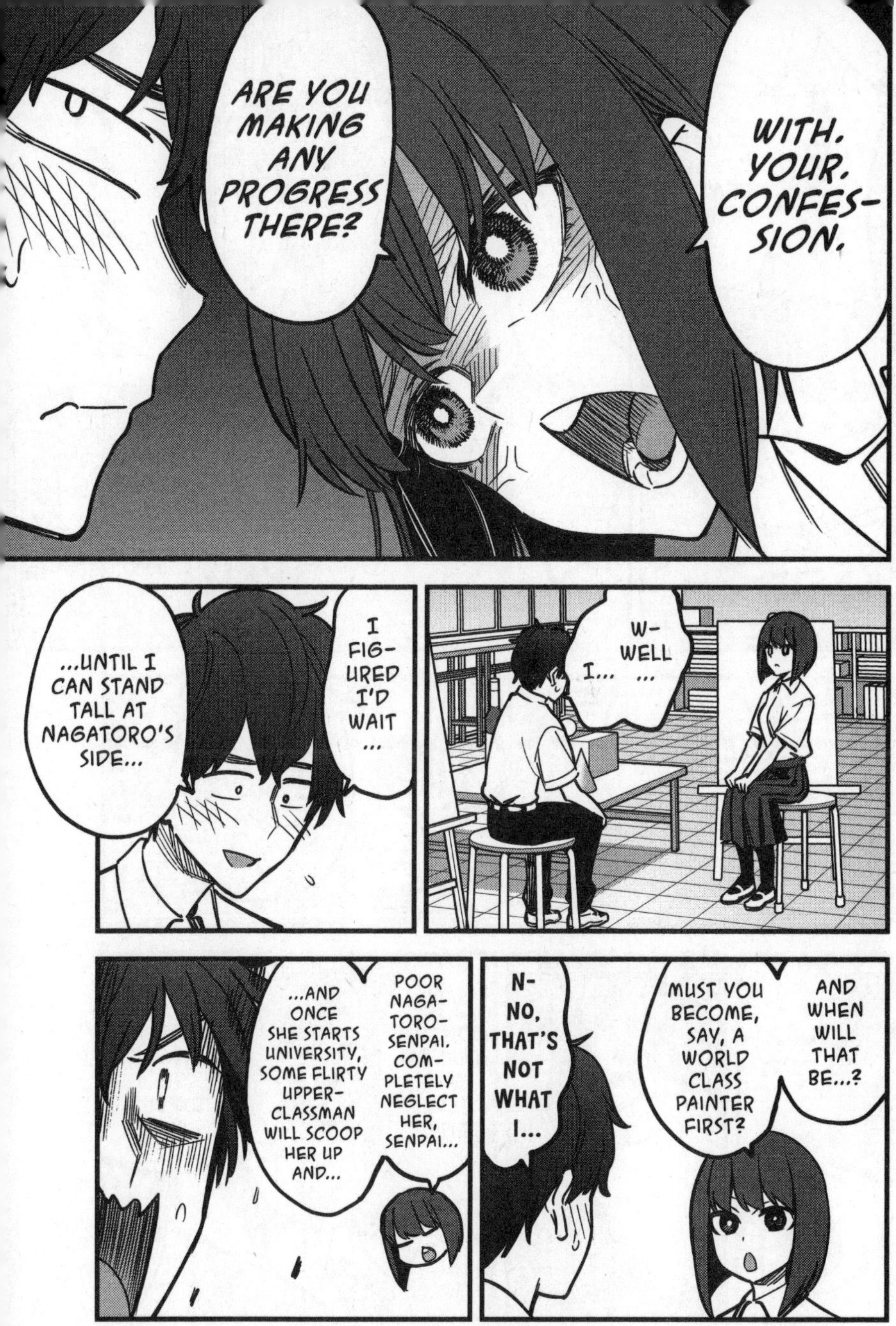
WITH. YOUR. CONFES-SION.
ARE YOU MAKING ANY PROGRESS THERE?
W-WELL...
I...
I FIGURED I'D WAIT...
...UNTIL I CAN STAND TALL AT NAGATORO'S SIDE...
AND WHEN WILL THAT BE...?
MUST YOU BECOME, SAY, A WORLD CLASS PAINTER FIRST?
N-NO, THAT'S NOT WHAT I...
POOR NAGATORO-SENPAI. COMPLETELY NEGLECT HER, SENPAI...
...AND ONCE SHE STARTS UNIVERSITY, SOME FLIRTY UPPERCLASSMAN WILL SCOOP HER UP AND...

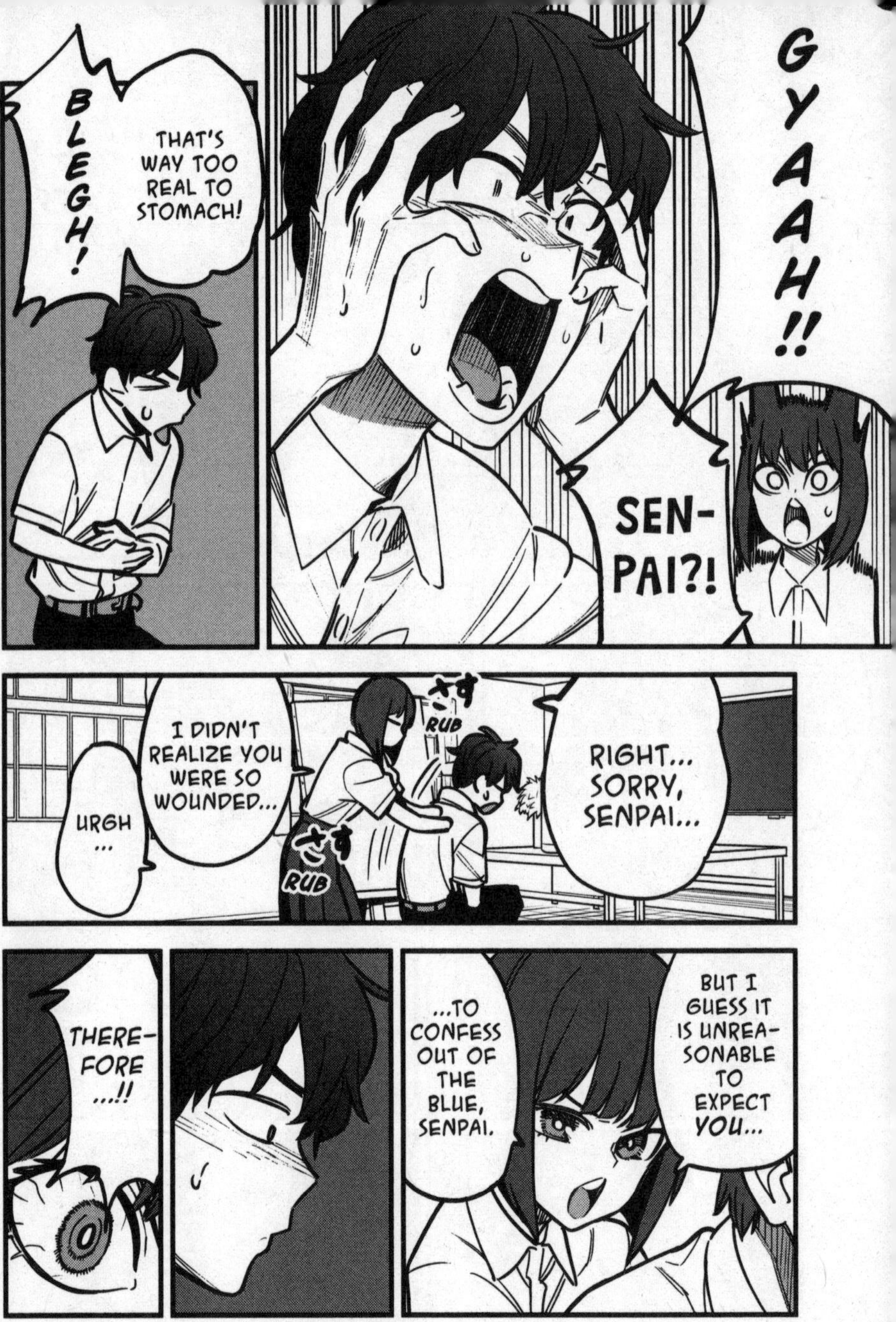
GYAAAH!!
SEN-PAI?!
BLEGH!
THAT'S WAY TOO REAL TO STOMACH!
RIGHT... SORRY, SENPAI...
さす RUB
I DIDN'T REALIZE YOU WERE SO WOUNDED...
URGH...
さす RUB
BUT I GUESS IT IS UNREA-SONABLE TO EXPECT YOU...
...TO CONFESS OUT OF THE BLUE, SENPAI.
THERE-FORE ...!!

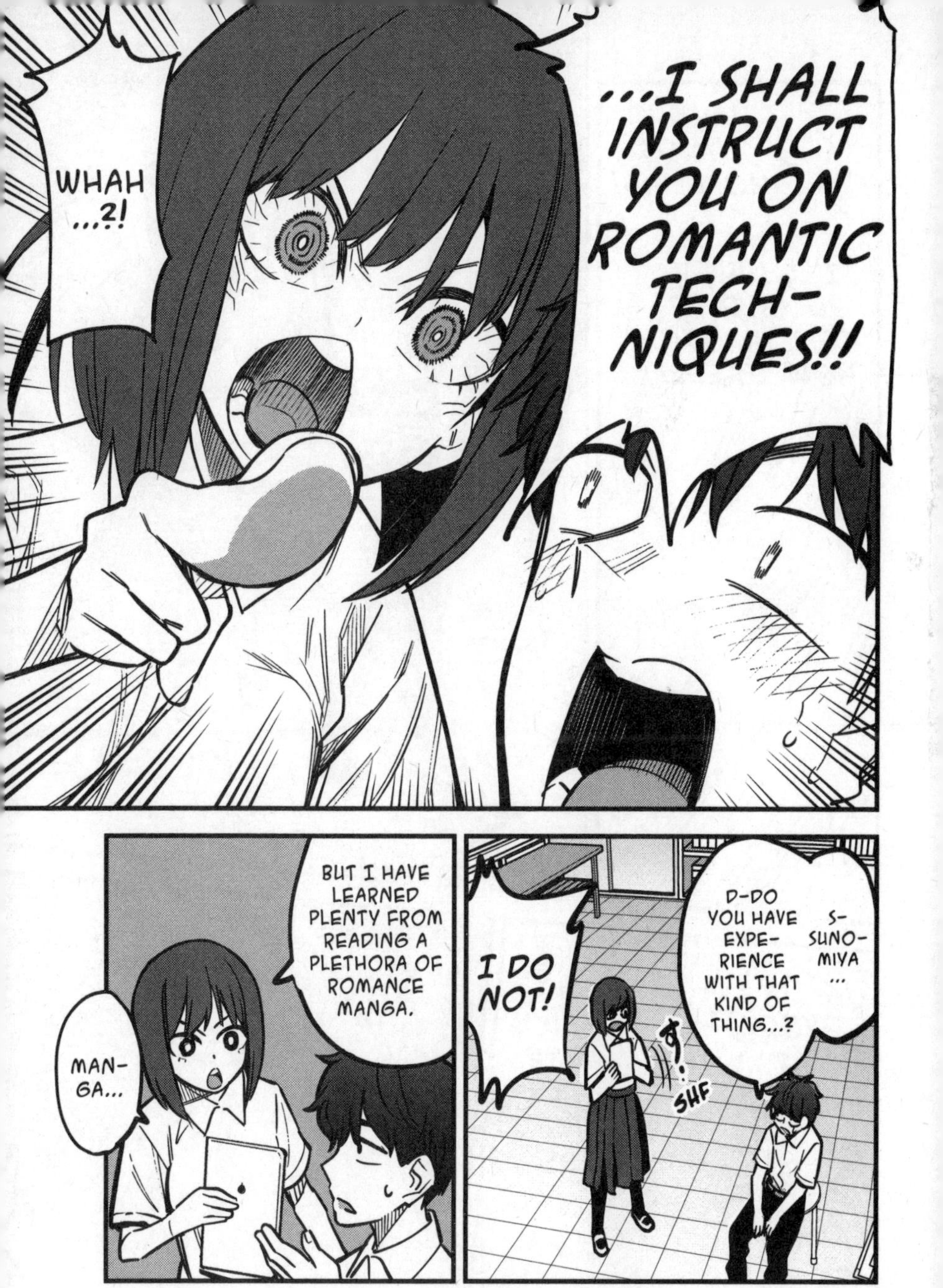
...I SHALL INSTRUCT YOU ON ROMANTIC TECH-NIQUES!!
WHAH ...?!
S-SUNOMIYA ...
D-DO YOU HAVE EXPE-RIENCE WITH THAT KIND OF THING...?
I DO NOT!
SHF
BUT I HAVE LEARNED PLENTY FROM READING A PLETHORA OF ROMANCE MANGA.
MAN-GA...

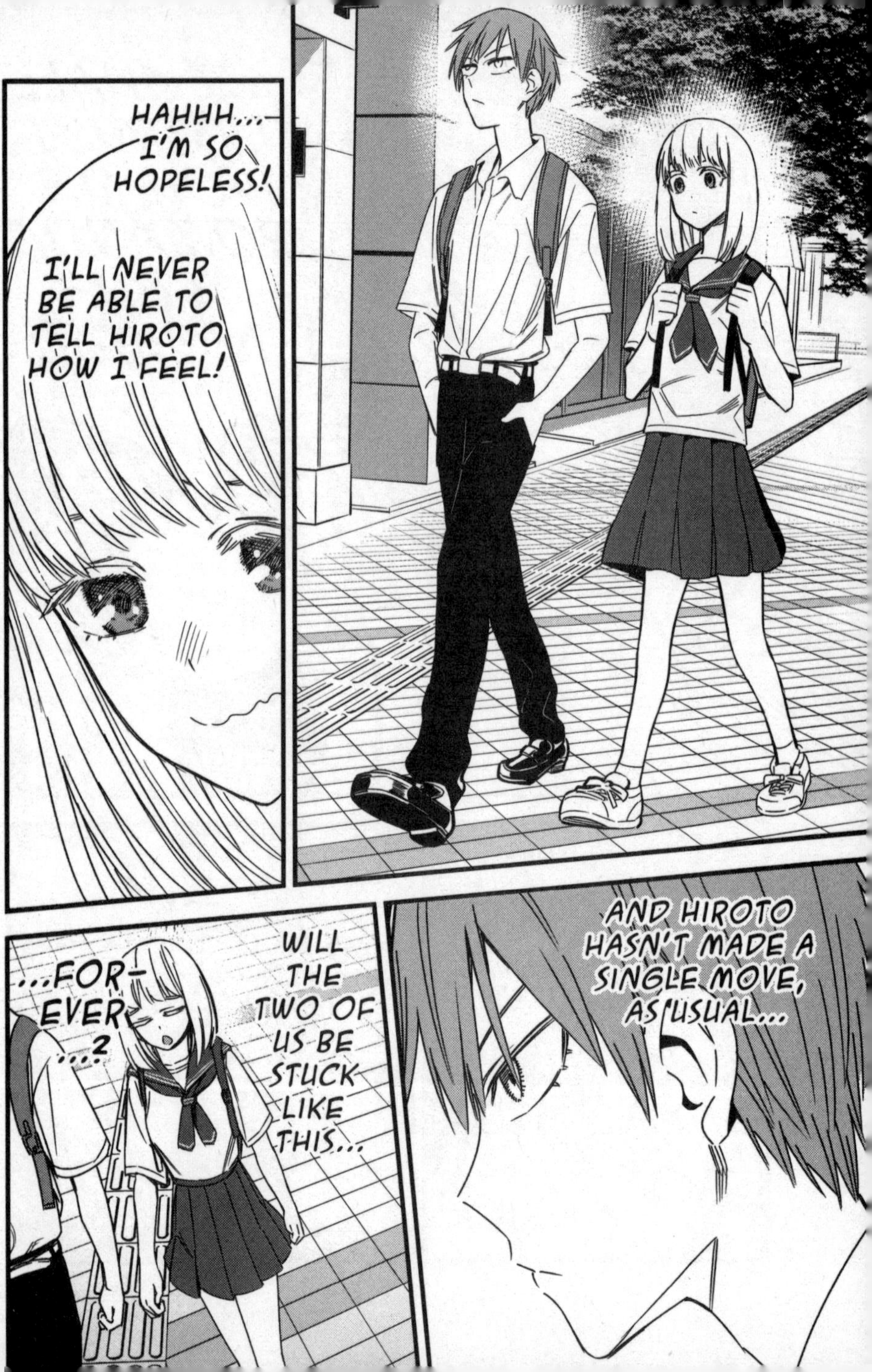
HAHHH... I'M SO HOPELESS!
I'LL NEVER BE ABLE TO TELL HIROTO HOW I FEEL!
AND HIROTO HASN'T MADE A SINGLE MOVE, AS USUAL...
WILL THE TWO OF US BE STUCK LIKE THIS...
...FOR-EVER...?

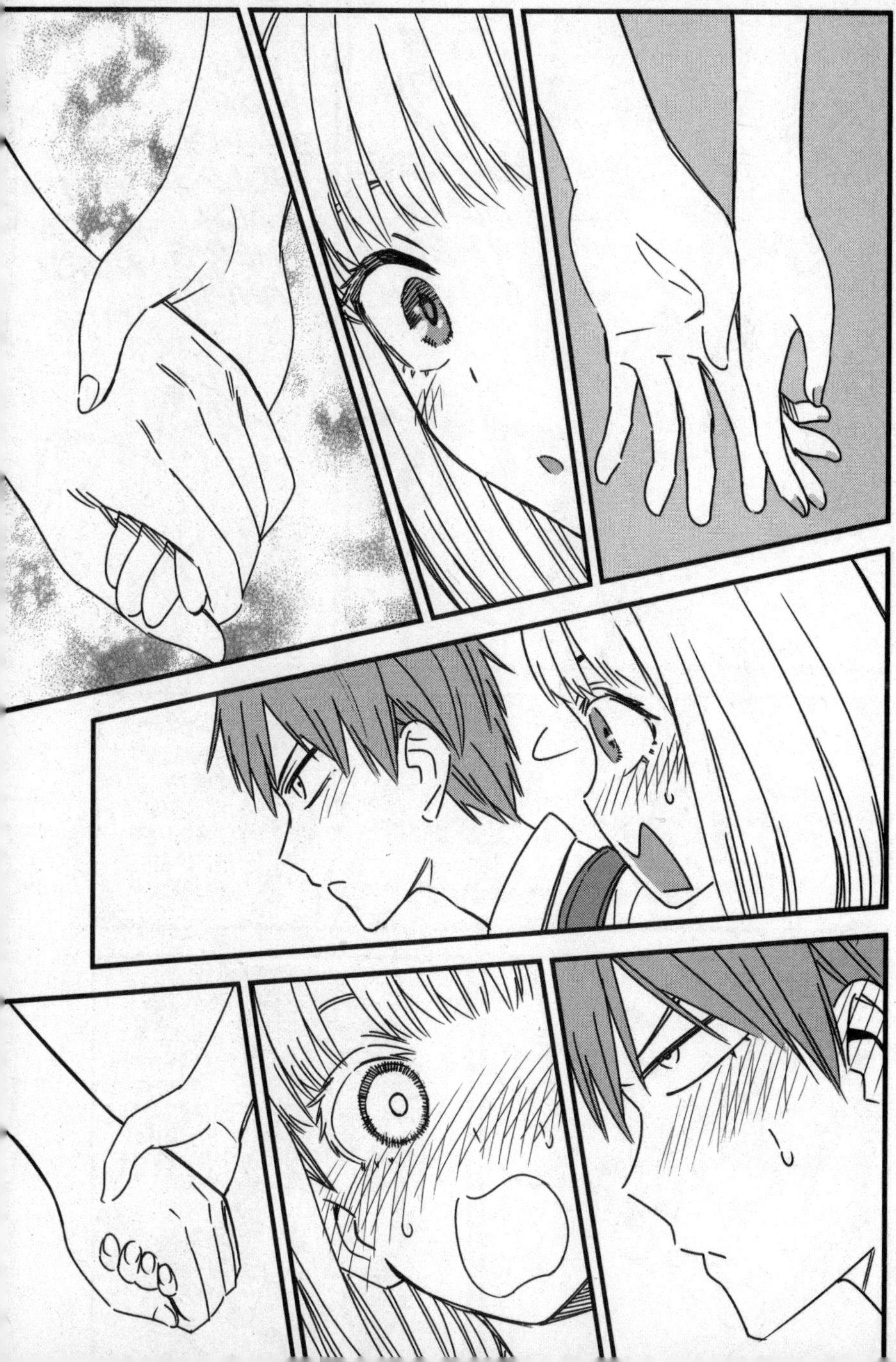

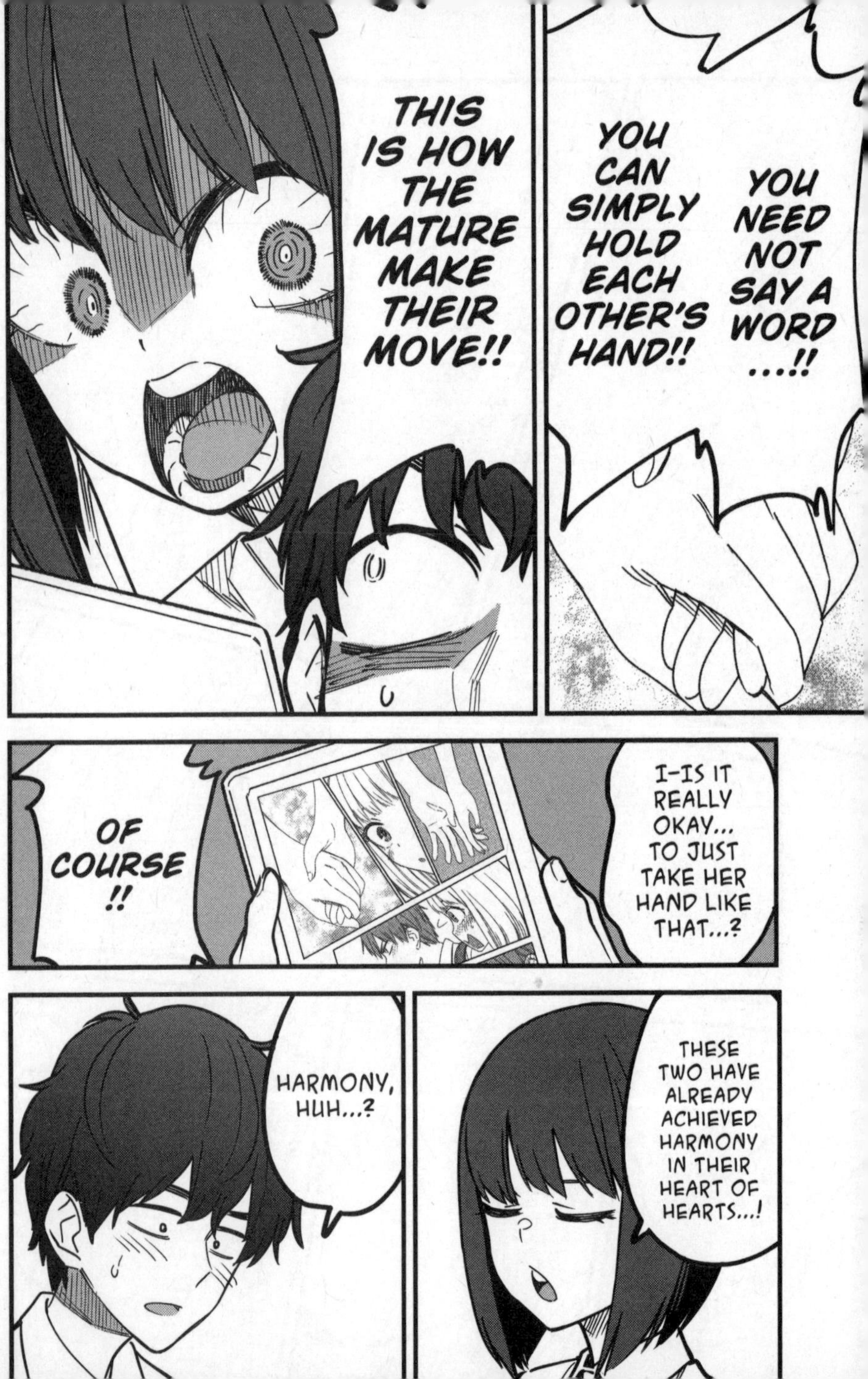
YOU NEED NOT SAY A WORD ...!!
YOU CAN SIMPLY HOLD EACH OTHER'S HAND!!
THIS IS HOW THE MATURE MAKE THEIR MOVE!!
I-IS IT REALLY OKAY... TO JUST TAKE HER HAND LIKE THAT...?
OF COURSE !!
THESE TWO HAVE ALREADY ACHIEVED HARMONY IN THEIR HEART OF HEARTS...!
HARMONY, HUH...?

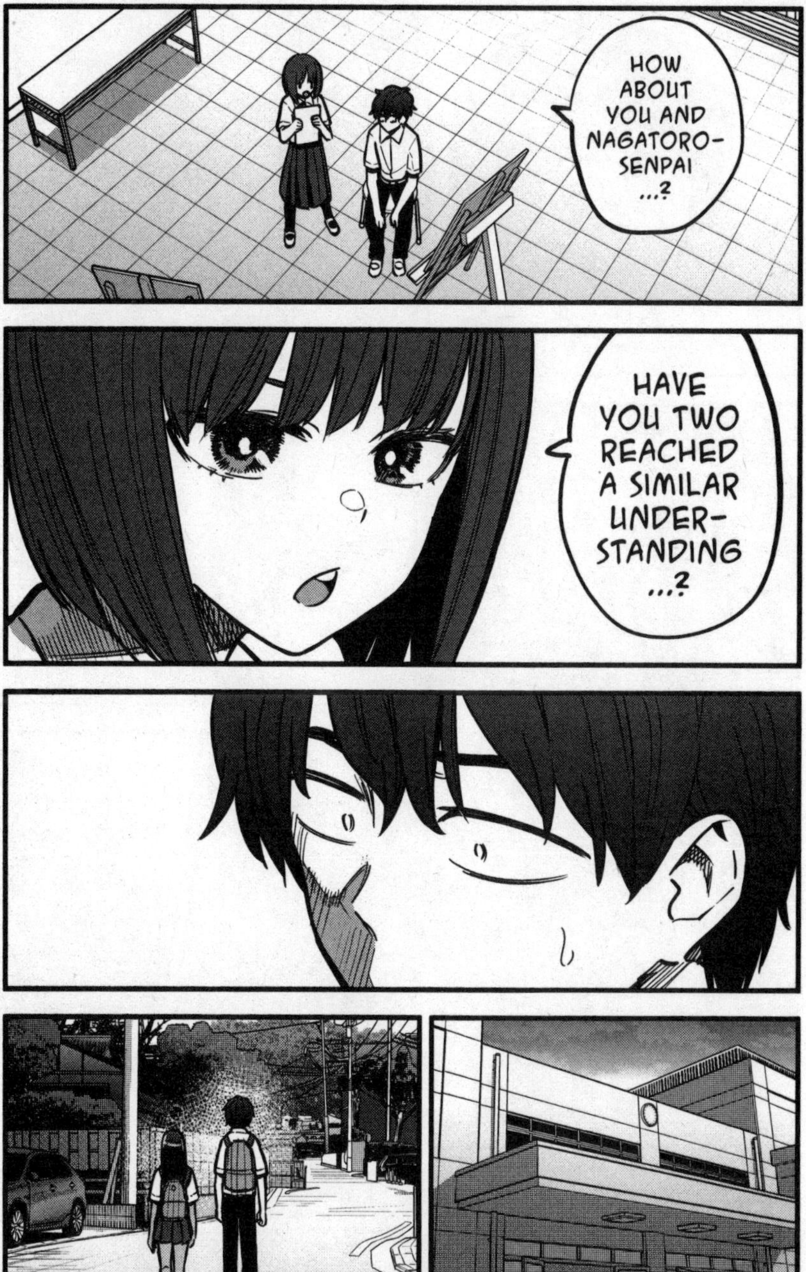
HOW ABOUT YOU AND NAGATORO-SENPAI ...?
HAVE YOU TWO REACHED A SIMILAR UNDER-STANDING ...?

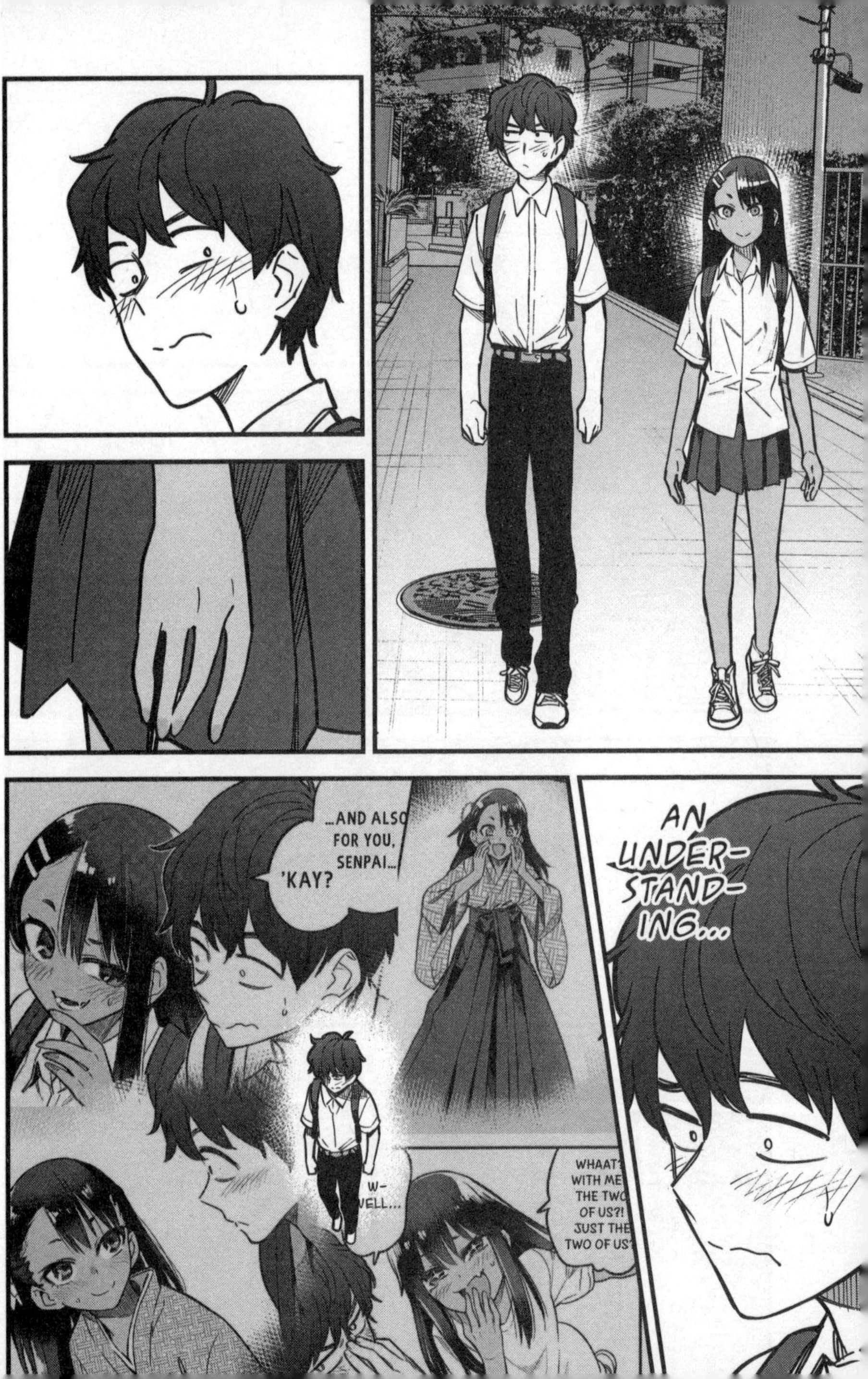
AN UNDER-STAND-ING...
...AND ALSO FOR YOU, SENPAI...
'KAY?
WHAAT'S WITH ME THE TWO OF US?! JUST THE TWO OF US?
W-WELL...

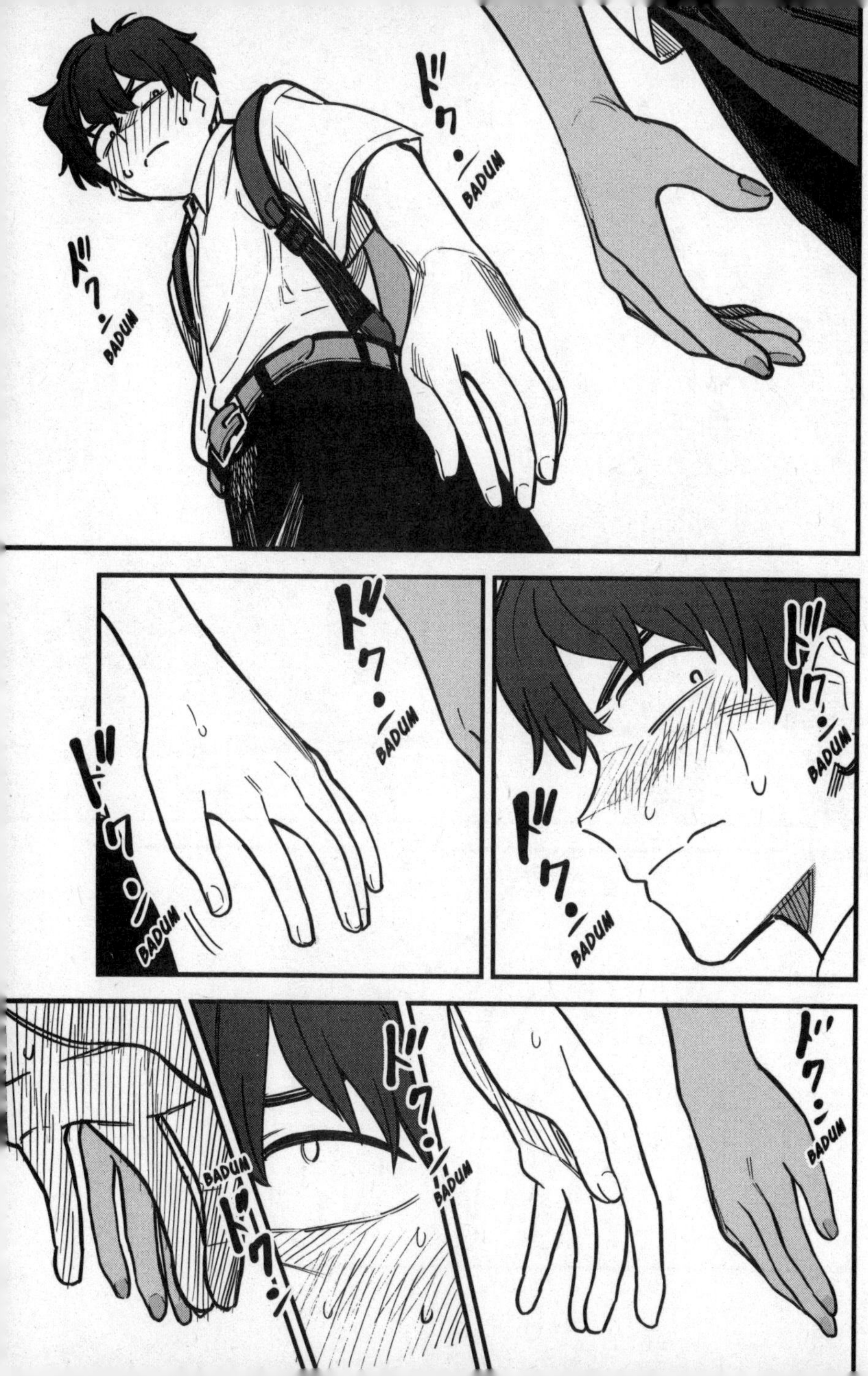

ドク
BADUM
ドク
BADUM
ドク
BADUM
ドク
BADUM
ドク
BADUM
ドク
BADUM
ドク
BADUM
ドク
BADUM
ドク
BADUM

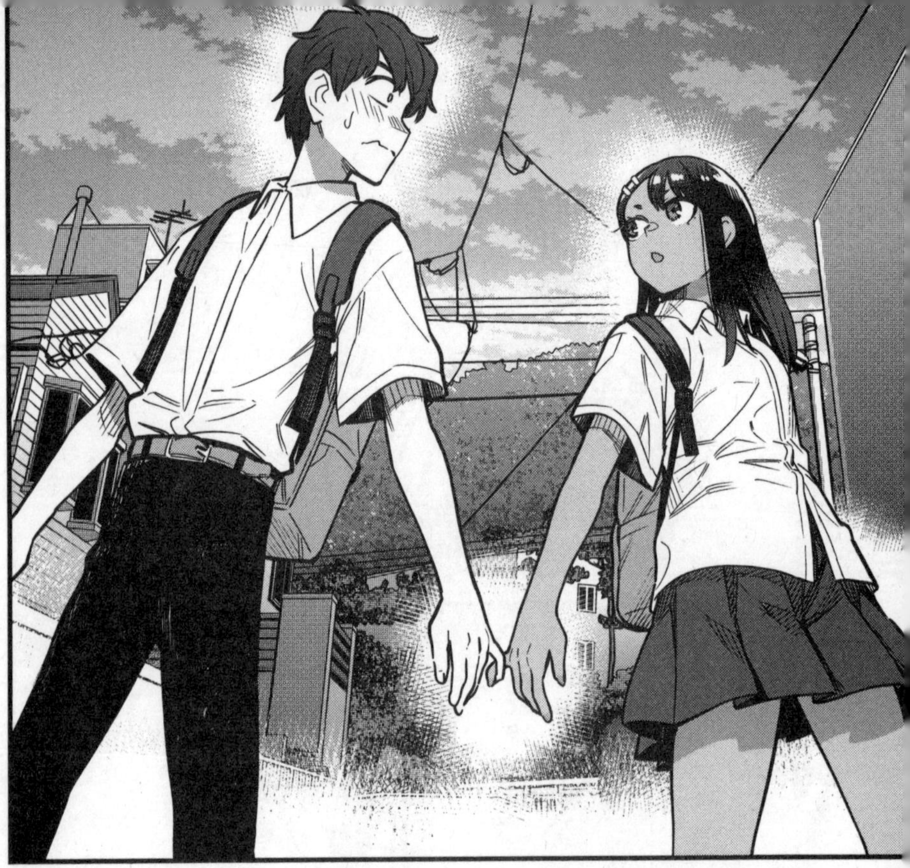

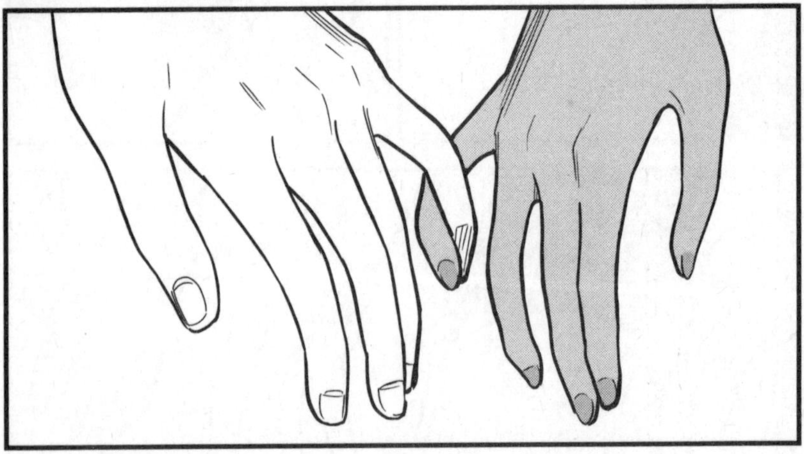

I CAME UP TOO SHO-O-O-ORT!!

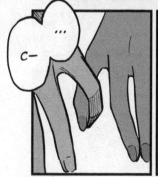

...

I-I'VE GOTTA SAY SOMETHING...!!

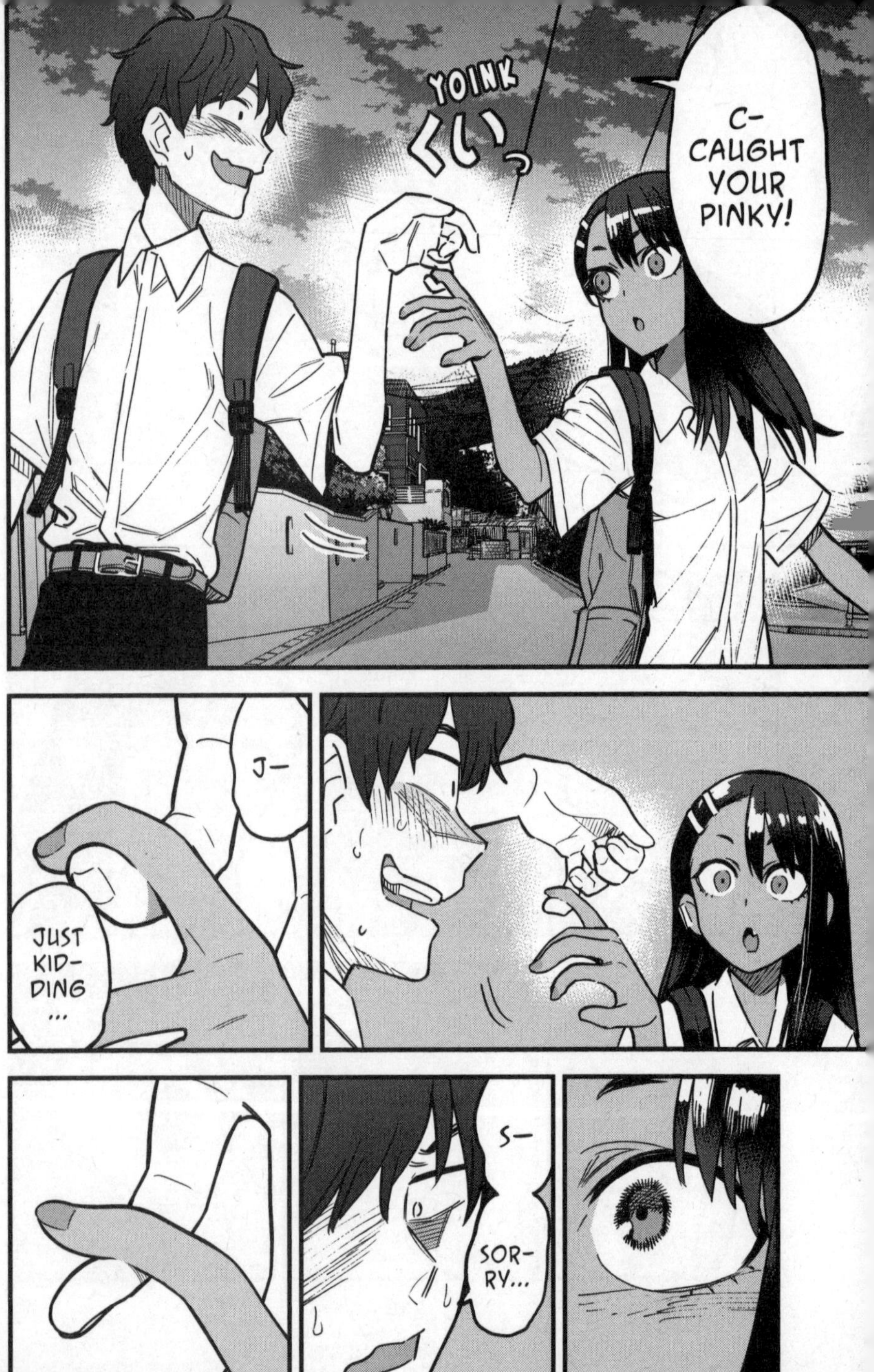
C-CAUGHT YOUR PINKY!
YOINK
くいっ
J—
JUST KID-DING...
S—
SOR-RY...

SKWEEZ
ギュ

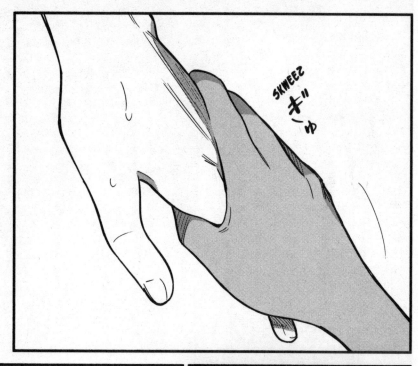

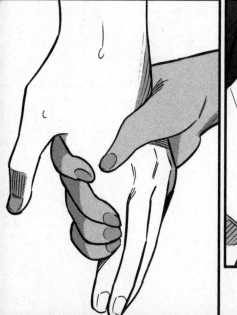

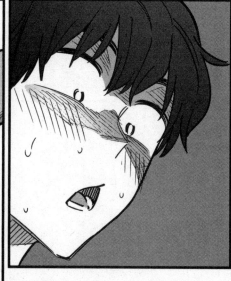

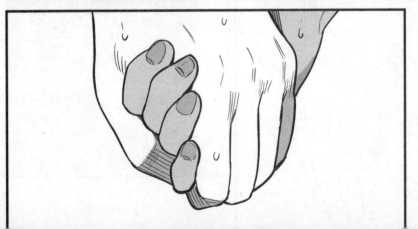

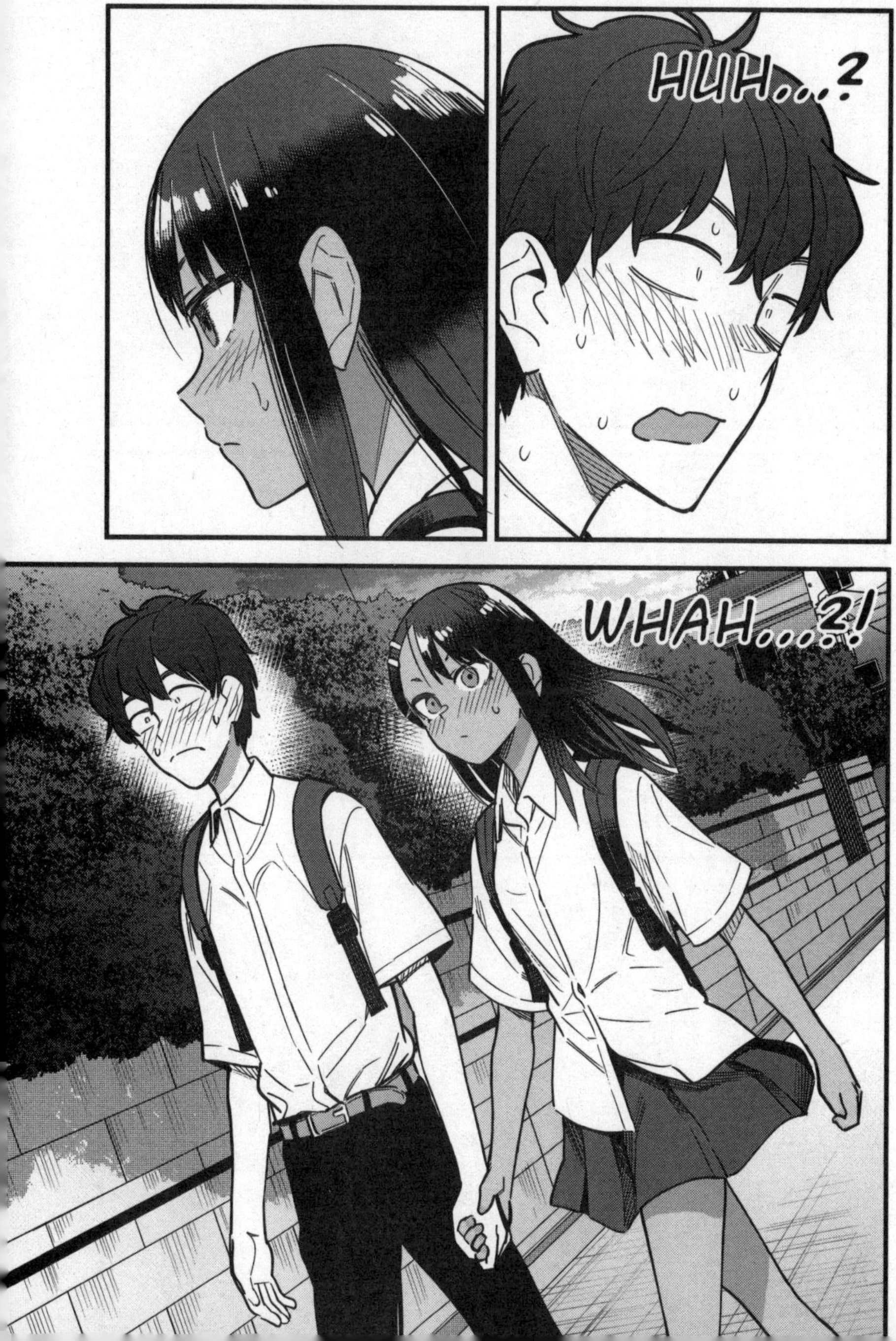
HUH...?
WHAH...?!

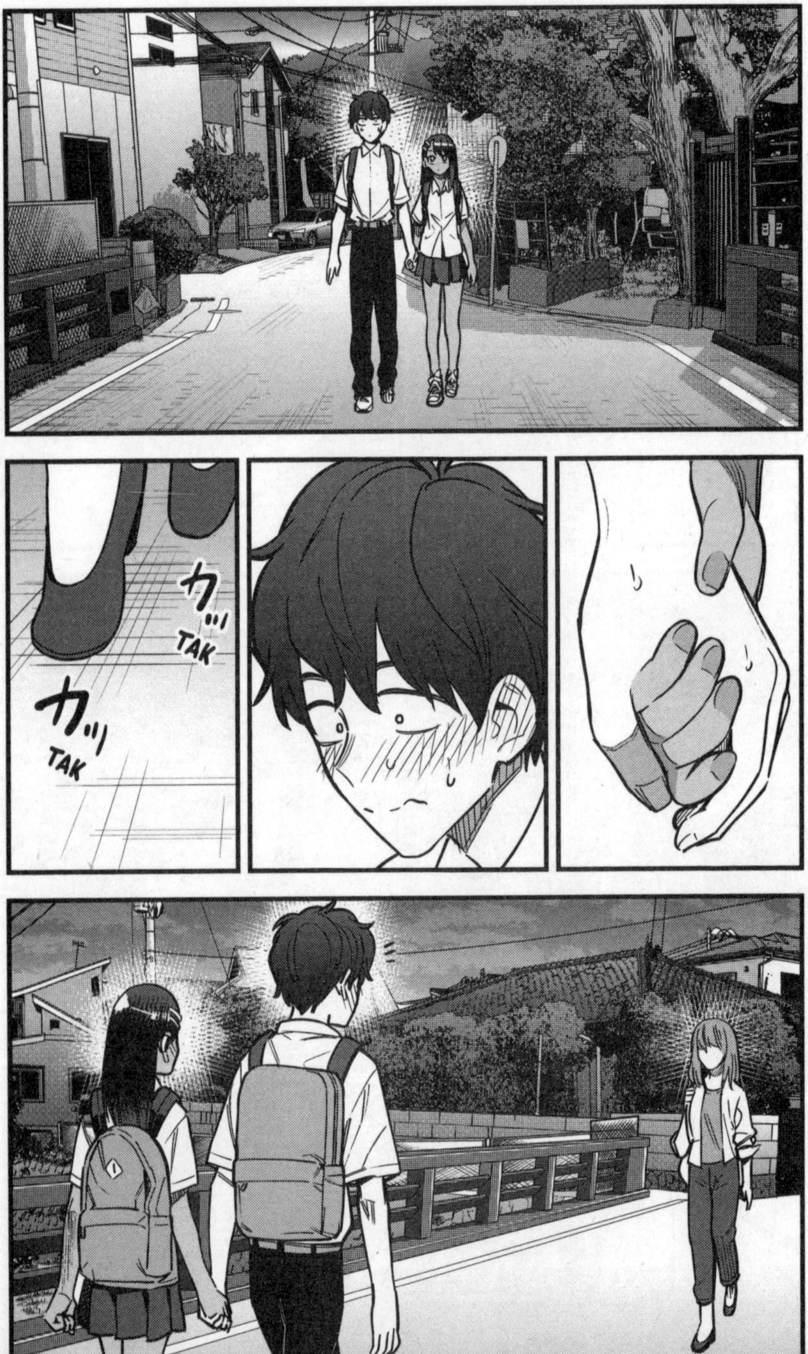
カッ
TAK
カッ
TAK

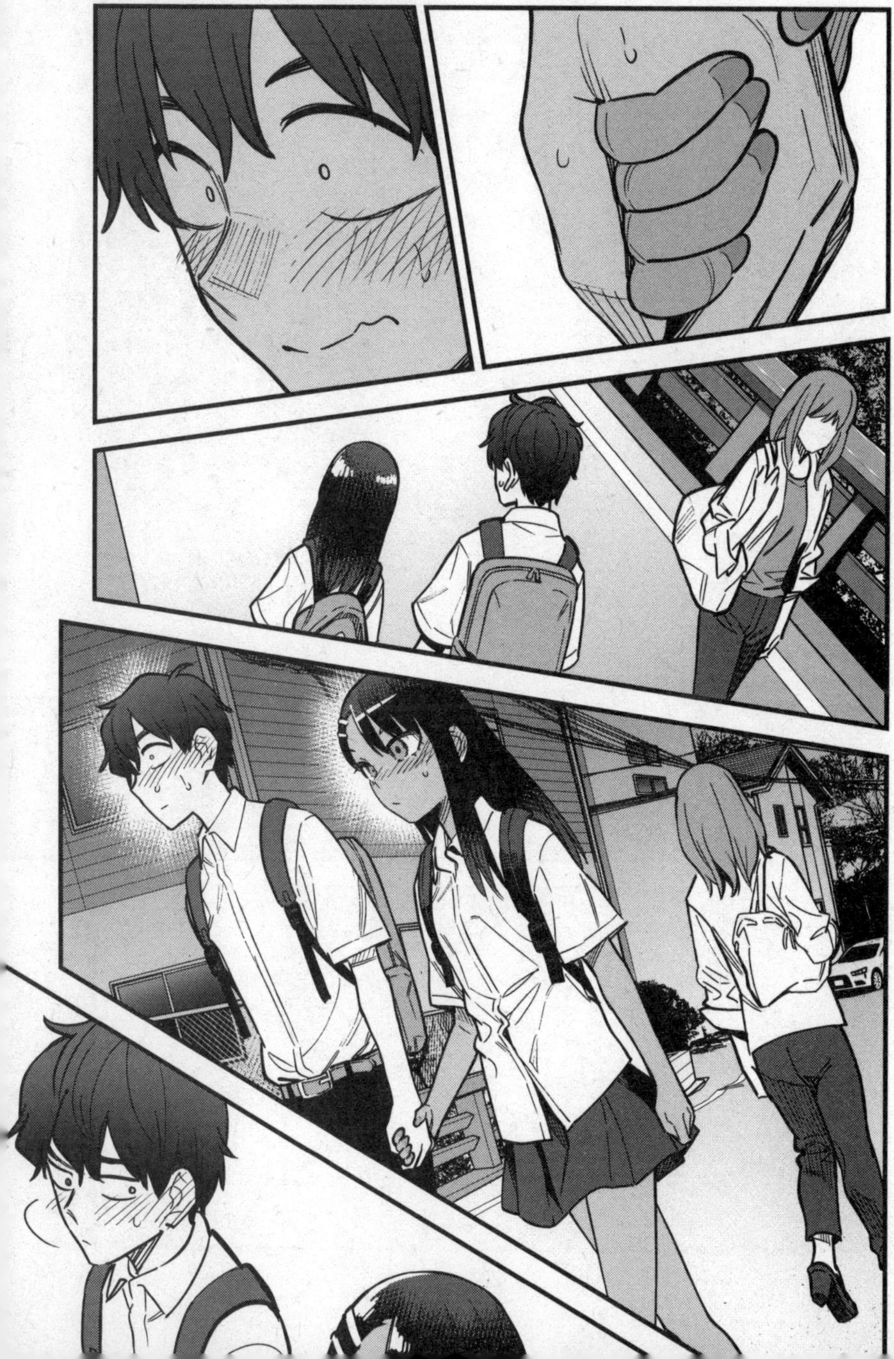

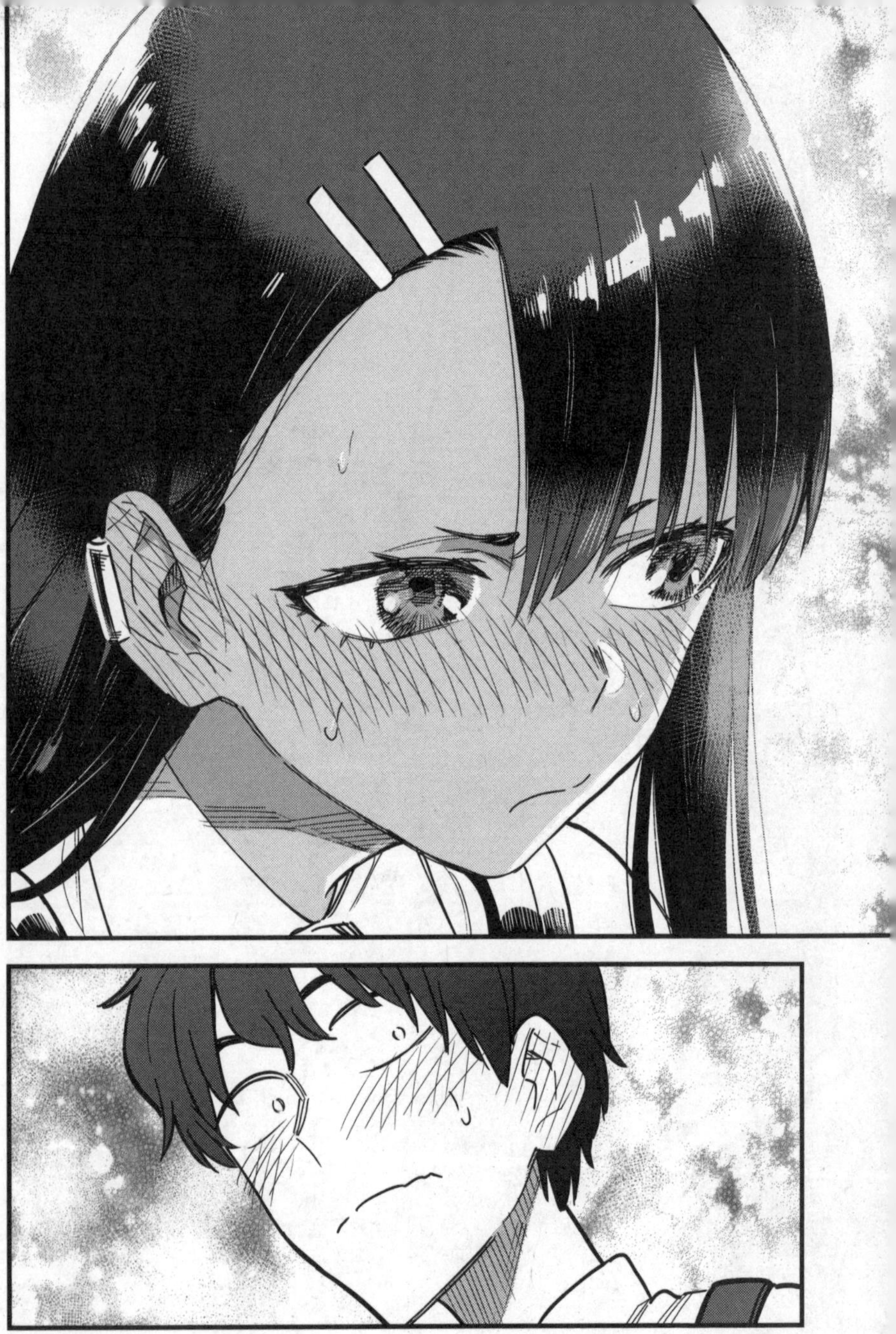

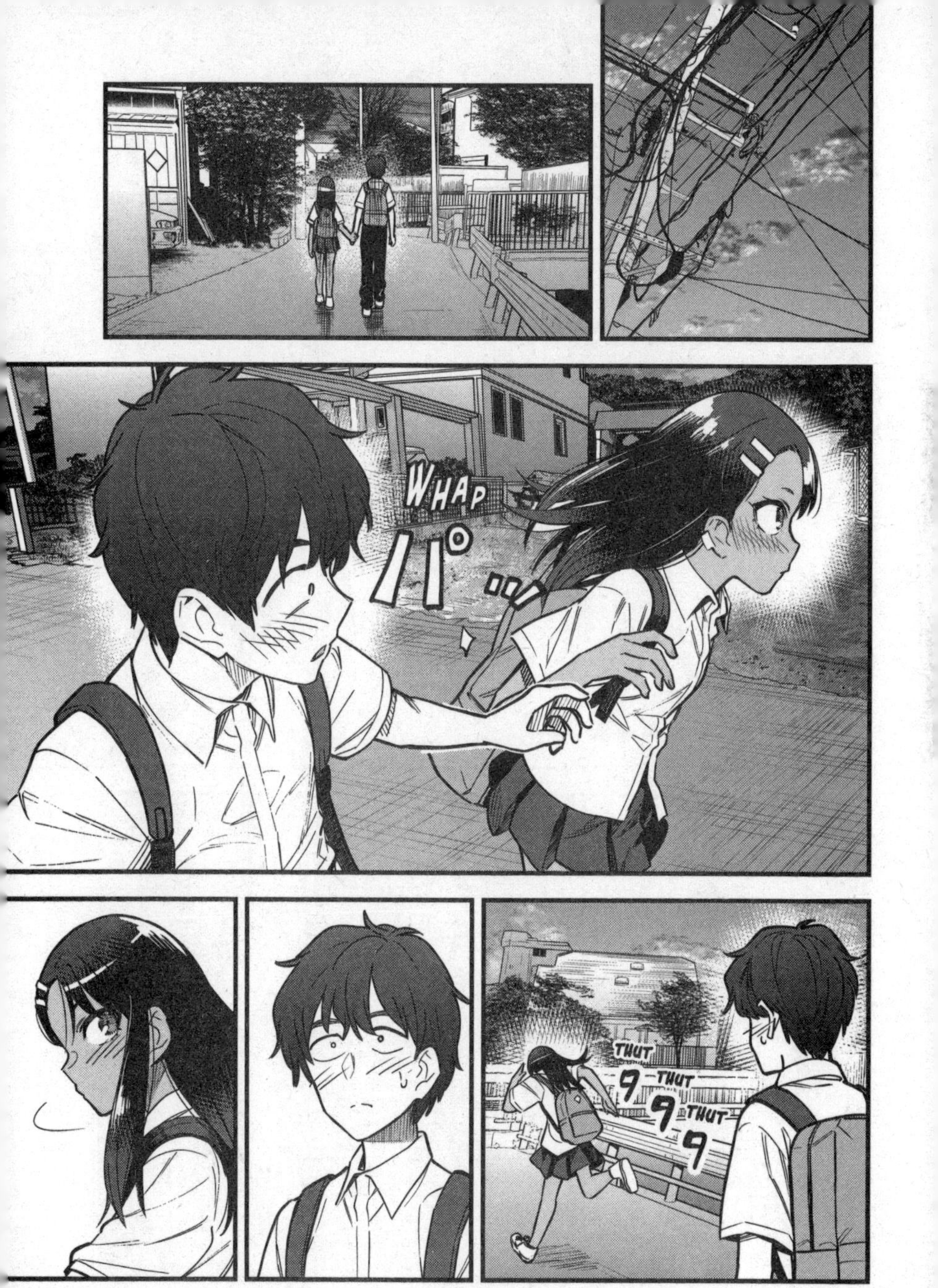
WHAP
THUT
THUT
THUT

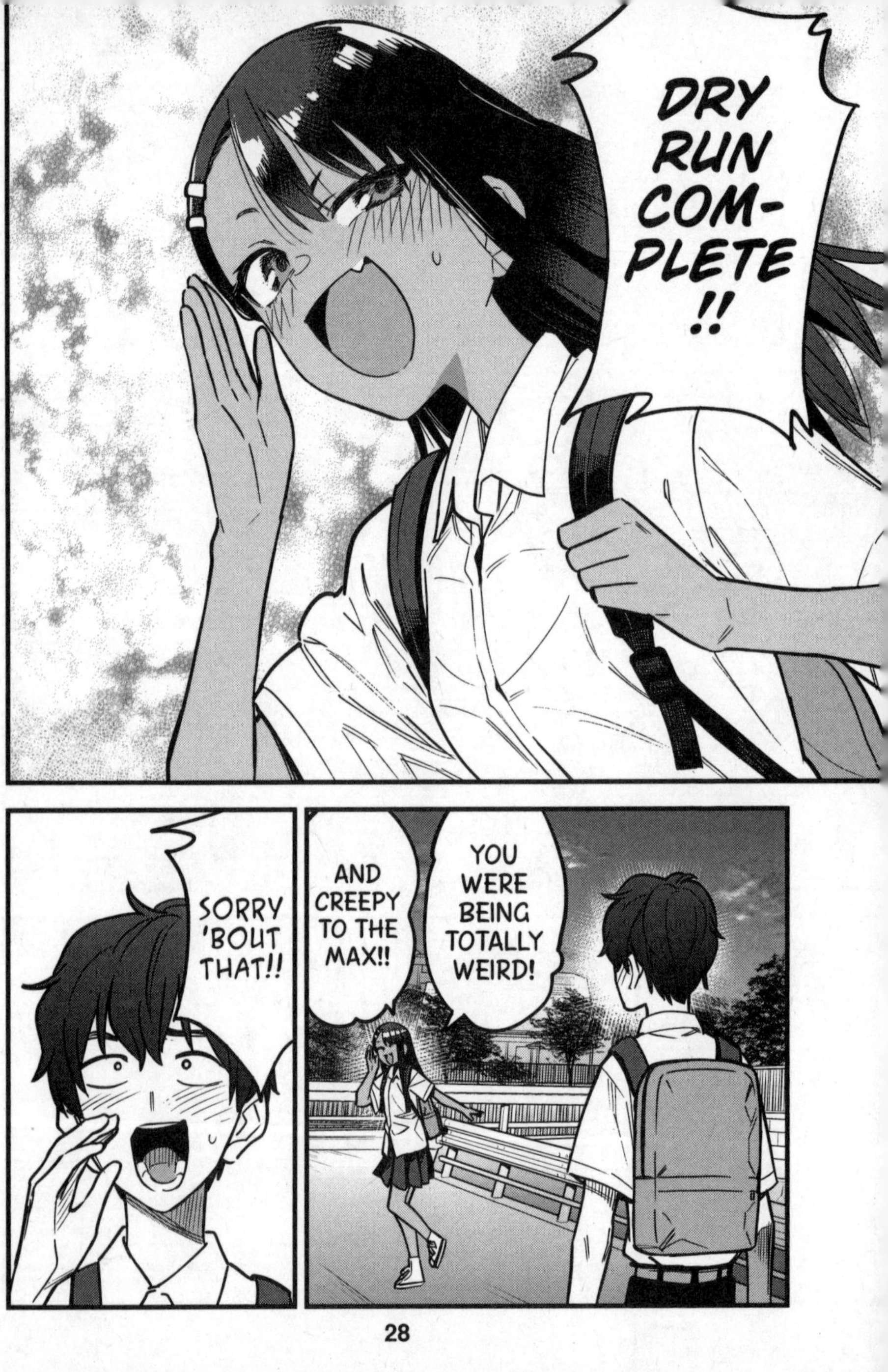
DRY RUN COM-PLETE!!
YOU WERE BEING TOTALLY WEIRD!
AND CREEPY TO THE MAX!!
SORRY 'BOUT THAT!!

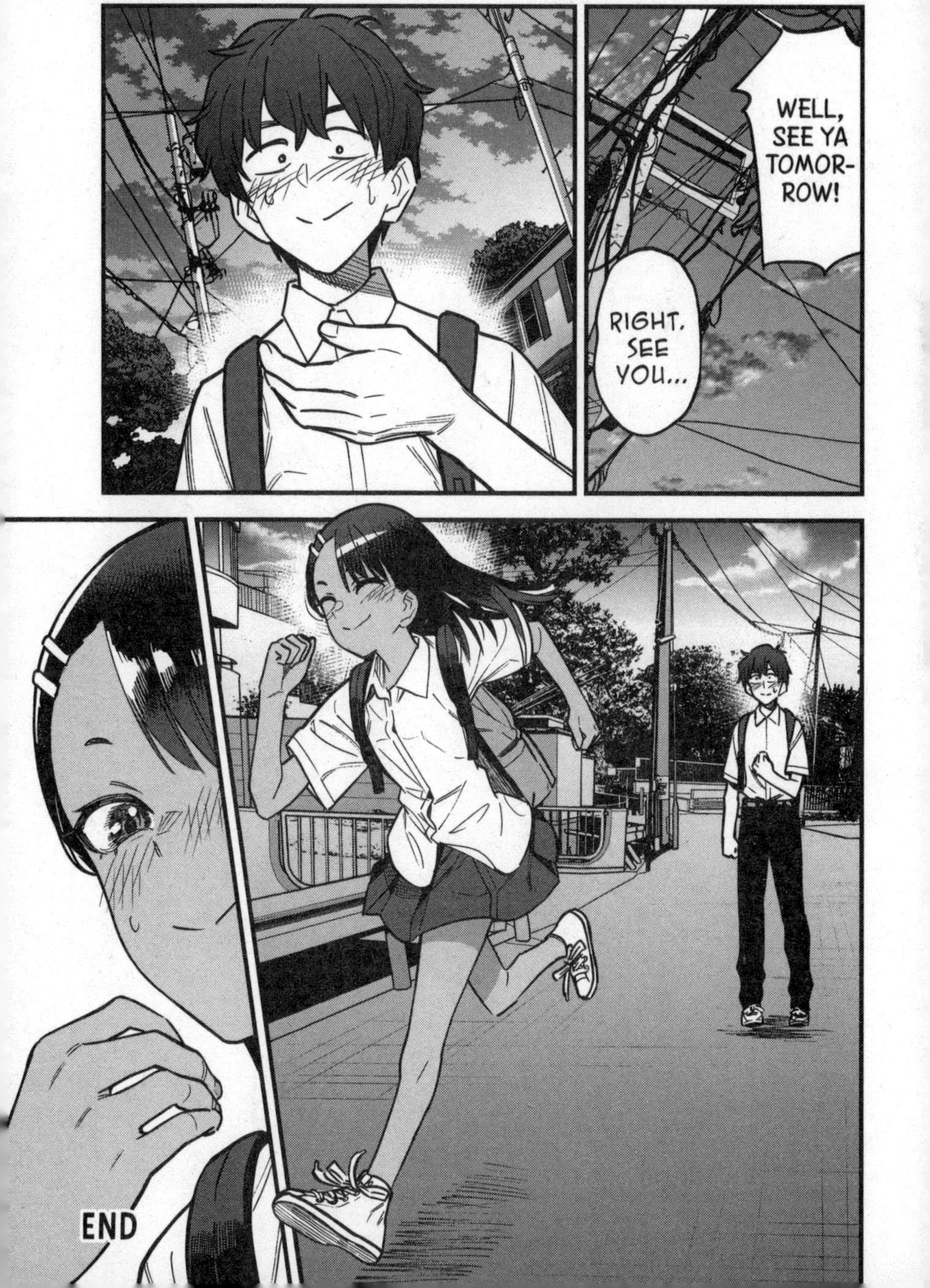
WELL, SEE YA TOMOR-ROW!
RIGHT. SEE YOU...
END

HAYASE-CHAN, DINNER'S READY. GO WASH YOUR HANDS!
NOPE.
WHY NOT...?
DON'T WANNA.

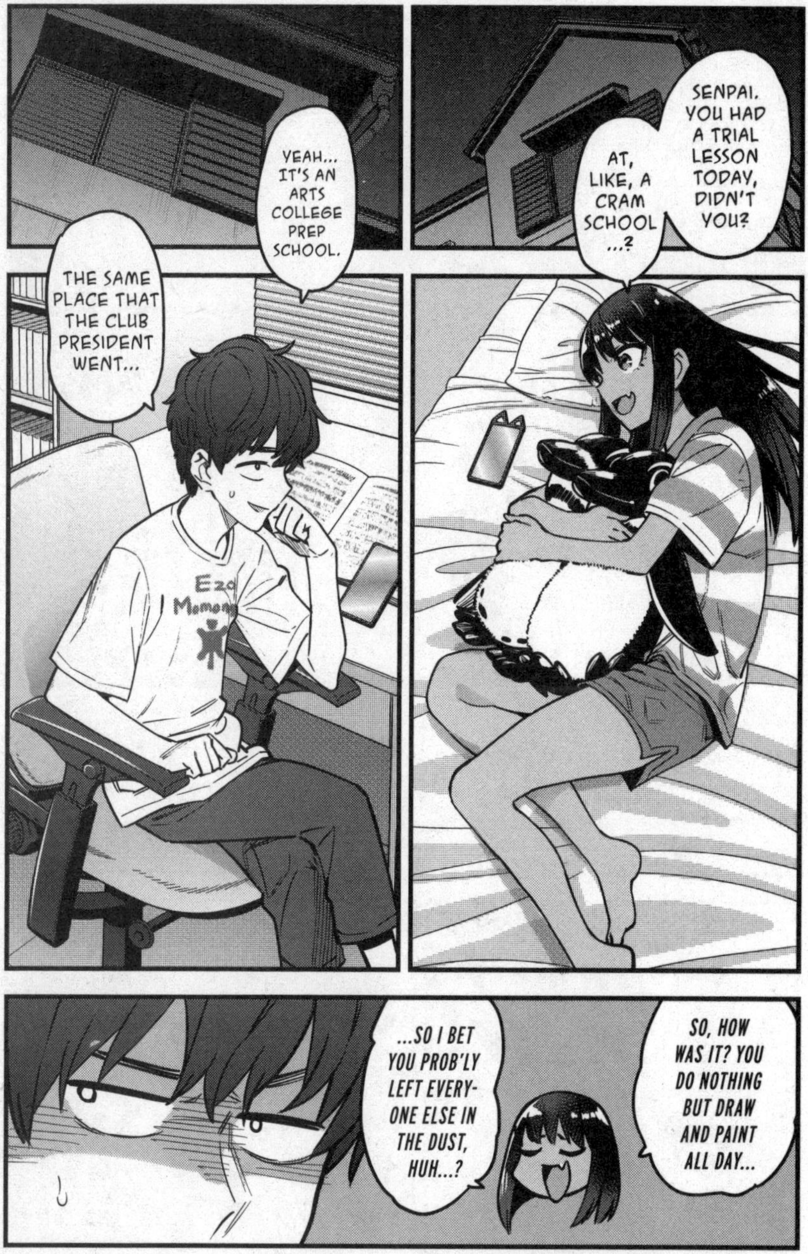
SENPAI. YOU HAD A TRIAL LESSON TODAY, DIDN'T YOU?
AT, LIKE, A CRAM SCHOOL ...?
YEAH... IT'S AN ARTS COLLEGE PREP SCHOOL.
THE SAME PLACE THAT THE CLUB PRESIDENT WENT...
SO, HOW WAS IT? YOU DO NOTHING BUT DRAW AND PAINT ALL DAY...
...SO I BET YOU PROB'LY LEFT EVERY-ONE ELSE IN THE DUST, HUH...?

CHAPTER III: GIVE SENPAI SOME ADVICE...PLEASE!!

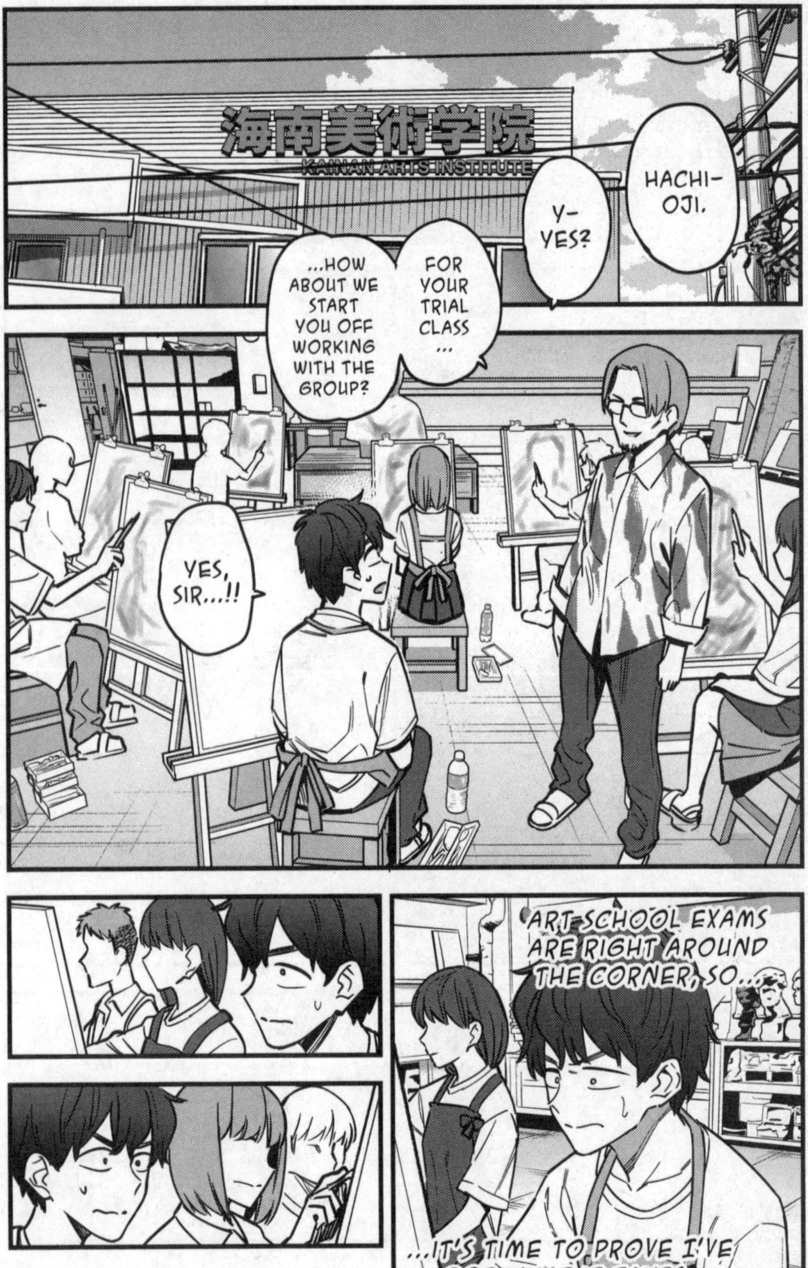
海南美術学院
KAINAN ARTS INSTITUTE
HACHI-OJI.
Y-YES?
FOR YOUR TRIAL CLASS...
...HOW ABOUT WE START YOU OFF WORKING WITH THE GROUP?
YES, SIR...!!
ART-SCHOOL EXAMS ARE RIGHT AROUND THE CORNER, SO...
...IT'S TIME TO PROVE I'VE GOT WHAT IT TAKES...

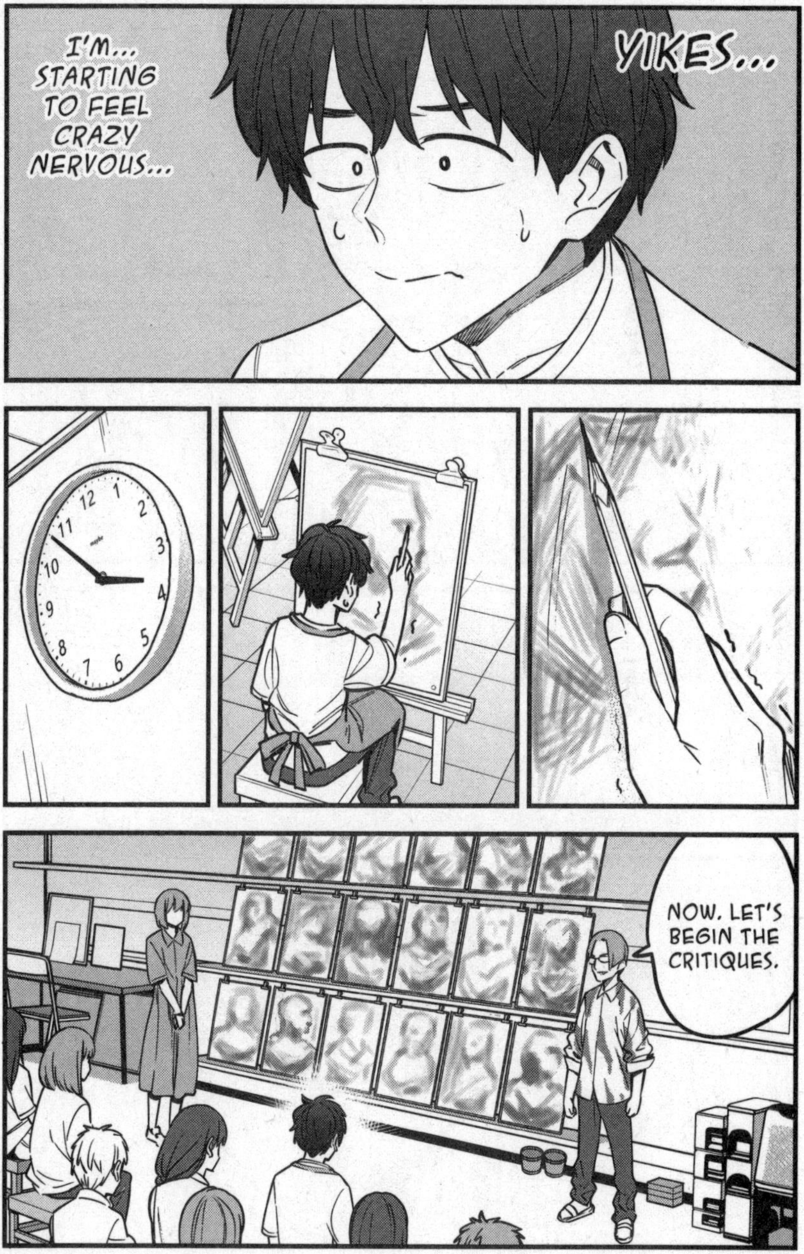
YIKES...
I'M... STARTING TO FEEL CRAZY NERVOUS...
NOW. LET'S BEGIN THE CRITIQUES.

EVERYONE'S SO TALENTED...

E2D Mananga

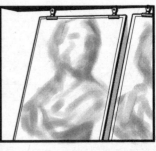

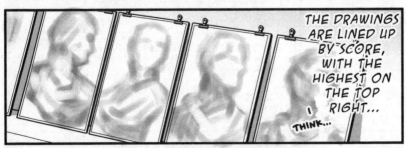

THE DRAWINGS ARE LINED UP BY SCORE, WITH THE HIGHEST ON THE TOP RIGHT...

I THINK...

...THAT MINE IS...

SO THAT MEANS...

34

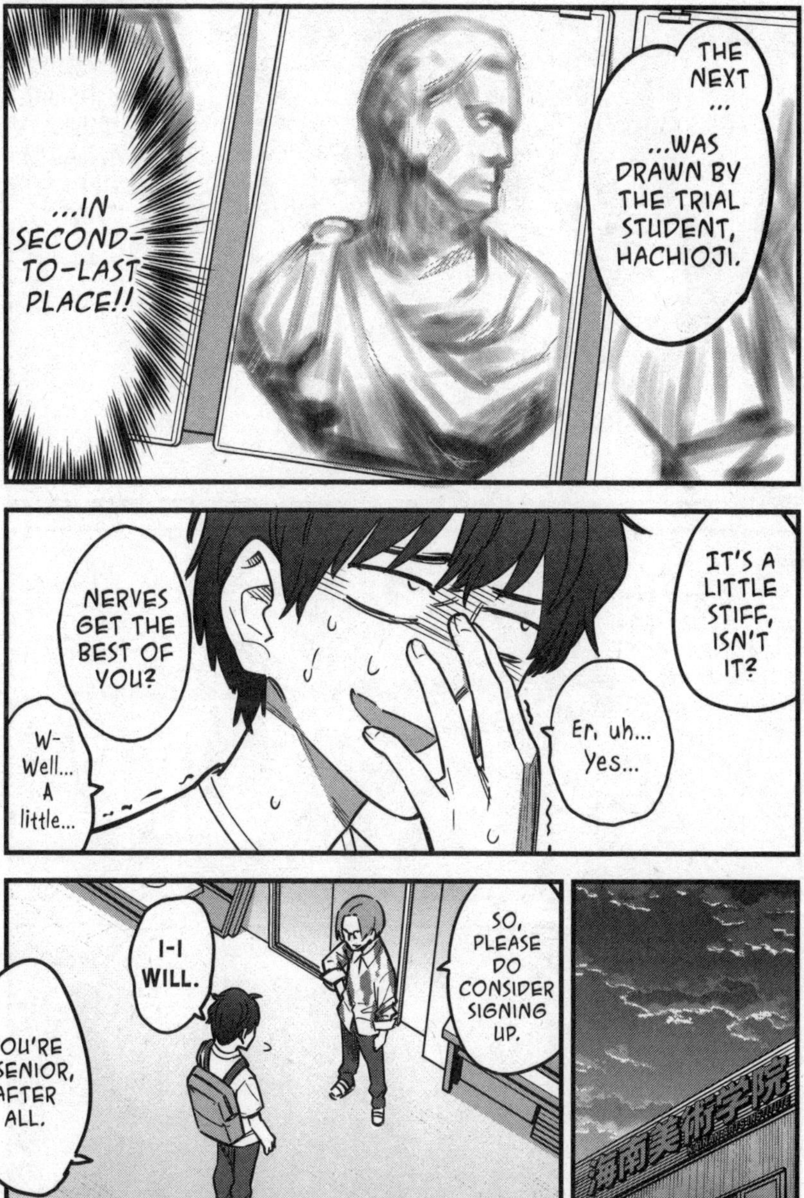
THE NEXT ...
...WAS DRAWN BY THE TRIAL STUDENT, HACHIOJI.
...IN SECOND-TO-LAST PLACE!!
IT'S A LITTLE STIFF, ISN'T IT?
Er, uh... yes...
NERVES GET THE BEST OF YOU?
W-Well... A little...
海南美術学院
SO, PLEASE DO CONSIDER SIGNING UP.
I-I WILL.
YOU'RE A SENIOR, AFTER ALL.

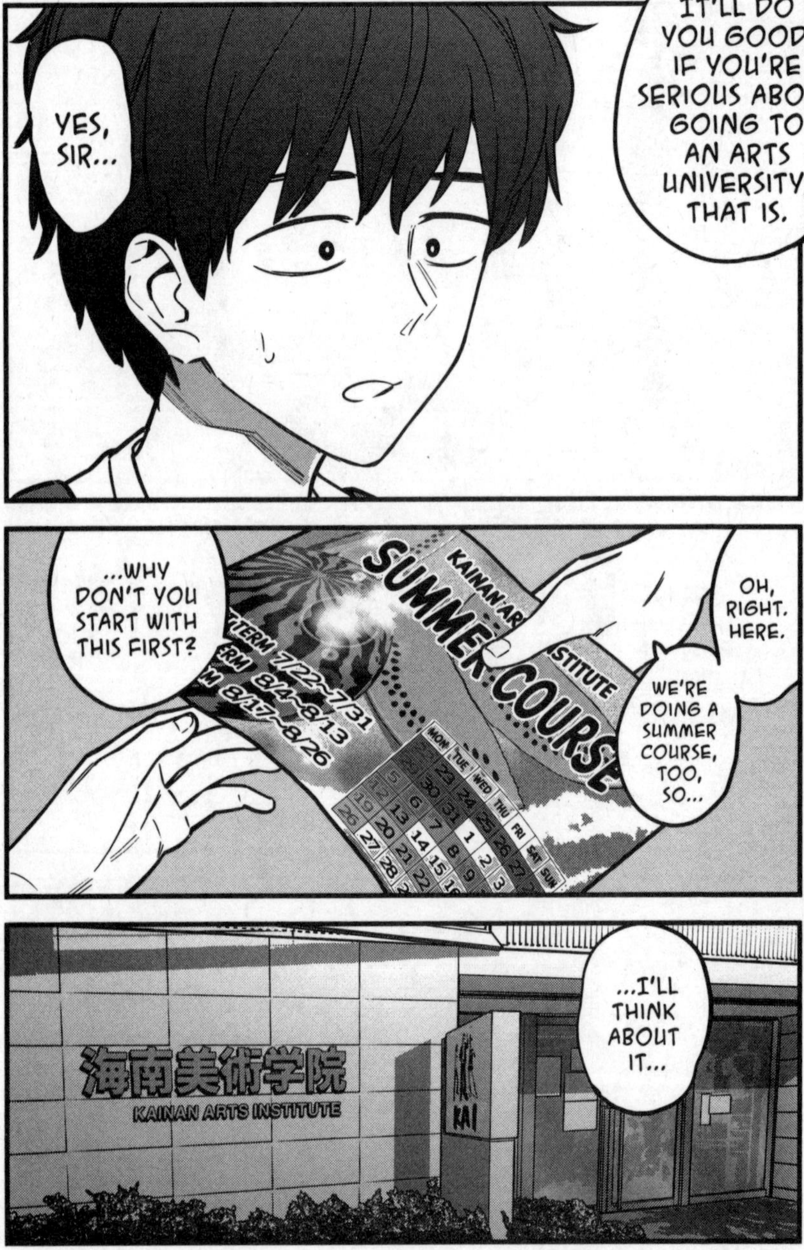
IT'LL DO YOU GOOD, IF YOU'RE SERIOUS ABOUT GOING TO AN ARTS UNIVERSITY, THAT IS.
YES, SIR...
OH, RIGHT. HERE.
WE'RE DOING A SUMMER COURSE, TOO, SO...
SUMMER COURSE
...WHY DON'T YOU START WITH THIS FIRST?
...I'LL THINK ABOUT IT...
海南美術学院
KAINAN ARTS INSTITUTE
KAI

SO, YEAH...
IT DIDN'T GO TOO WELL...
ぎゅうう
SKWEEZ
BUT I THOUGHT YOU'D BUILT UP A LITTLE CONFIDENCE RECENTLY.
WELL... IT'S JUST NOT THAT STRAIGHT-FORWARD WHEN IT COMES TO ART.
AND I'VE NEVER REALLY DONE WELL IN THAT KIND OF ENVIRONMENT, TO BEGIN WITH...

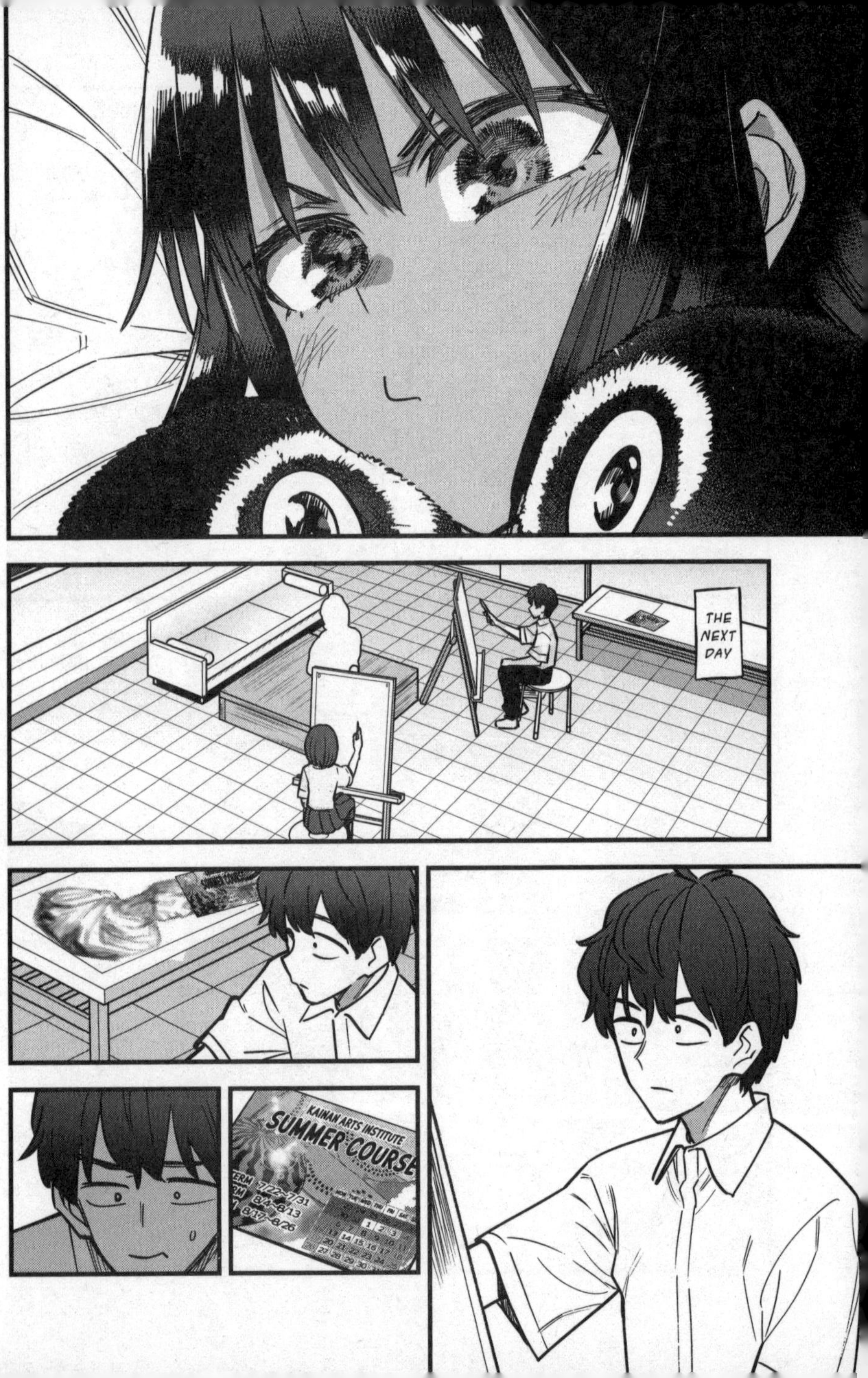
THE NEXT DAY
KAINAN ARTS INSTITUTE
SUMMER COURSE
7/22~7/31
8/4~8/13
8/17~8/26

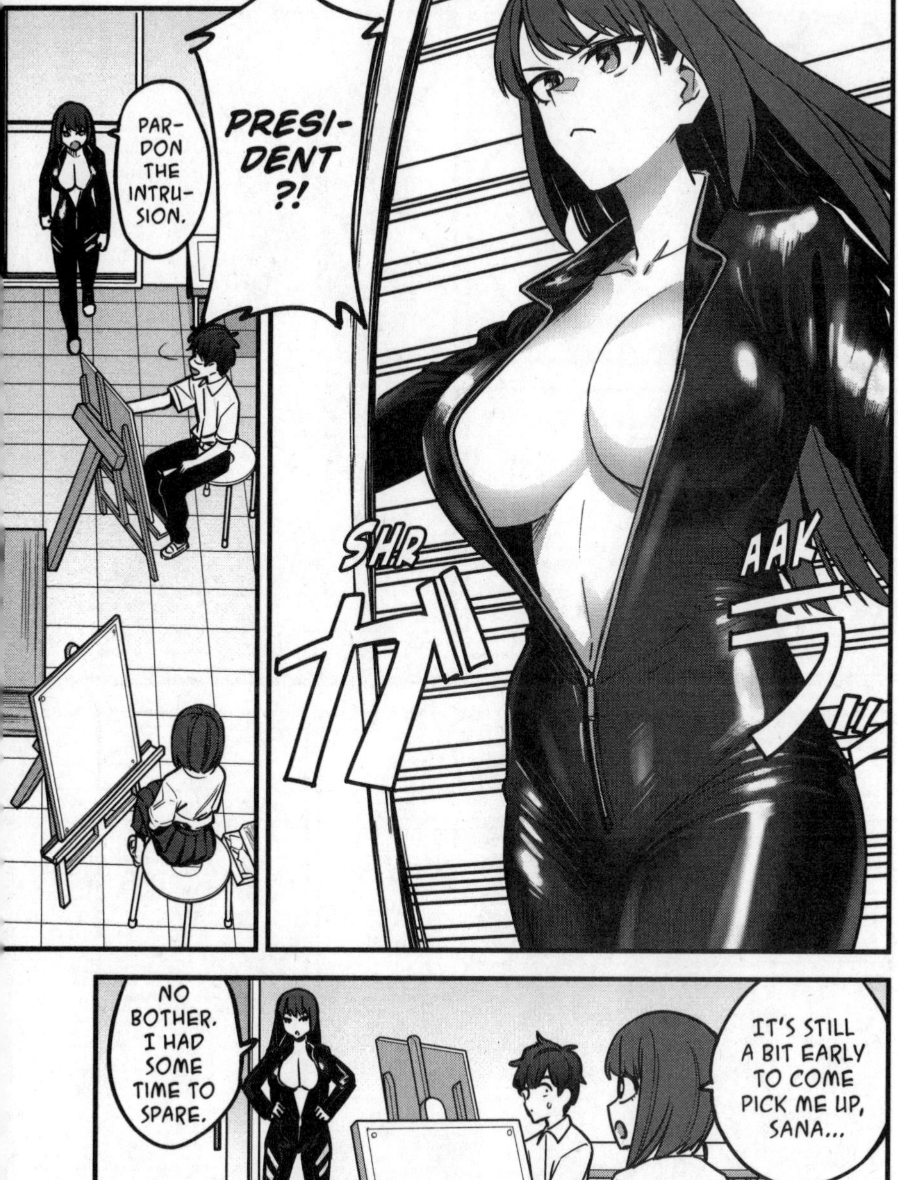
SHR AAK
ガラッ
PRESI-DENT?!
PAR-DON THE INTRU-SION.
IT'S STILL A BIT EARLY TO COME PICK ME UP, SANA...
NO BOTHER. I HAD SOME TIME TO SPARE.

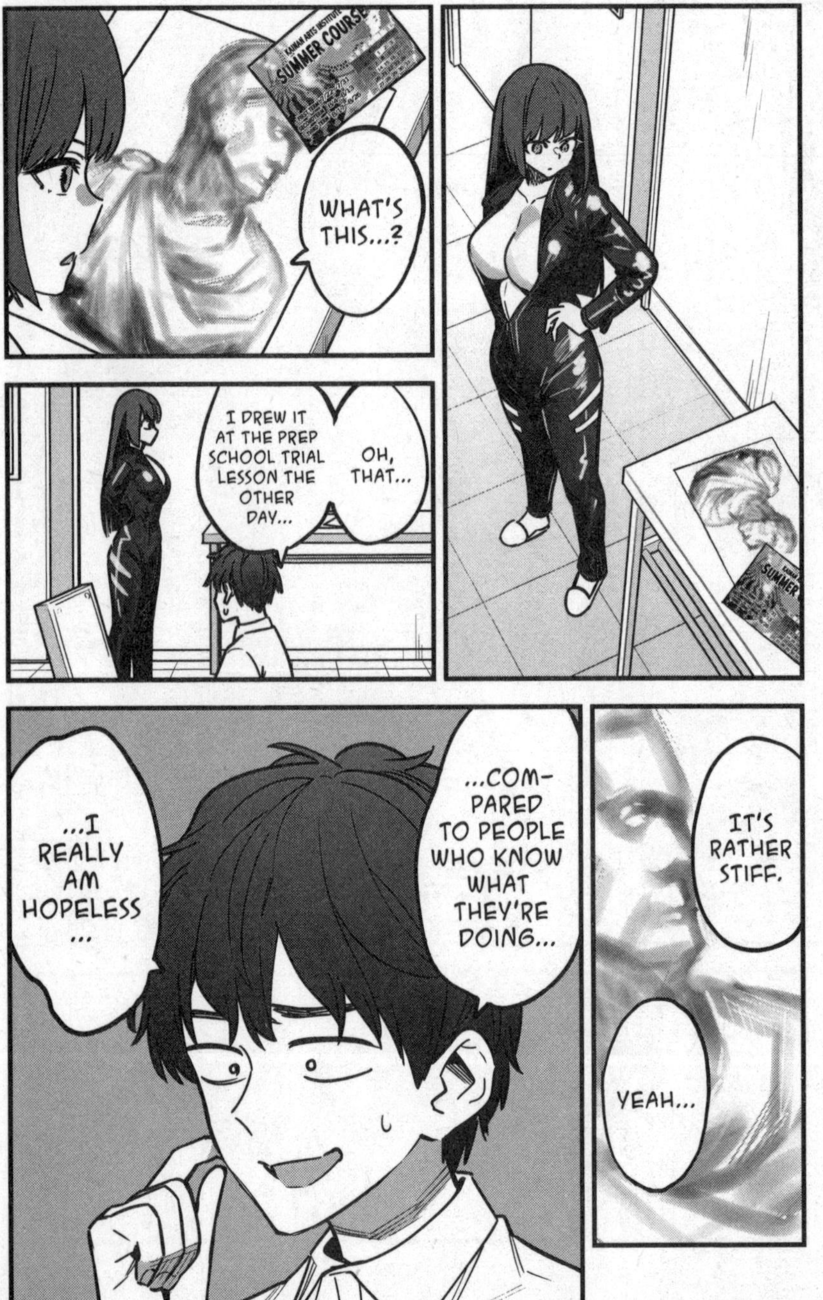
SUMMER COURSE
WHAT'S THIS...?
OH, THAT...
I DREW IT AT THE PREP SCHOOL TRIAL LESSON THE OTHER DAY...
IT'S RATHER STIFF.
YEAH...
...COMPARED TO PEOPLE WHO KNOW WHAT THEY'RE DOING...
...I REALLY AM HOPELESS...

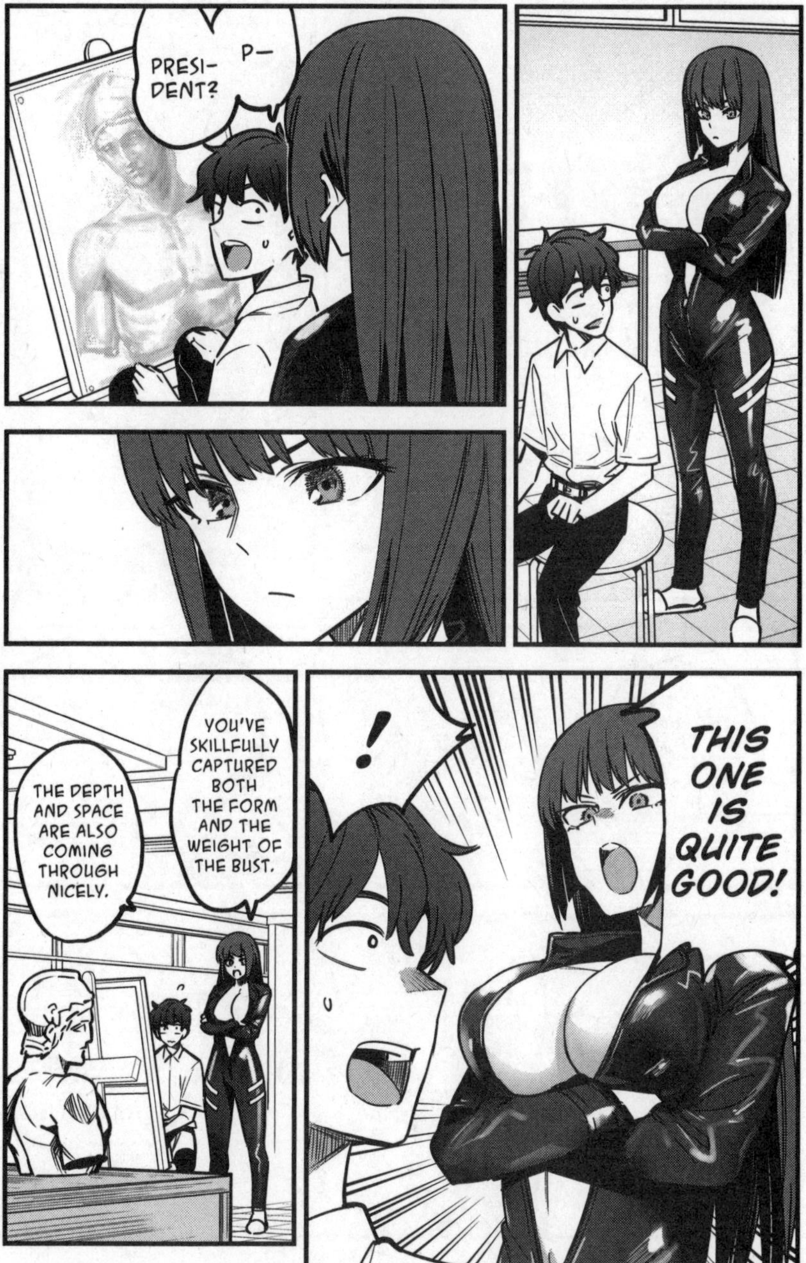
P— PRESI-DENT?
!
THIS ONE IS QUITE GOOD!
YOU'VE SKILLFULLY CAPTURED BOTH THE FORM AND THE WEIGHT OF THE BUST.
THE DEPTH AND SPACE ARE ALSO COMING THROUGH NICELY.

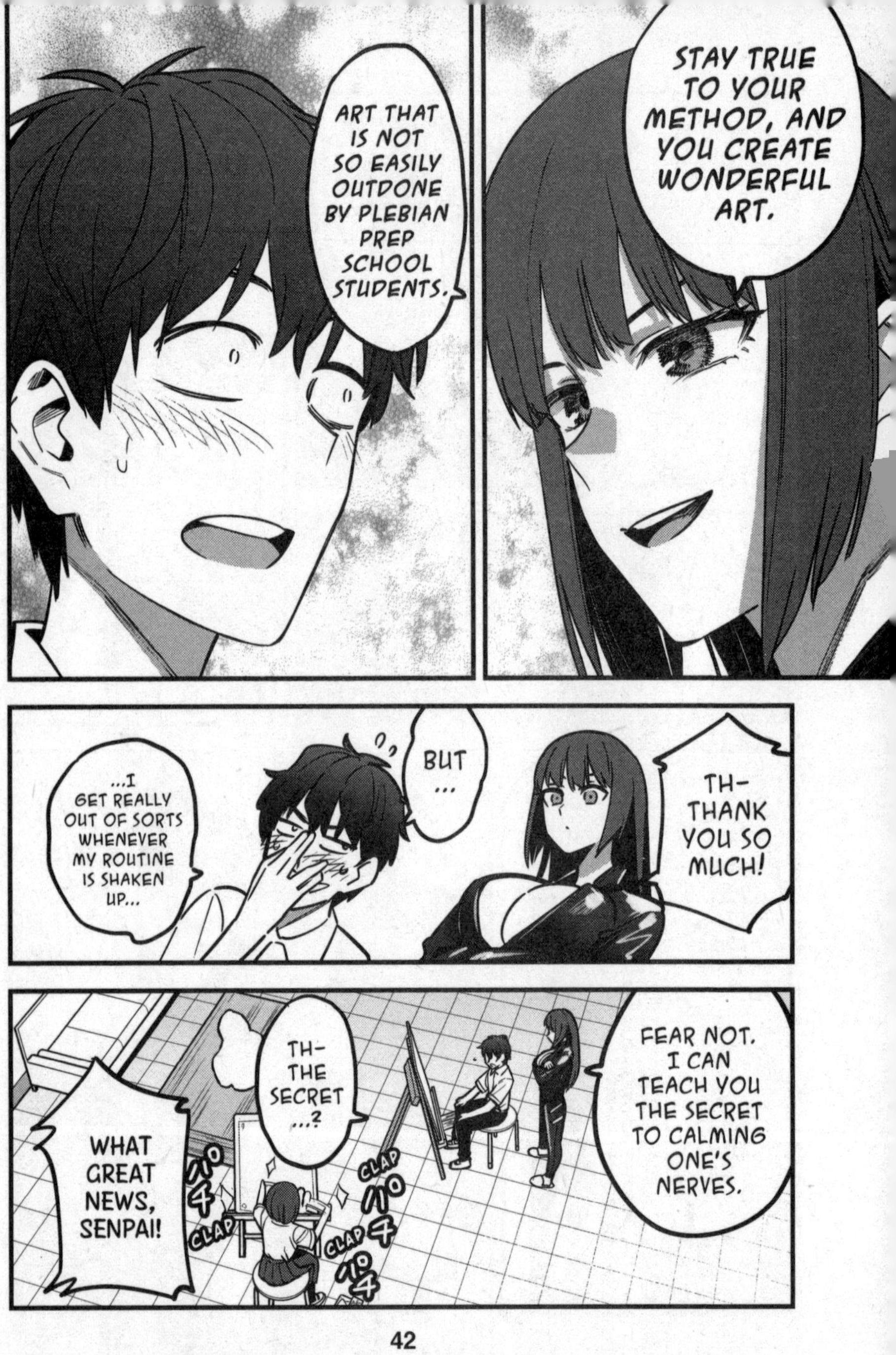
STAY TRUE TO YOUR METHOD, AND YOU CREATE WONDERFUL ART.
ART THAT IS NOT SO EASILY OUTDONE BY PLEBIAN PREP SCHOOL STUDENTS.
TH- THANK YOU SO MUCH!
BUT ...
...I GET REALLY OUT OF SORTS WHENEVER MY ROUTINE IS SHAKEN UP...
FEAR NOT. I CAN TEACH YOU THE SECRET TO CALMING ONE'S NERVES.
TH- THE SECRET ...?
CLAP
WHAT GREAT NEWS, SENPAI!
CLAP
CLAP

B-BUT PRESIDENT, AREN'T YOU BUSY WITH UNIVER-SITY...?
I DON'T MIND. ESPECIALLY GIVEN ALL THE TROUBLE I CAUSED YOU LAST YEAR.
I-I WOULDN'T SAY YOU—
ALSO ...
VRRUMM
KRSH
...

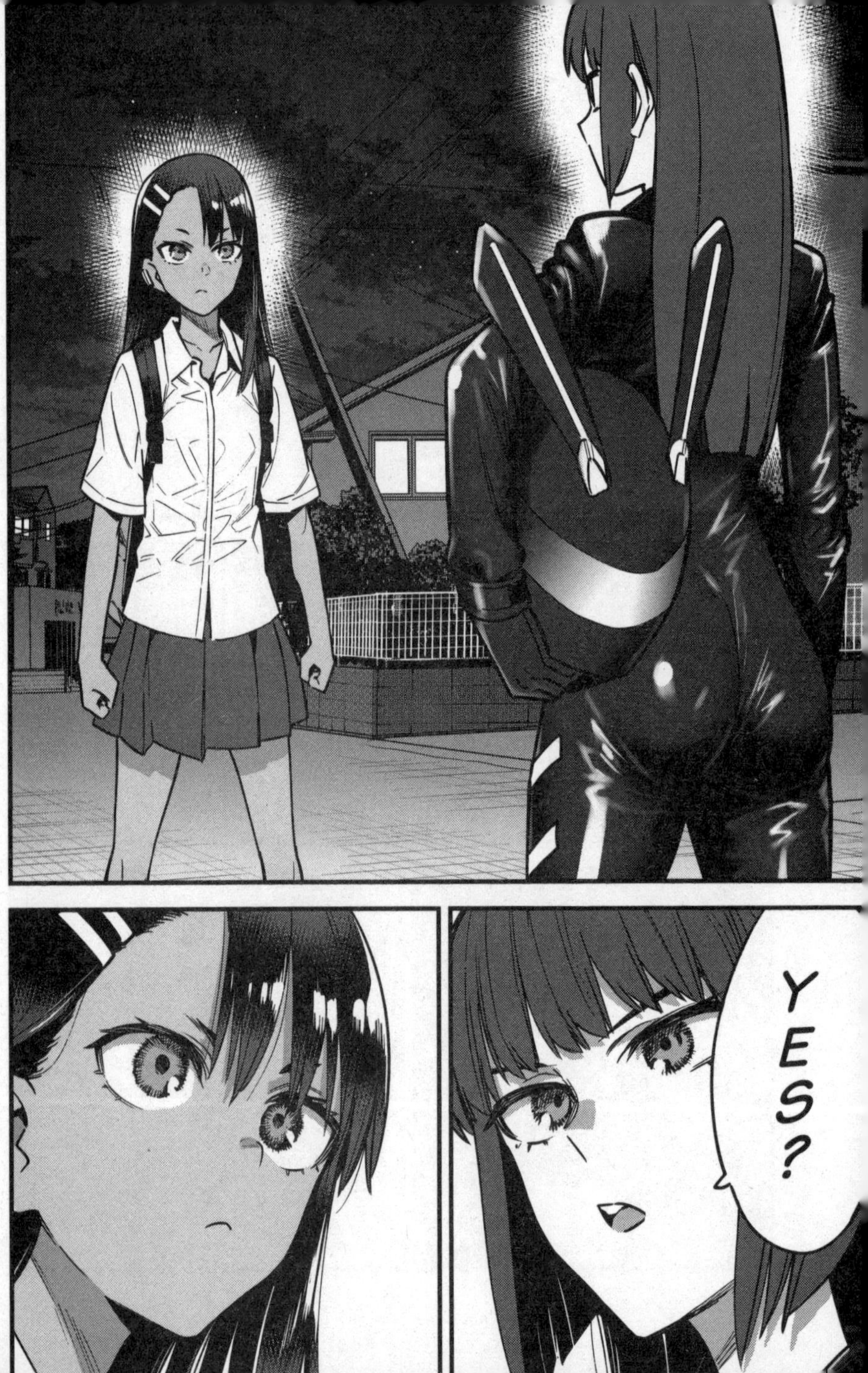
YES?

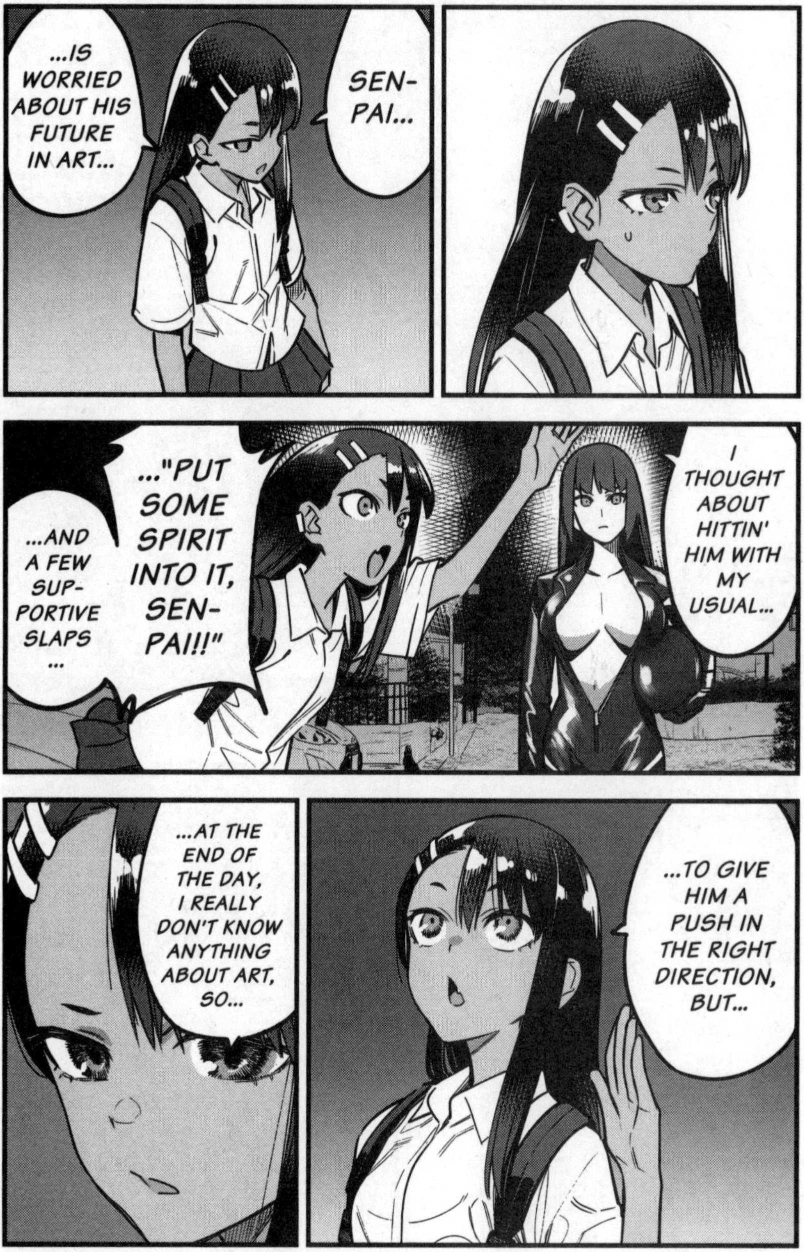
SEN-PAI...
...IS WORRIED ABOUT HIS FUTURE IN ART...
I THOUGHT ABOUT HITTIN' HIM WITH MY USUAL...
..."PUT SOME SPIRIT INTO IT, SEN-PAI!!"
...AND A FEW SUP-PORTIVE SLAPS ...
...TO GIVE HIM A PUSH IN THE RIGHT DIRECTION, BUT...
...AT THE END OF THE DAY, I REALLY DON'T KNOW ANYTHING ABOUT ART, SO...

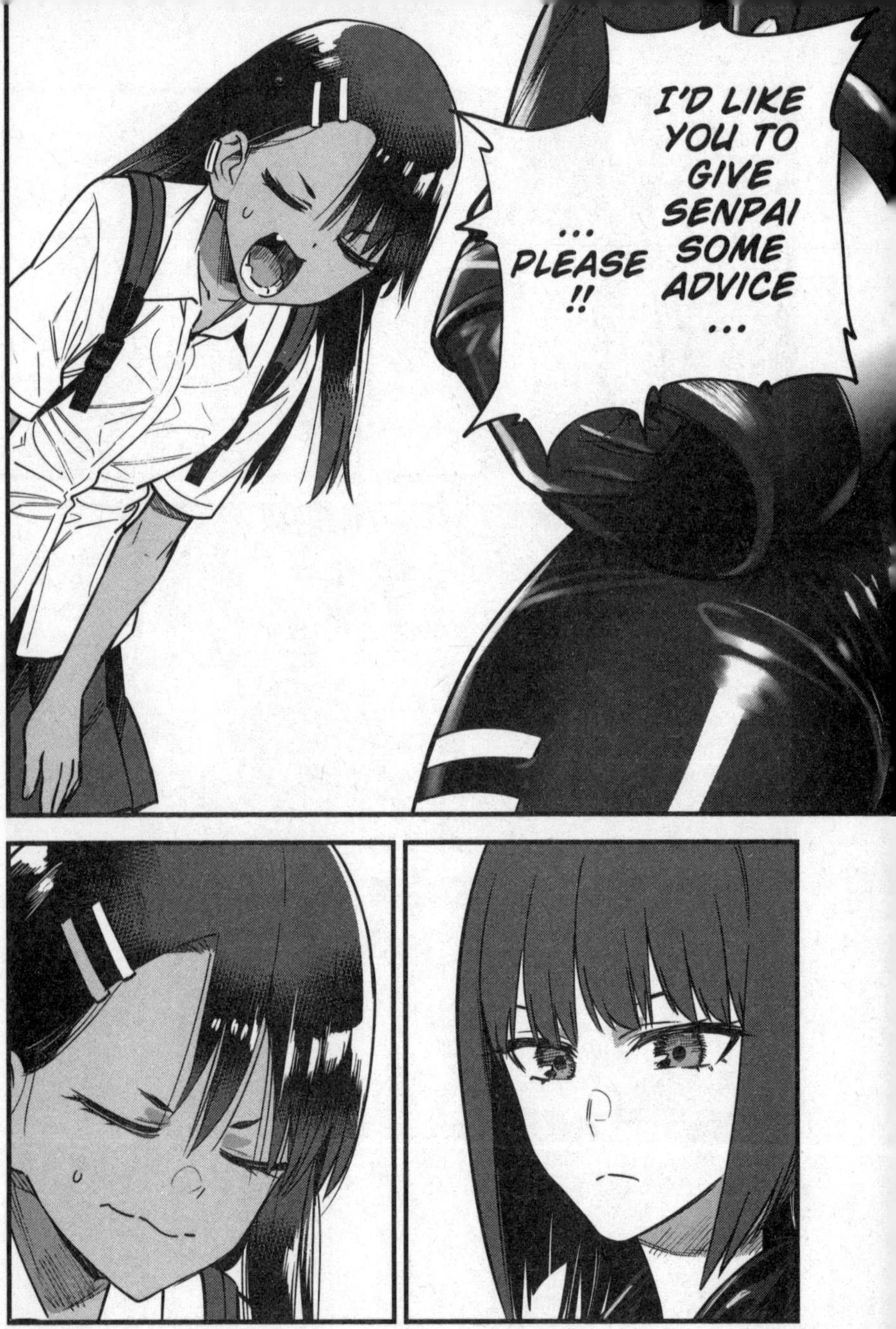
I'D LIKE YOU TO GIVE SENPAI SOME ADVICE ...
... PLEASE !!

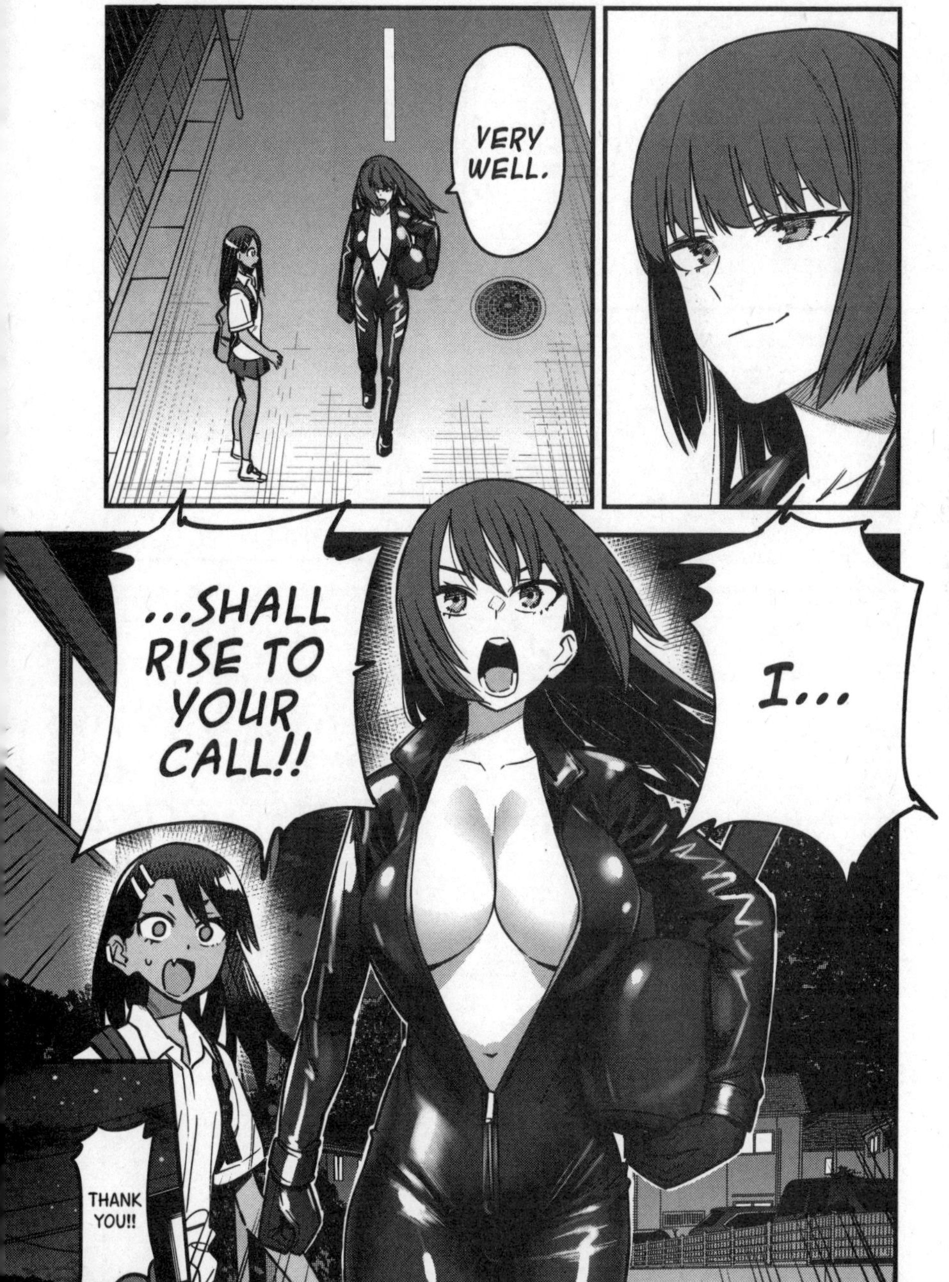
VERY WELL.
I...
...SHALL RISE TO YOUR CALL!!
THANK YOU!!

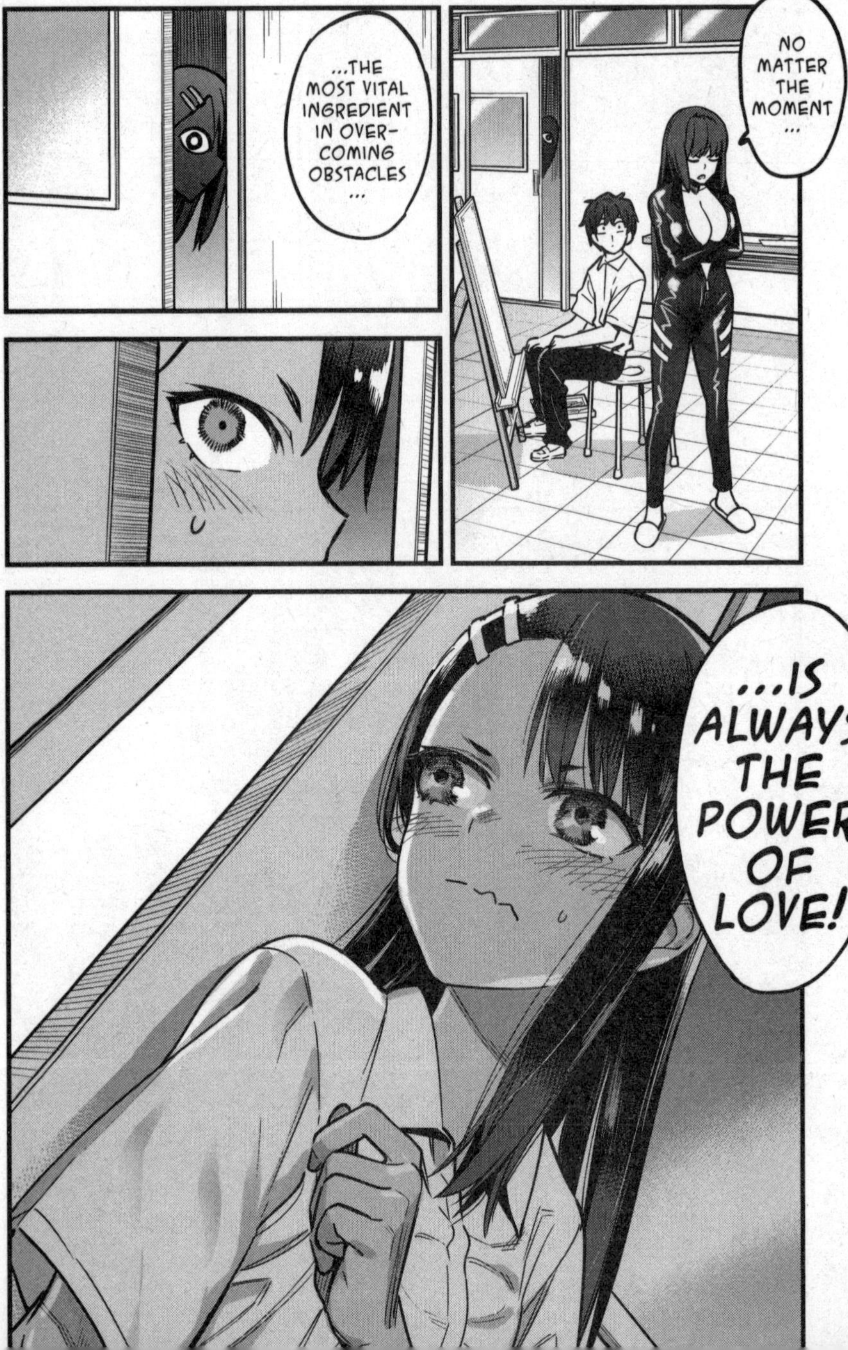
NO MATTER THE MOMENT...
...THE MOST VITAL INGREDIENT IN OVER-COMING OBSTACLES...
...IS ALWAYS THE POWER OF LOVE!

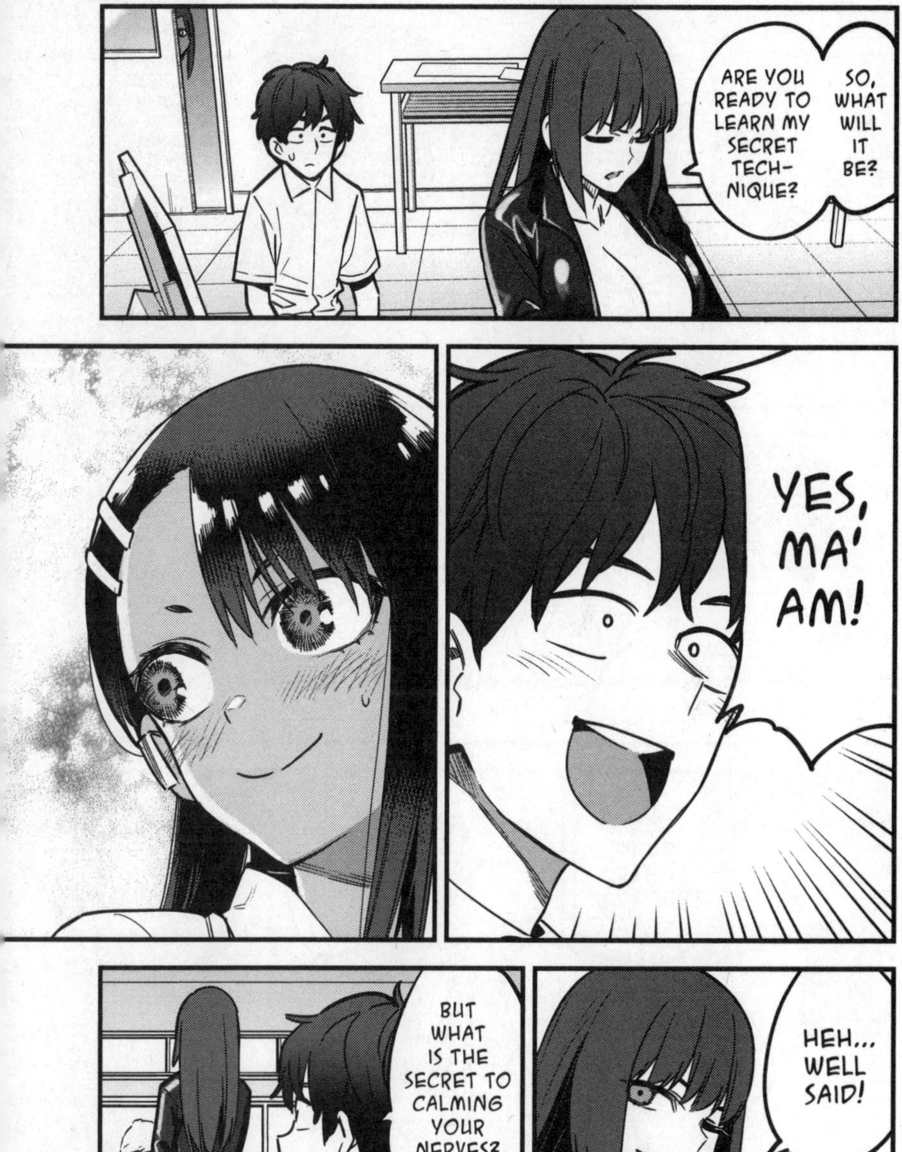
SO, WHAT WILL IT BE?
ARE YOU READY TO LEARN MY SECRET TECH-NIQUE?
YES, MA'AM!
HEH... WELL SAID!
BUT WHAT IS THE SECRET TO CALMING YOUR NERVES?

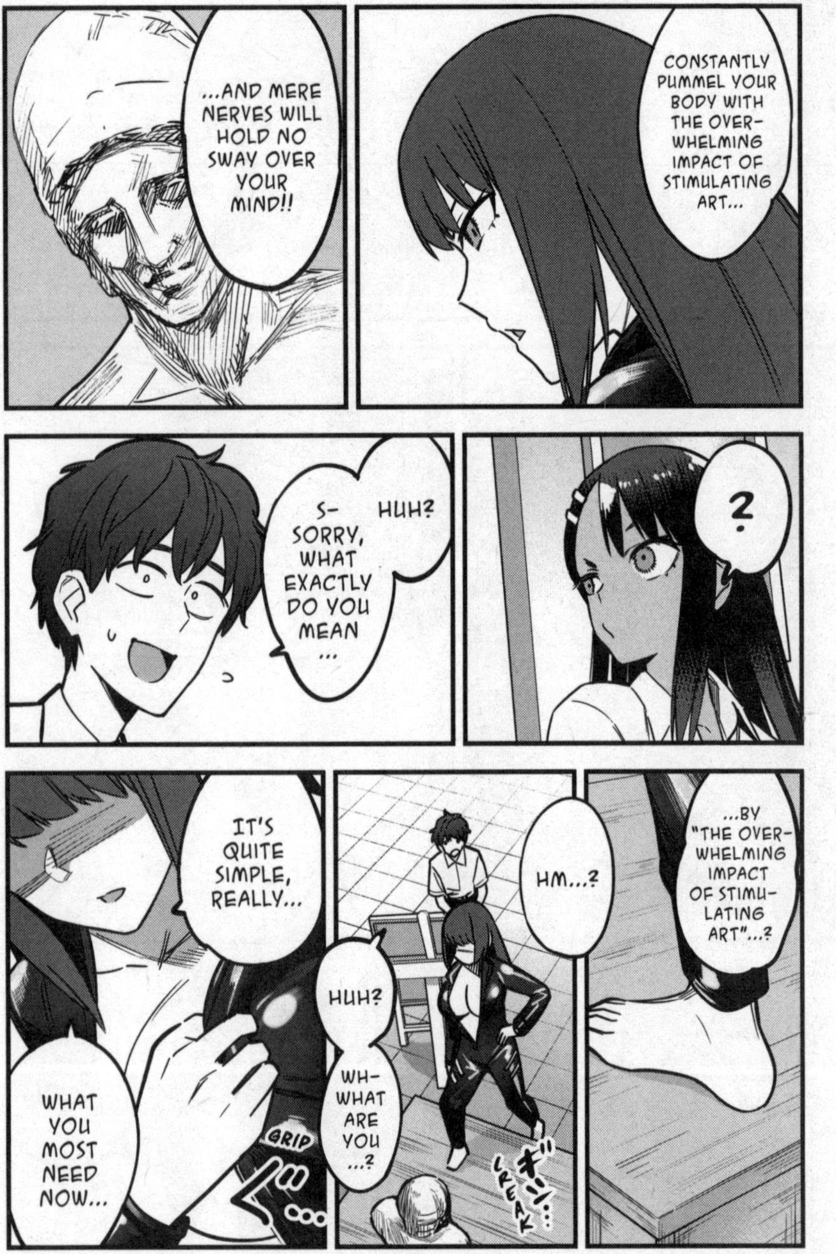
CONSTANTLY PUMMEL YOUR BODY WITH THE OVER-WHELMING IMPACT OF STIMULATING ART...
...AND MERE NERVES WILL HOLD NO SWAY OVER YOUR MIND!!
?
HUH?
S-SORRY, WHAT EXACTLY DO YOU MEAN...
...BY "THE OVER-WHELMING IMPACT OF STIMU-LATING ART"...?
HM...?
HUH?
WH-WHAT ARE YOU...?
CREAK
IT'S QUITE SIMPLE, REALLY...
WHAT YOU MOST NEED NOW...
GRIP

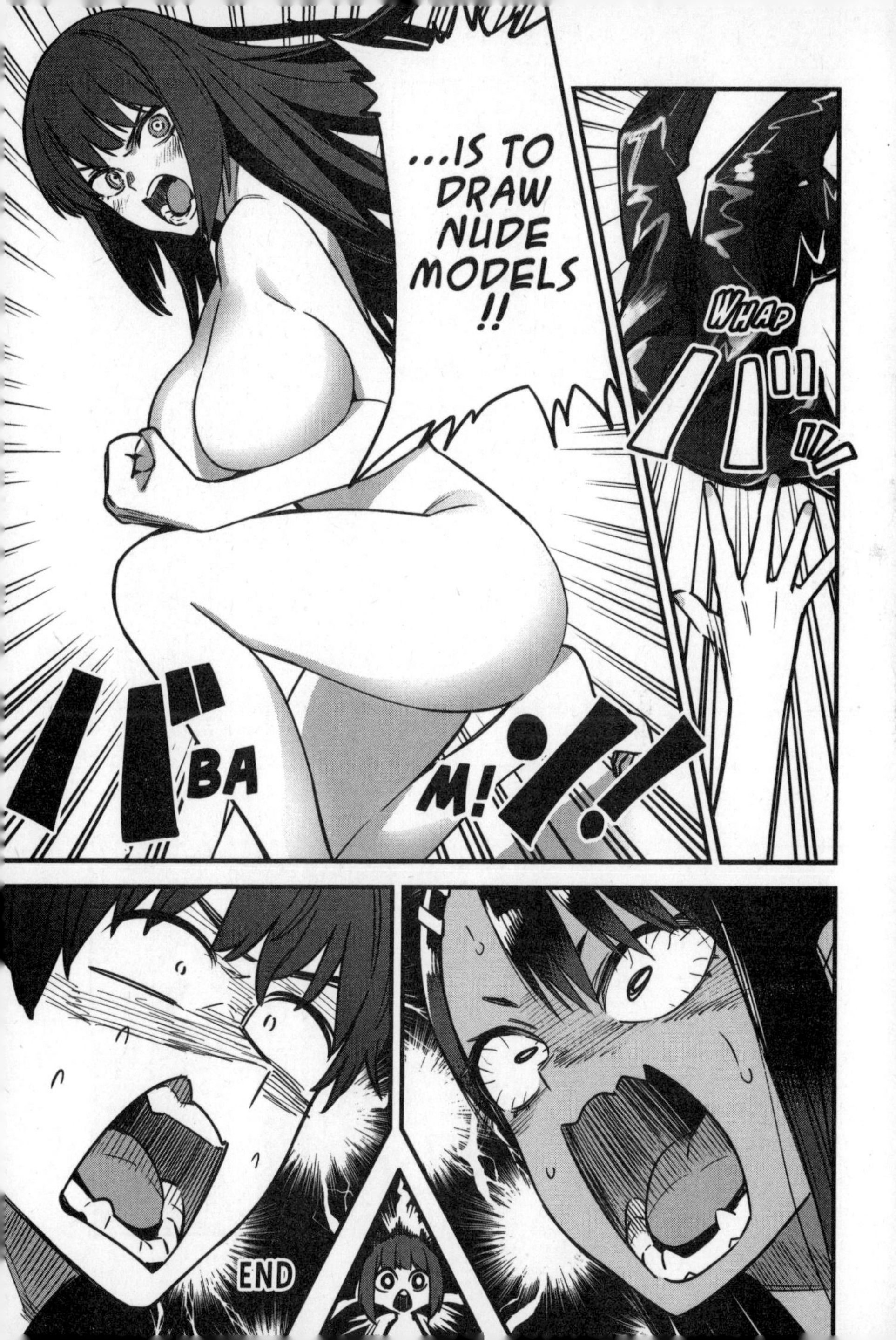
WHAP
...IS TO DRAW NUDE MODELS!!
BAM!
END

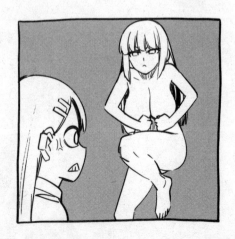

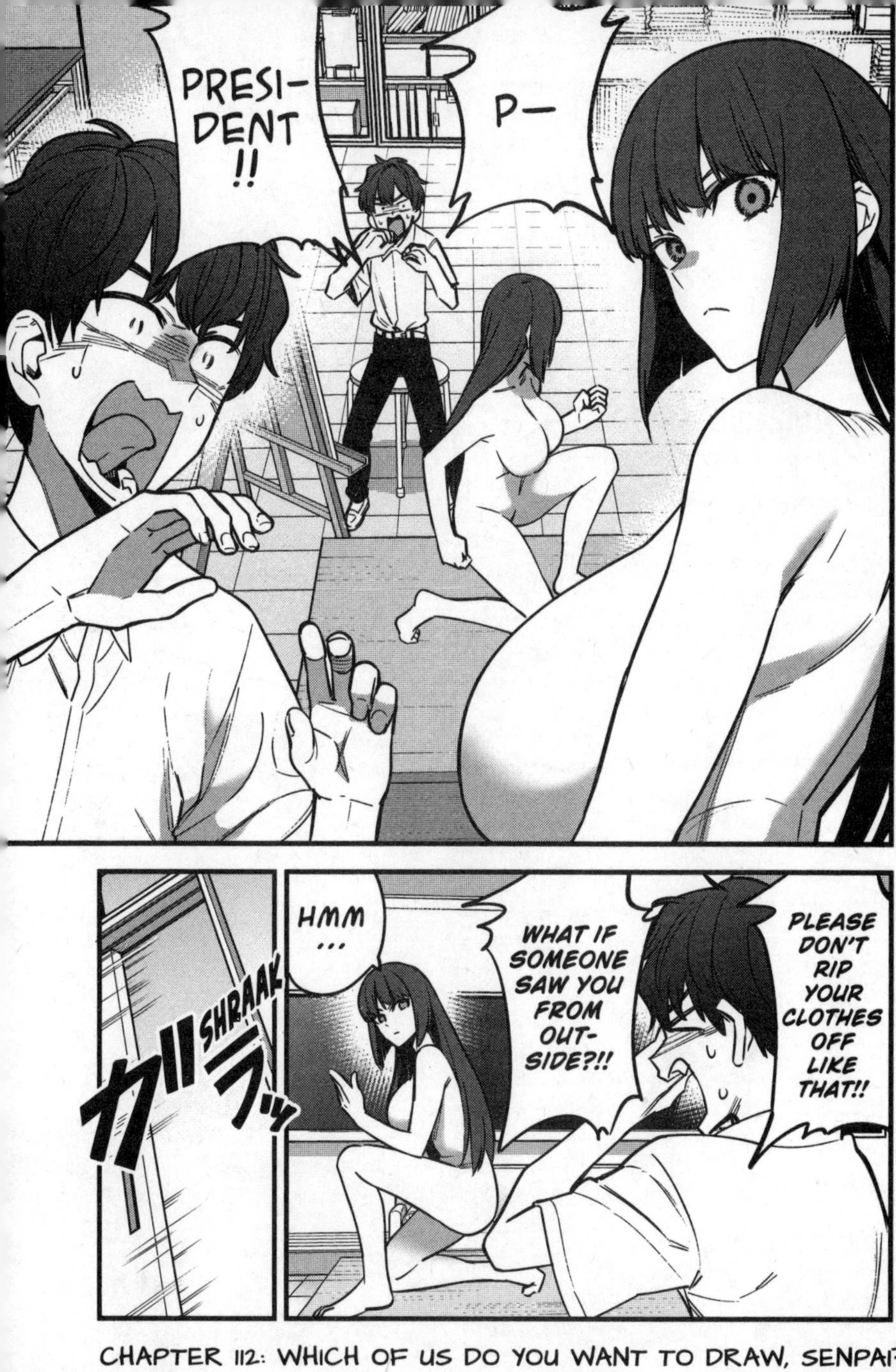
P—
PRESI-DENT!!
PLEASE DON'T RIP YOUR CLOTHES OFF LIKE THAT!!
WHAT IF SOMEONE SAW YOU FROM OUT-SIDE?!!
HMM...
カラッ
SHRAAK

CHAPTER 112: WHICH OF US DO YOU WANT TO DRAW, SENPAI?

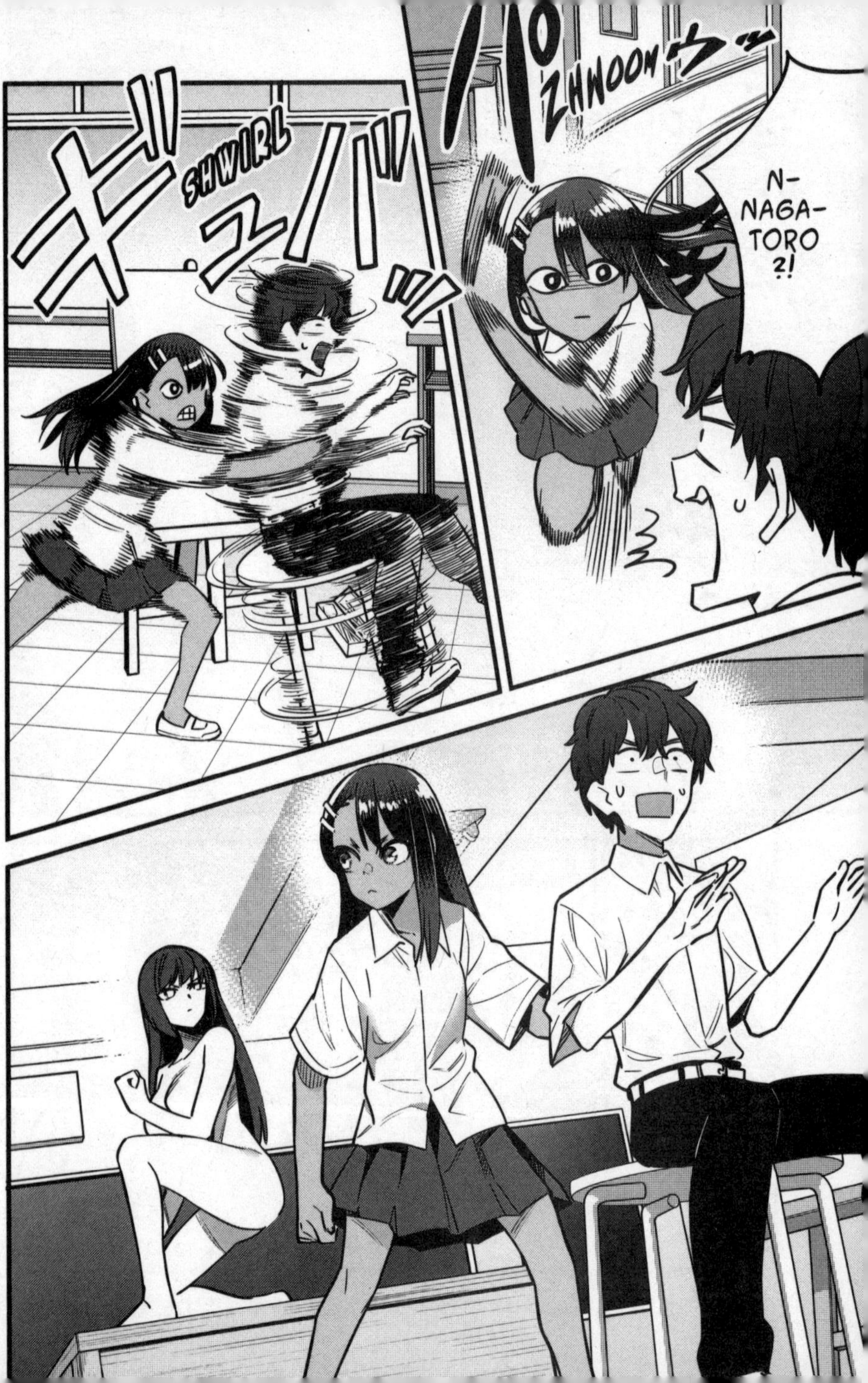
ZHWOOM
N-NAGATORO?!
SHWIRL

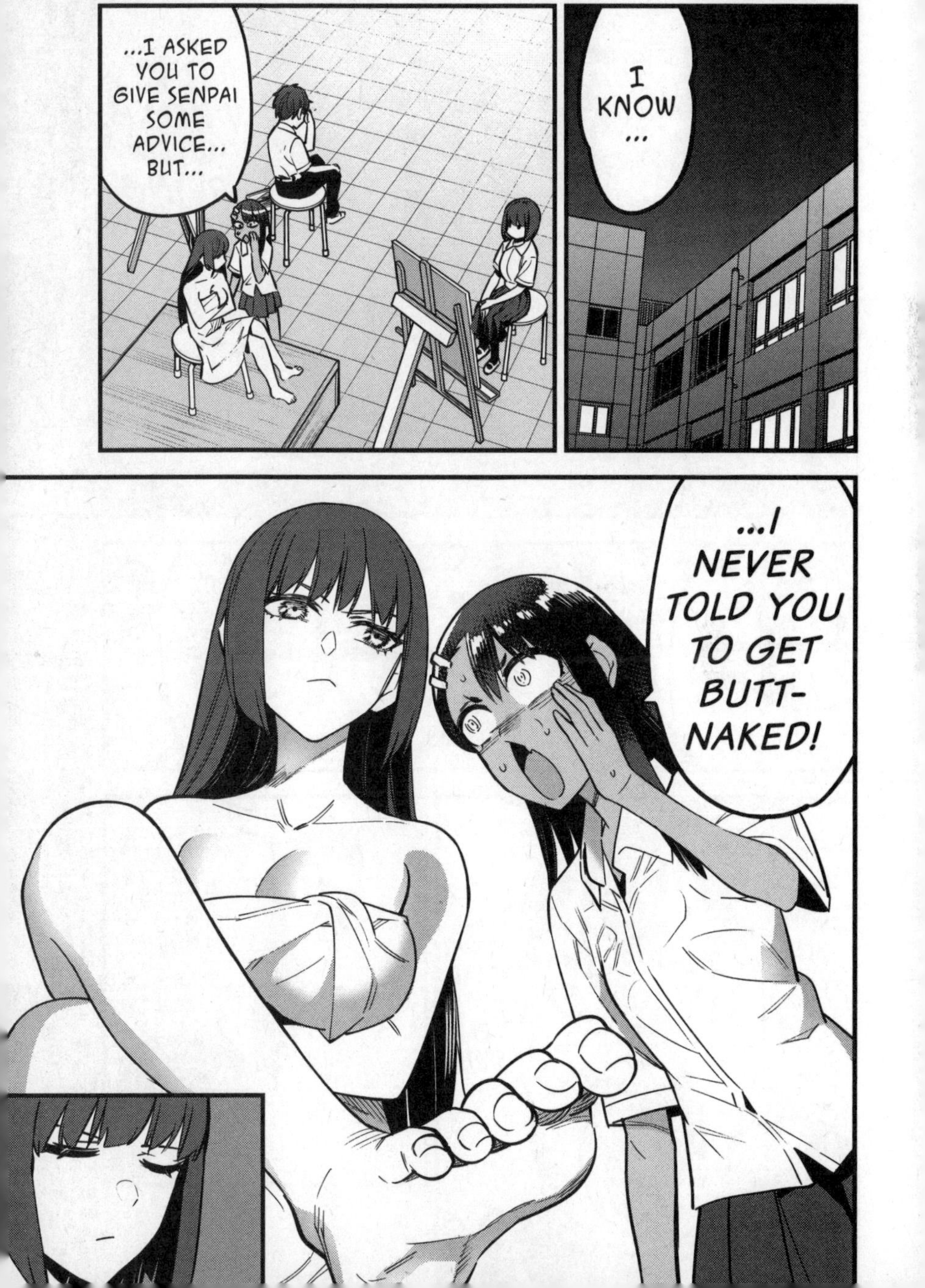
I KNOW ...
...I ASKED YOU TO GIVE SENPAI SOME ADVICE... BUT...
...I NEVER TOLD YOU TO GET BUTT-NAKED!

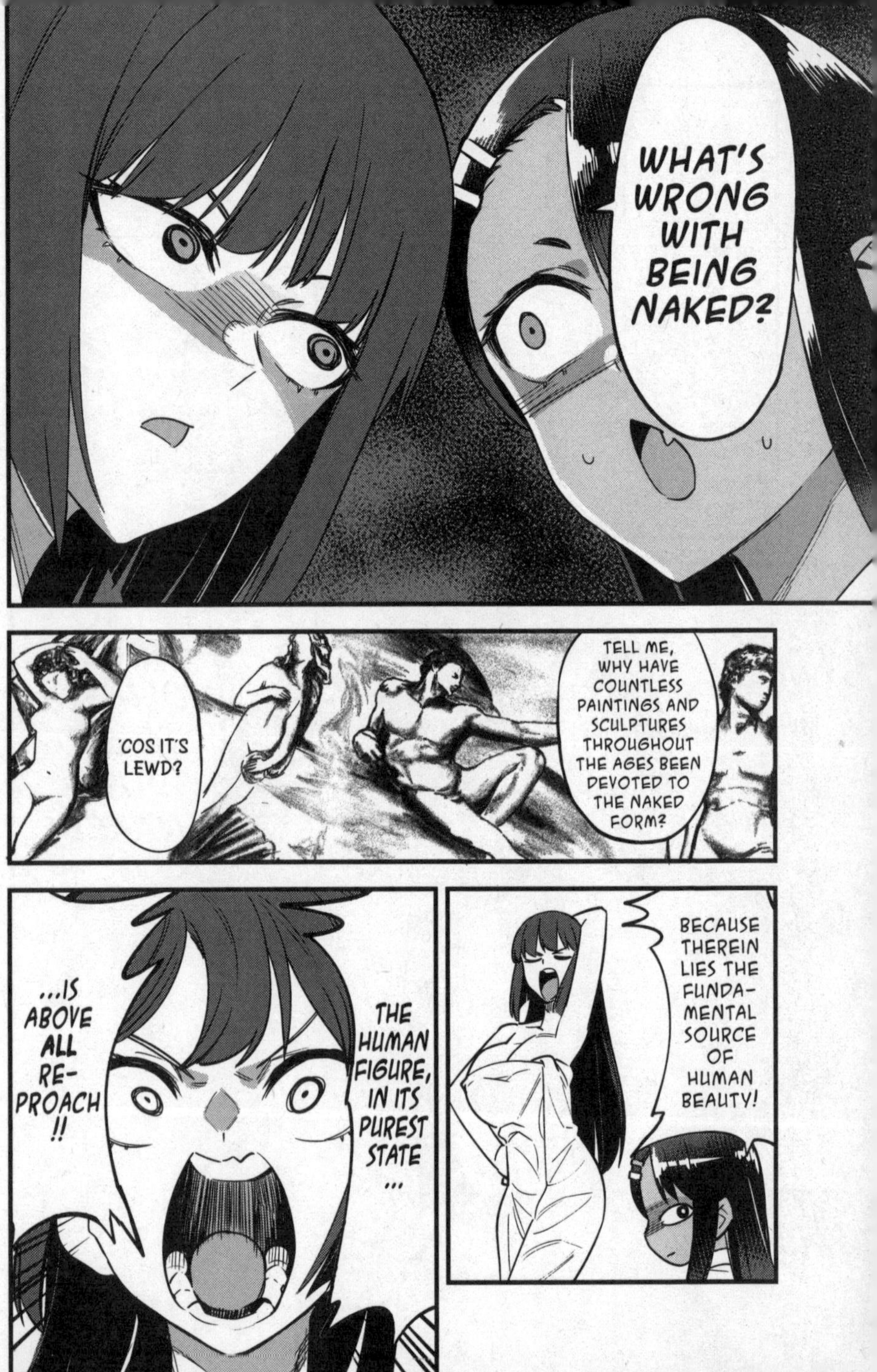
WHAT'S WRONG WITH BEING NAKED?
TELL ME, WHY HAVE COUNTLESS PAINTINGS AND SCULPTURES THROUGHOUT THE AGES BEEN DEVOTED TO THE NAKED FORM?
'COS IT'S LEWD?
BECAUSE THEREIN LIES THE FUNDA-MENTAL SOURCE OF HUMAN BEAUTY!
THE HUMAN FIGURE, IN ITS PUREST STATE...
...IS ABOVE ALL RE-PROACH!!

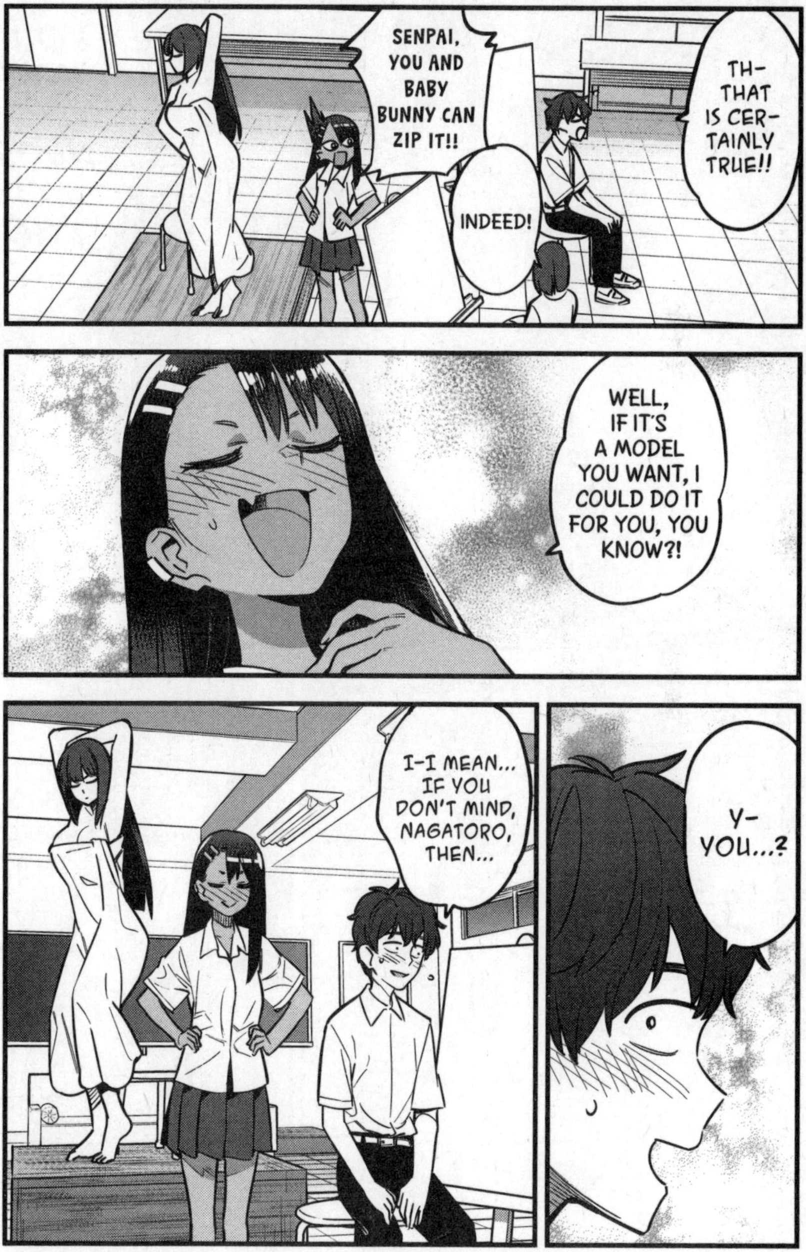

TH-THAT IS CER-TAINLY TRUE!!
SENPAI, YOU AND BABY BUNNY CAN ZIP IT!!
INDEED!
WELL, IF IT'S A MODEL YOU WANT, I COULD DO IT FOR YOU, YOU KNOW?!
Y-YOU...?
I-I MEAN... IF YOU DON'T MIND, NAGATORO, THEN...

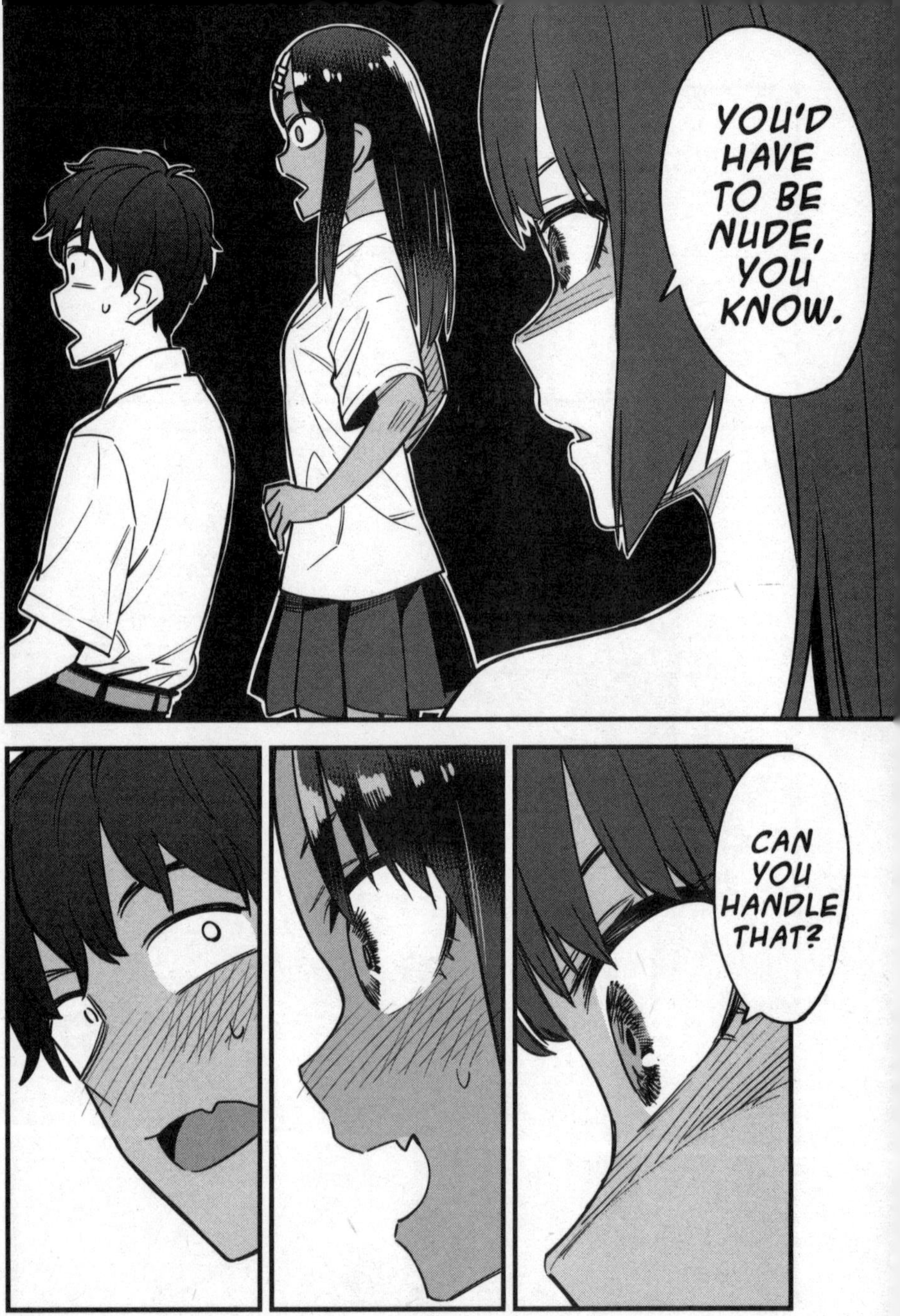
YOU'D HAVE TO BE NUDE, YOU KNOW.
CAN YOU HANDLE THAT?

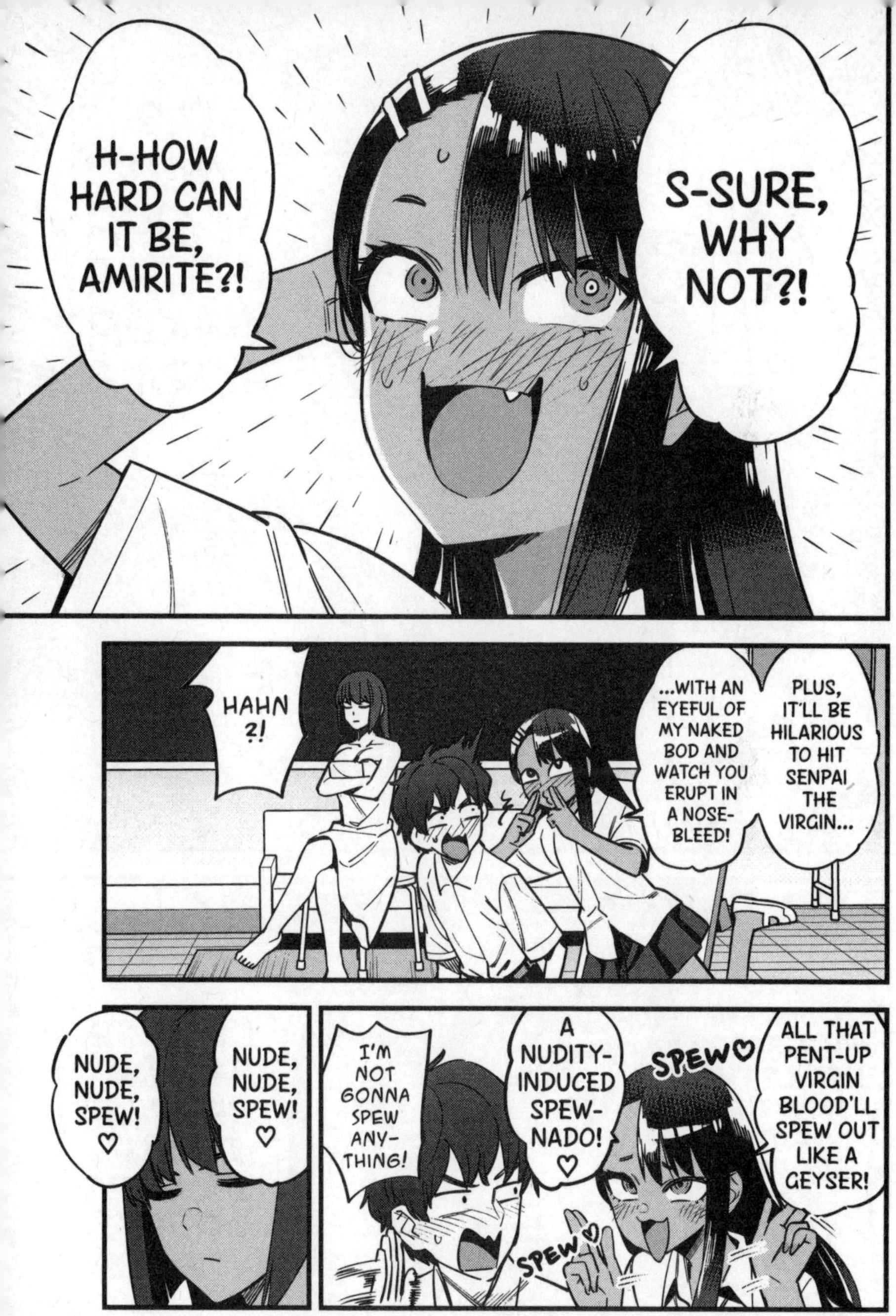
S-SURE, WHY NOT?!
H-HOW HARD CAN IT BE, AMIRITE?!
PLUS, IT'LL BE HILARIOUS TO HIT SENPAI THE VIRGIN...
...WITH AN EYEFUL OF MY NAKED BOD AND WATCH YOU ERUPT IN A NOSE-BLEED!
HAHN ?!
ALL THAT PENT-UP VIRGIN BLOOD'LL SPEW OUT LIKE A GEYSER!
SPEW♡
A NUDITY-INDUCED SPEW-NADO! ♡
I'M NOT GONNA SPEW ANY-THING!
SPEW♡
NUDE, NUDE, SPEW! ♡
NUDE, NUDE, SPEW! ♡

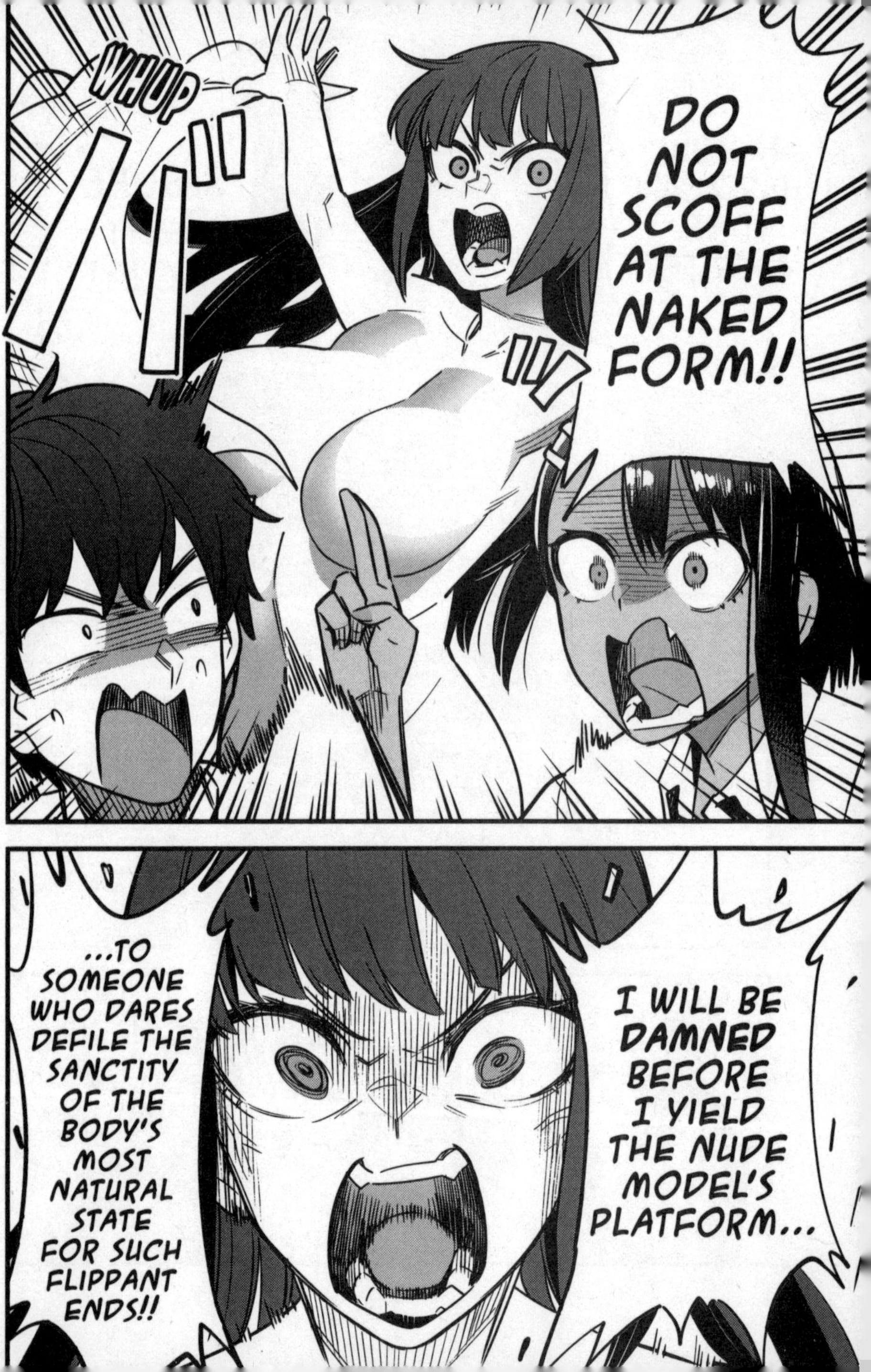
DO NOT SCOFF AT THE NAKED FORM!!
WHUP
I WILL BE DAMNED BEFORE I YIELD THE NUDE MODEL'S PLATFORM...
...TO SOMEONE WHO DARES DEFILE THE SANCTITY OF THE BODY'S MOST NATURAL STATE FOR SUCH FLIPPANT ENDS!!

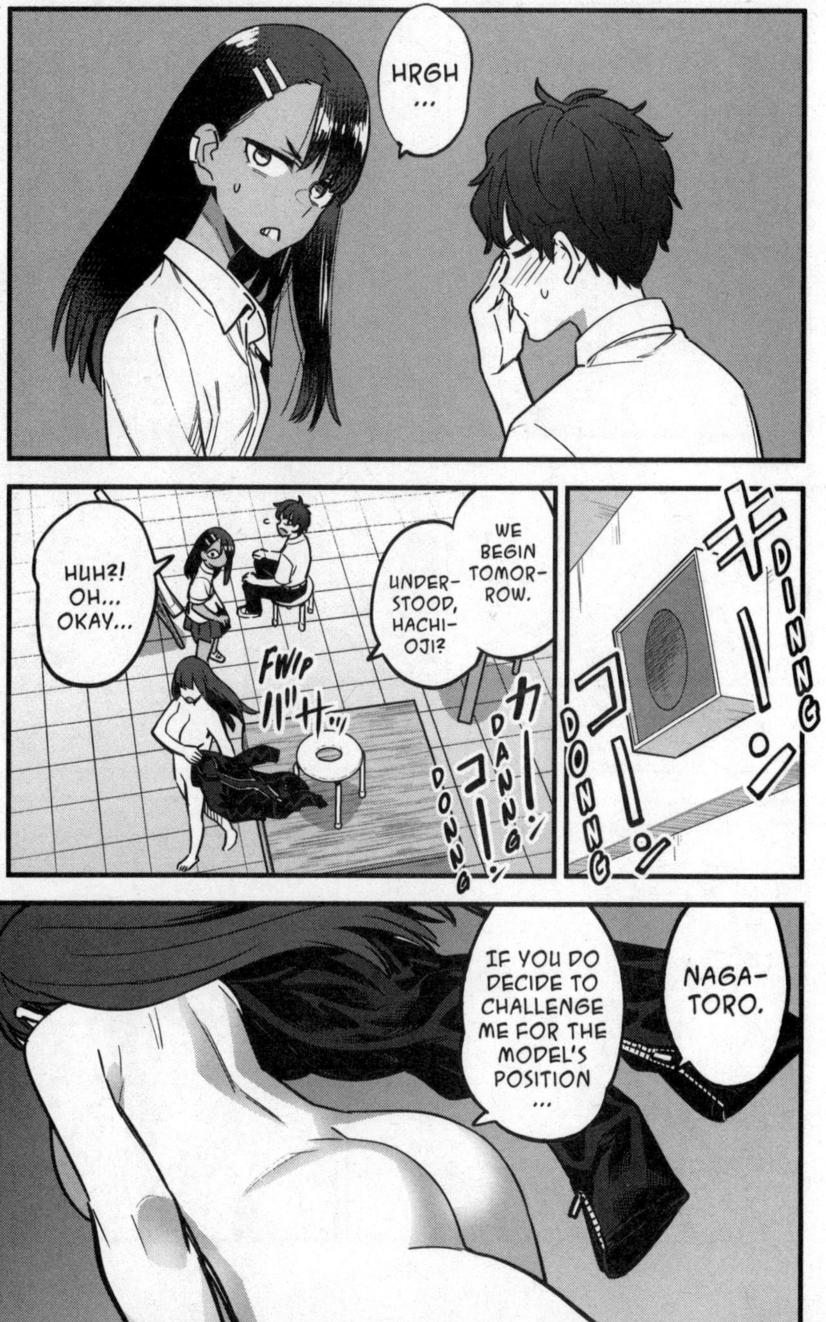
HRGH ...
キーンコーン
DINNG
DONNG
WE BEGIN TOMORROW.
UNDERSTOOD, HACHIOJI?
HUH?! OH... OKAY...
FWIP
バサッ
カーンコーン
DANNG
DONNG
NAGATORO.
IF YOU DO DECIDE TO CHALLENGE ME FOR THE MODEL'S POSITION ...

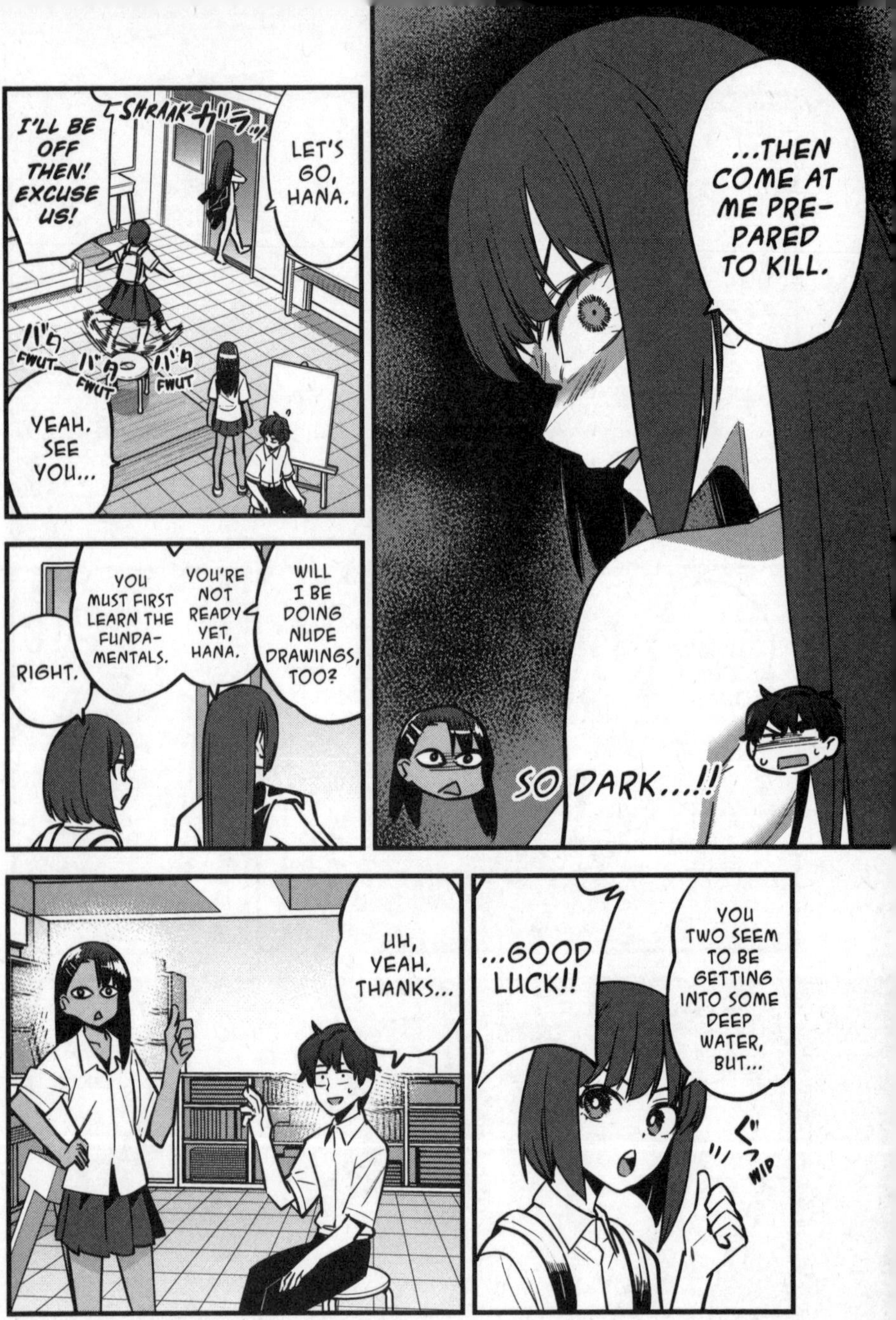
...THEN COME AT ME PRE-PARED TO KILL.
SO DARK...!!
LET'S GO, HANA.
SHRAAK ガラッ
I'LL BE OFF THEN! EXCUSE US!
バタ FWUT
バタ FWUT
バタ FWUT
YEAH. SEE YOU...
WILL I BE DOING NUDE DRAWINGS, TOO?
YOU'RE NOT READY YET, HANA.
YOU MUST FIRST LEARN THE FUNDA-MENTALS.
RIGHT.
YOU TWO SEEM TO BE GETTING INTO SOME DEEP WATER, BUT...
...GOOD LUCK!!
ぐっ WIP
UH, YEAH. THANKS...

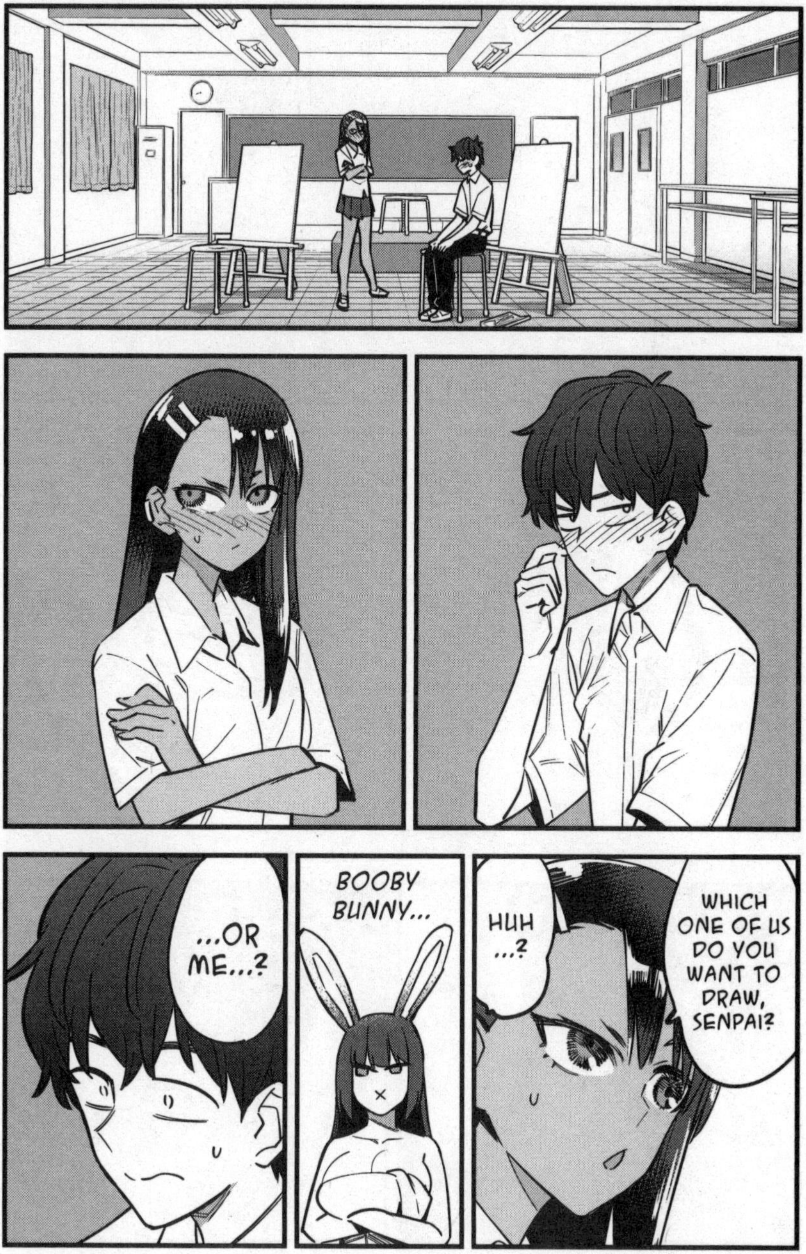
WHICH ONE OF US DO YOU WANT TO DRAW, SENPAI?
HUH ...?
BOOBY BUNNY...
...OR ME...?

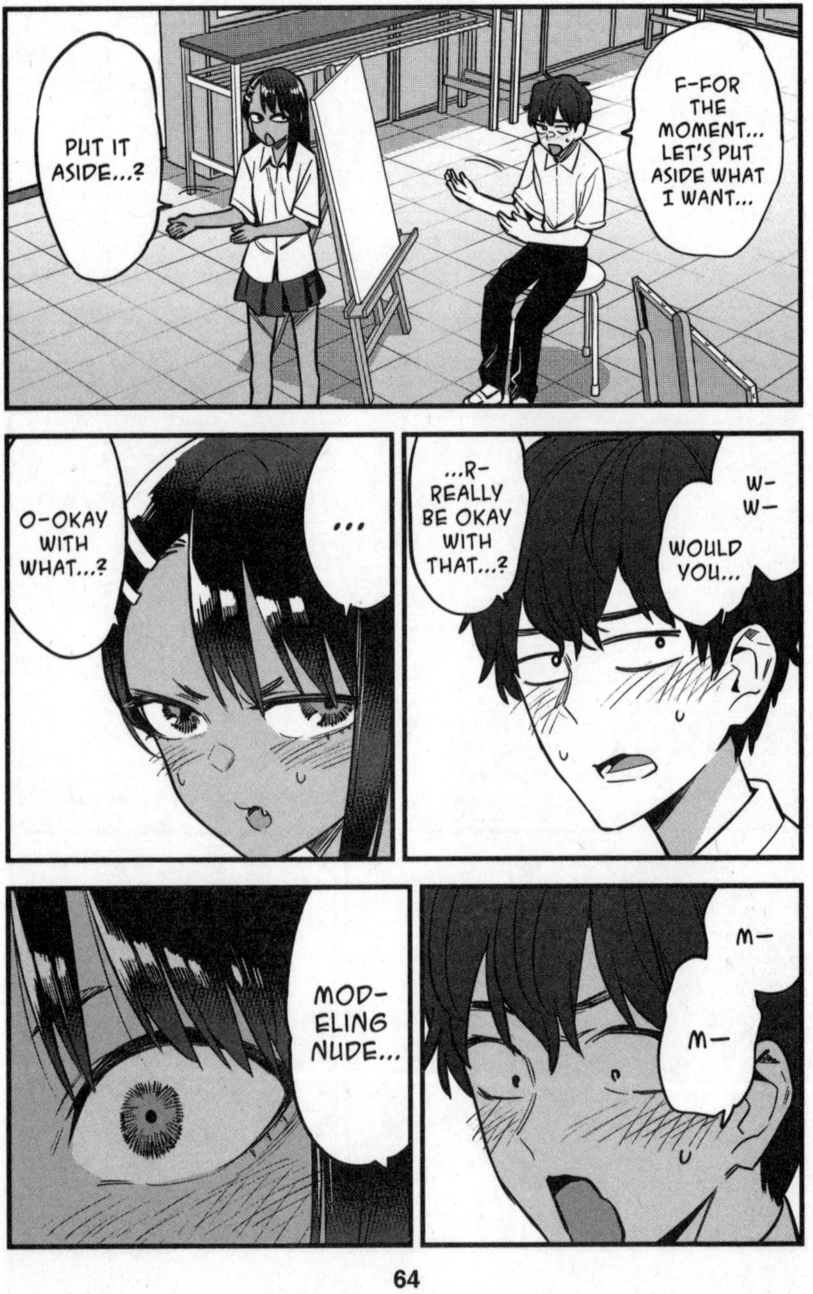
F-FOR THE MOMENT... LET'S PUT ASIDE WHAT I WANT...
PUT IT ASIDE...?
W- W- WOULD YOU...
...R- REALLY BE OKAY WITH THAT...?
...
O-OKAY WITH WHAT...?
M- M-
MOD-ELING NUDE...

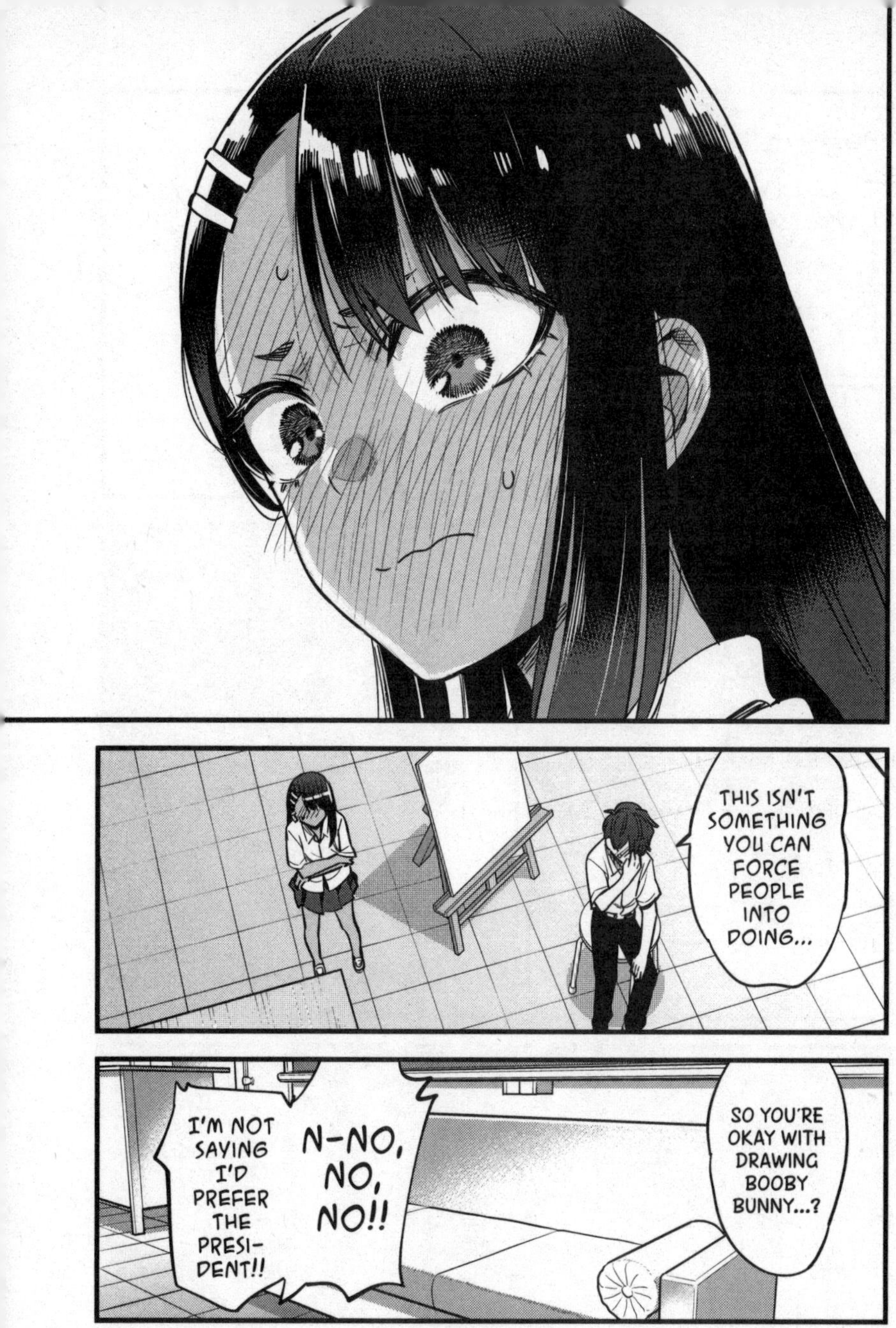
THIS ISN'T SOMETHING YOU CAN FORCE PEOPLE INTO DOING...
SO YOU'RE OKAY WITH DRAWING BOOBY BUNNY...?
N-NO, NO, NO!!
I'M NOT SAYING I'D PREFER THE PRESI-DENT!!

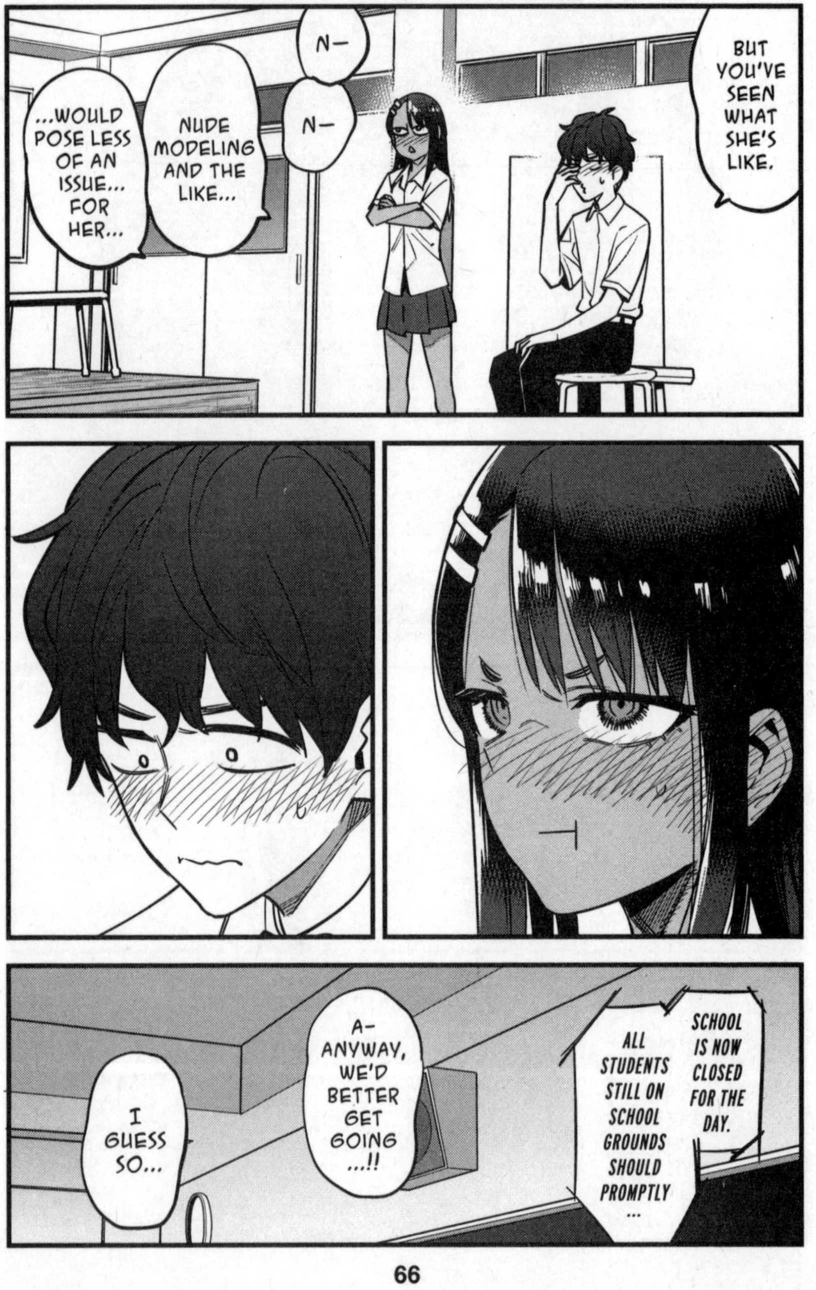
BUT YOU'VE SEEN WHAT SHE'S LIKE.
N—
N—
NUDE MODELING AND THE LIKE...
...WOULD POSE LESS OF AN ISSUE... FOR HER...
SCHOOL IS NOW CLOSED FOR THE DAY.
ALL STUDENTS STILL ON SCHOOL GROUNDS SHOULD PROMPTLY ...
A- ANYWAY, WE'D BETTER GET GOING ...!!
I GUESS SO...

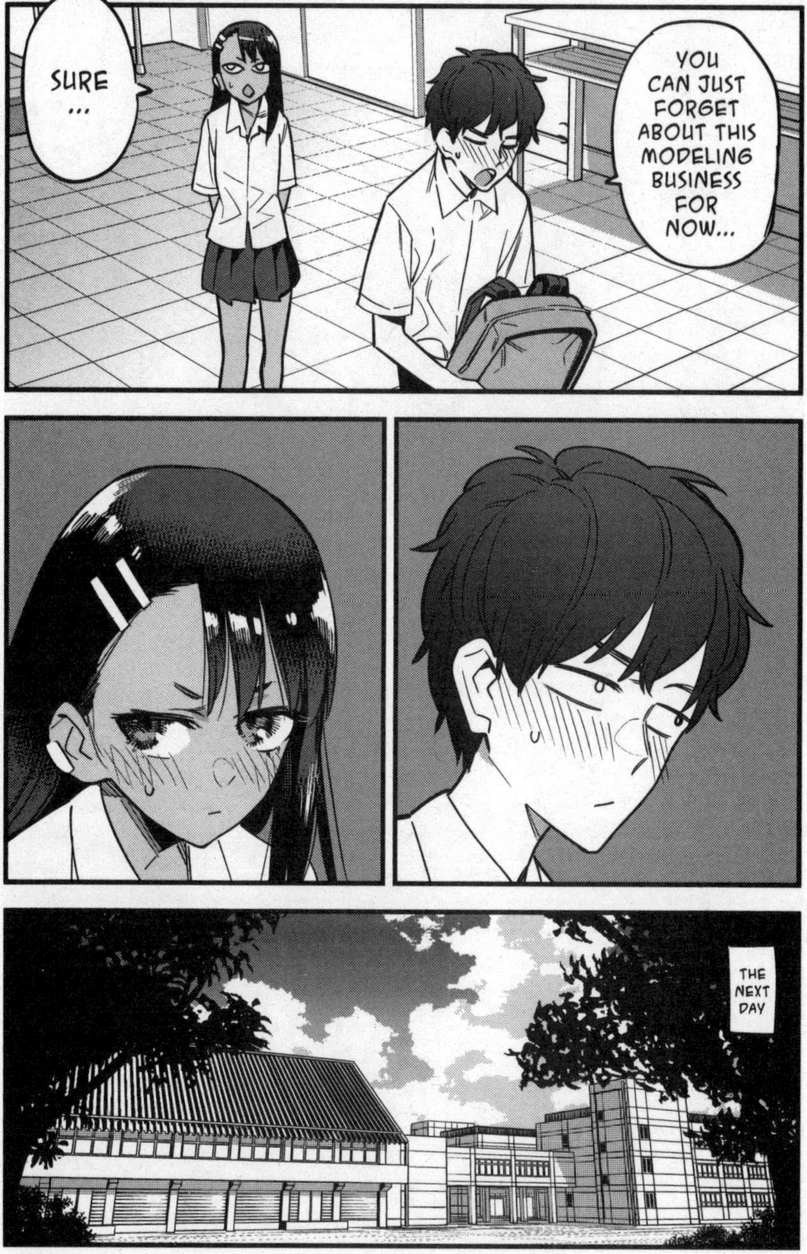
YOU CAN JUST FORGET ABOUT THIS MODELING BUSINESS FOR NOW...
SURE ...
THE NEXT DAY

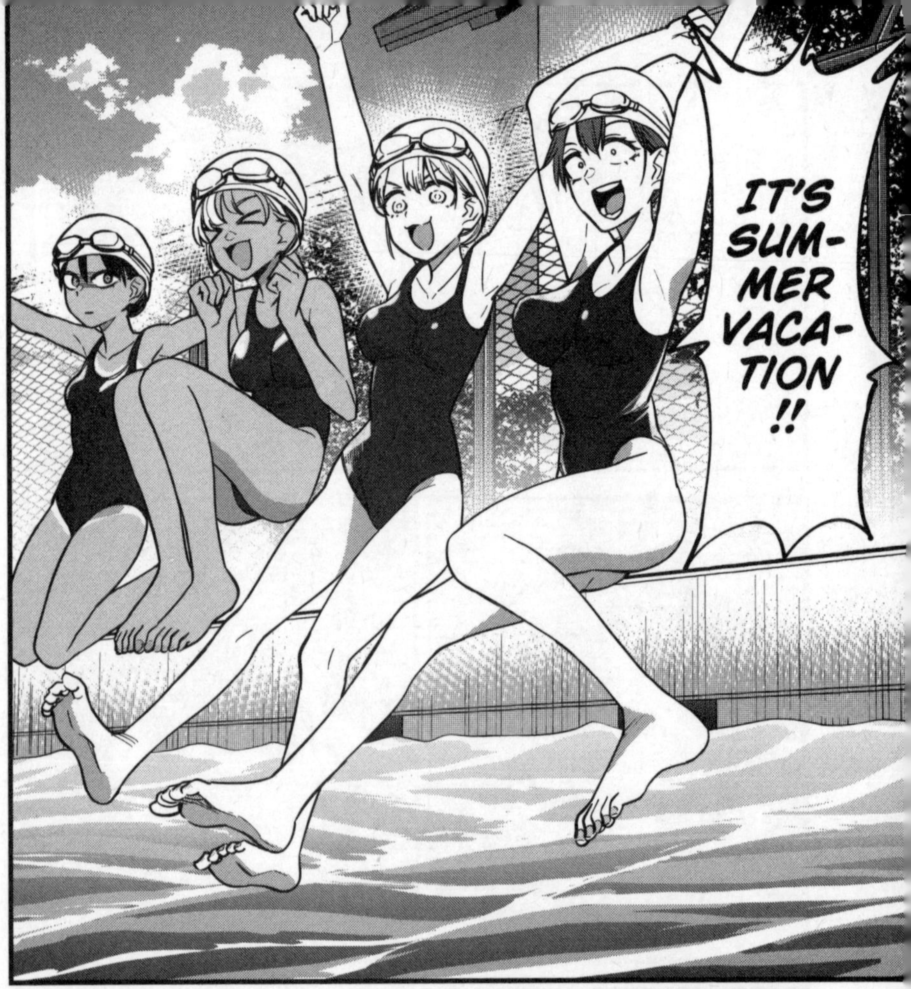
IT'S SUM-MER VACA-TION !!

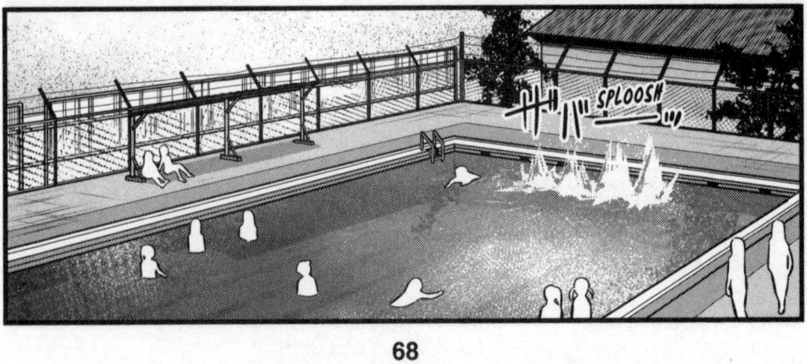
SPLOOSH

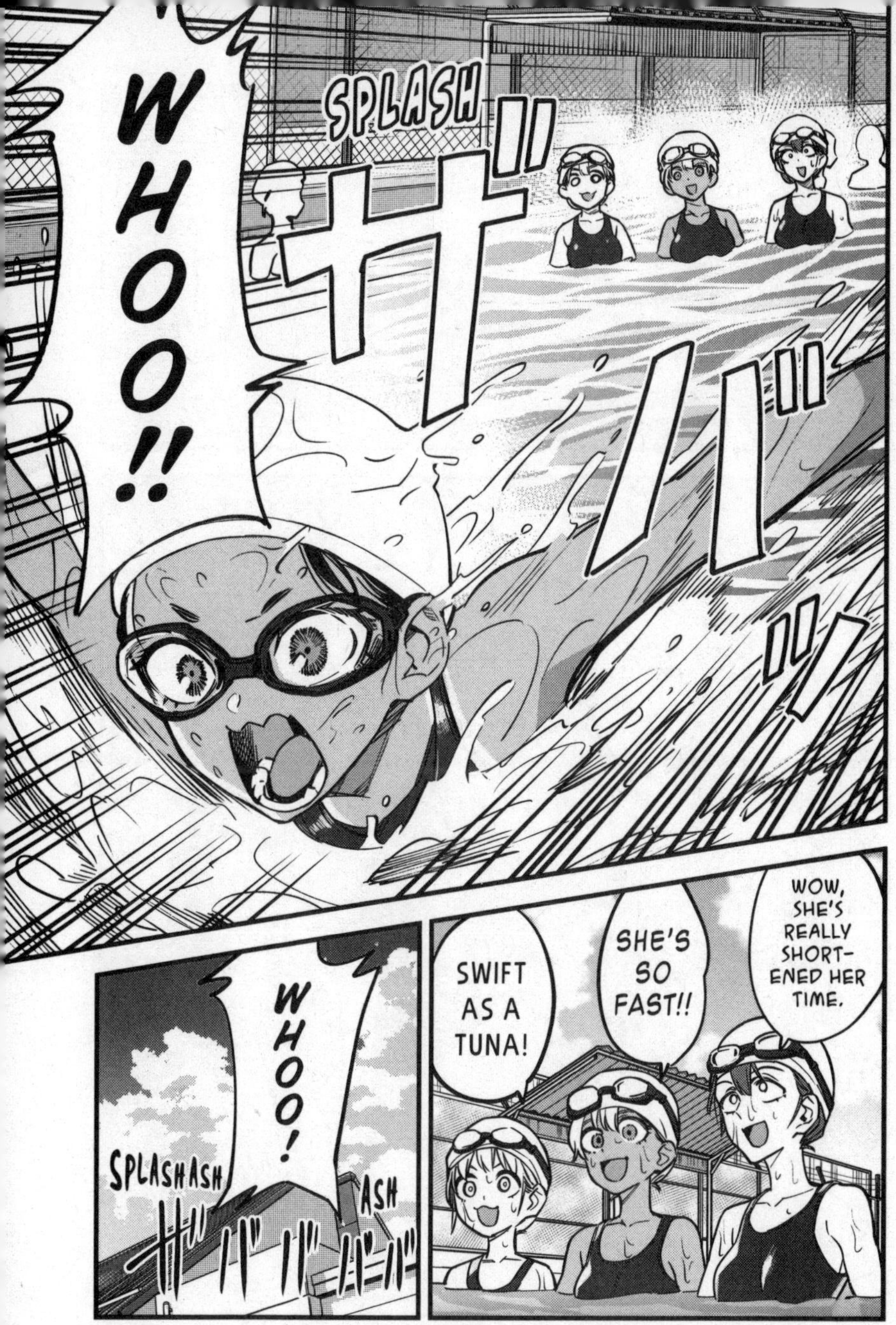
WHOO!!
SPLASH
WOW, SHE'S REALLY SHORT-ENED HER TIME.
SHE'S SO FAST!!
SWIFT AS A TUNA!
WHOO!
SPLASHASH
ASH

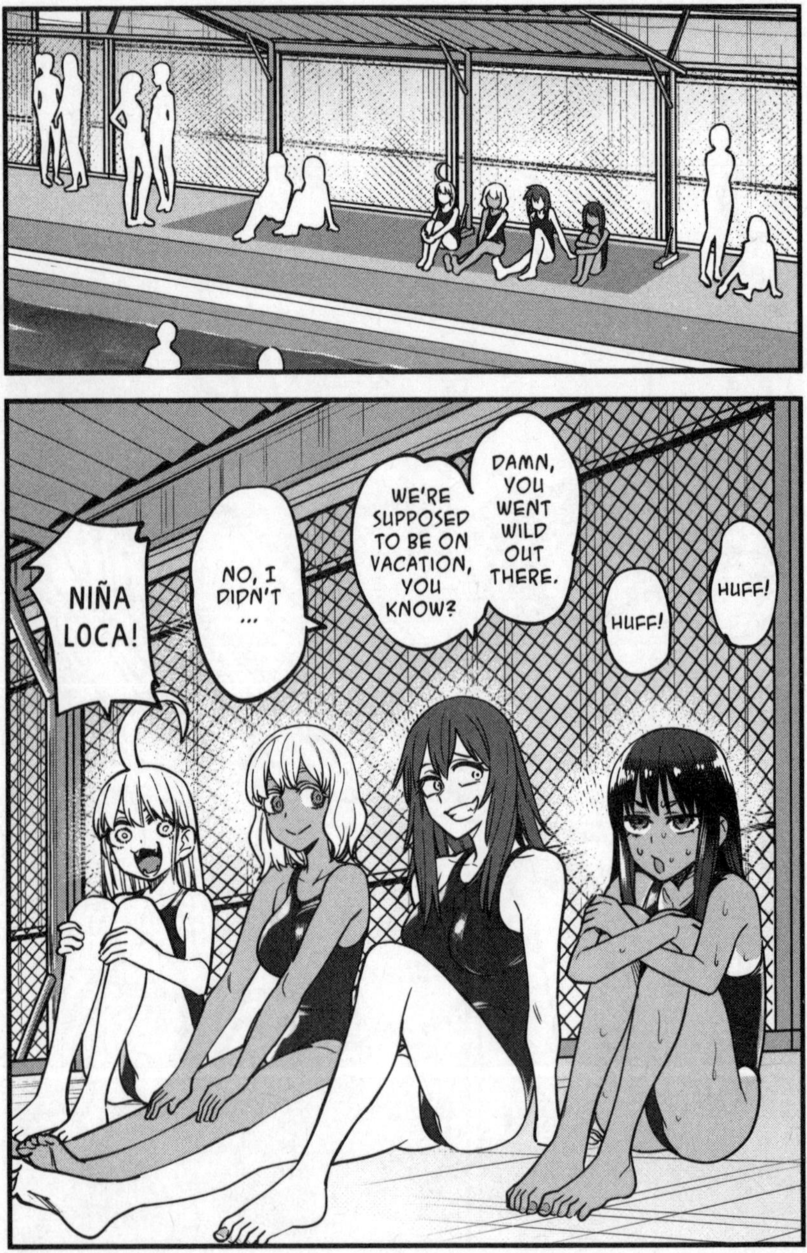
HUFF!
HUFF!
DAMN, YOU WENT WILD OUT THERE.
WE'RE SUPPOSED TO BE ON VACATION, YOU KNOW?
NO, I DIDN'T ...
NIÑA LOCA!

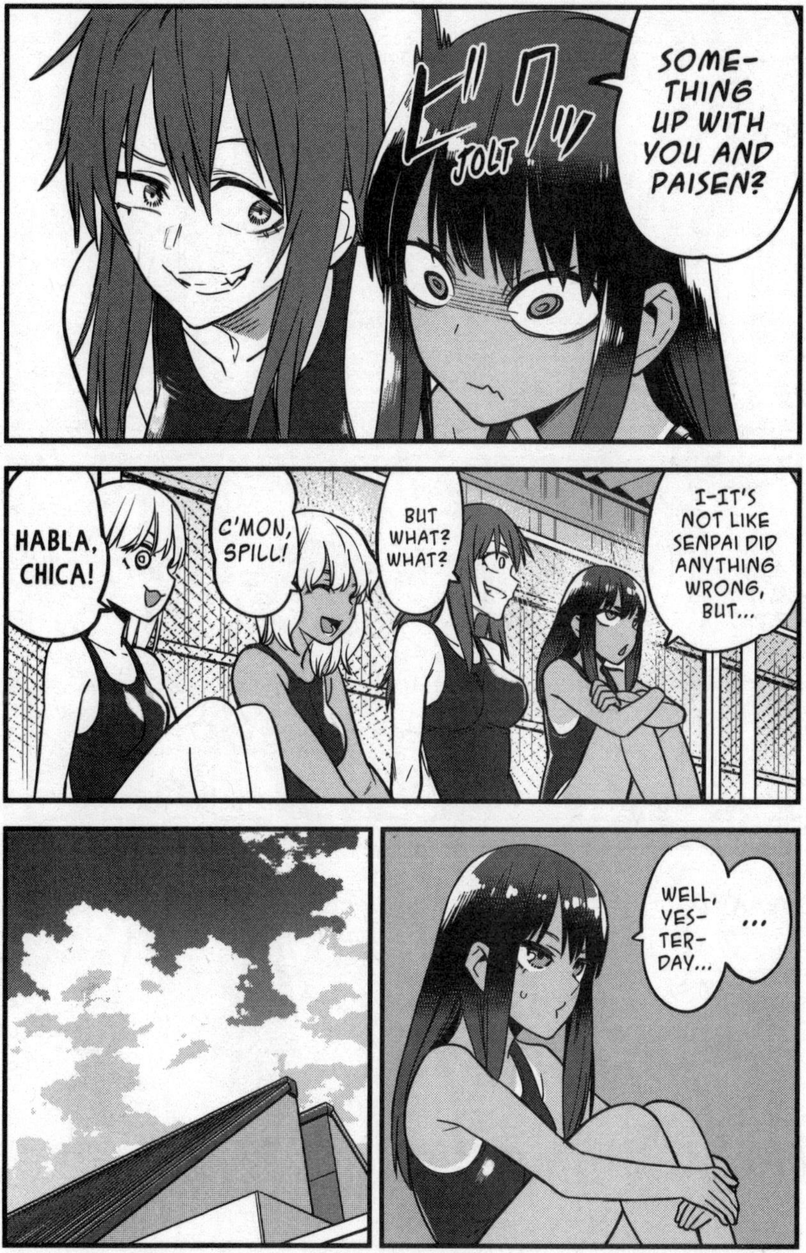
SOME-THING UP WITH YOU AND PAISEN?
ビクッ
JOLT
I-IT'S NOT LIKE SENPAI DID ANYTHING WRONG, BUT...
BUT WHAT? WHAT?
C'MON, SPILL!
HABLA, CHICA!
...
WELL, YES-TER-DAY...

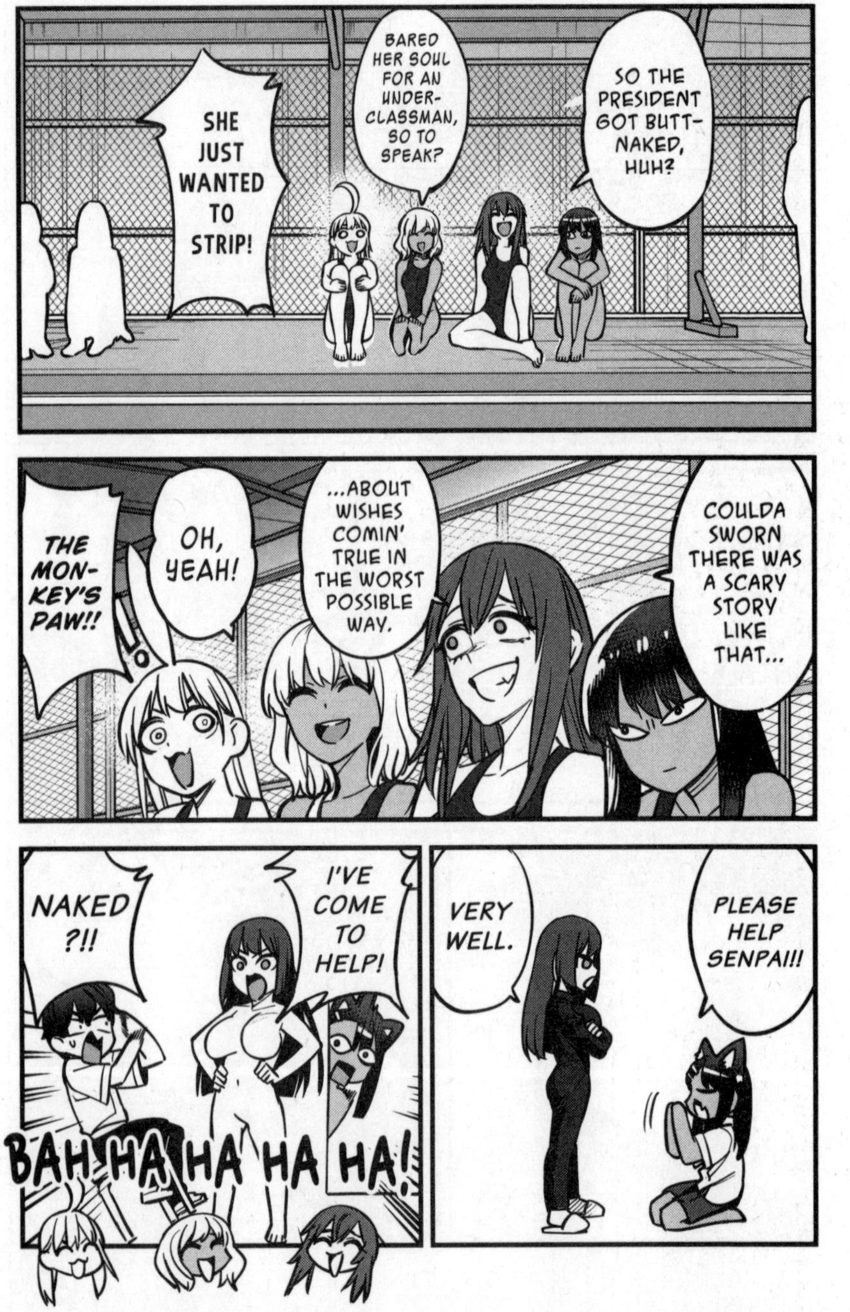
SO THE PRESIDENT GOT BUTT-NAKED, HUH?
BARED HER SOUL FOR AN UNDER-CLASSMAN, SO TO SPEAK?
SHE JUST WANTED TO STRIP!
COULDA SWORN THERE WAS A SCARY STORY LIKE THAT...
...ABOUT WISHES COMIN' TRUE IN THE WORST POSSIBLE WAY.
OH, YEAH!
THE MON-KEY'S PAW!!
PLEASE HELP SENPAI!!
VERY WELL.
I'VE COME TO HELP!
NAKED?!!
BAH HA HA HA HA!

IT'S NOT FUNNY.
SORZ, SORZ!
SORRY!
SOWWY!
BUT YOU KNOW, THE SOLUTION'S SIMPLE.
YOU'VE JUST GOTTA GO FOR IT, HAYATCHI!!
BUST OUT THAT BIRTHDAY SUIT!!

END

CHAPTER 113: I LOOK FORWARD TO WORKING WITH YOU, SENPAI ♡ (1)

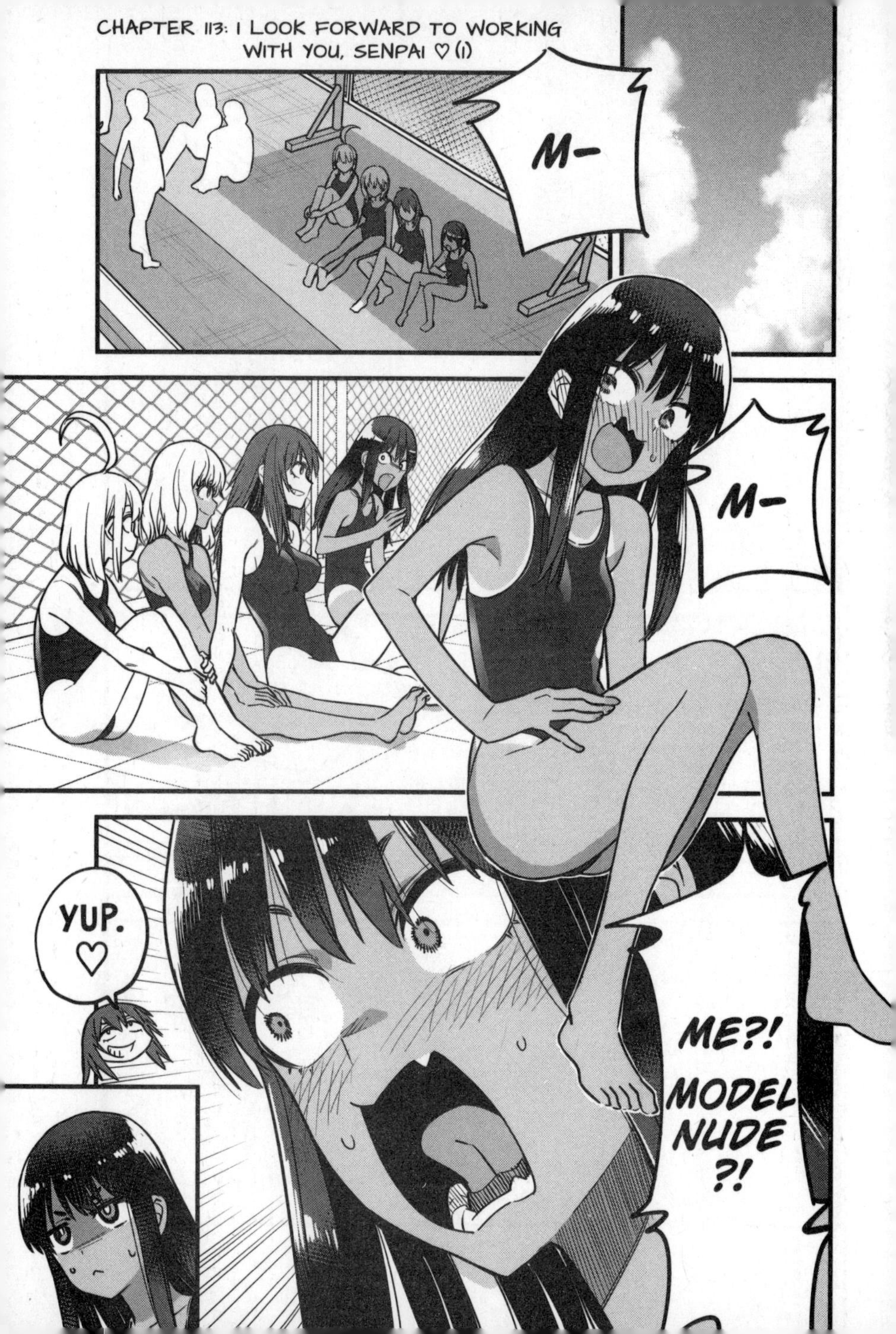
M-
M-
ME?!
MODEL NUDE ?!
YUP. ♡

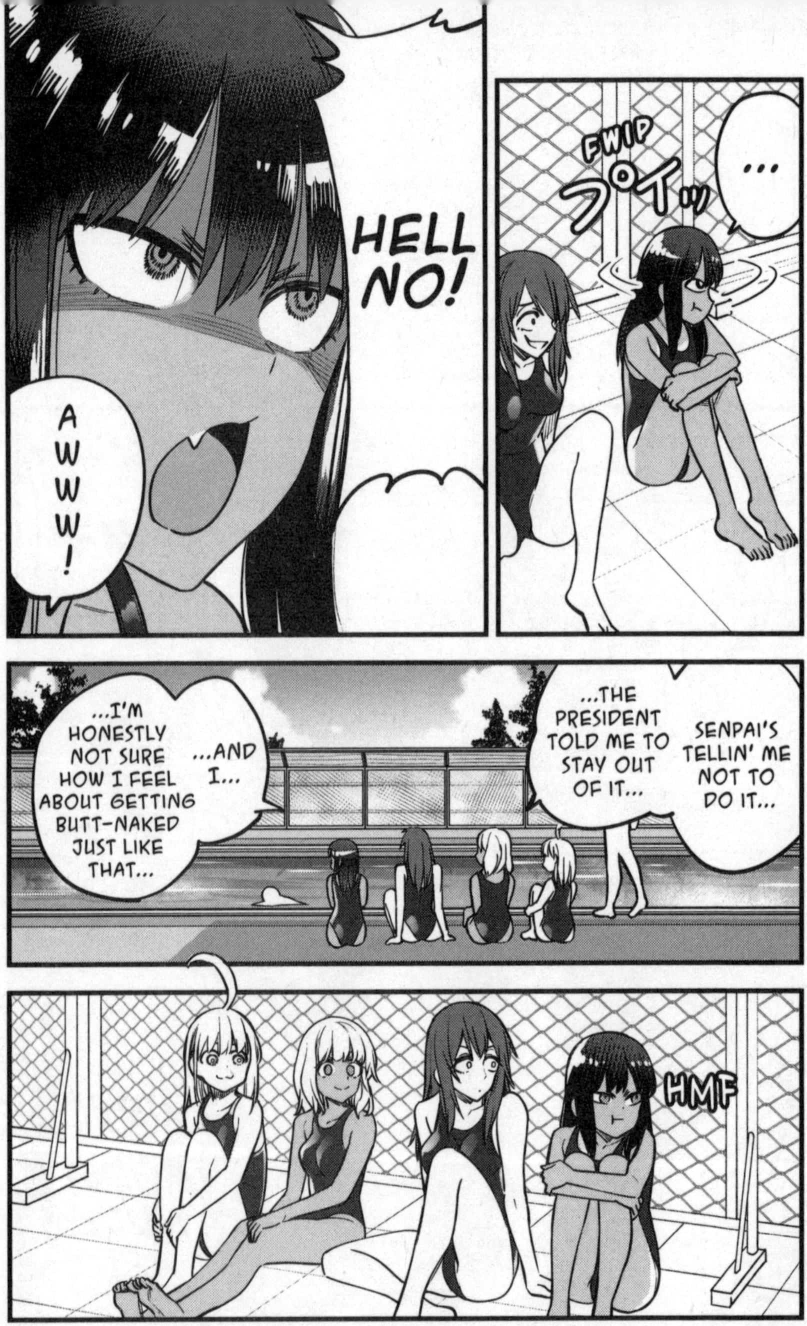
...
FWIP
プイッ
HELL NO!
AWWWW!
SENPAI'S TELLIN' ME NOT TO DO IT...
...THE PRESIDENT TOLD ME TO STAY OUT OF IT...
...AND I...
...I'M HONESTLY NOT SURE HOW I FEEL ABOUT GETTING BUTT-NAKED JUST LIKE THAT...
HMF

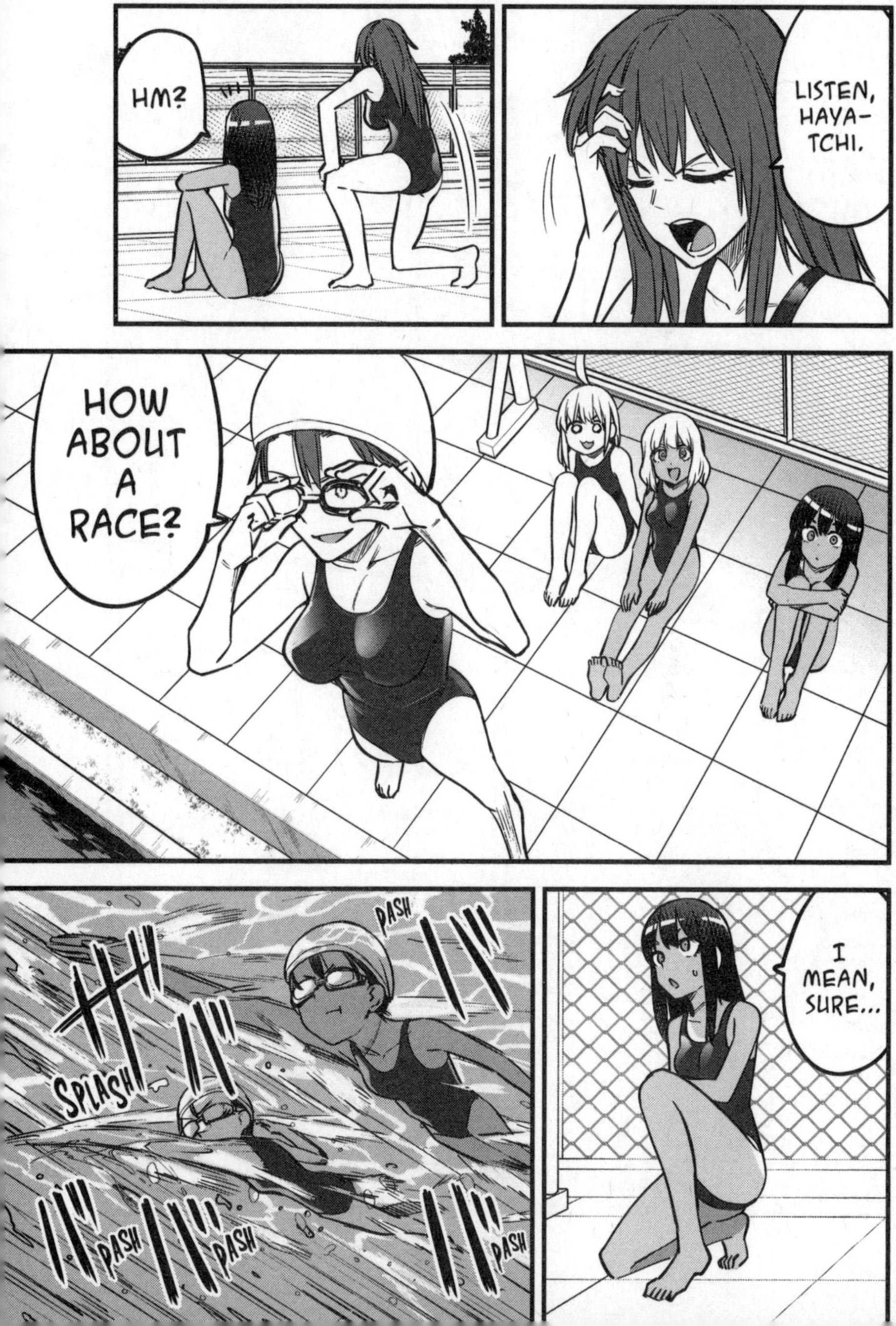
LISTEN, HAYA-TCHI.
HM?
HOW ABOUT A RACE?
I MEAN, SURE...
PASH
SPLASH
PASH
PASH
PASH

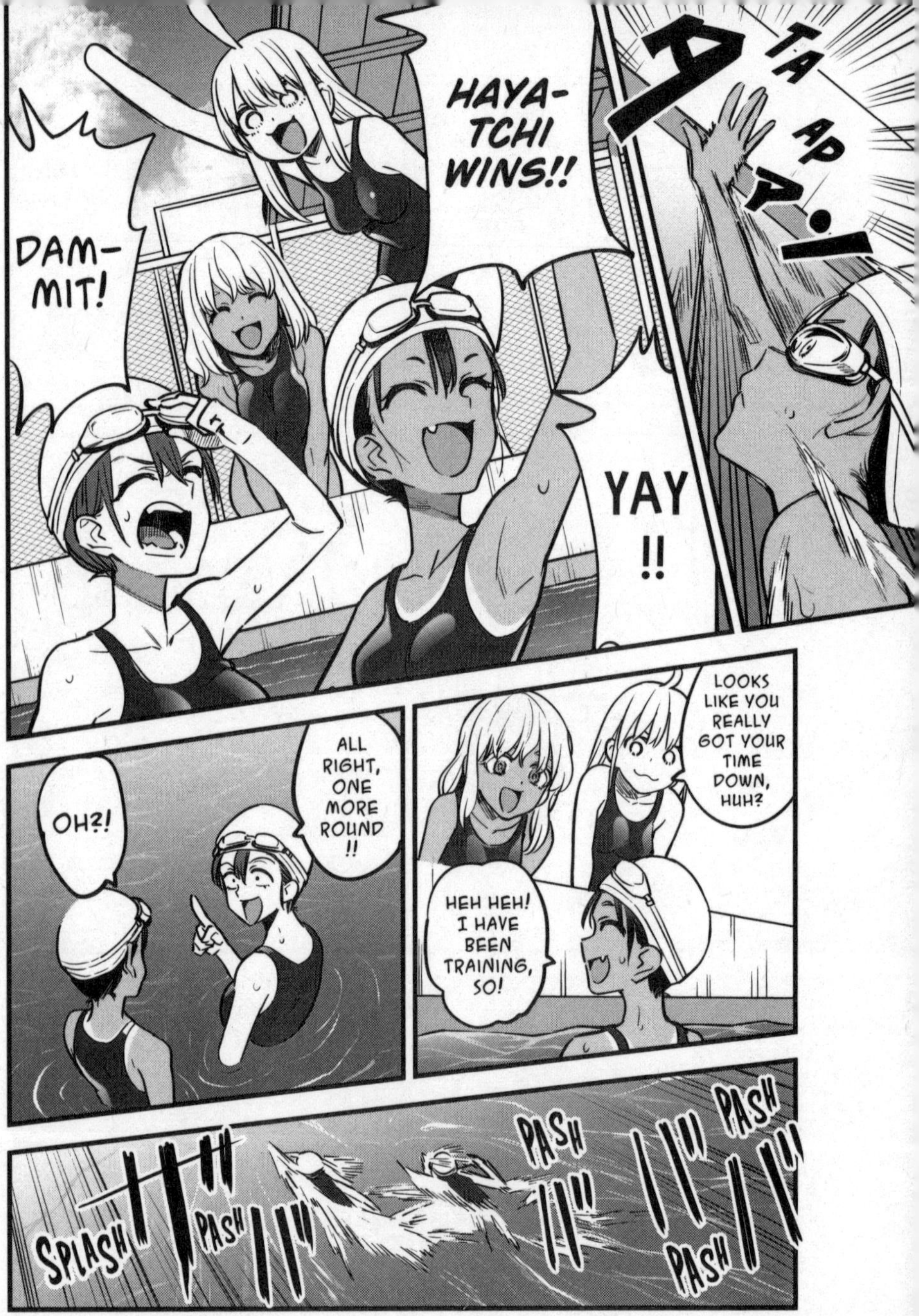
TAAAP!
HAYA-TCHI WINS!!
YAY!!
DAM-MIT!
LOOKS LIKE YOU REALLY GOT YOUR TIME DOWN, HUH?
HEH HEH! I HAVE BEEN TRAINING, SO!
ALL RIGHT, ONE MORE ROUND!!
OH?!
PASH
PASH
PASH
PASH
SPLASH

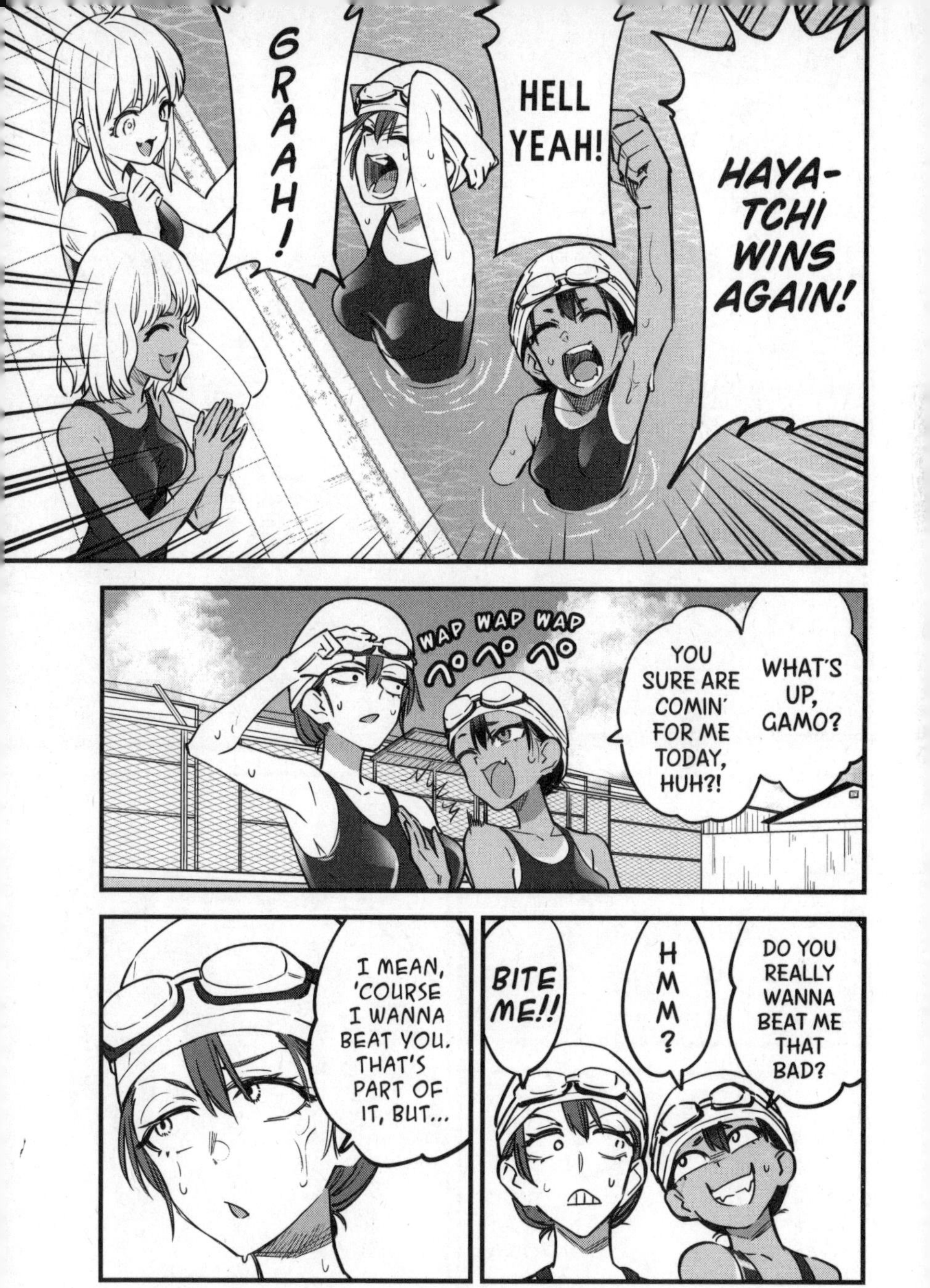
HAYA-TCHI WINS AGAIN!
HELL YEAH!
GRAAH!
WHAT'S UP, GAMO?
YOU SURE ARE COMIN' FOR ME TODAY, HUH?!
WAP WAP WAP
DO YOU REALLY WANNA BEAT ME THAT BAD?
HMM?
BITE ME!!
I MEAN, 'COURSE I WANNA BEAT YOU. THAT'S PART OF IT, BUT...

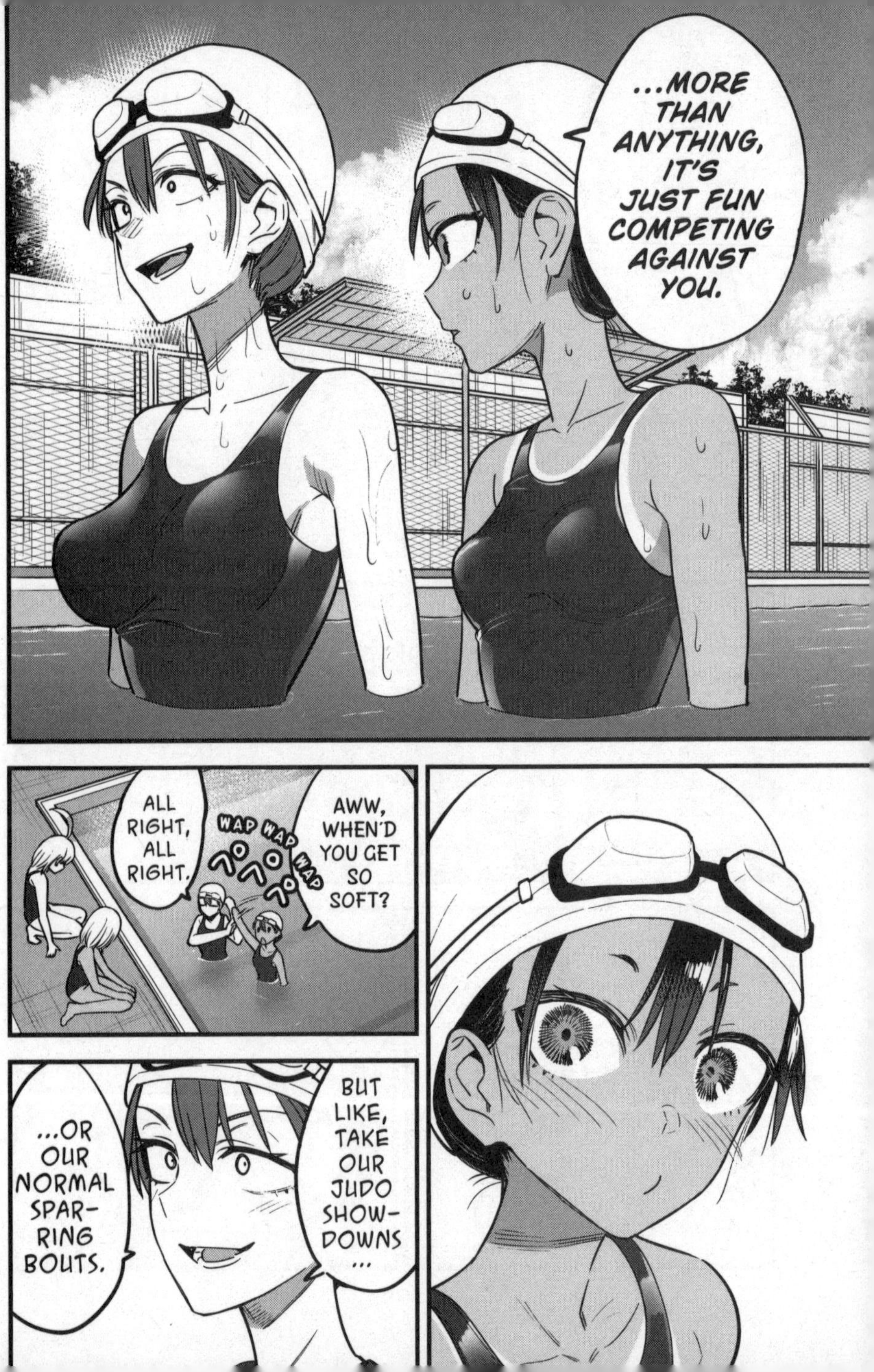
...MORE THAN ANYTHING, IT'S JUST FUN COMPETING AGAINST YOU.
AWW, WHEN'D YOU GET SO SOFT?
WAP WAP WAP
ALL RIGHT, ALL RIGHT.
BUT LIKE, TAKE OUR JUDO SHOW-DOWNS...
...OR OUR NORMAL SPAR-RING BOUTS.

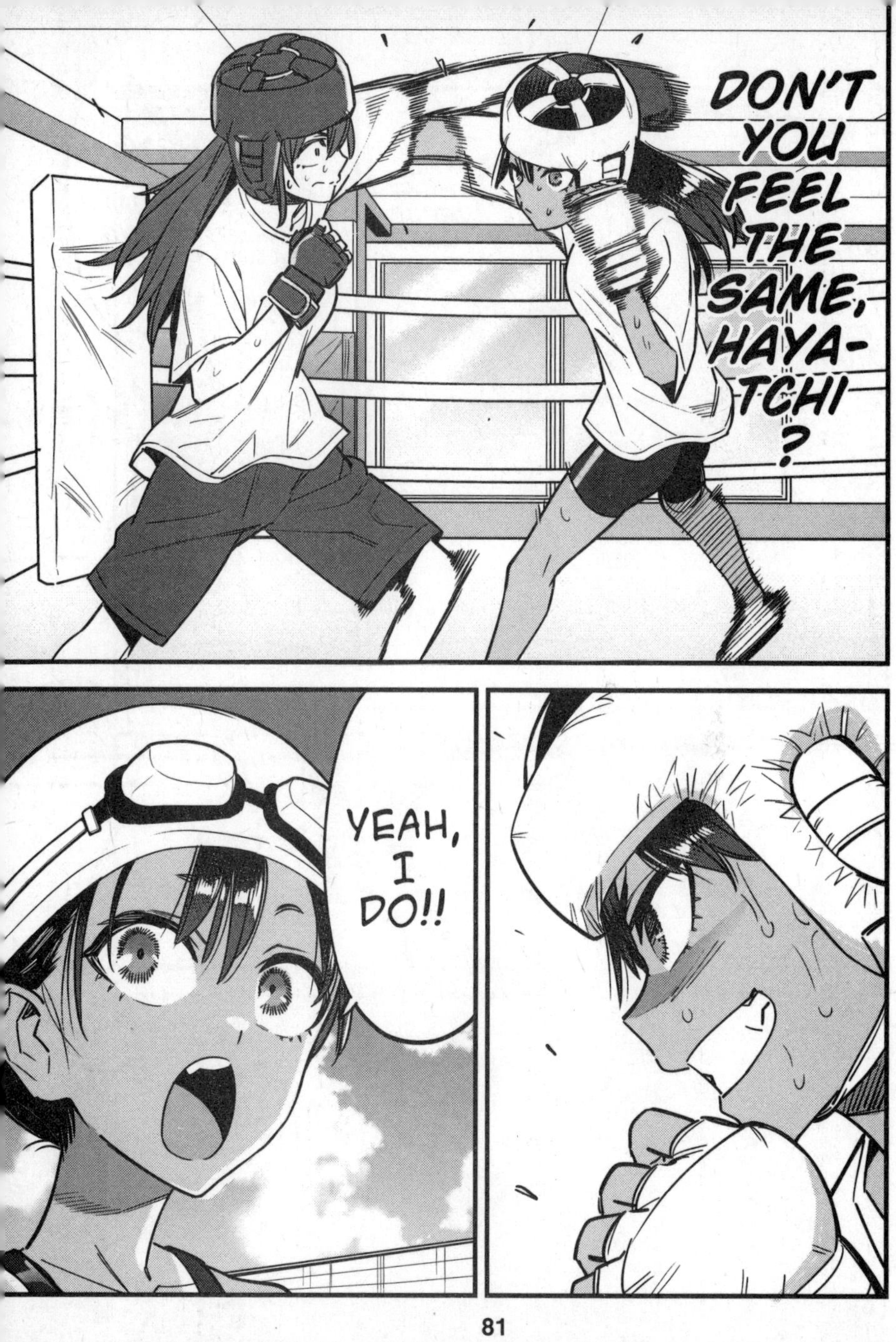
DON'T YOU FEEL THE SAME, HAYA-TCHI?
YEAH, I DO!!

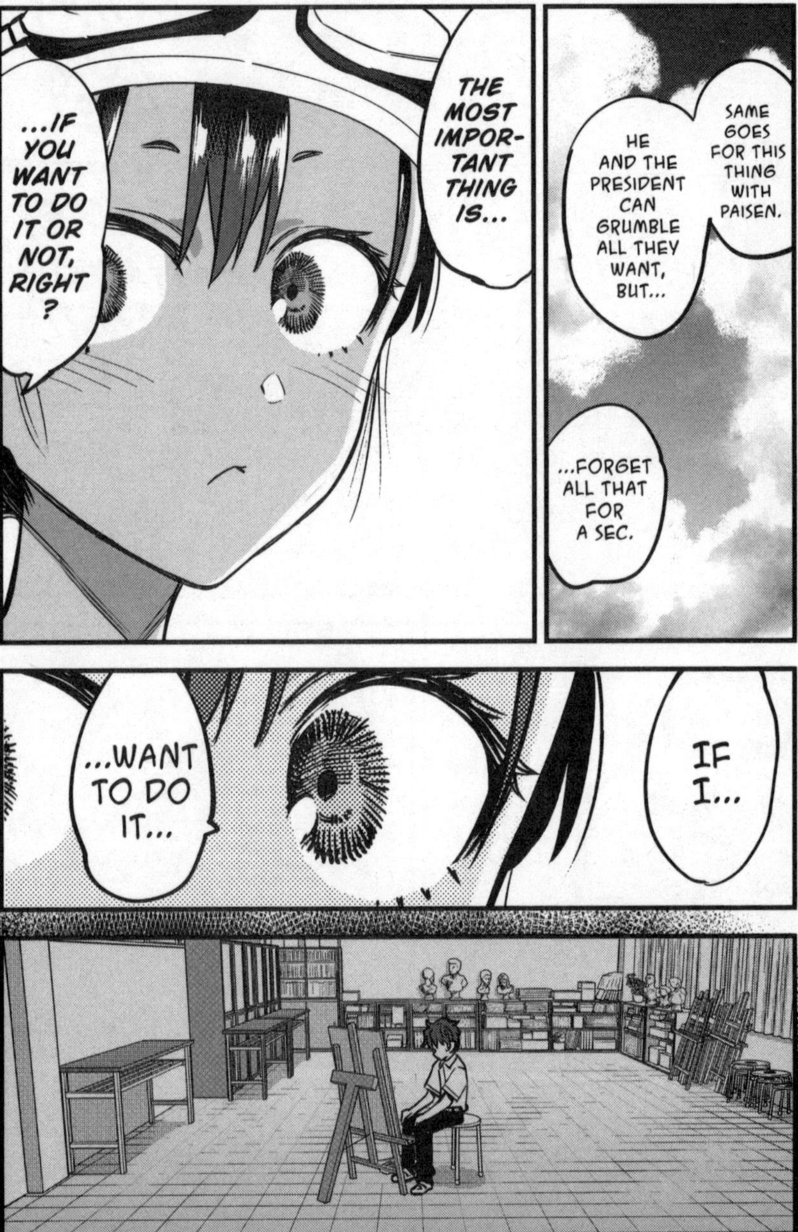
SAME GOES FOR THIS THING WITH PAISEN.
HE AND THE PRESIDENT CAN GRUMBLE ALL THEY WANT, BUT...
...FORGET ALL THAT FOR A SEC.
THE MOST IMPOR-TANT THING IS...
...IF YOU WANT TO DO IT OR NOT, RIGHT?
IF I...
...WANT TO DO IT...

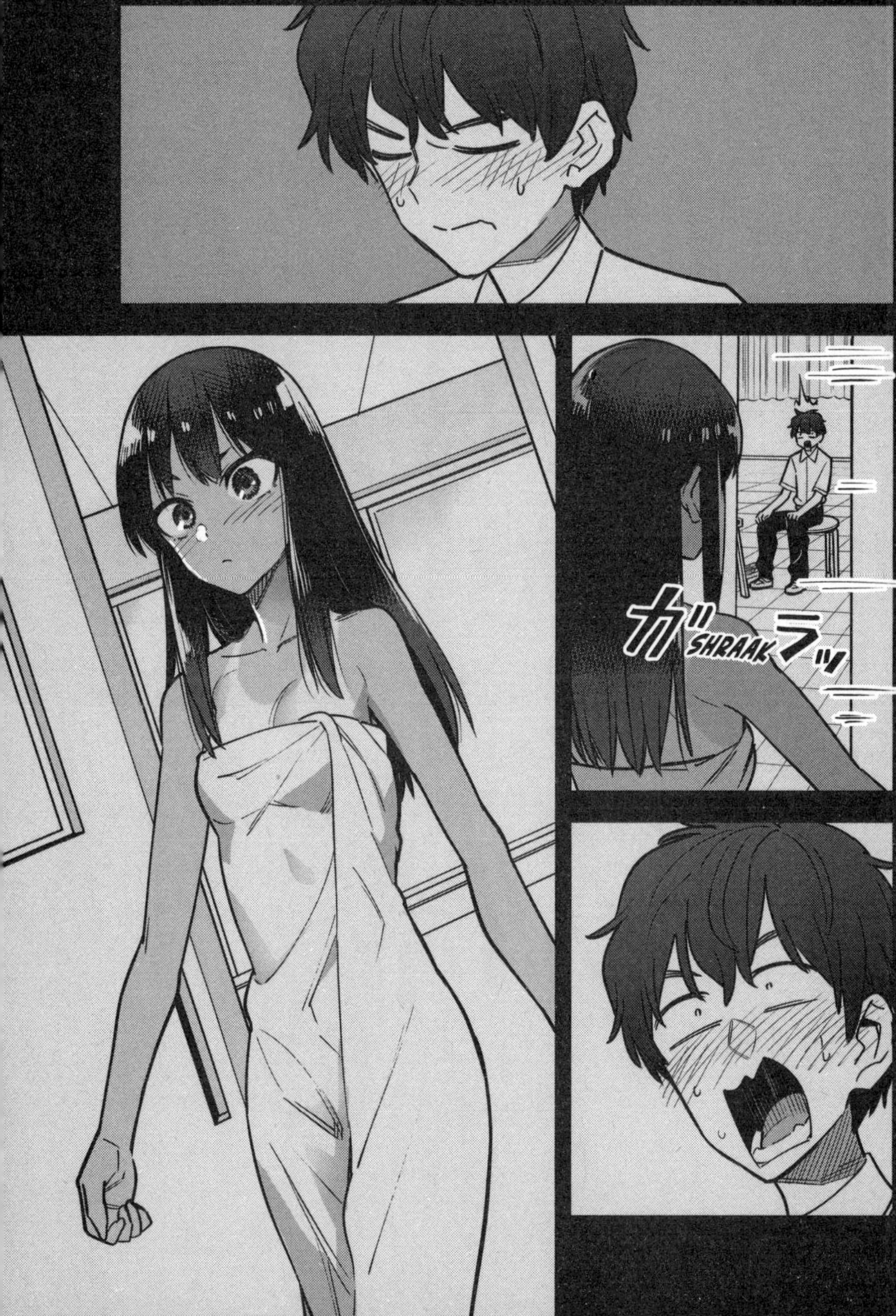
ガラッ
SHRAAK

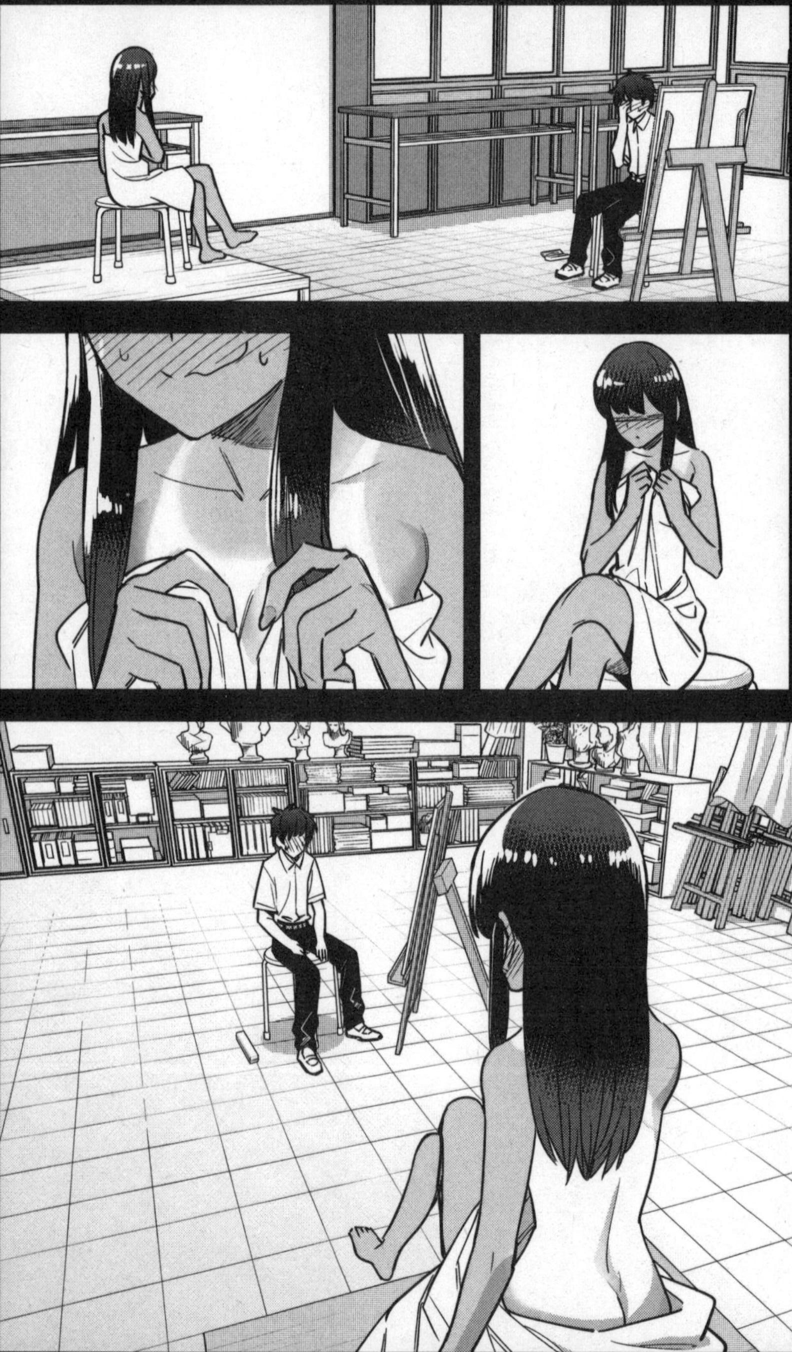

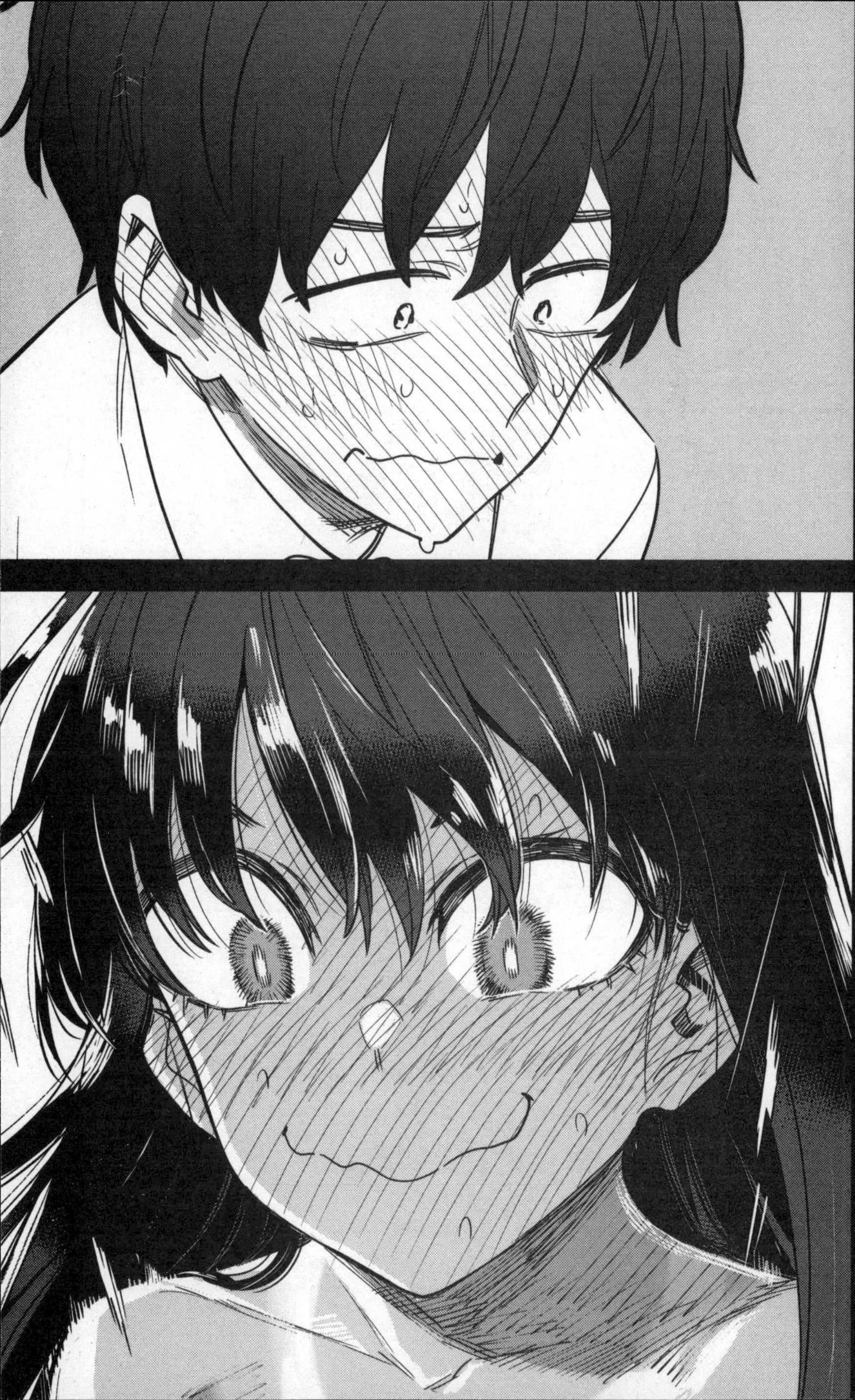

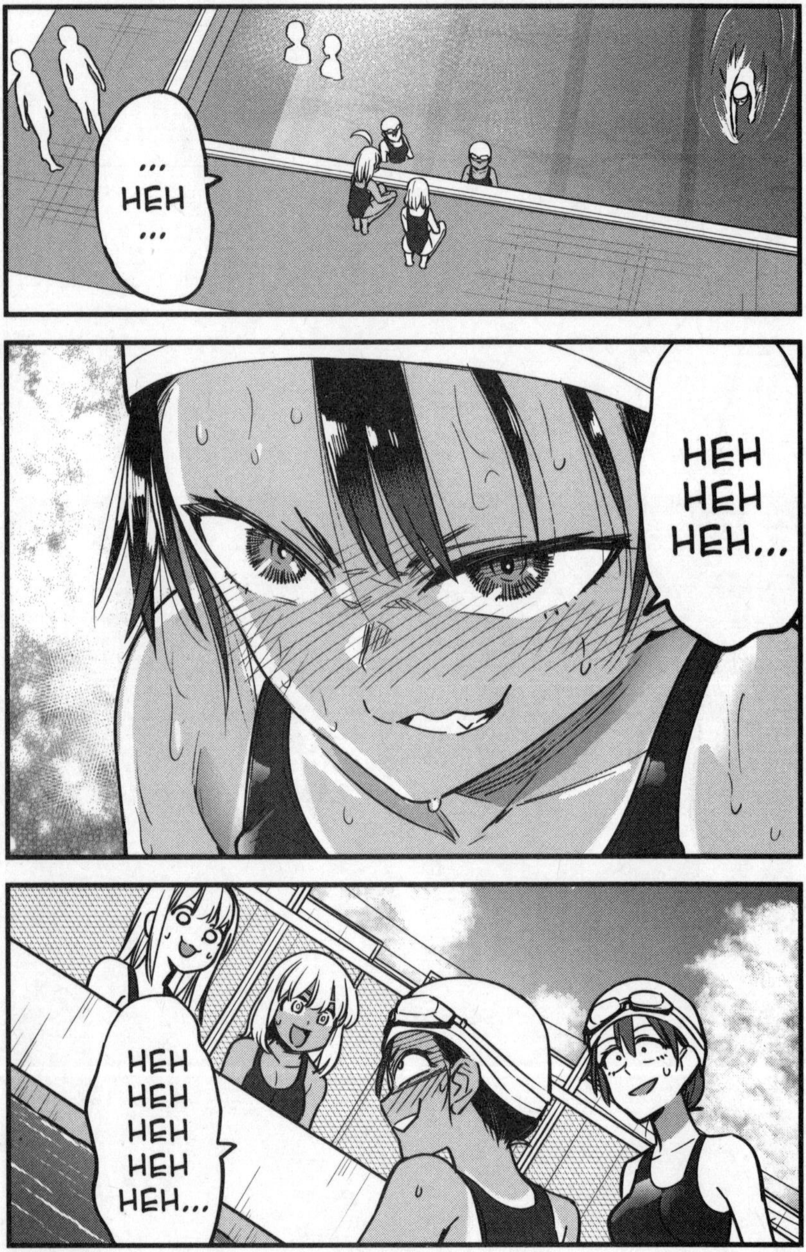
... HEH ...
HEH HEH HEH...
HEH HEH HEH HEH HEH...

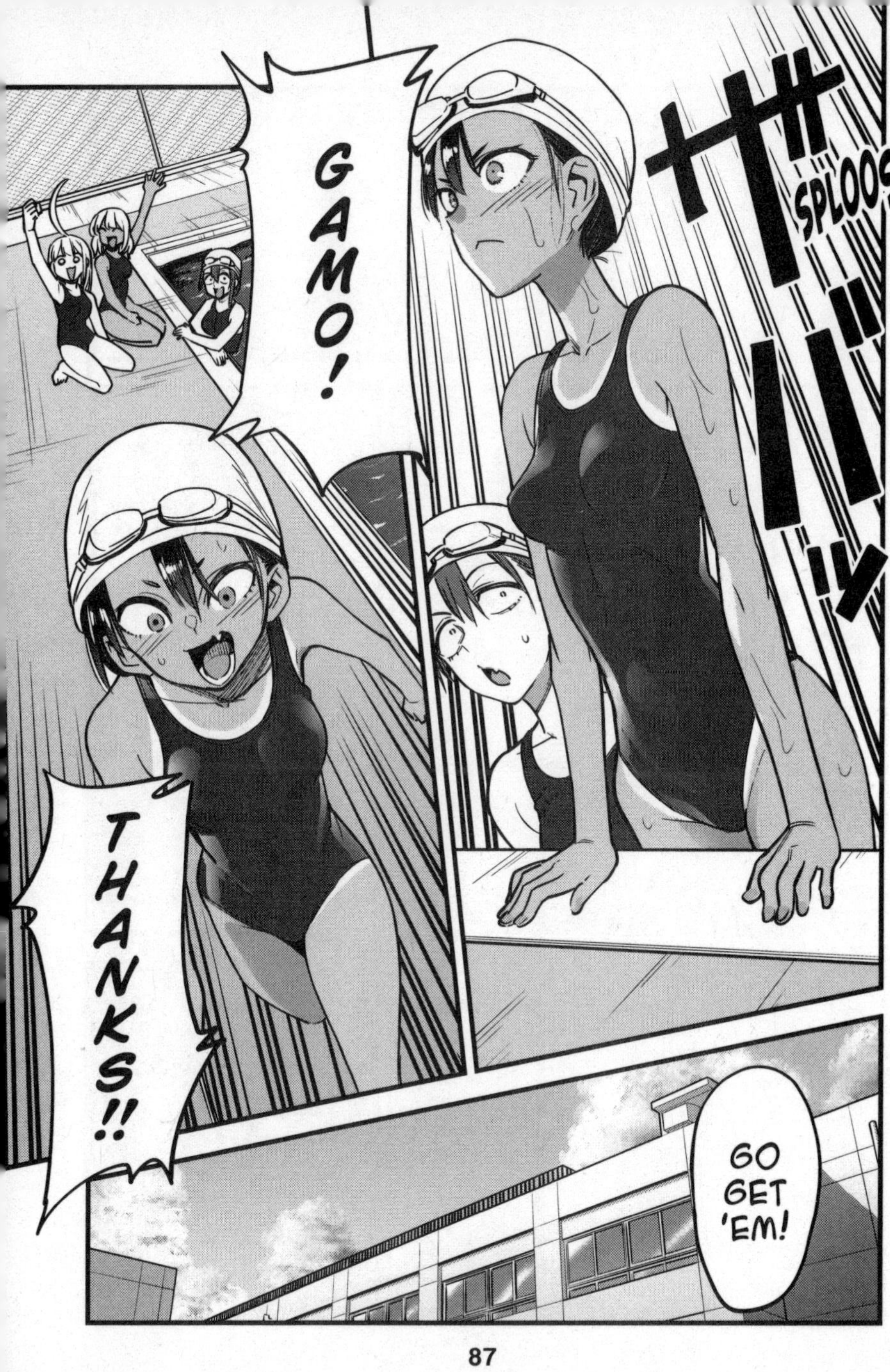
ザバッ
SPLOOSH
GAMO!
THANKS!!
GO GET 'EM!

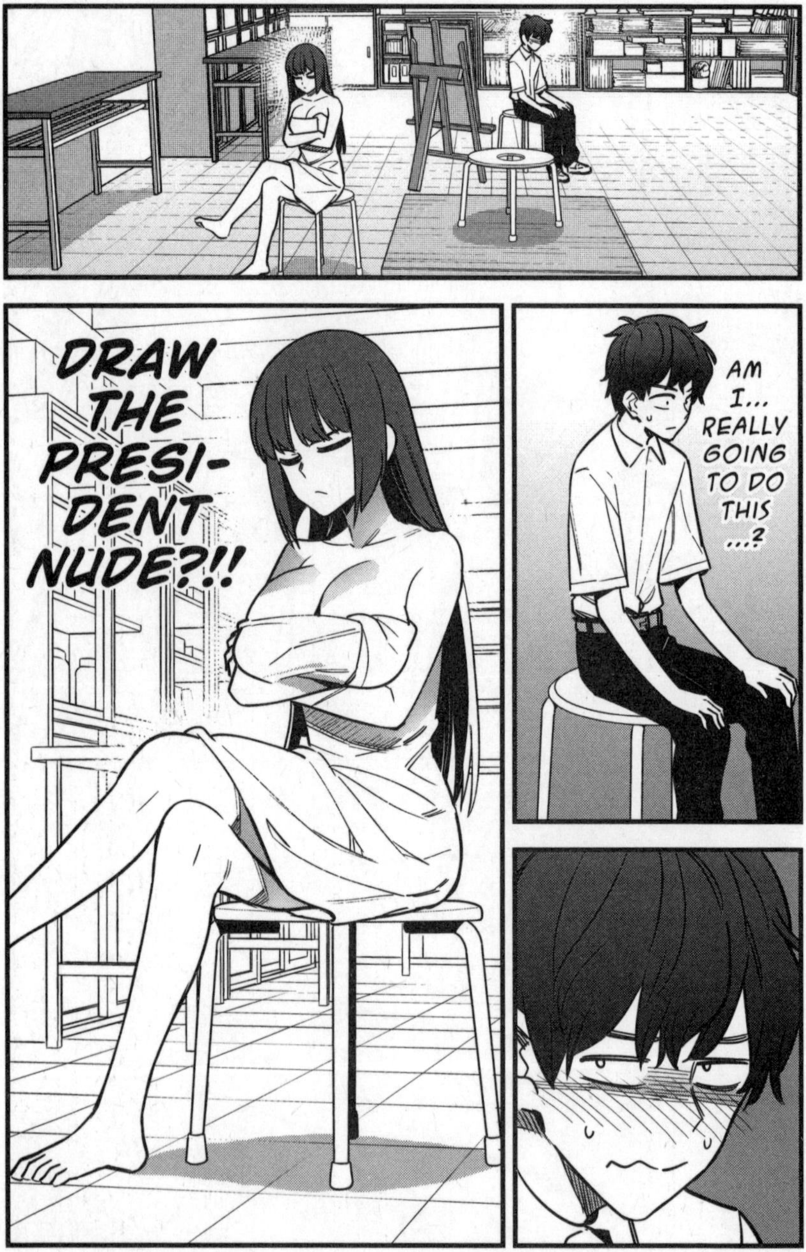
AM I... REALLY GOING TO DO THIS ...?
DRAW THE PRESI-DENT NUDE?!!

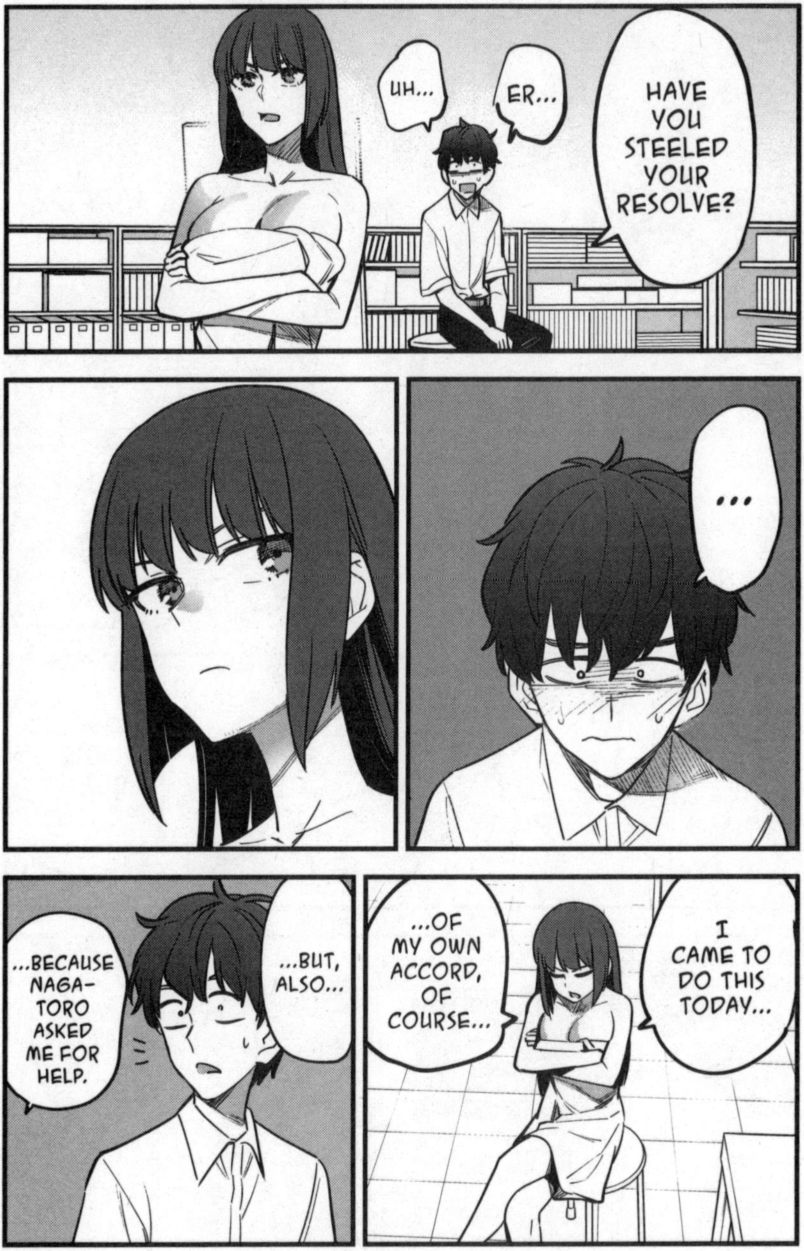
HAVE YOU STEELED YOUR RESOLVE?
ER...
UH...
...
I CAME TO DO THIS TODAY...
...OF MY OWN ACCORD, OF COURSE...
...BUT, ALSO...
...BECAUSE NAGA-TORO ASKED ME FOR HELP.

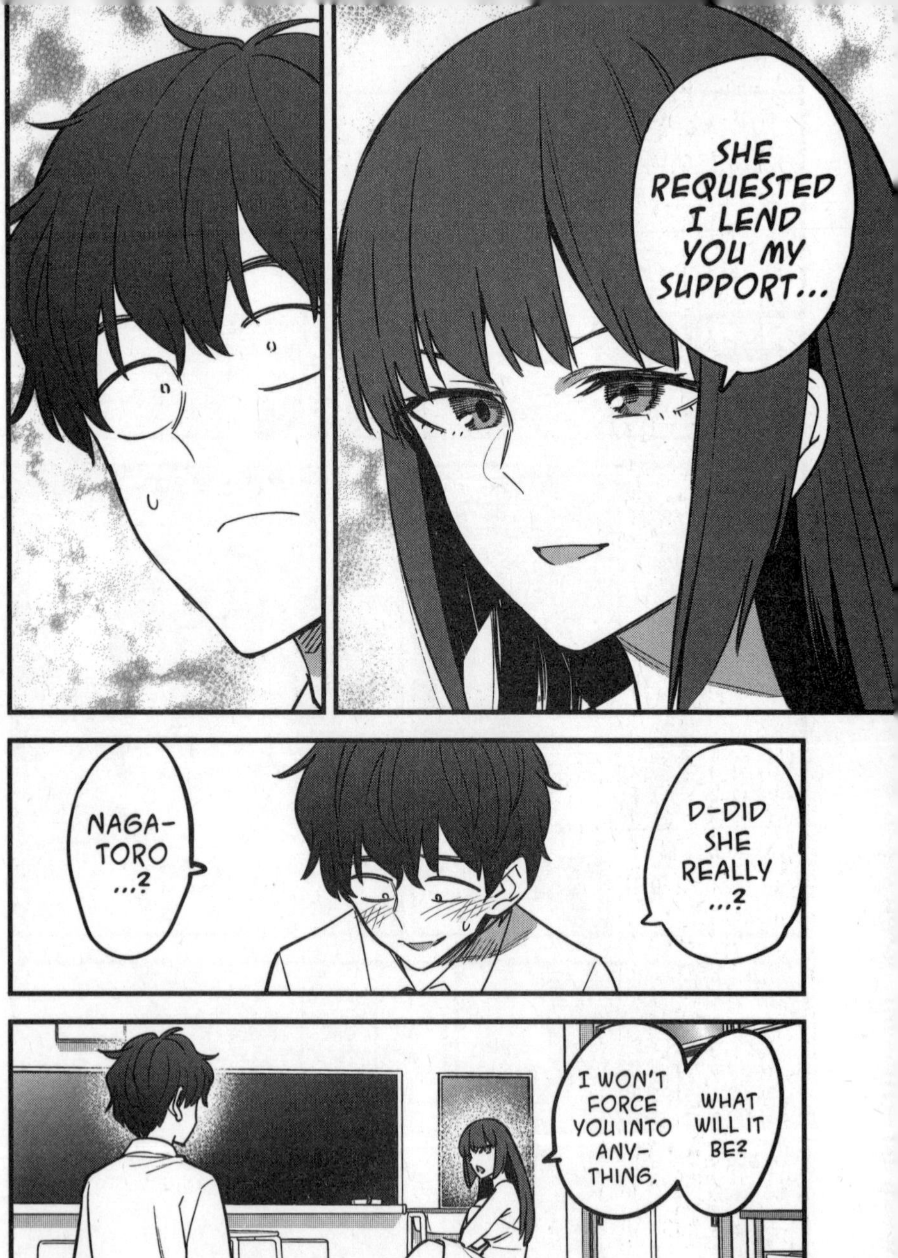
SHE REQUESTED I LEND YOU MY SUPPORT...
D-DID SHE REALLY ...?
NAGA-TORO ...?
WHAT WILL IT BE?
I WON'T FORCE YOU INTO ANY-THING.

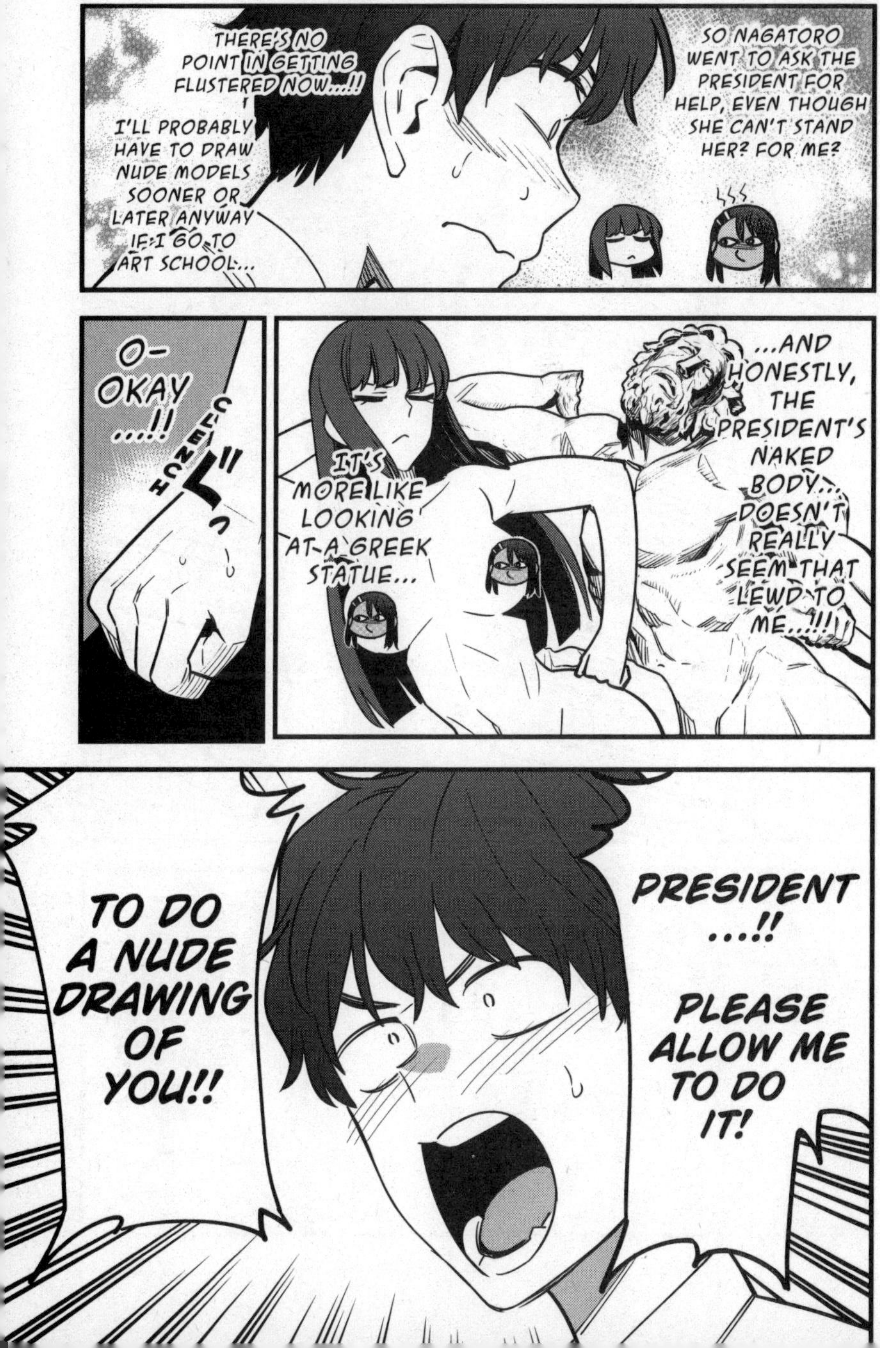
SO NAGATORO WENT TO ASK THE PRESIDENT FOR HELP, EVEN THOUGH SHE CAN'T STAND HER? FOR ME?
THERE'S NO POINT IN GETTING FLUSTERED NOW...!!
I'LL PROBABLY HAVE TO DRAW NUDE MODELS SOONER OR LATER ANYWAY IF I GO TO ART SCHOOL...
...AND HONESTLY, THE PRESIDENT'S NAKED BODY... DOESN'T REALLY SEEM THAT LEWD TO ME...!!!
IT'S MORE LIKE LOOKING AT A GREEK STATUE...
O-OKAY ...!!
CLENCH
PRESIDENT ...!!
PLEASE ALLOW ME TO DO IT!
TO DO A NUDE DRAWING OF YOU!!

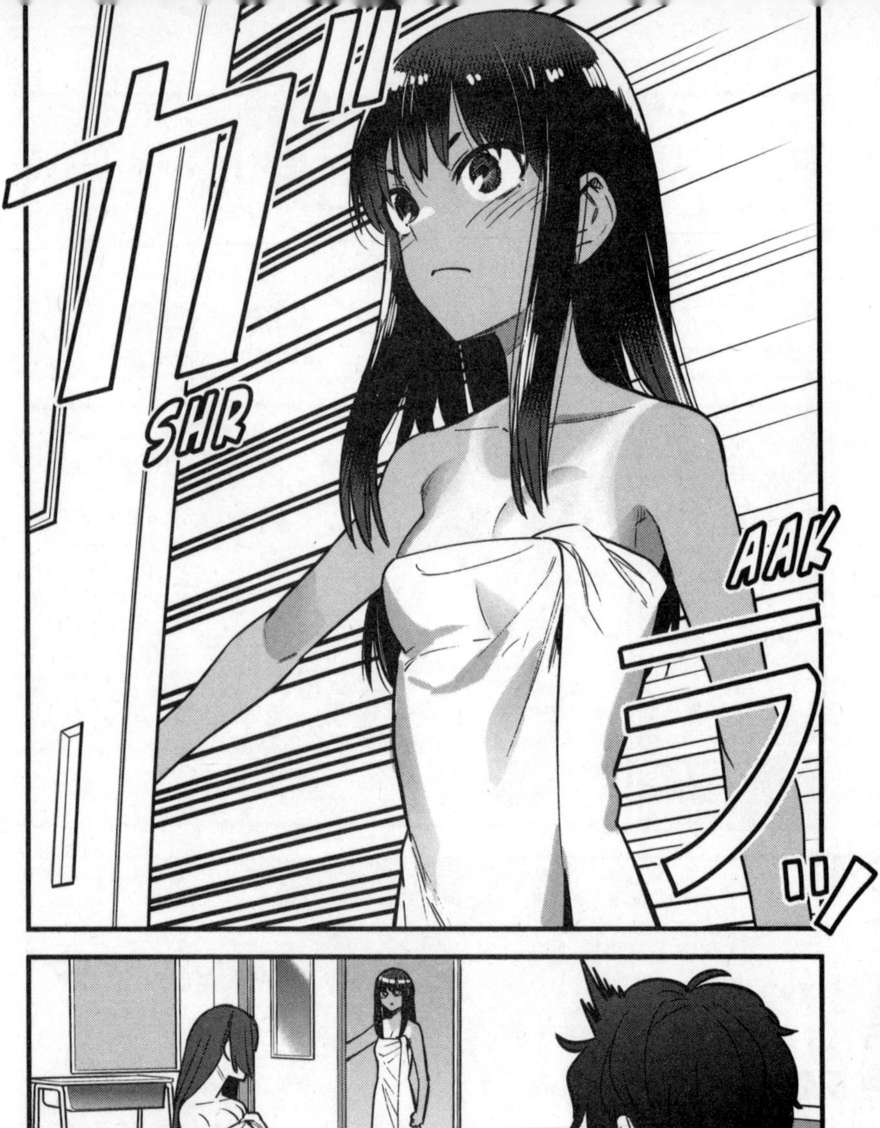
SHR
AAK

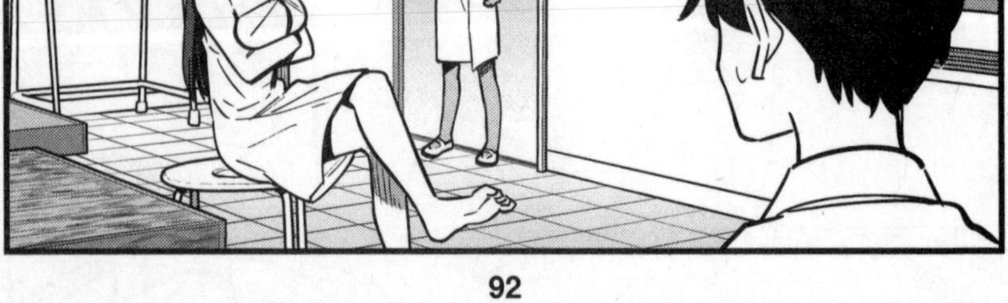

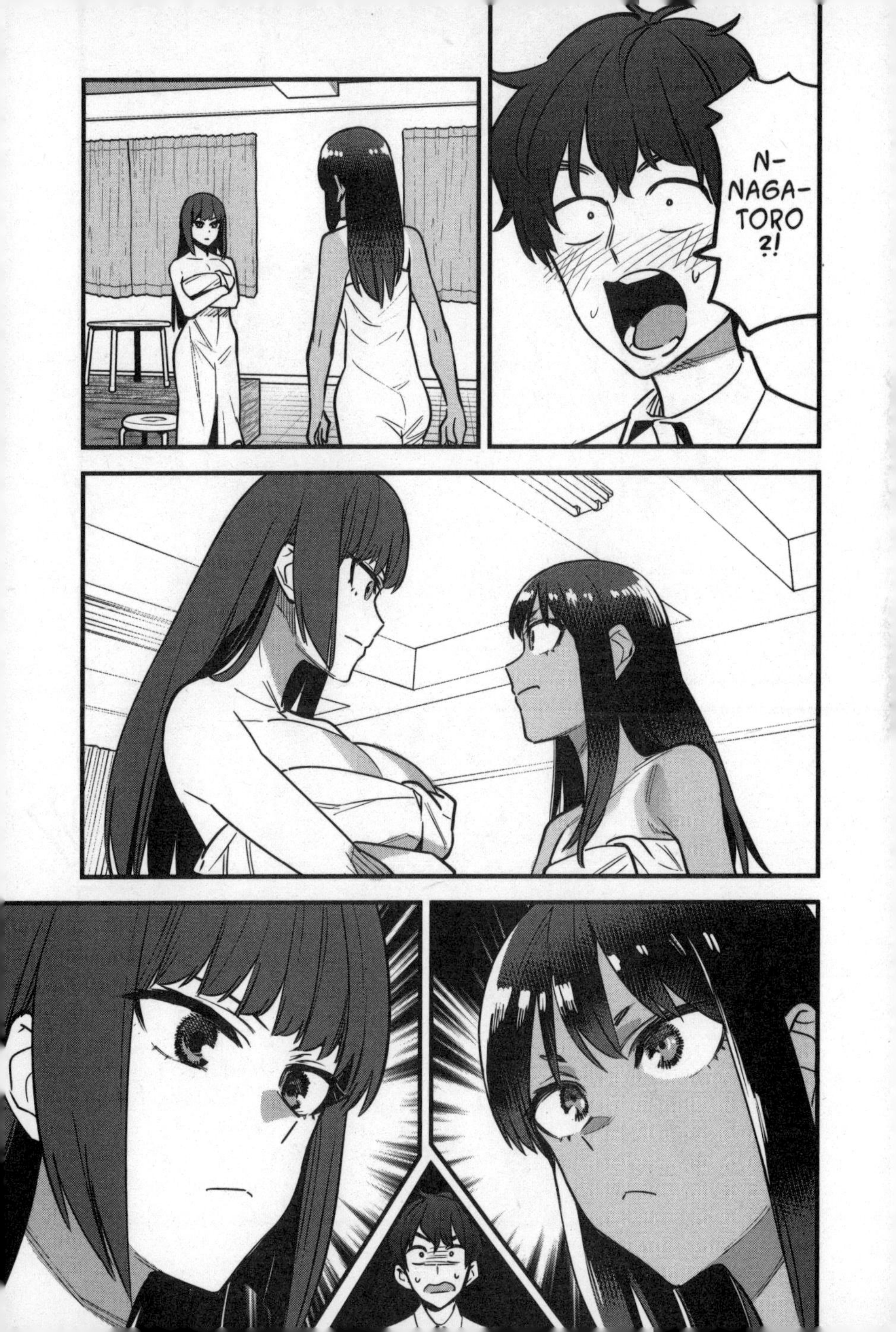
N-NAGATORO?!

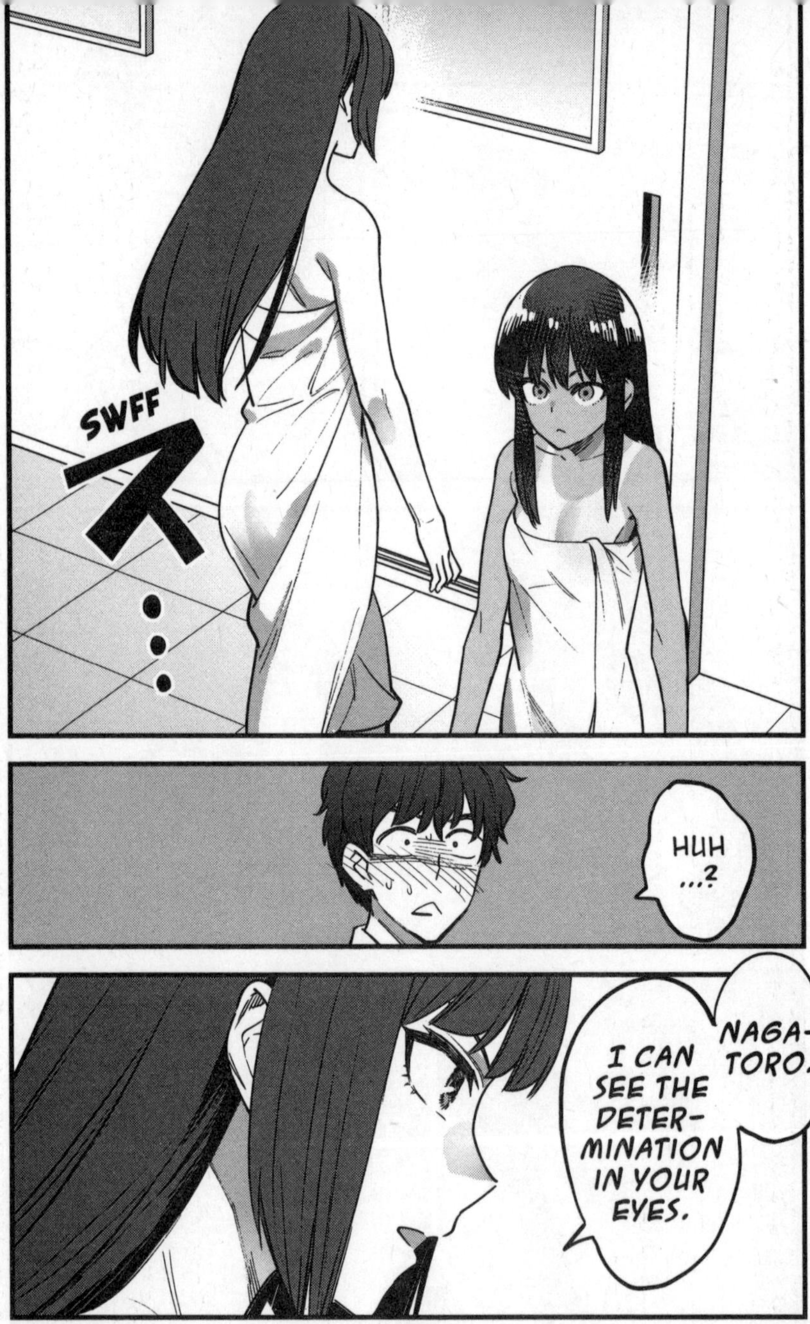

SWFF
...
HUH ...?
NAGA-TORO.
I CAN SEE THE DETERMINATION IN YOUR EYES.

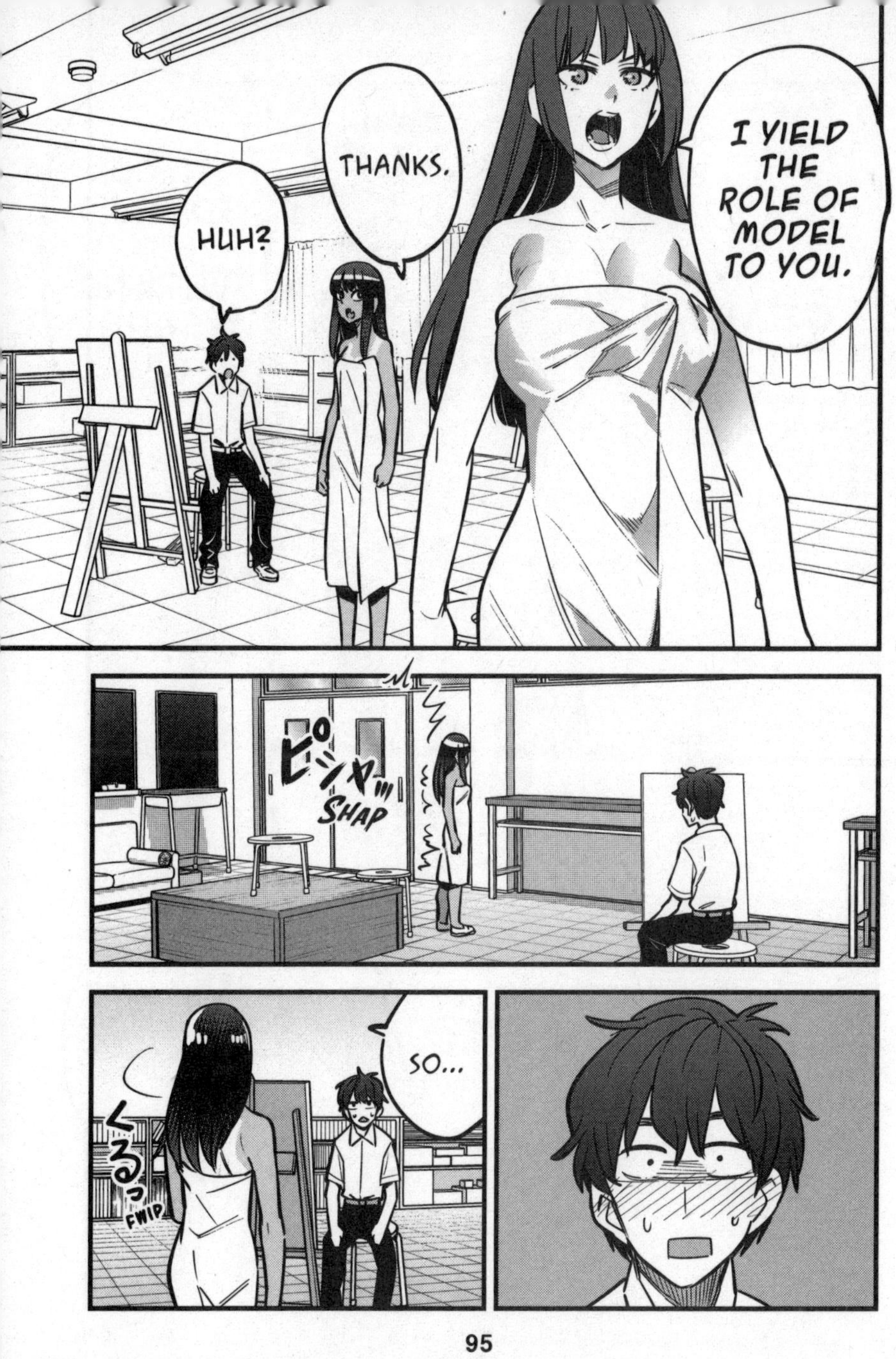
I YIELD THE ROLE OF MODEL TO YOU.
THANKS.
HUH?
ピシャ
SHAP
SO...
くるっ
FWIP

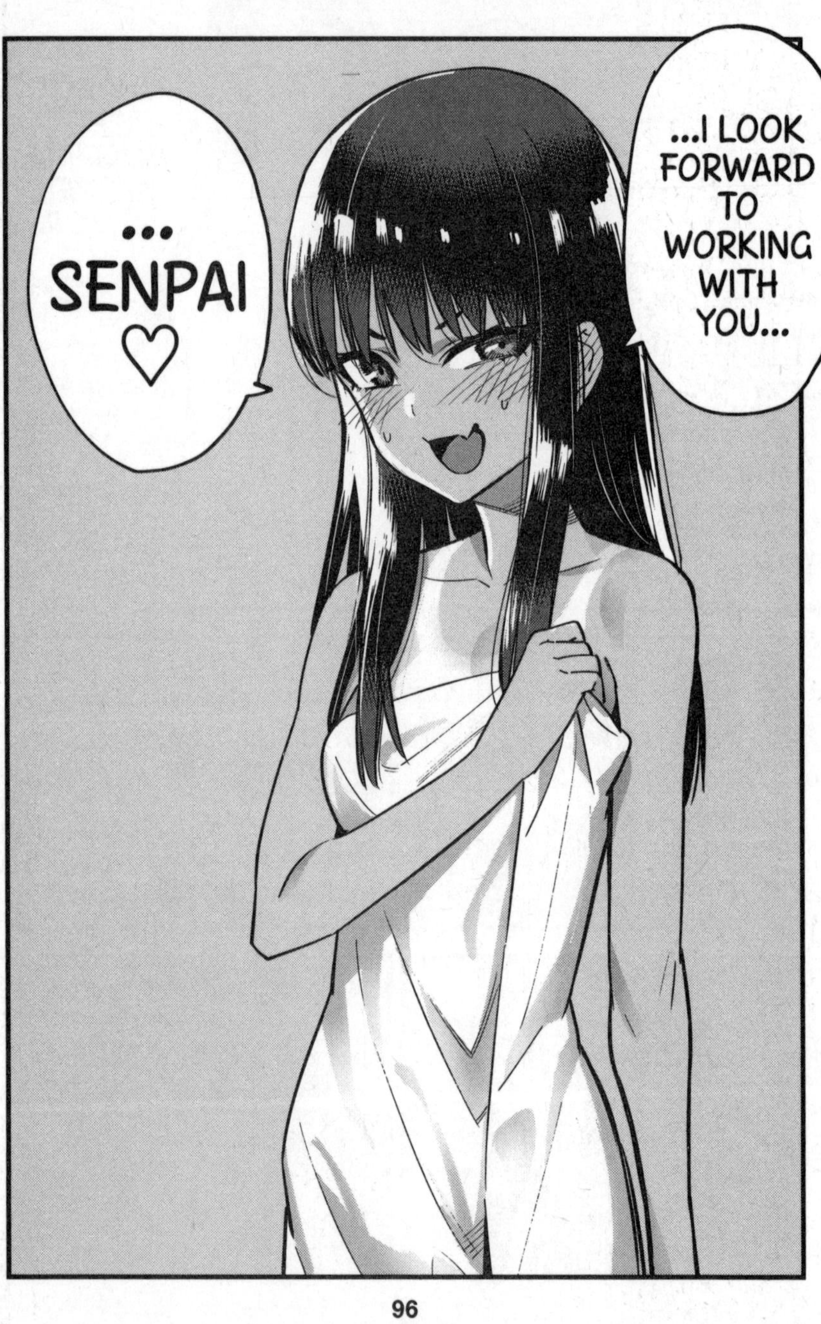
...I LOOK FORWARD TO WORKING WITH YOU...
... SENPAI ♡

HUH?
UH!
HUH ?!
P—
P—
P—
PLEASE AND THANK ...
...YOU ...

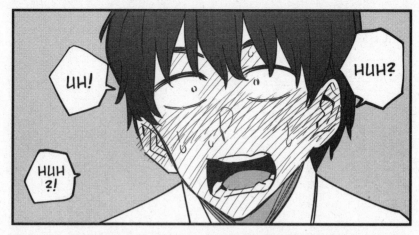

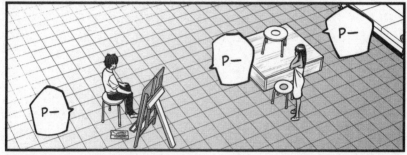

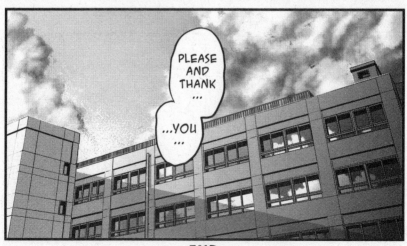

END

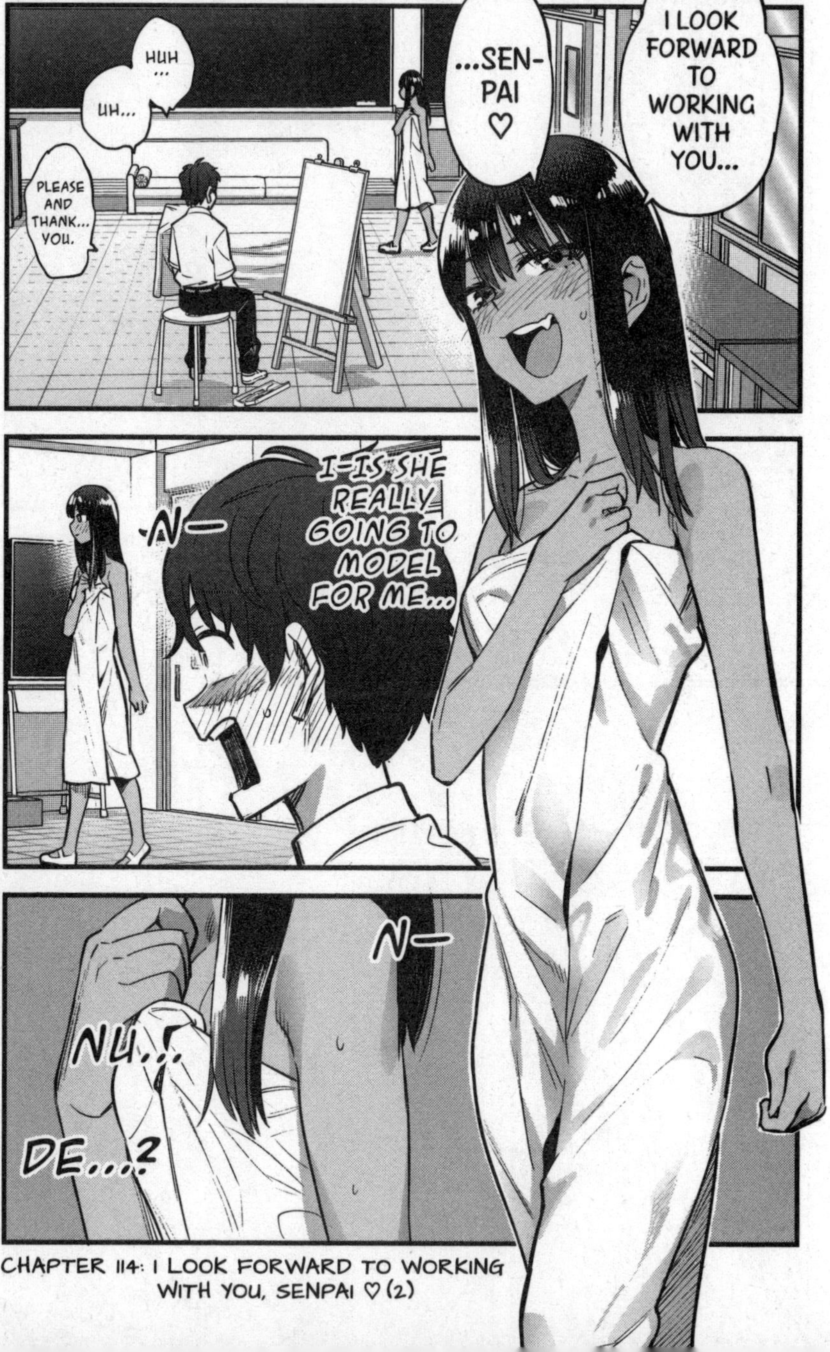
I LOOK FORWARD TO WORKING WITH YOU...
...SEN-PAI ♡
HUH...
UH...
PLEASE AND THANK... YOU.
I-IS SHE REALLY GOING TO MODEL FOR ME...
-N—
N—
NU..!
DE...?

CHAPTER 114: I LOOK FORWARD TO WORKING WITH YOU, SENPAI ♡ (2)

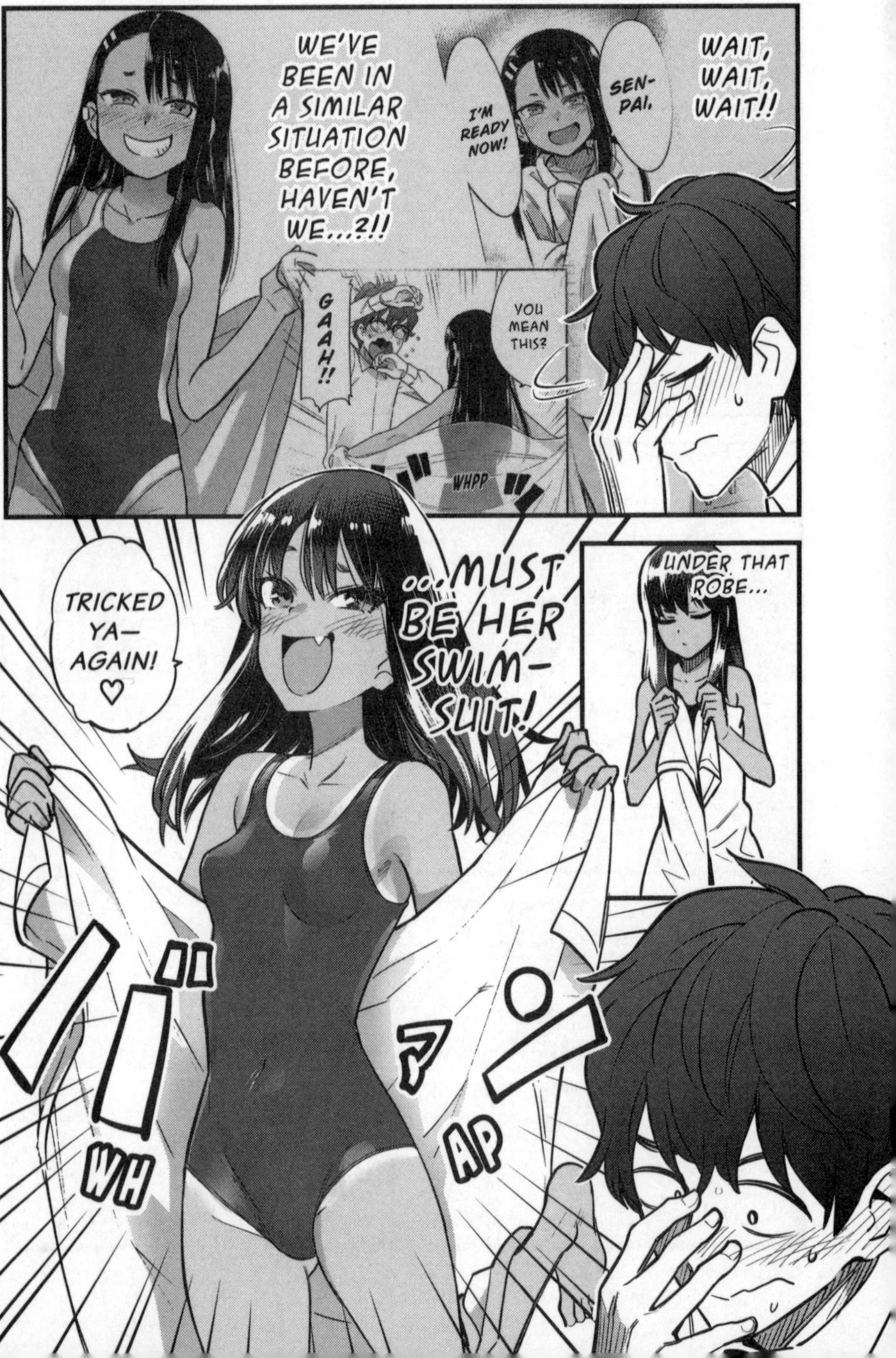
WAIT, WAIT, WAIT!!
SEN-PAI, I'M READY NOW!
WE'VE BEEN IN A SIMILAR SITUATION BEFORE, HAVEN'T WE...?!!
YOU MEAN THIS?
GAAAH!!
WHPP
UNDER THAT ROBE...
...MUST BE HER SWIM-SUIT!
TRICKED YA—AGAIN! ♡
AP
WH

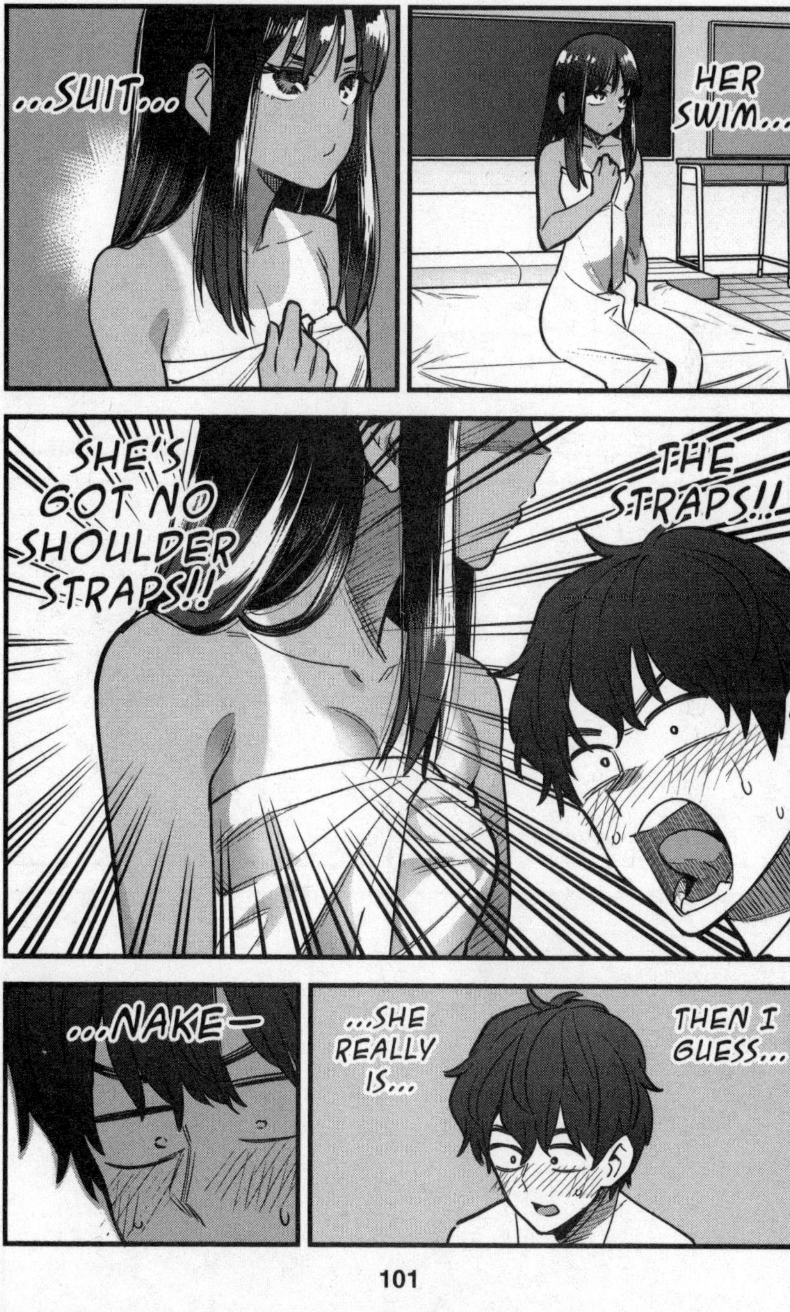
HER SWIM...
...SUIT...
THE STRAPS!!
SHE'S GOT NO SHOULDER STRAPS!!
THEN I GUESS...
...SHE REALLY IS...
...NAKE—

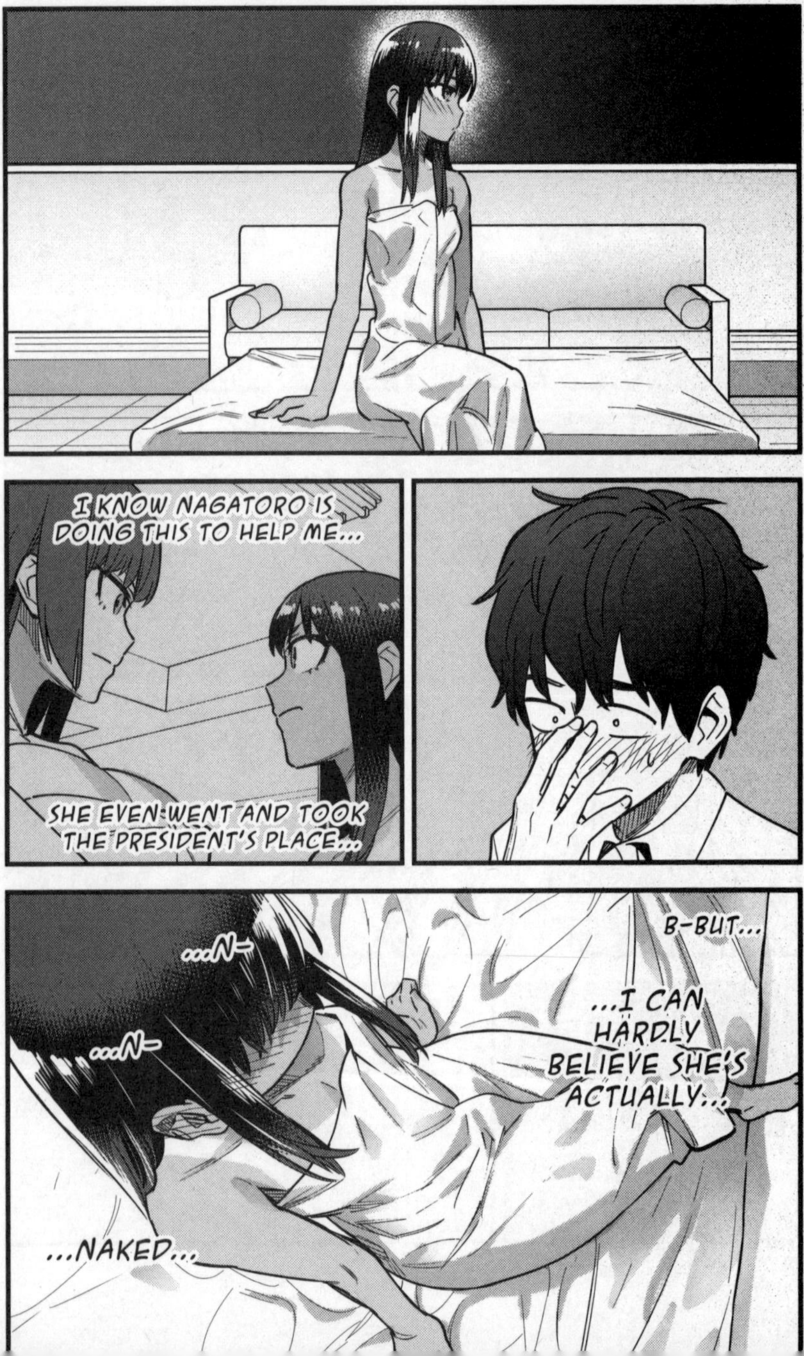
I KNOW NAGATORO IS DOING THIS TO HELP ME...
SHE EVEN WENT AND TOOK THE PRESIDENT'S PLACE...
B-BUT...
...N-
...I CAN HARDLY BELIEVE SHE'S ACTUALLY...
...N-
...NAKED...

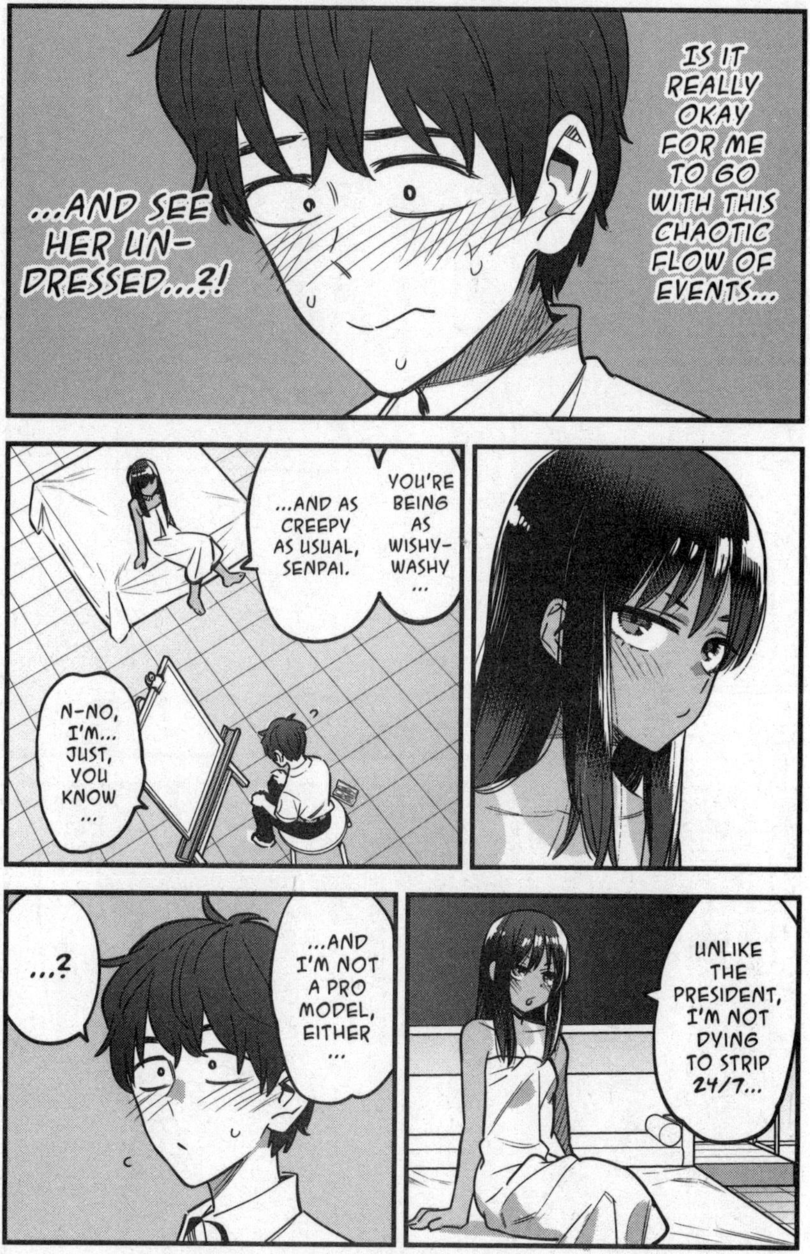
IS IT REALLY OKAY FOR ME TO GO WITH THIS CHAOTIC FLOW OF EVENTS...
...AND SEE HER UN-DRESSED...?!
YOU'RE BEING AS WISHY-WASHY...
...AND AS CREEPY AS USUAL, SENPAI.
N-NO, I'M... JUST, YOU KNOW...
UNLIKE THE PRESIDENT, I'M NOT DYING TO STRIP 24/7...
...AND I'M NOT A PRO MODEL, EITHER...
...?

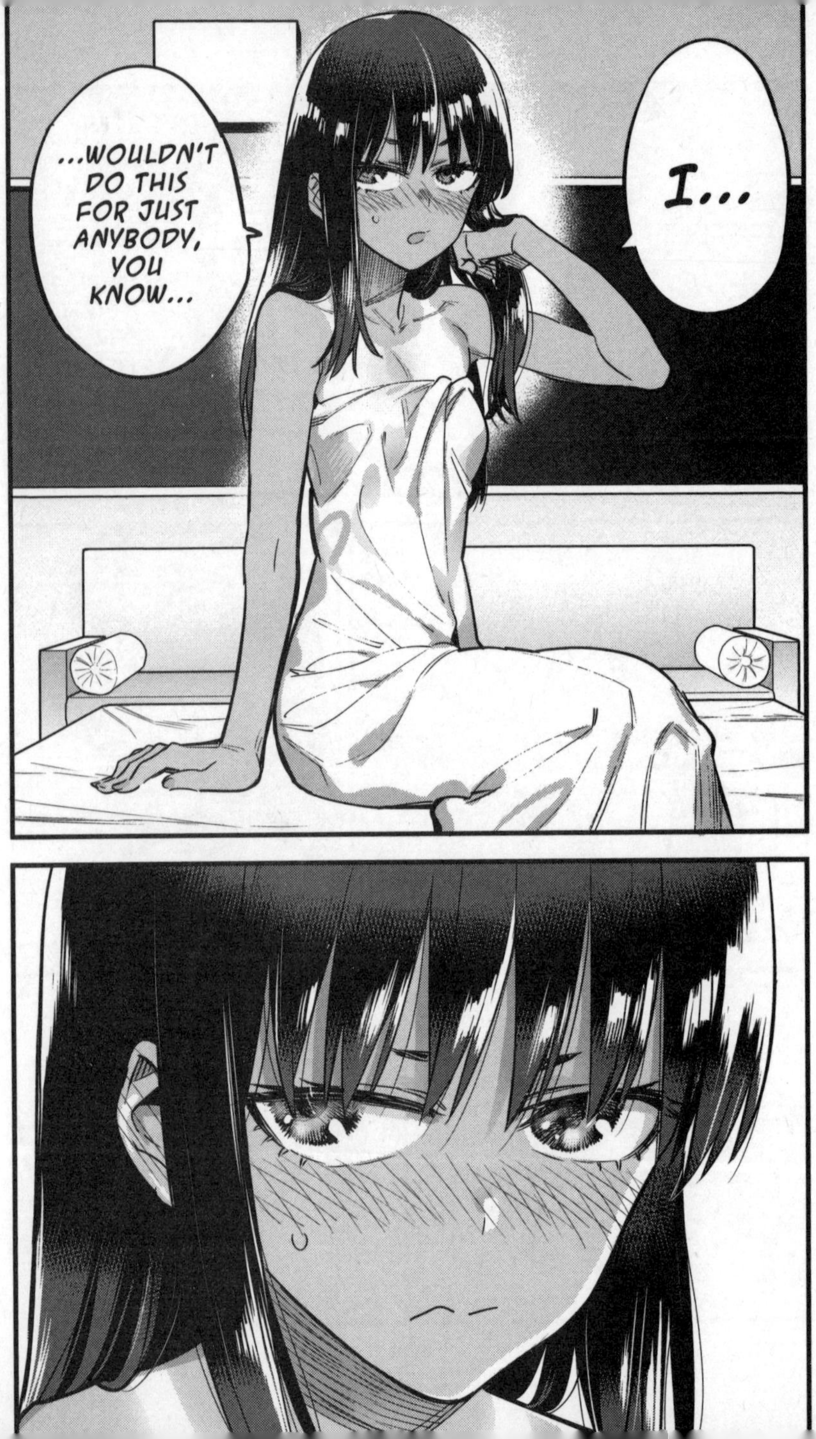
I...
...WOULDN'T DO THIS FOR JUST ANYBODY, YOU KNOW...

BUT IF YOU DON'T WANT TO DRAW ME, THEN—

NO!!

I...

...

...

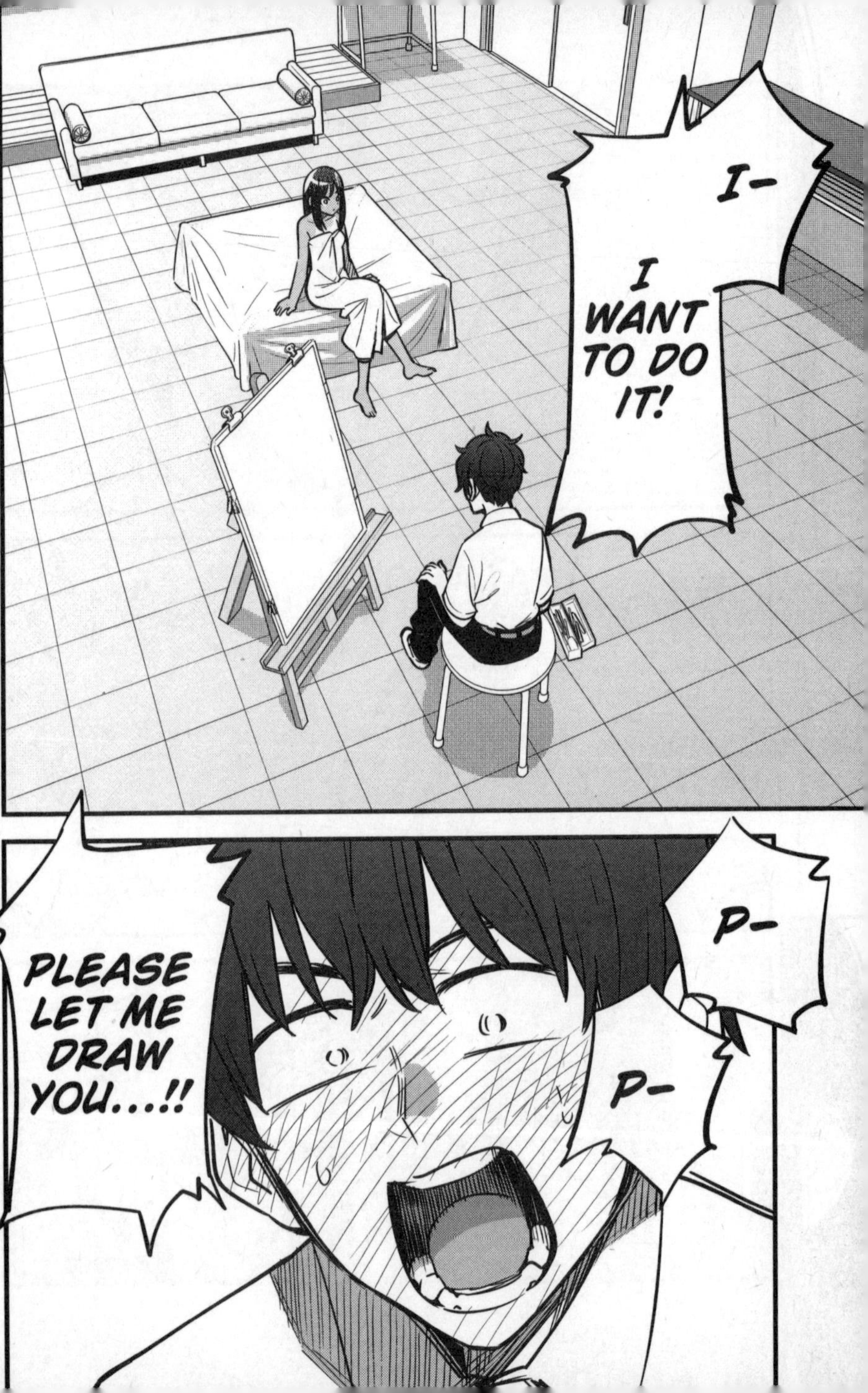
I–
I WANT TO DO IT!
P–
P–
PLEASE LET ME DRAW YOU...!!

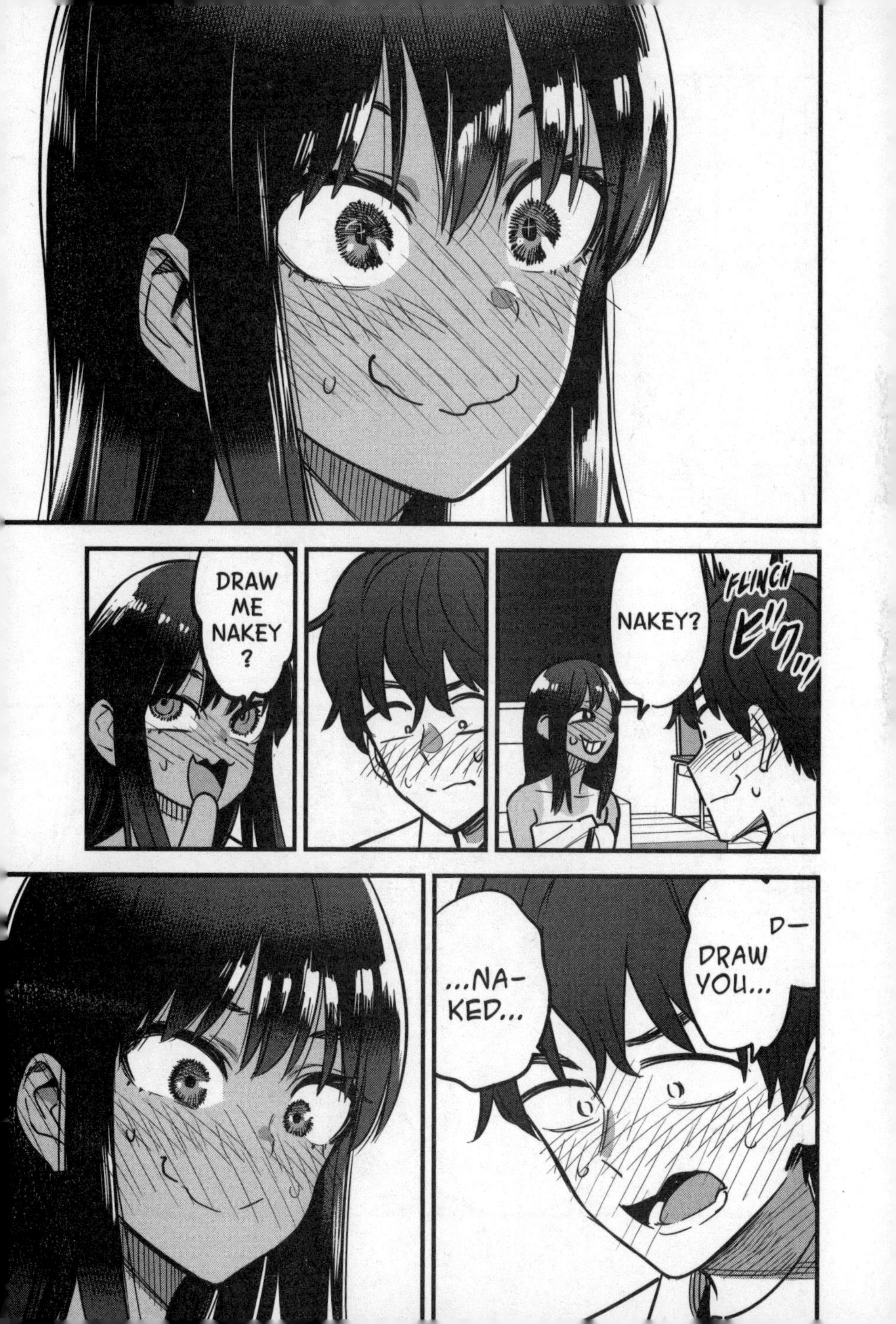
FLINCH
ビクッ
NAKEY?
DRAW ME NAKEY?
D— DRAW YOU...
...NA-KED...

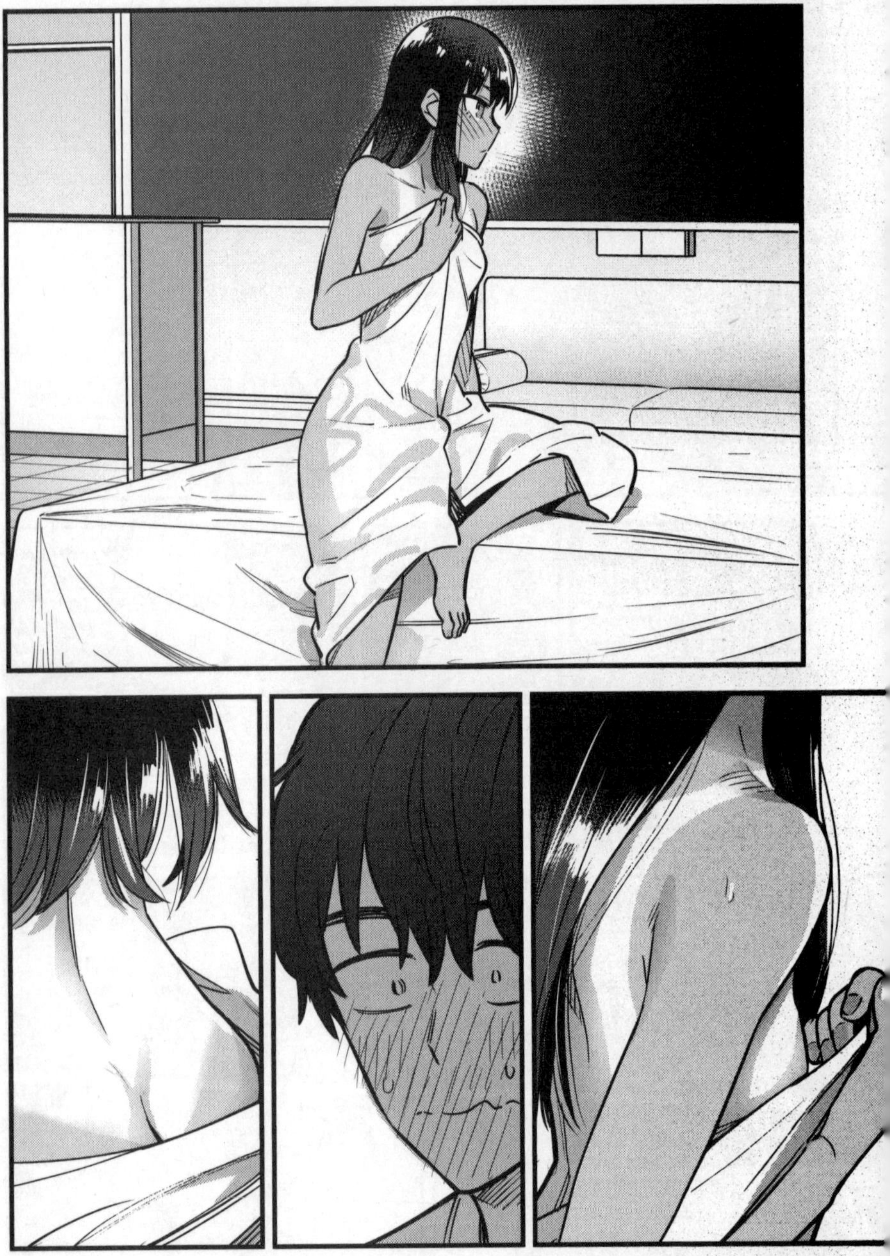

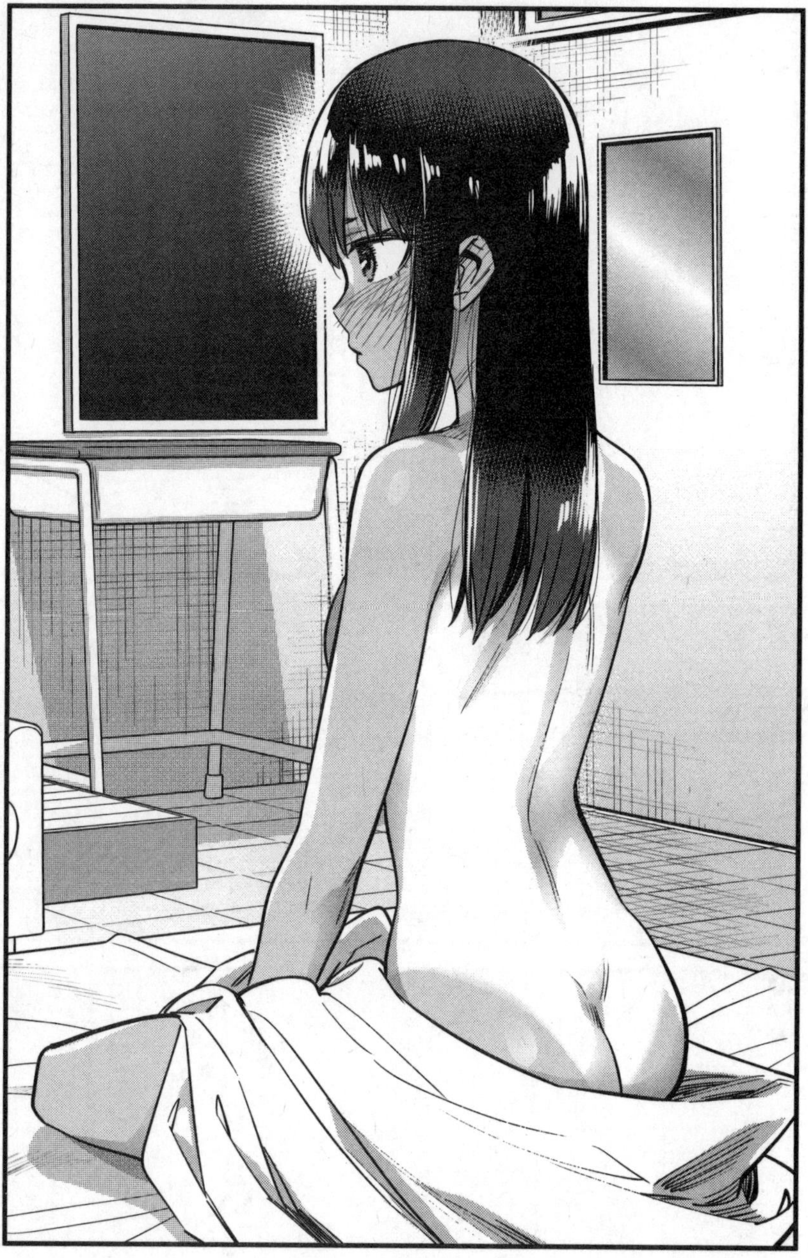

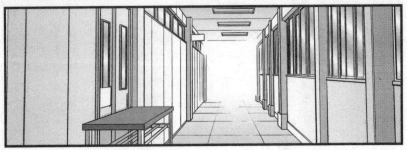

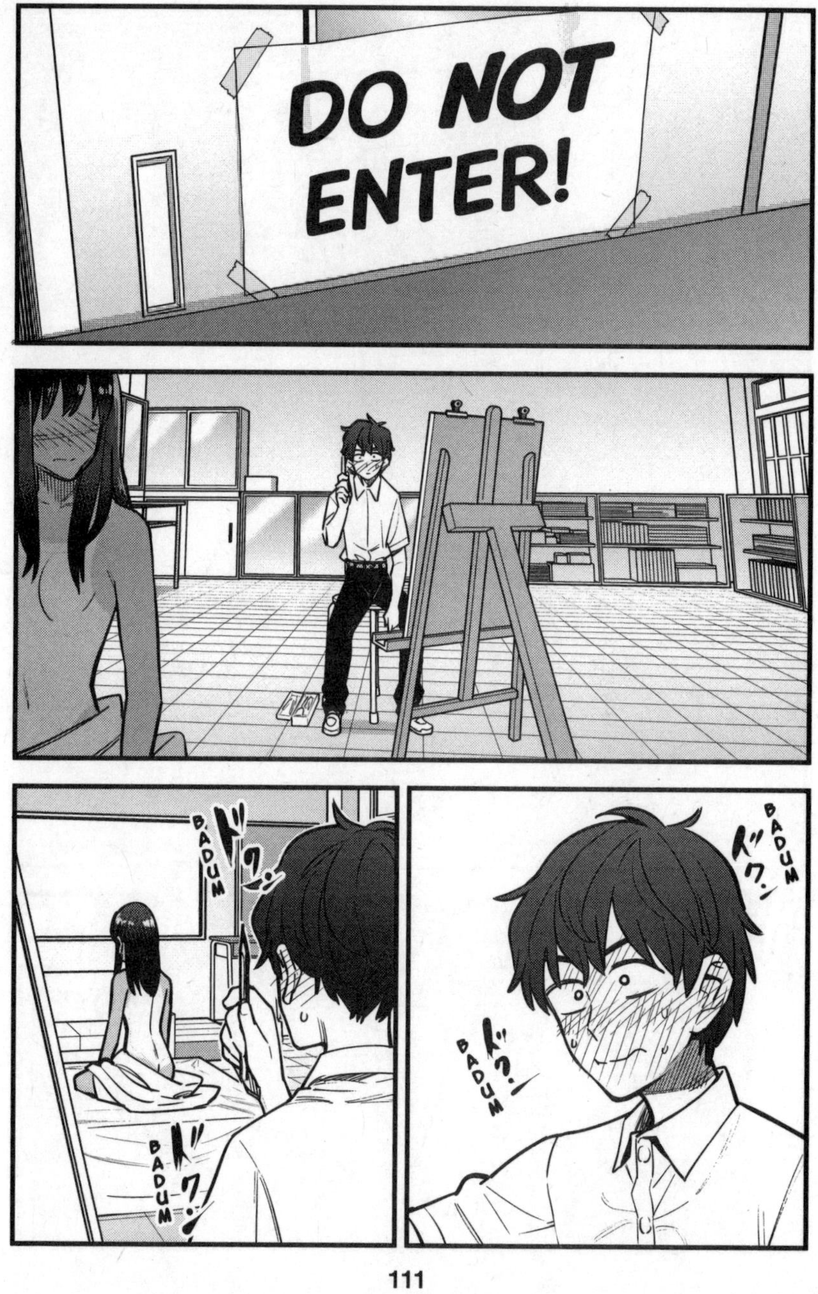
DO NOT ENTER!
BADUM
BADUM
BADUM
BADUM

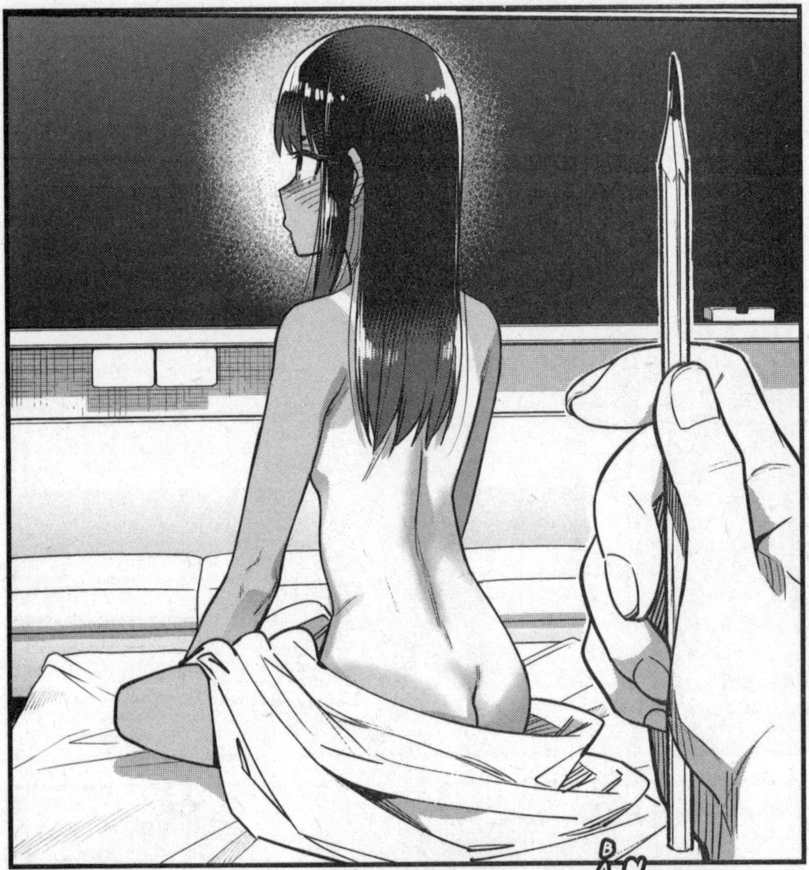

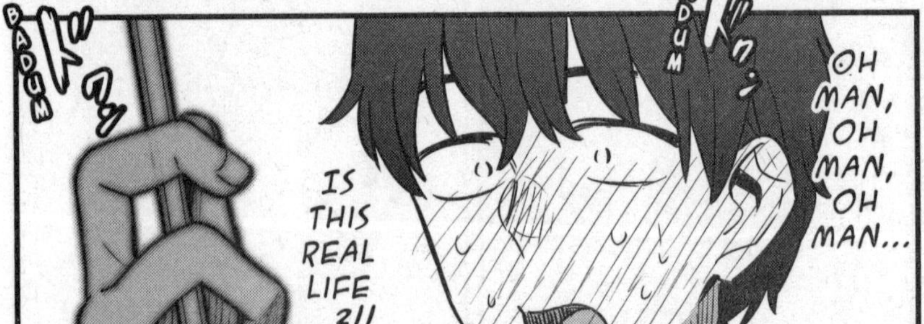
BADUM
OH MAN, OH MAN, OH MAN...
IS THIS REAL LIFE ...?!!
HUFF
HUFF
BADUM

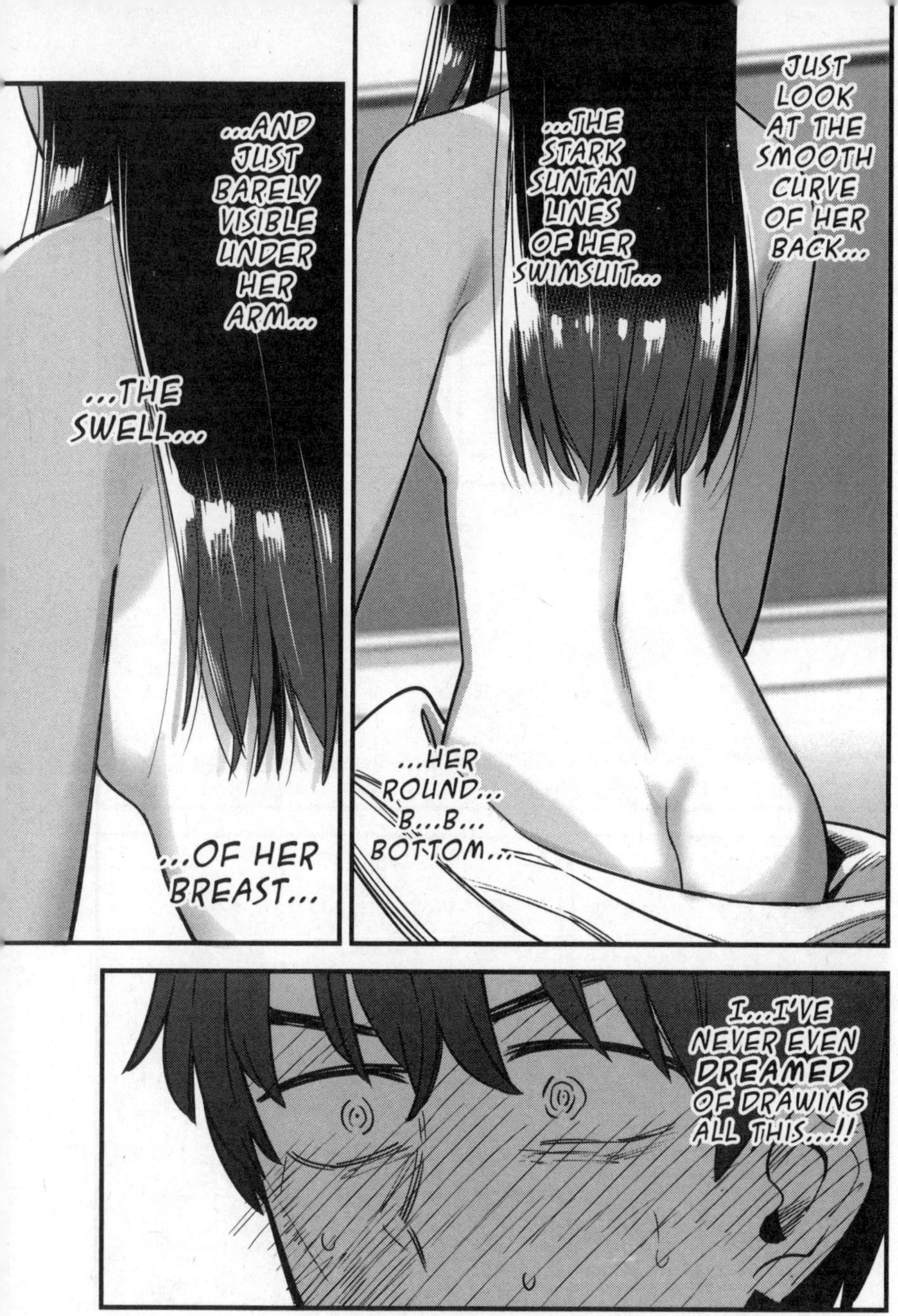
JUST LOOK AT THE SMOOTH CURVE OF HER BACK...
...THE STARK SUNTAN LINES OF HER SWIMSUIT...
...HER ROUND... B...B... BOTTOM...
...AND JUST BARELY VISIBLE UNDER HER ARM...
...THE SWELL...
...OF HER BREAST...
I...I'VE NEVER EVEN DREAMED OF DRAWING ALL THIS...!!

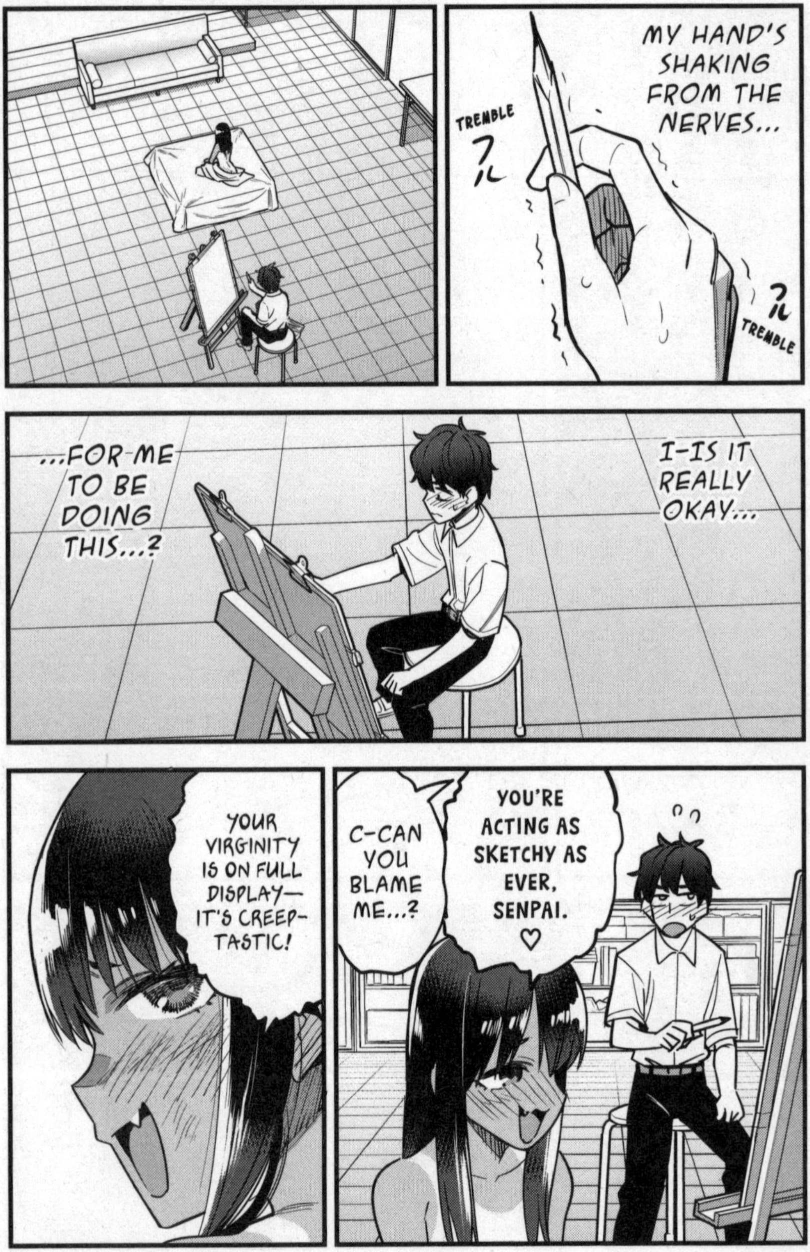
MY HAND'S SHAKING FROM THE NERVES...
TREMBLE
TREMBLE
I-IS IT REALLY OKAY...
...FOR ME TO BE DOING THIS...?
YOU'RE ACTING AS SKETCHY AS EVER, SENPAI. ♡
C-CAN YOU BLAME ME...?
YOUR VIRGINITY IS ON FULL DISPLAY—IT'S CREEP-TASTIC!

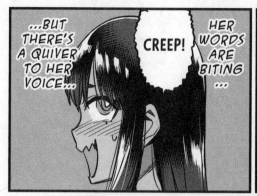

HER WORDS ARE BITING ...
CREEP!
...BUT THERE'S A QUIVER TO HER VOICE...
NAGATORO MUST BE NERVOUS, TOO...
I MEAN, OF COURSE SHE IS...
CREEEEP!
I ONCE READ SOME-WHERE...
...THAT IT'S AN ARTIST'S DUTY TO HELP THEIR MODELS RELAX...
I'VE GOTTA SAY SOMETHING TO PUT HER AT EASE...!!

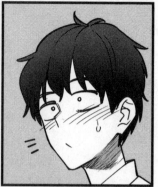

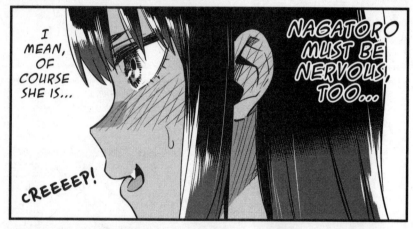

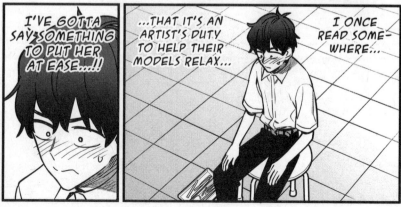

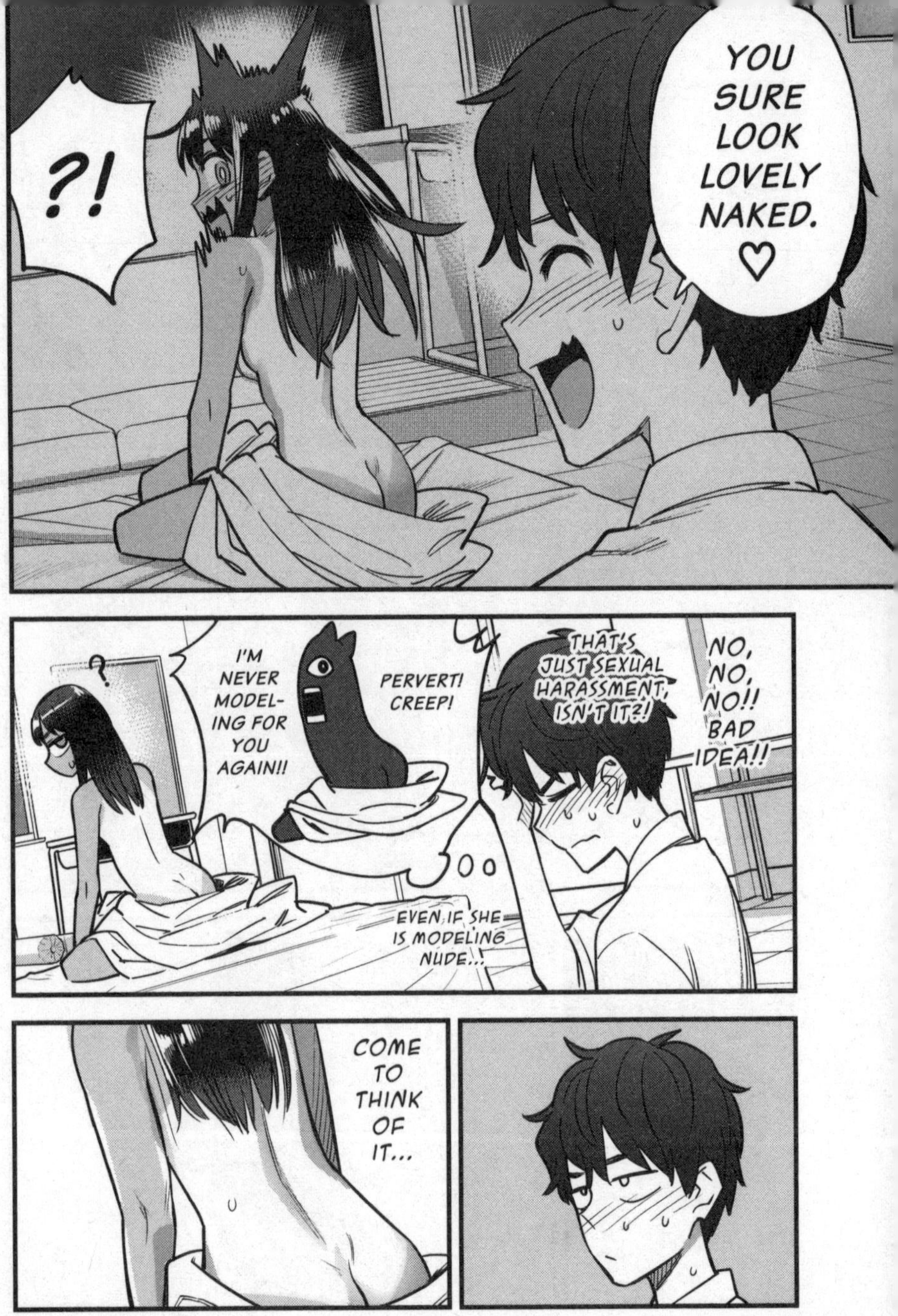
YOU SURE LOOK LOVELY NAKED. ♡
?!
NO, NO, NO!! BAD IDEA!!
THAT'S JUST SEXUAL HARASSMENT, ISN'T IT?!
PERVERT! CREEP!
I'M NEVER MODEL-ING FOR YOU AGAIN!!
?
EVEN IF SHE IS MODELING NUDE...
COME TO THINK OF IT...

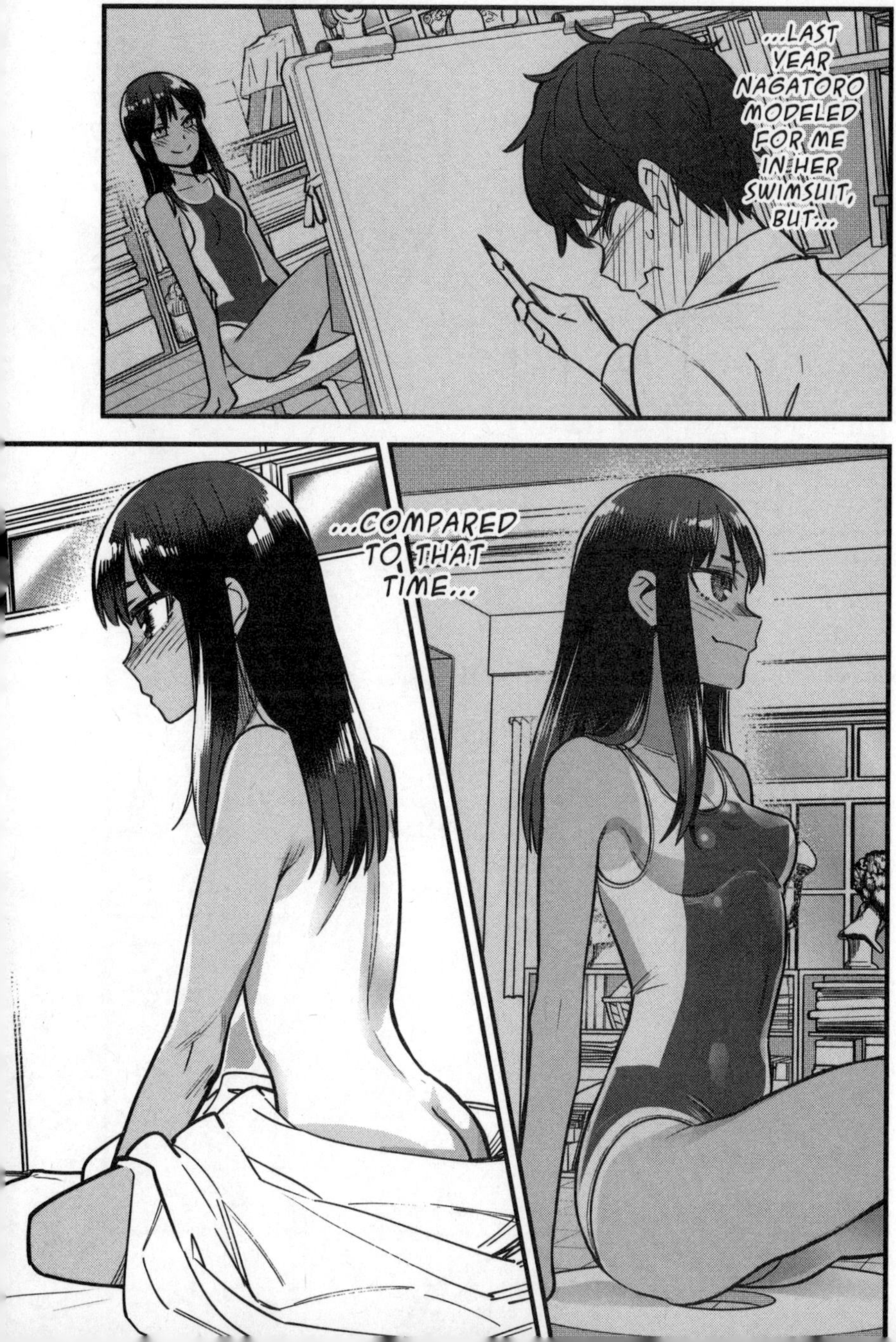
...LAST YEAR NAGATORO MODELED FOR ME IN HER SWIMSUIT, BUT...
...COMPARED TO THAT TIME...

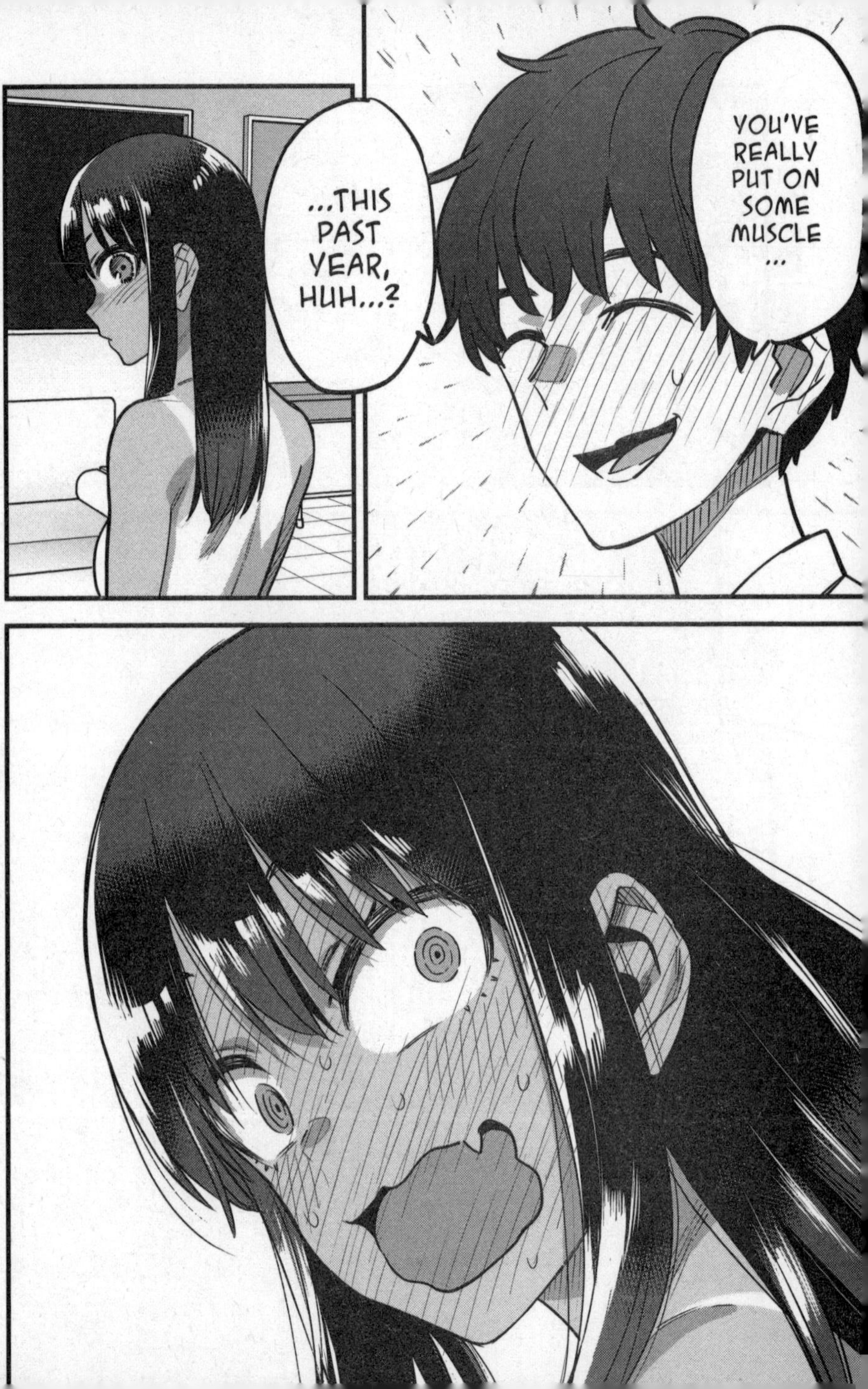
YOU'VE REALLY PUT ON SOME MUSCLE ...
...THIS PAST YEAR, HUH...?

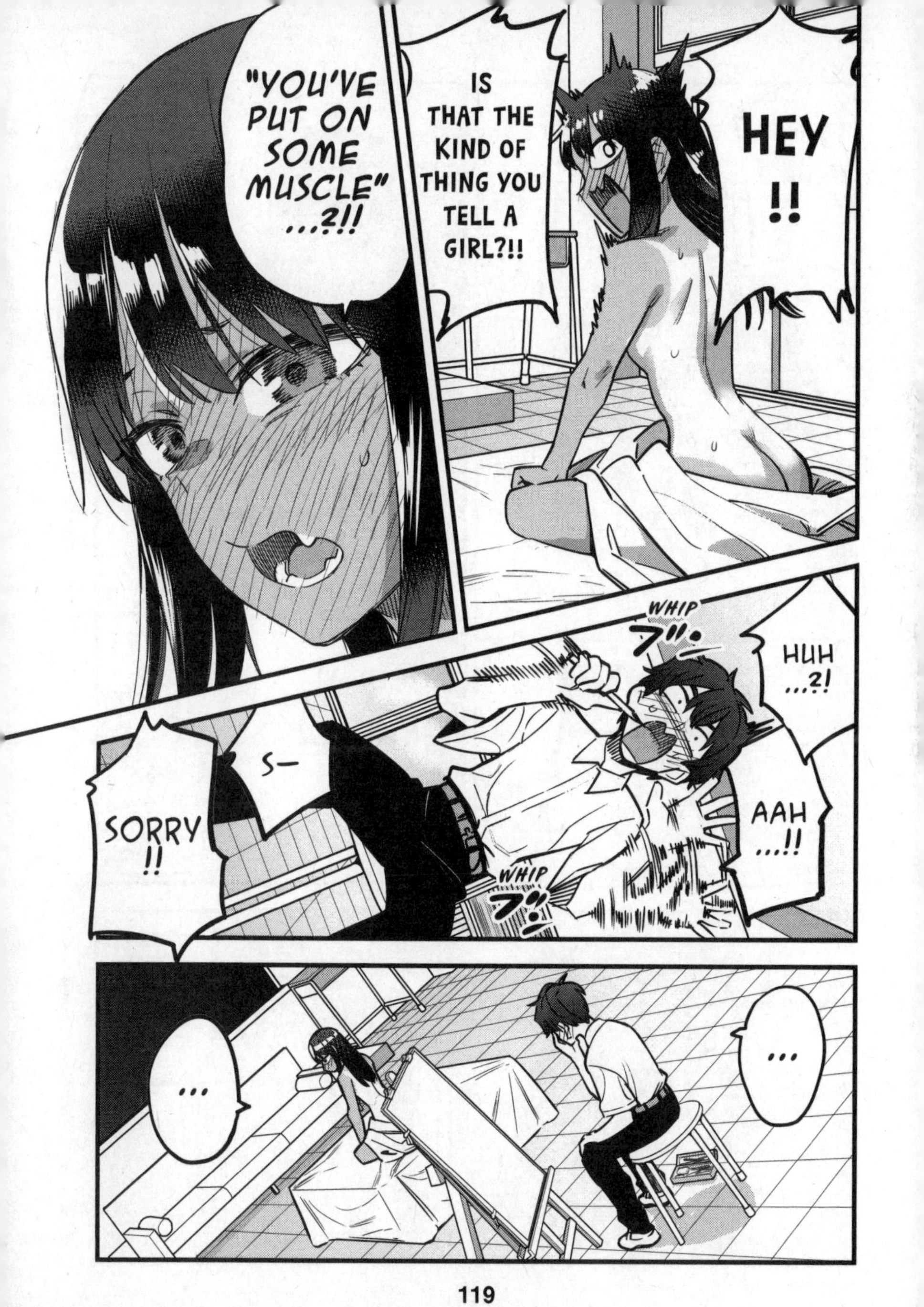
HEY !!
IS THAT THE KIND OF THING YOU TELL A GIRL?!!
"YOU'VE PUT ON SOME MUSCLE" ...?!!
HUH ...?!
WHIP
AAH ...!!
WHIP
S—
SORRY !!
...
...

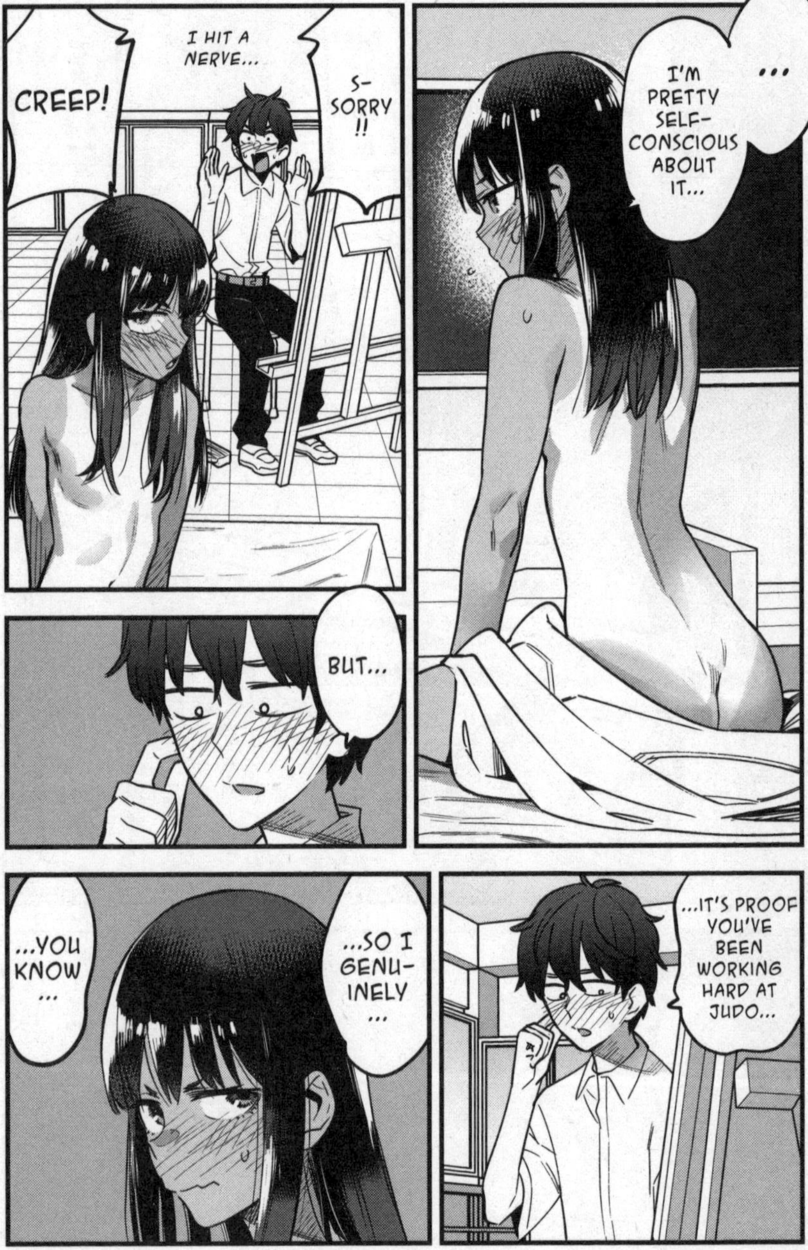
...
I'M PRETTY SELF-CONSCIOUS ABOUT IT...
S-SORRY !!
I HIT A NERVE...
CREEP!
BUT...
...IT'S PROOF YOU'VE BEEN WORKING HARD AT JUDO...
...SO I GENUINELY ...
...YOU KNOW ...

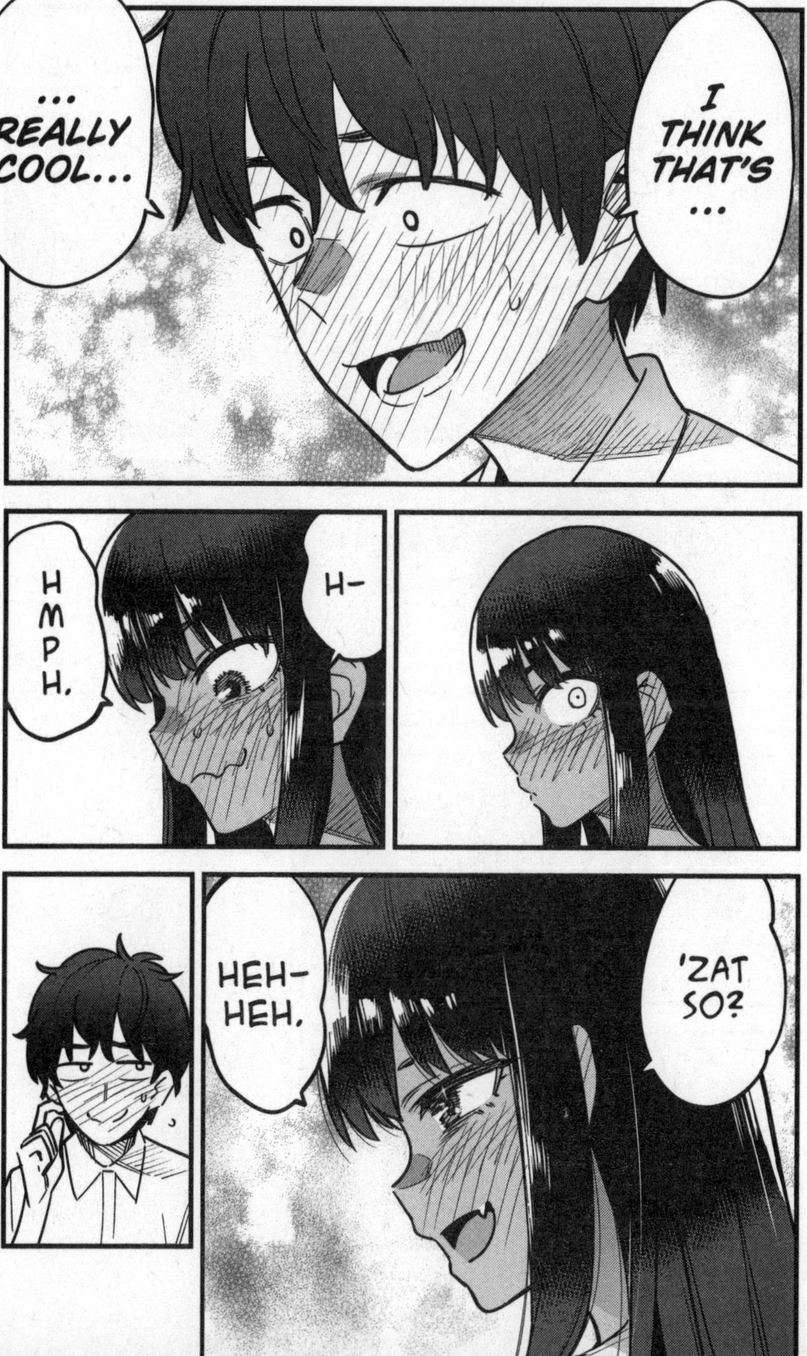
I THINK THAT'S ...
... REALLY COOL...
H-
HMPH.
'ZAT SO?
HEH-HEH.

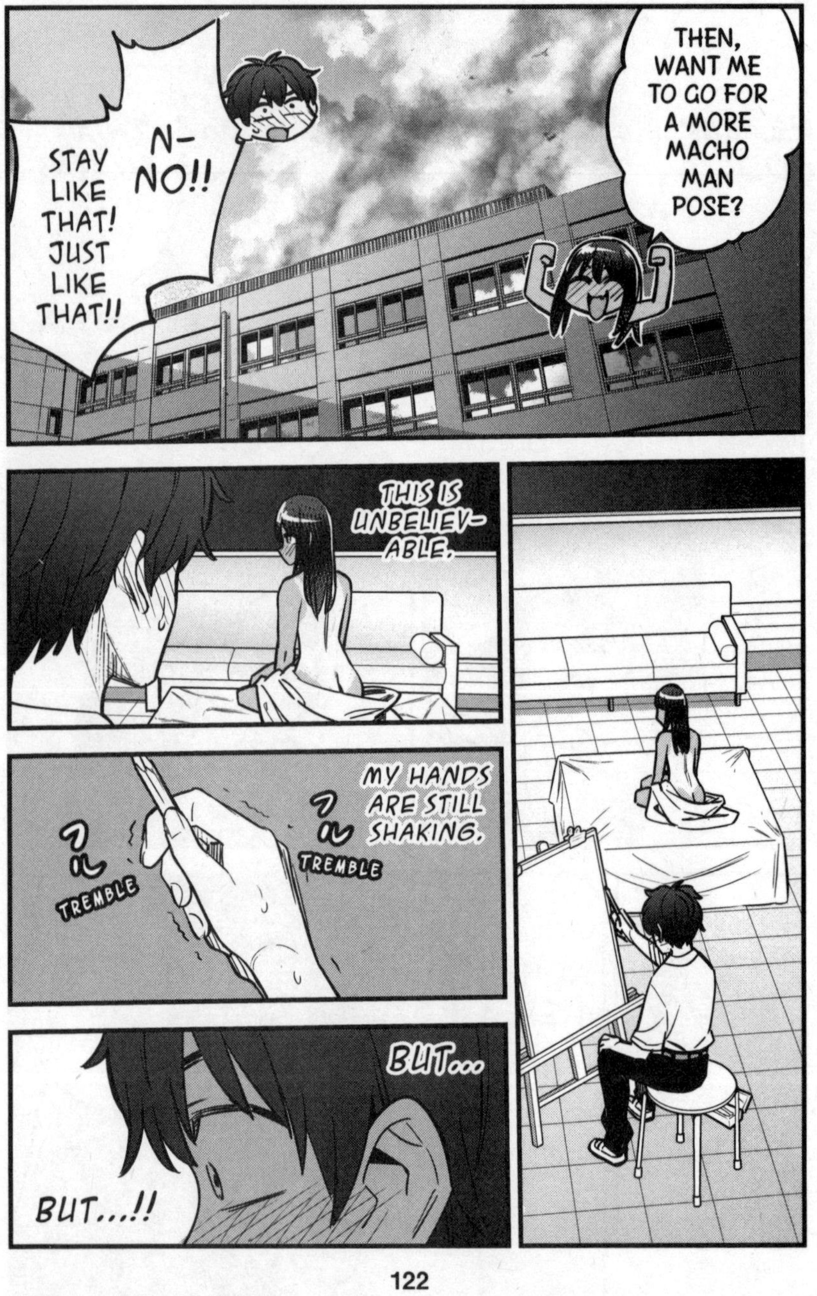
THEN, WANT ME TO GO FOR A MORE MACHO MAN POSE?
N- NO!!
STAY LIKE THAT! JUST LIKE THAT!!
THIS IS UNBELIEV- ABLE.
MY HANDS ARE STILL SHAKING.
TREMBLE
TREMBLE
BUT...
BUT...!!

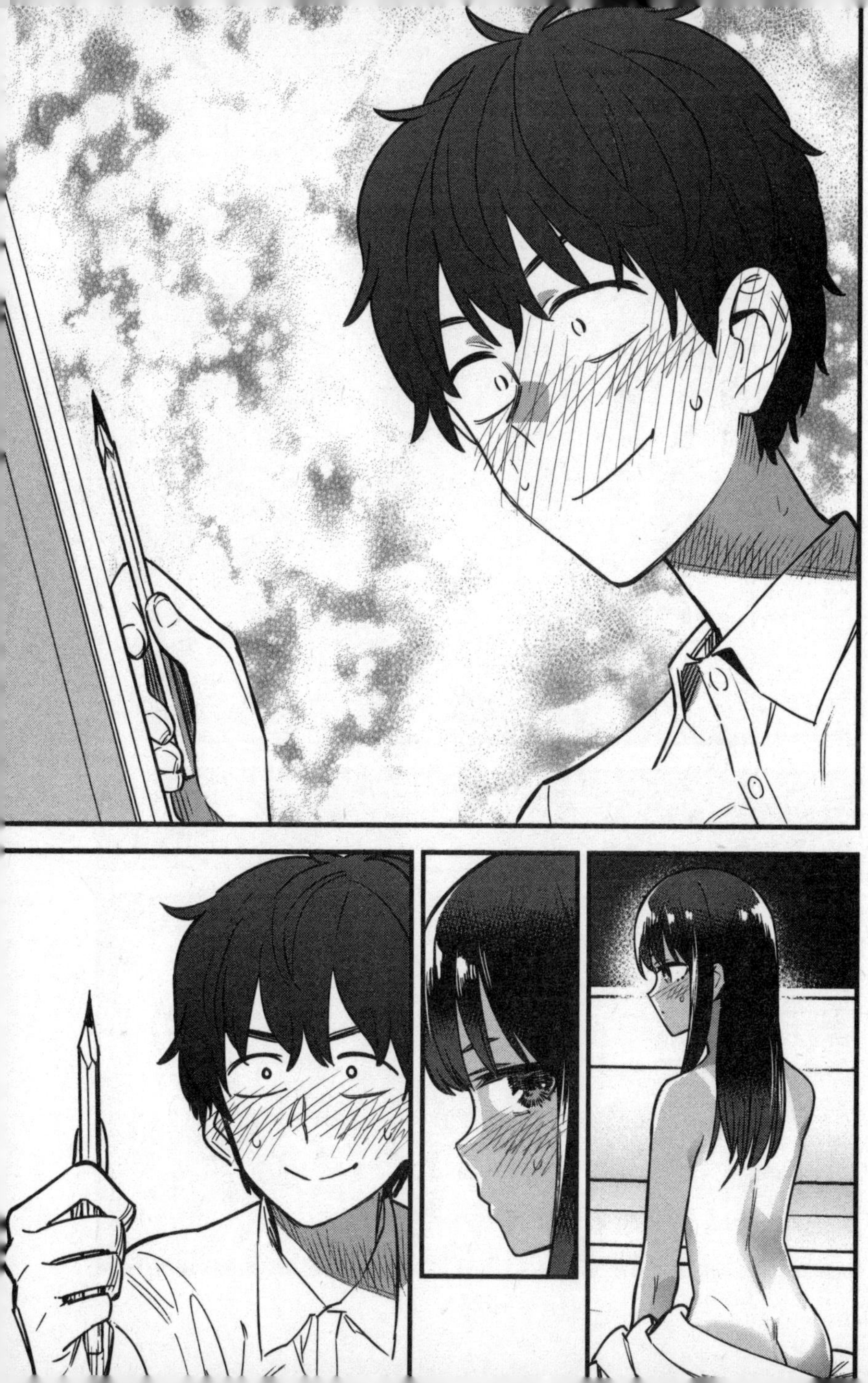

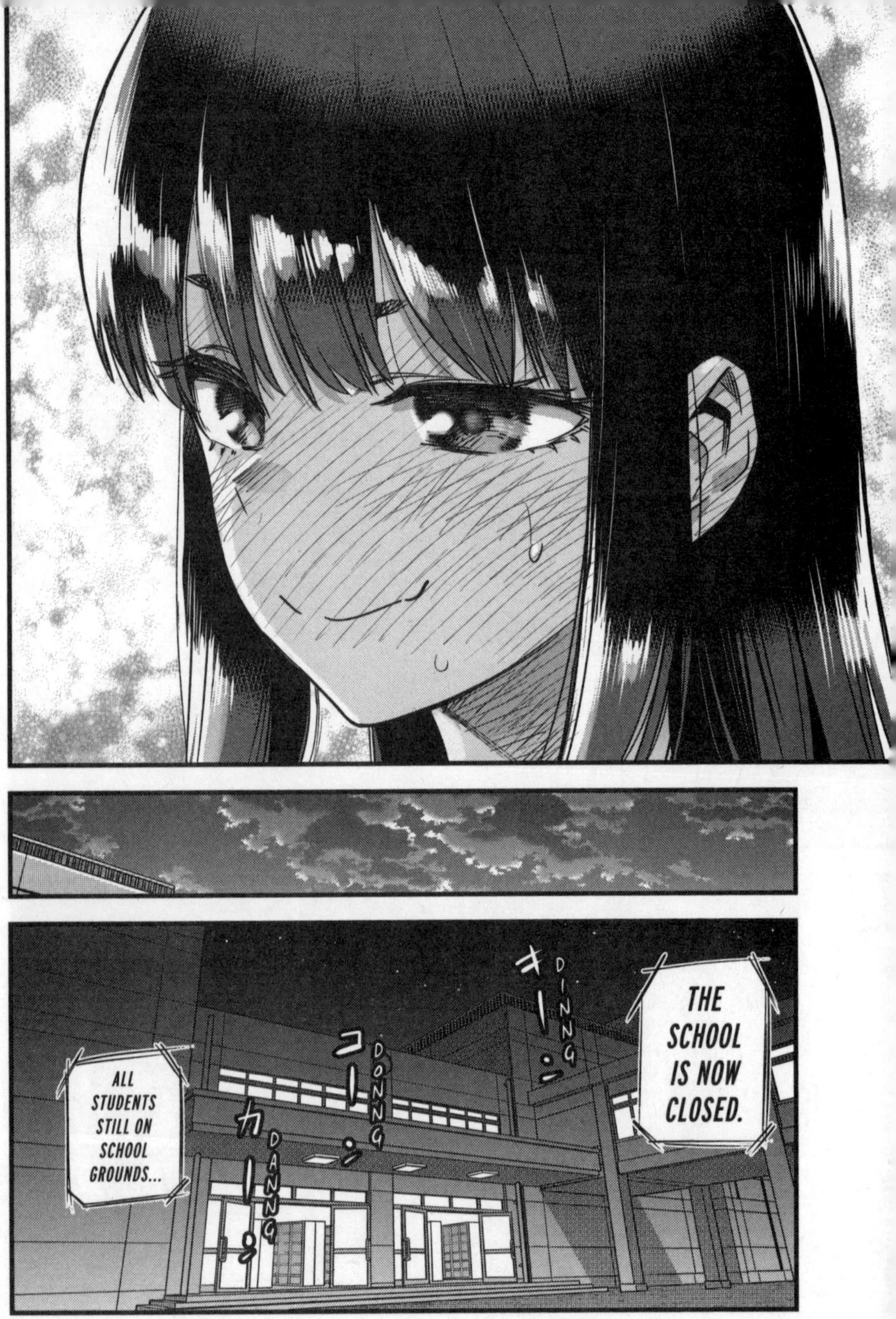
THE SCHOOL IS NOW CLOSED.
DINNG
DONNG
DANNG
ALL STUDENTS STILL ON SCHOOL GROUNDS...

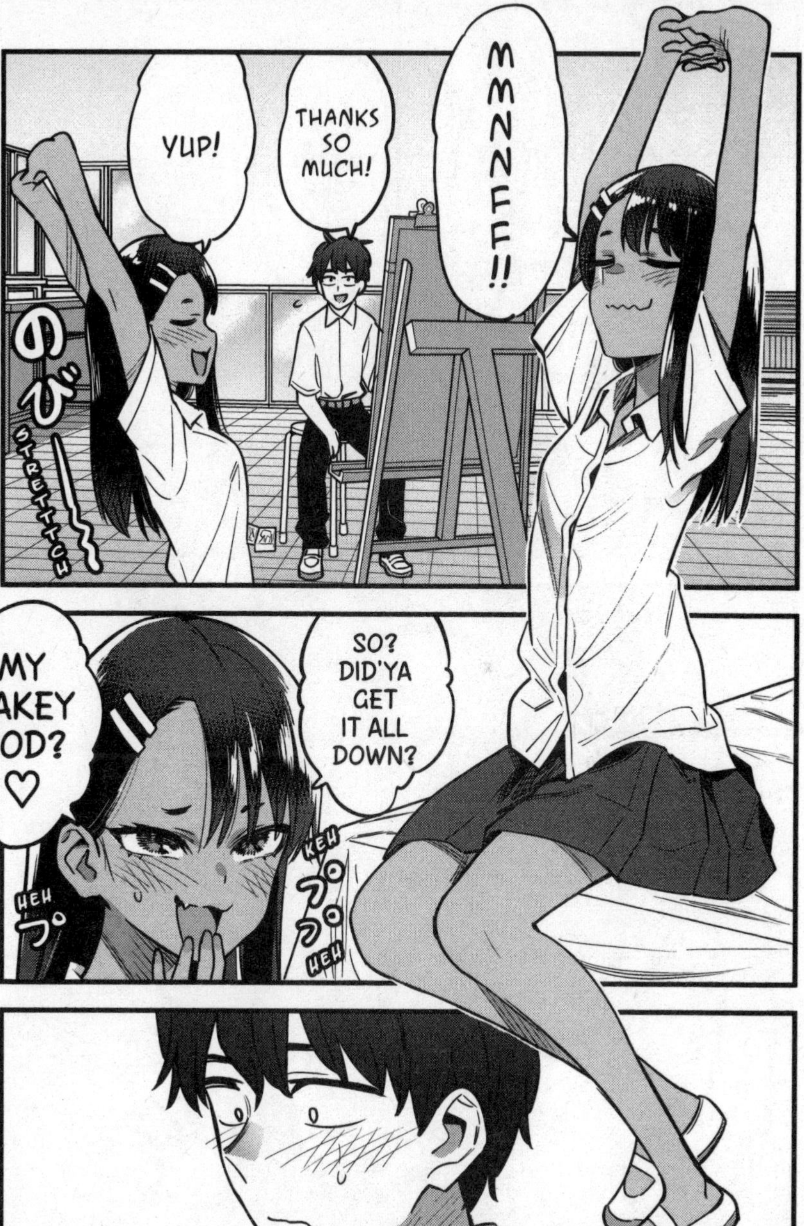
MMMNNFF!!
THANKS SO MUCH!
YUP!
のび
STRETTTCH
SO? DID'YA GET IT ALL DOWN?
MY NAKEY BOD? ♡
KEH
フ
フ
HEH
HEH
フ

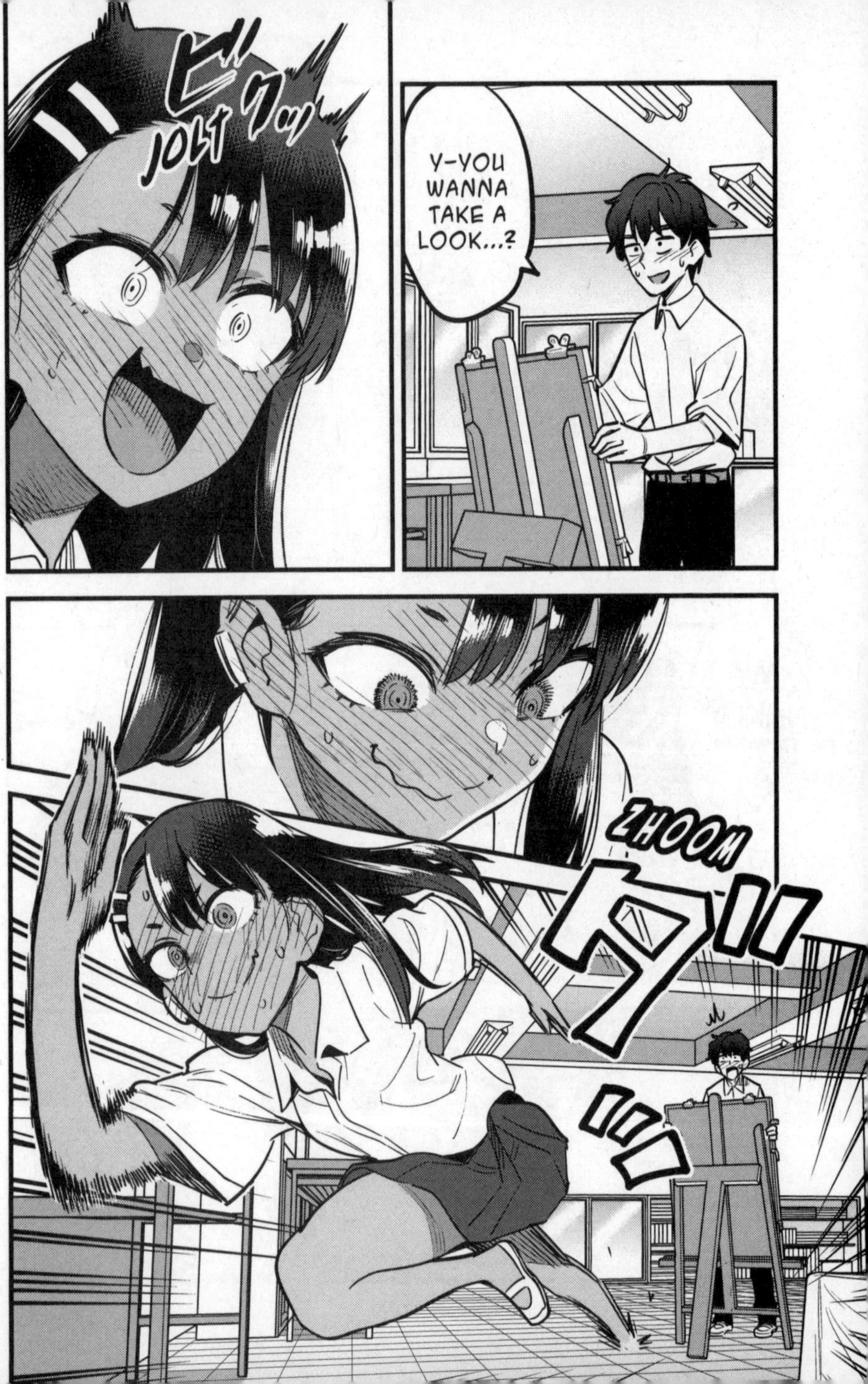
Y-YOU WANNA TAKE A LOOK...?
ビクッ
JOLT
ZHOOM

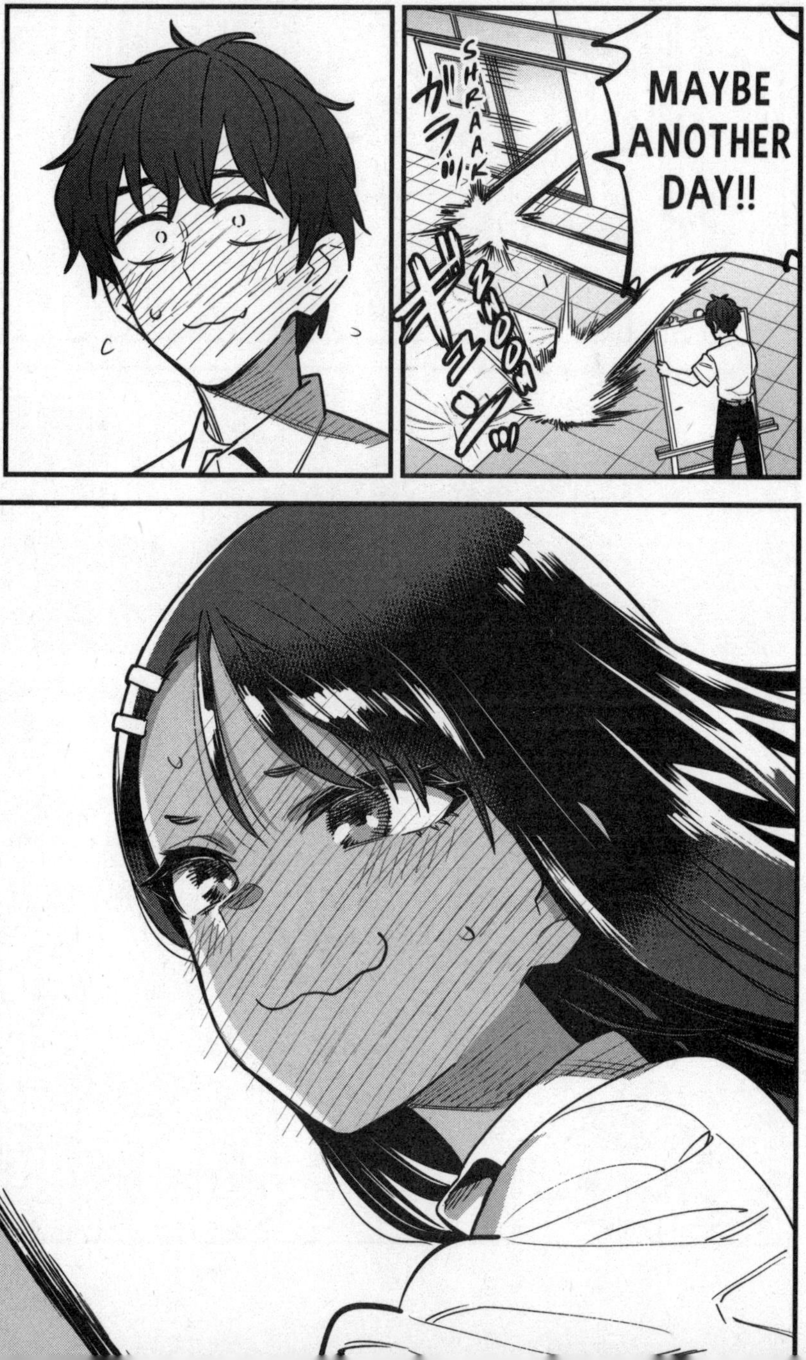
MAYBE ANOTHER DAY!!
SHRAAK
WHOOM

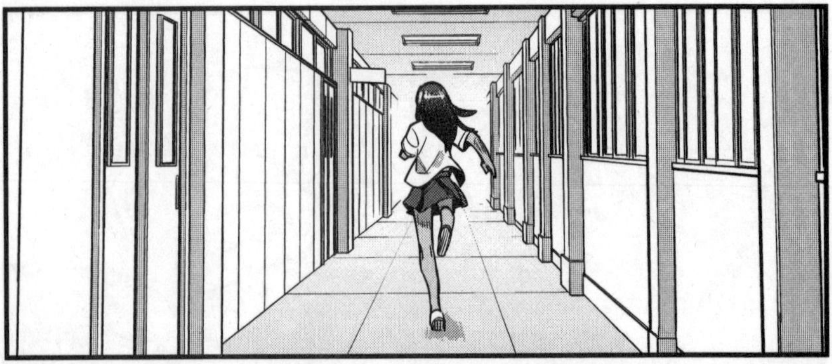

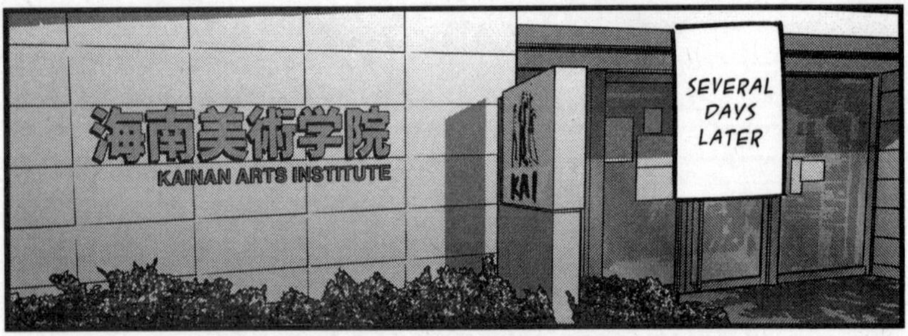
SEVERAL DAYS LATER
KAI
海南美術学院
KAINAN ARTS INSTITUTE

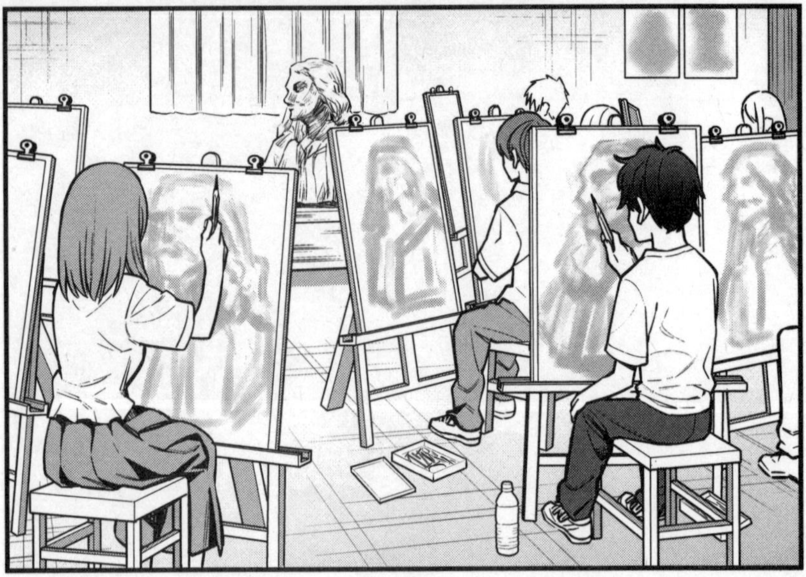

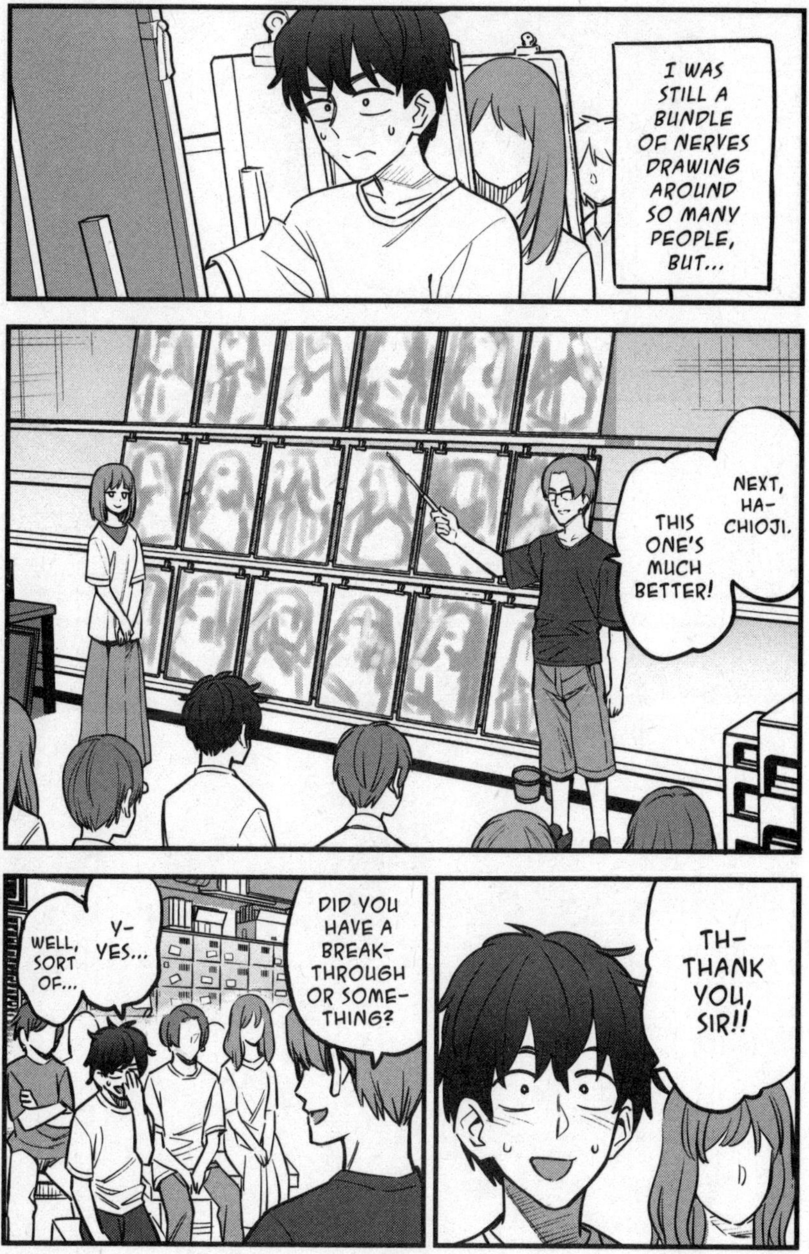
I WAS STILL A BUNDLE OF NERVES DRAWING AROUND SO MANY PEOPLE, BUT...
NEXT, HA-CHIOJI.
THIS ONE'S MUCH BETTER!
TH-THANK YOU, SIR!!
DID YOU HAVE A BREAK-THROUGH OR SOME-THING?
Y-YES...
WELL, SORT OF...

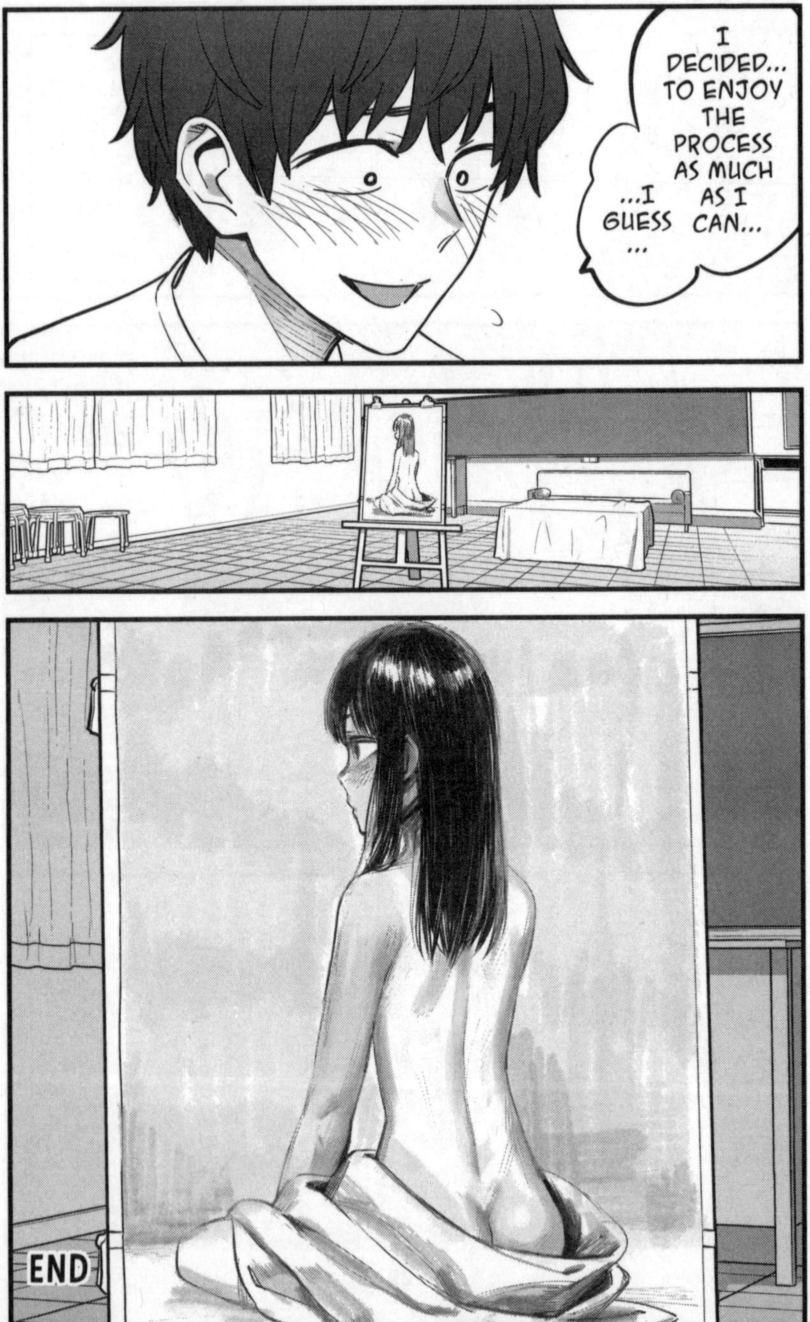
I DECIDED... TO ENJOY THE PROCESS AS MUCH AS I CAN...
...I GUESS ...
END

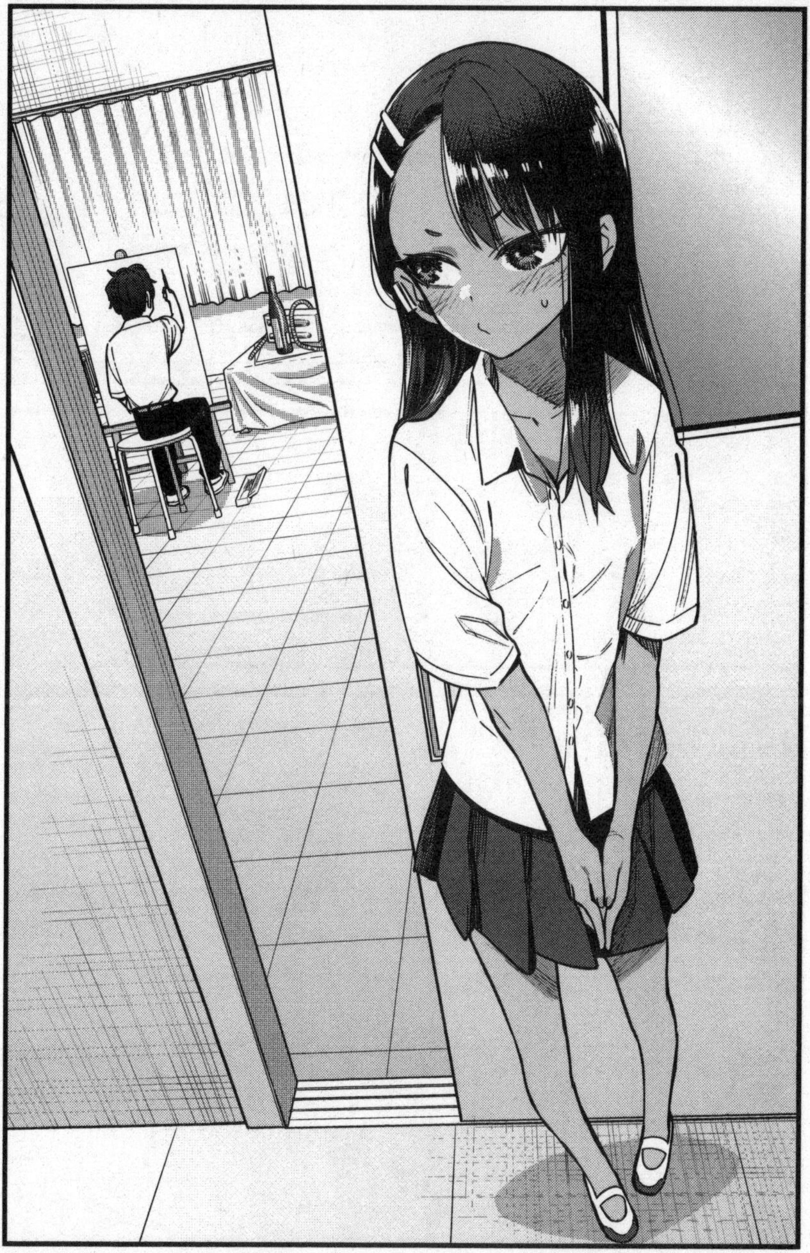

CHAPTER 115: YOU WANT ME TO KISS YOU, DON'T YOU, SENPAI? ♡

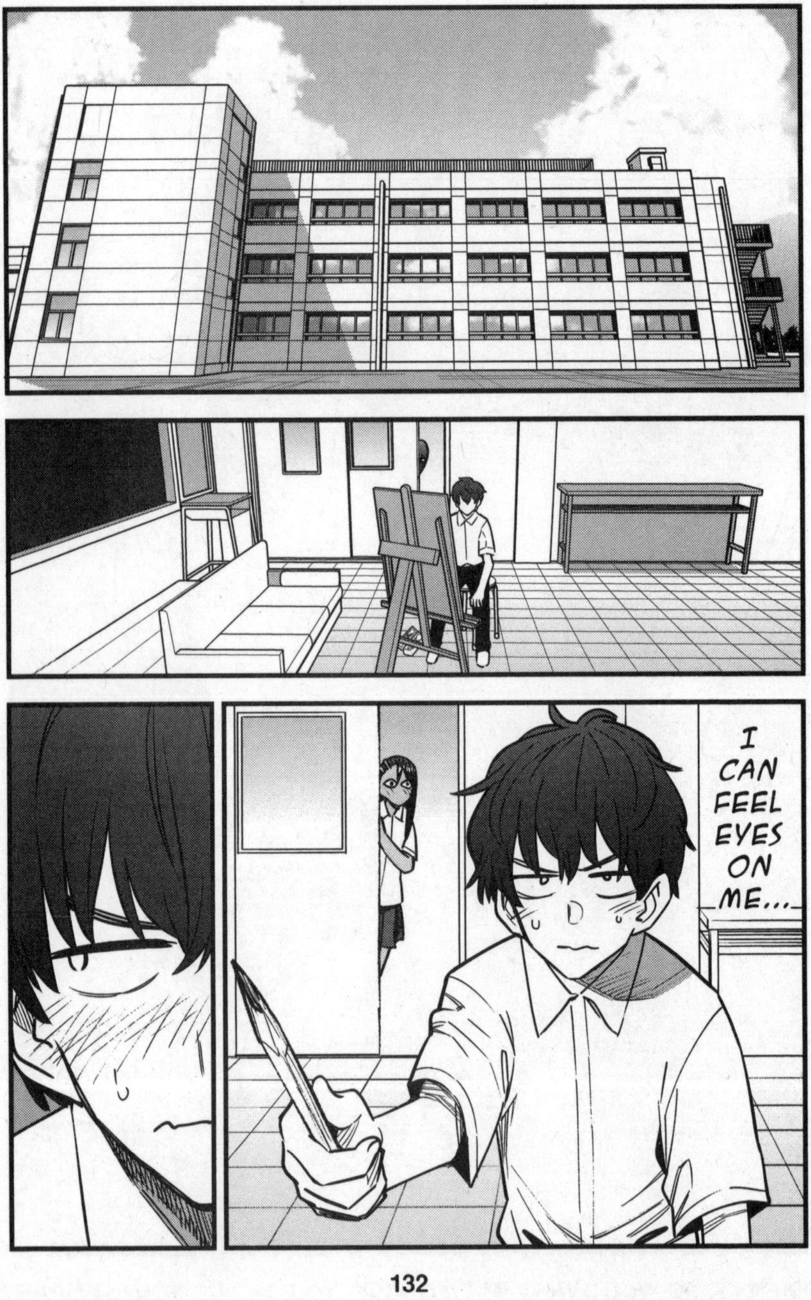
I CAN FEEL EYES ON ME...

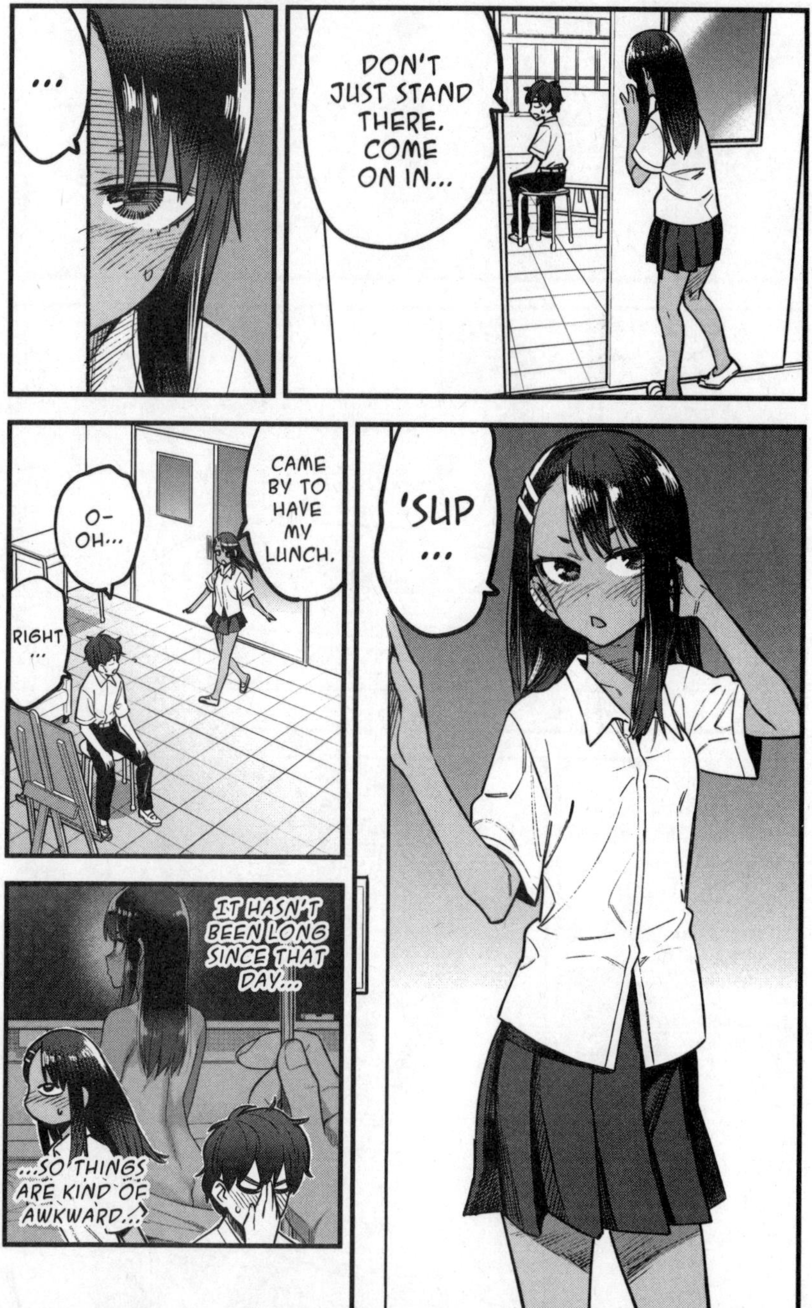
DON'T JUST STAND THERE. COME ON IN...
...
'SUP ...
CAME BY TO HAVE MY LUNCH.
O-OH...
RIGHT ...
IT HASN'T BEEN LONG SINCE THAT DAY...
...SO THINGS ARE KIND OF AWKWARD...

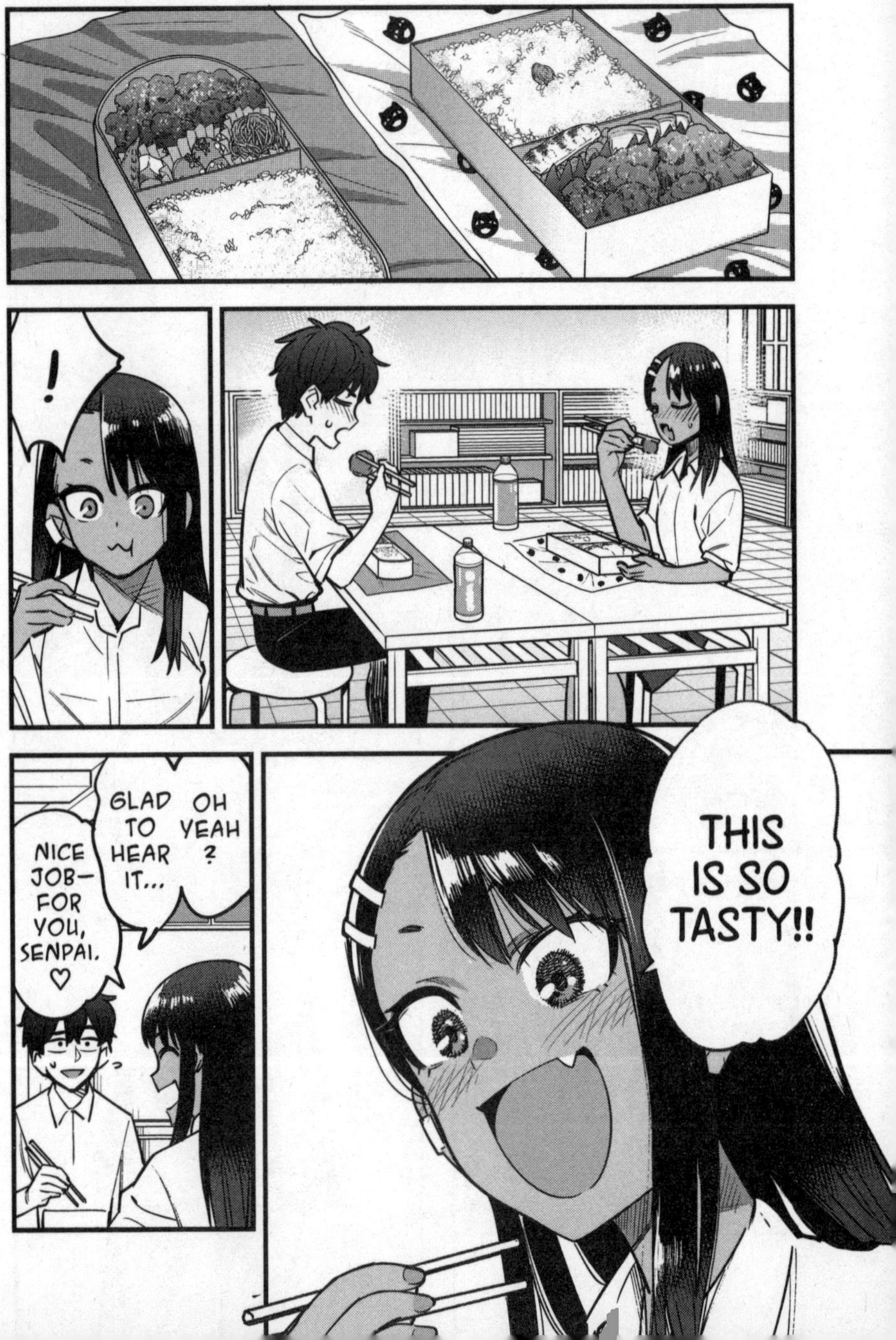
!
THIS IS SO TASTY!!
OH YEAH?
GLAD TO HEAR IT...
NICE JOB—FOR YOU, SENPAI. ♡

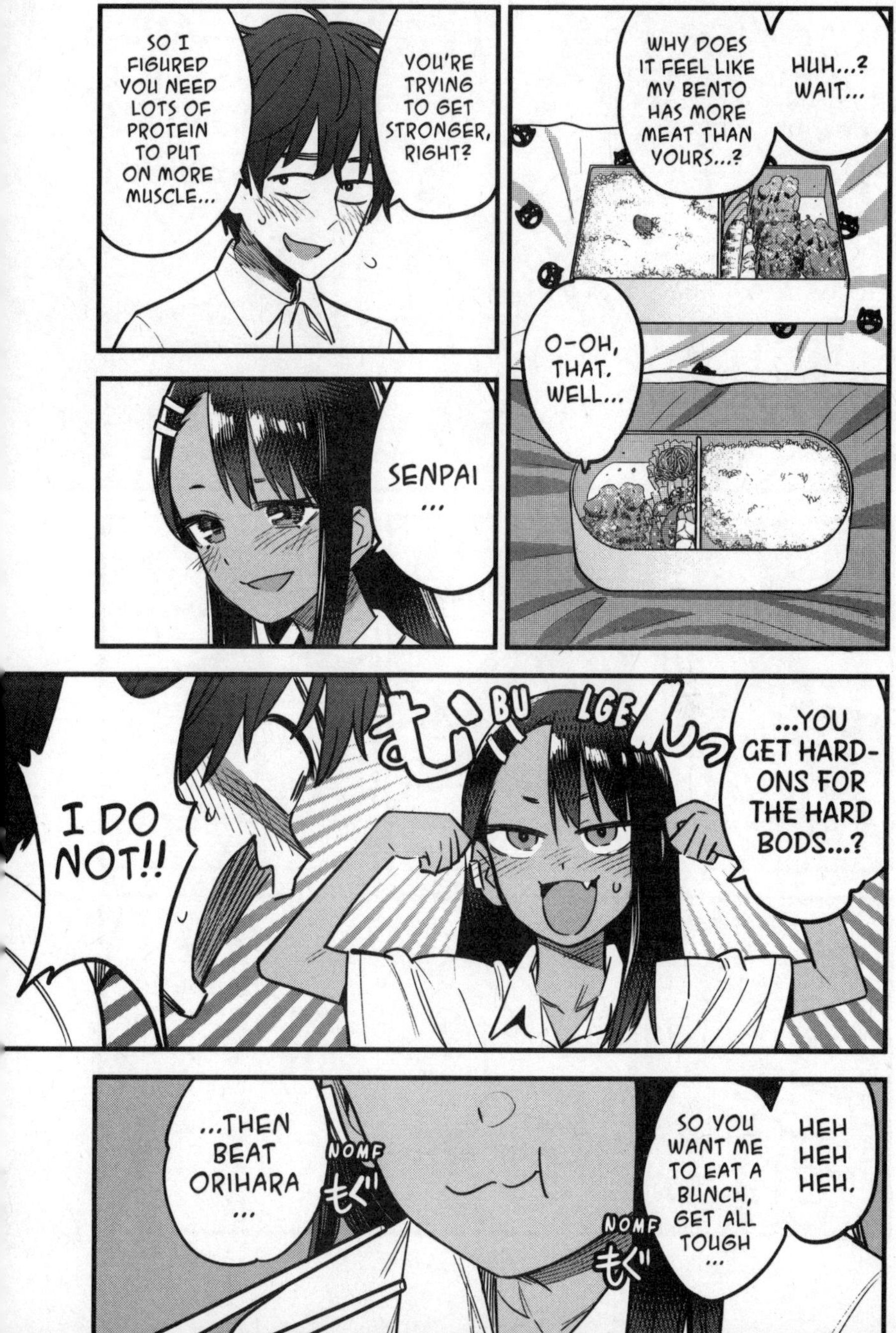
HUH...? WAIT...
WHY DOES IT FEEL LIKE MY BENTO HAS MORE MEAT THAN YOURS...?
O-OH, THAT. WELL...
YOU'RE TRYING TO GET STRONGER, RIGHT?
SO I FIGURED YOU NEED LOTS OF PROTEIN TO PUT ON MORE MUSCLE...
SENPAI ...
...YOU GET HARD-ONS FOR THE HARD BODS...?
むんっ BULGE
I DO NOT!!
HEH HEH HEH.
SO YOU WANT ME TO EAT A BUNCH, GET ALL TOUGH ...
NOMF もぐ
NOMF もぐ
...THEN BEAT ORIHARA ...

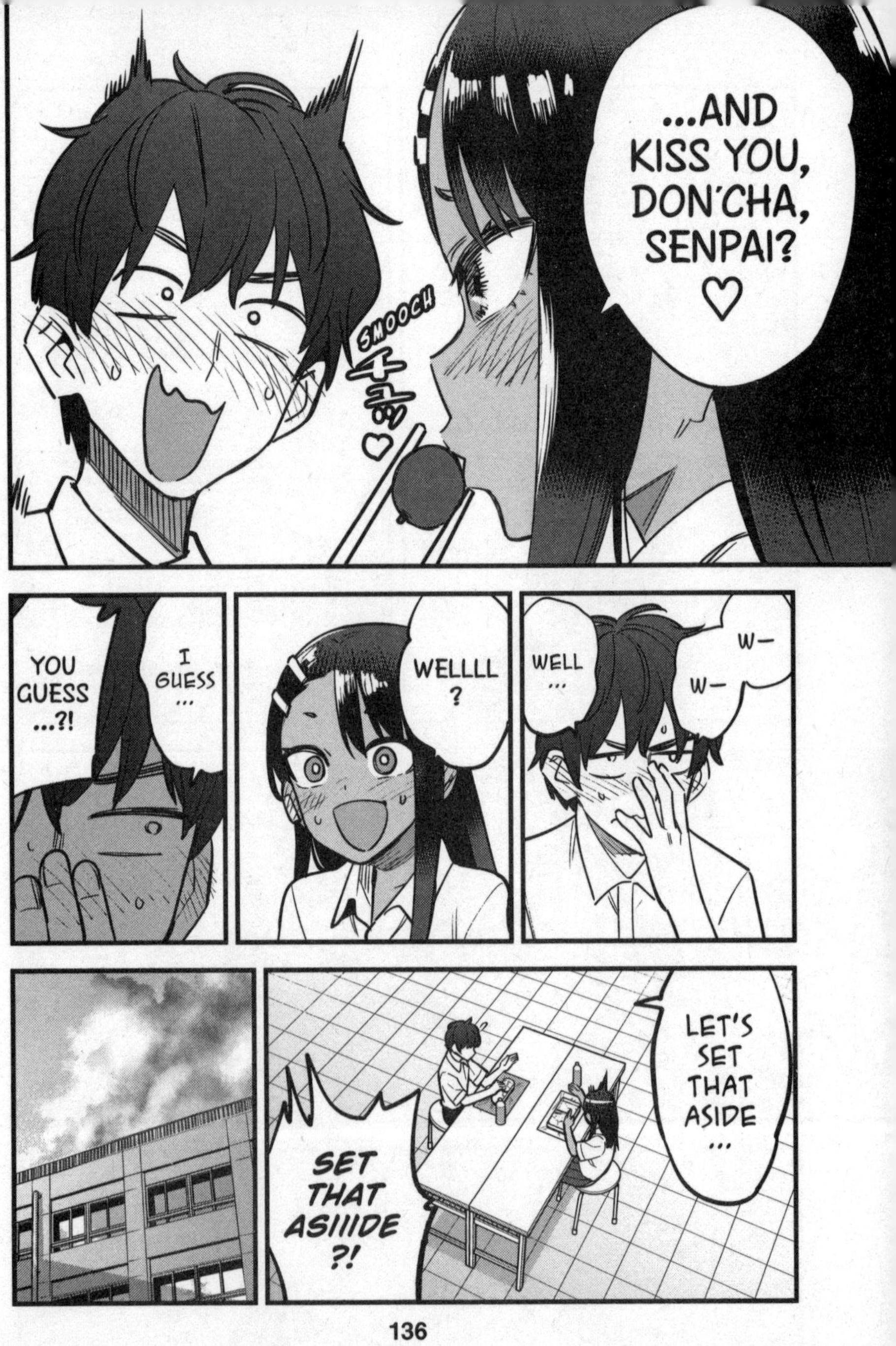
...AND KISS YOU, DON'CHA, SENPAI? ♡
SMOOCH
♡
W— W—
WELL ...
WELLLL ?
I GUESS ...
YOU GUESS ...?!
LET'S SET THAT ASIDE ...
SET THAT ASIIIDE ?!

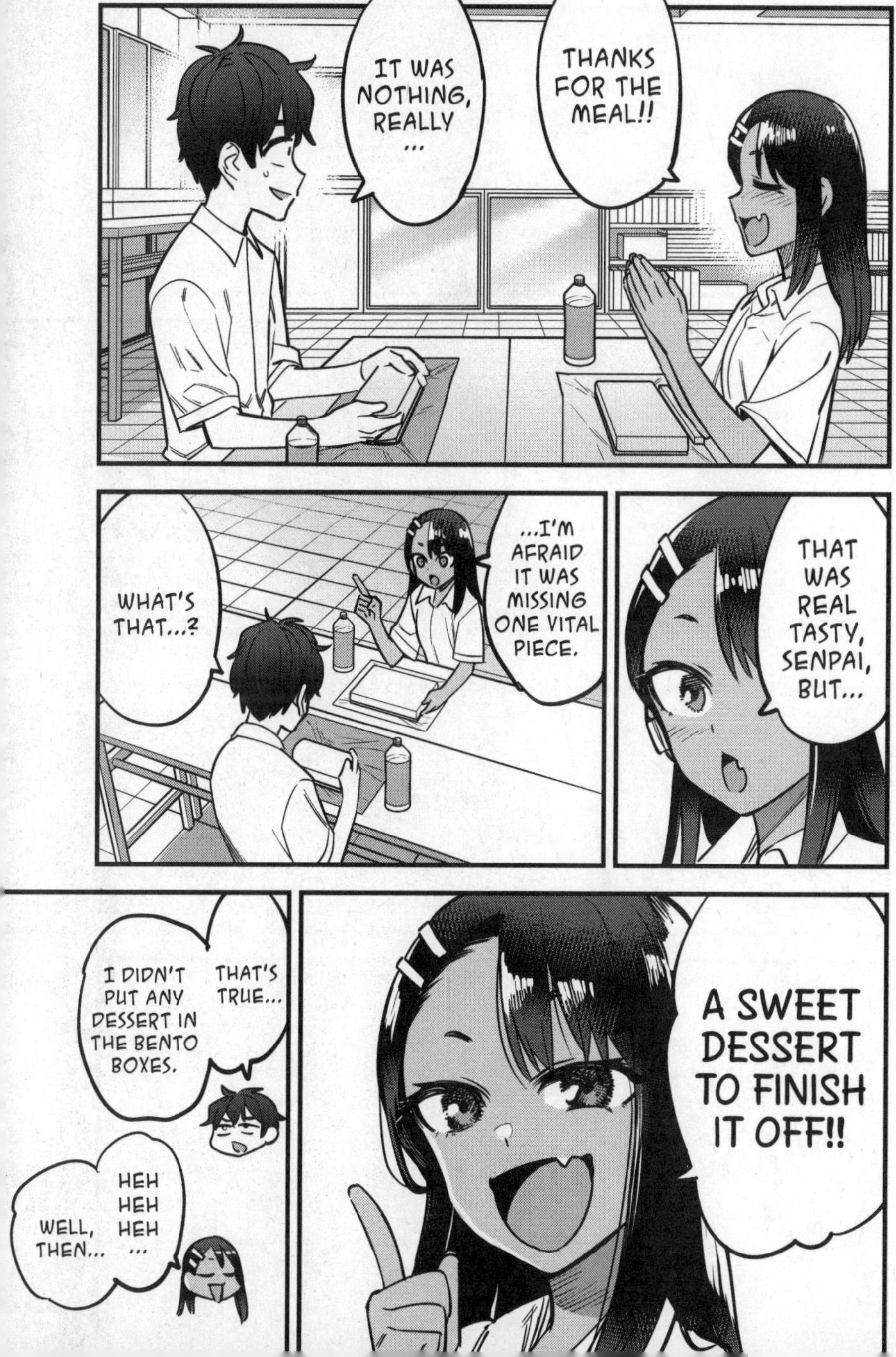
THANKS FOR THE MEAL!!
IT WAS NOTHING, REALLY ...
THAT WAS REAL TASTY, SENPAI, BUT...
...I'M AFRAID IT WAS MISSING ONE VITAL PIECE.
WHAT'S THAT...?
A SWEET DESSERT TO FINISH IT OFF!!
THAT'S TRUE...
I DIDN'T PUT ANY DESSERT IN THE BENTO BOXES.
HEH HEH HEH ...
WELL, THEN...

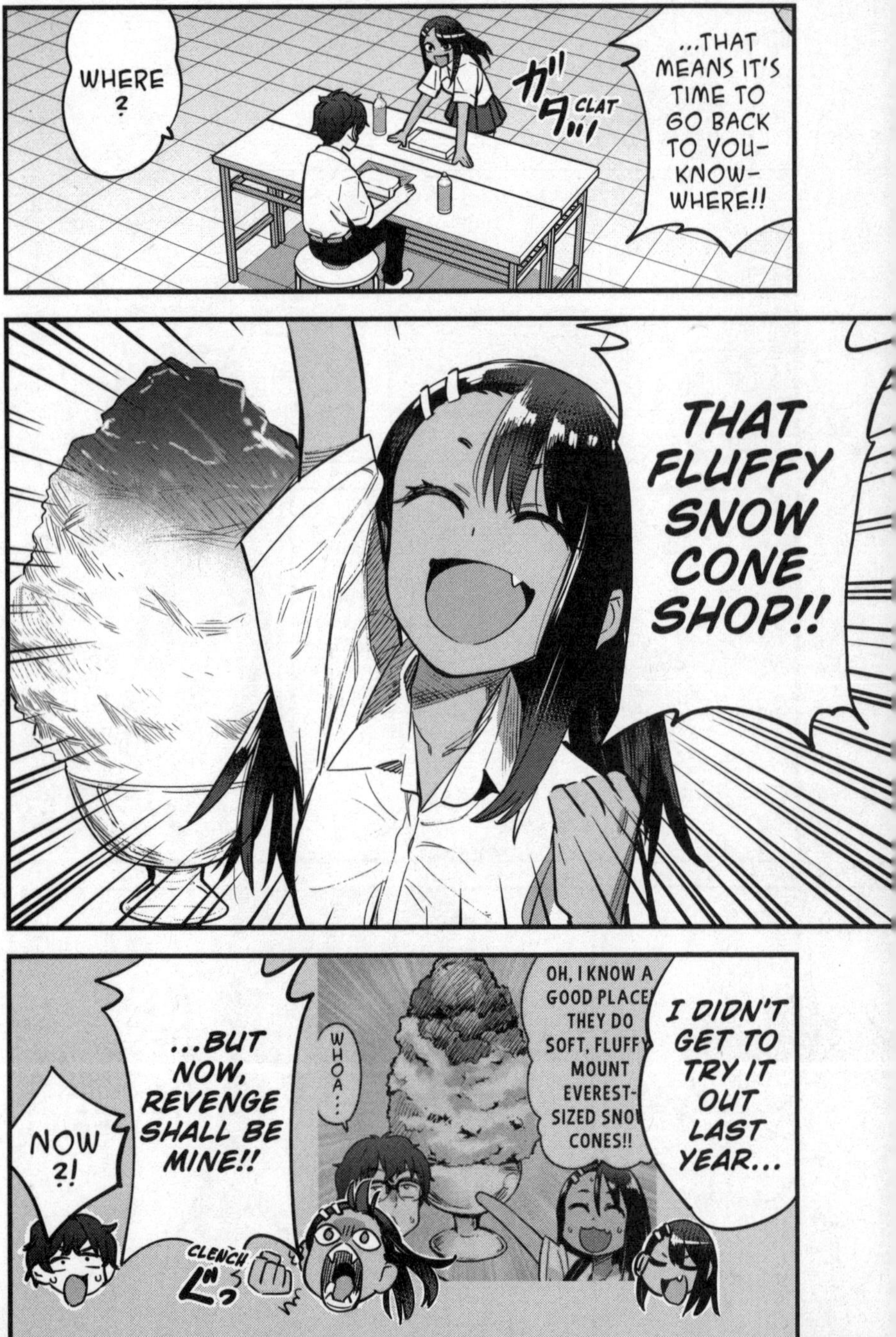
...THAT MEANS IT'S TIME TO GO BACK TO YOU-KNOW-WHERE!!
CLAT
WHERE?
THAT FLUFFY SNOW CONE SHOP!!
I DIDN'T GET TO TRY IT OUT LAST YEAR...
OH, I KNOW A GOOD PLACE! THEY DO SOFT, FLUFFY MOUNT EVEREST-SIZED SNO CONES!!
WHOA...
...BUT NOW, REVENGE SHALL BE MINE!!
CLENCH
NOW?!

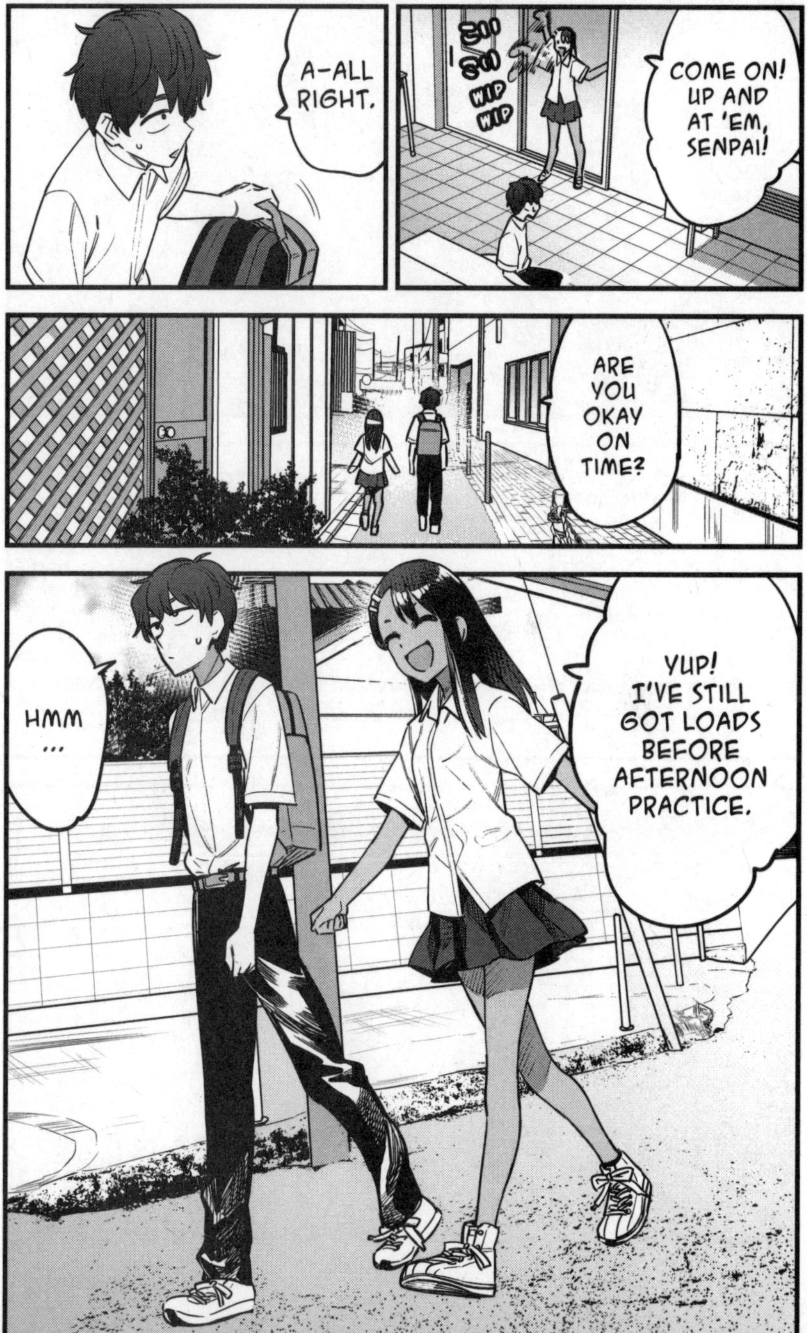
COME ON! UP AND AT 'EM, SENPAI!
WIP WIP
A-ALL RIGHT.
ARE YOU OKAY ON TIME?
YUP! I'VE STILL GOT LOADS BEFORE AFTERNOON PRACTICE.
HMM ...

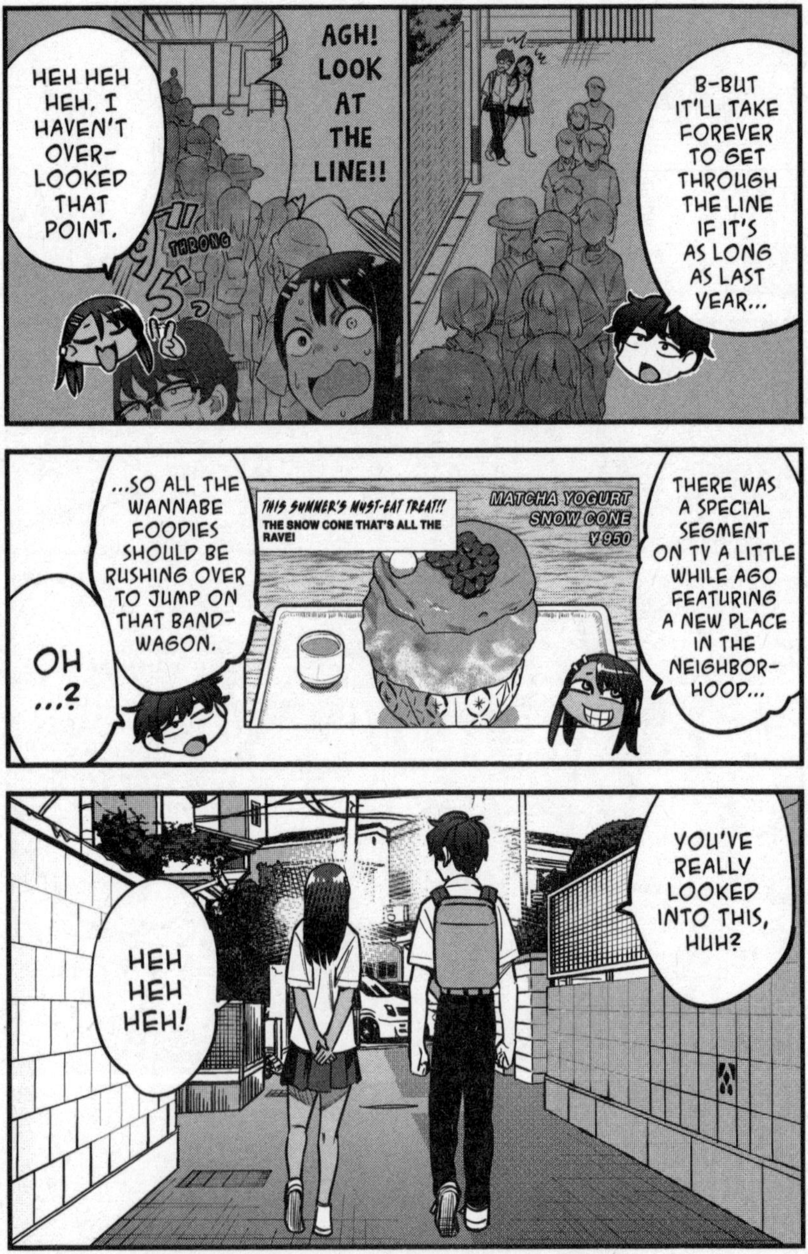
B-BUT IT'LL TAKE FOREVER TO GET THROUGH THE LINE IF IT'S AS LONG AS LAST YEAR...
AGH! LOOK AT THE LINE!!
HEH HEH HEH, I HAVEN'T OVERLOOKED THAT POINT.
THRONG
THERE WAS A SPECIAL SEGMENT ON TV A LITTLE WHILE AGO FEATURING A NEW PLACE IN THE NEIGHBORHOOD...
MATCHA YOGURT SNOW CONE ¥950
THIS SUMMER'S MUST-EAT TREAT!!
THE SNOW CONE THAT'S ALL THE RAVE!
...SO ALL THE WANNABE FOODIES SHOULD BE RUSHING OVER TO JUMP ON THAT BANDWAGON.
OH ...?
YOU'VE REALLY LOOKED INTO THIS, HUH?
HEH HEH HEH!

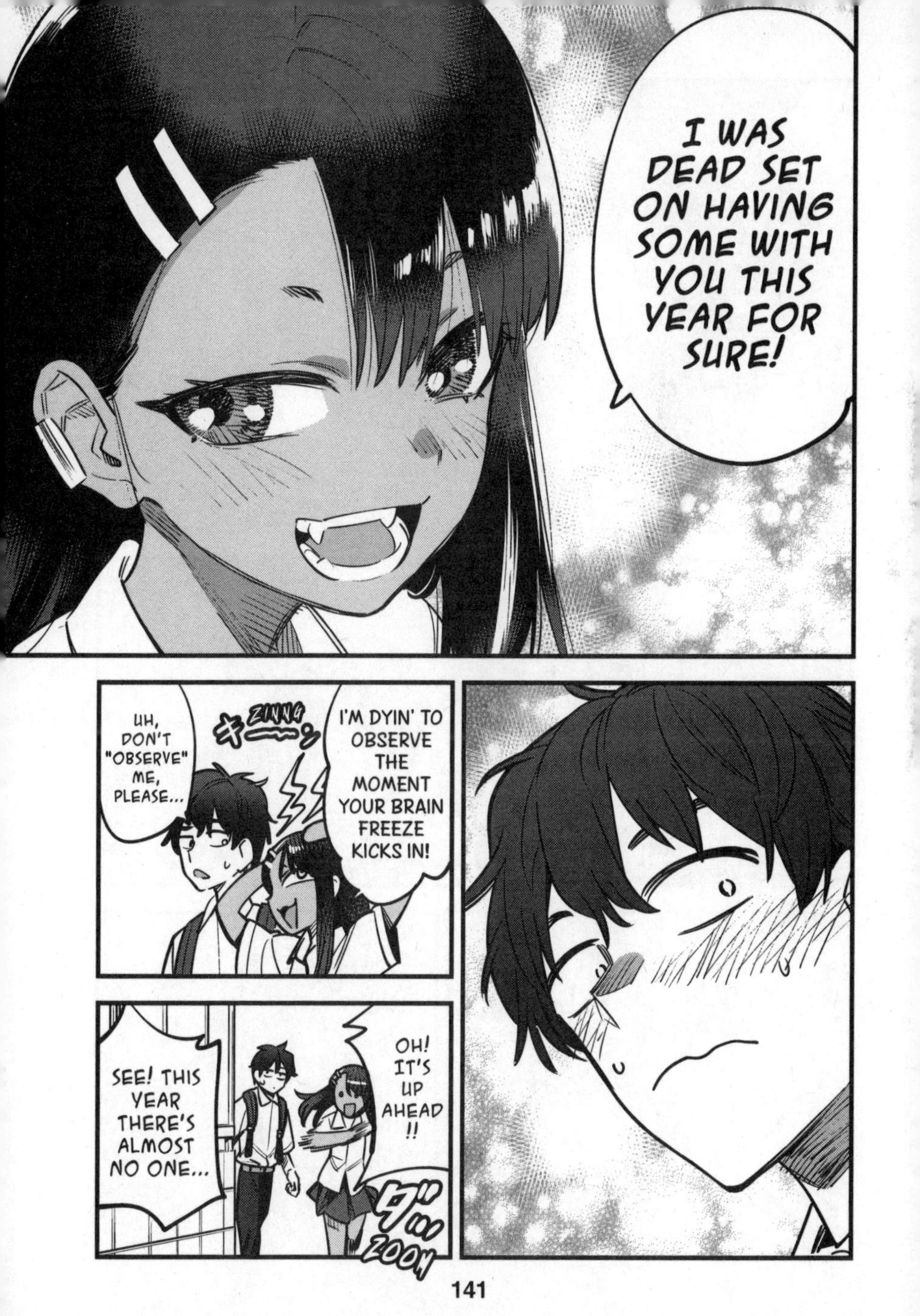
I WAS DEAD SET ON HAVING SOME WITH YOU THIS YEAR FOR SURE!
I'M DYIN' TO OBSERVE THE MOMENT YOUR BRAIN FREEZE KICKS IN!
ZINNG
UH, DON'T "OBSERVE" ME, PLEASE...
OH! IT'S UP AHEAD!!
ZOOM
SEE! THIS YEAR THERE'S ALMOST NO ONE...

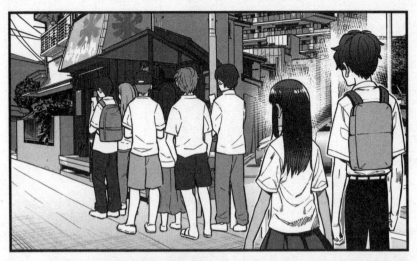

...
NOT EXACTLY "ALMOST NO ONE" HERE...
DIDN'T YOU SAY THE FOODIES WOULD BE PULLED AWAY...?
WAP WAP WAP
SHUT UP! SHUT UP!!
WAP WAP WAP
QUIT YER GRUMBLIN' AND GET IN LINE, SENPAI!!
ZOOM

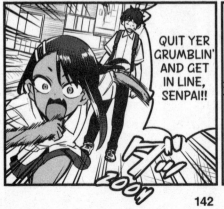

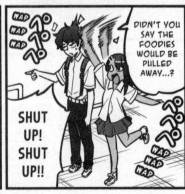

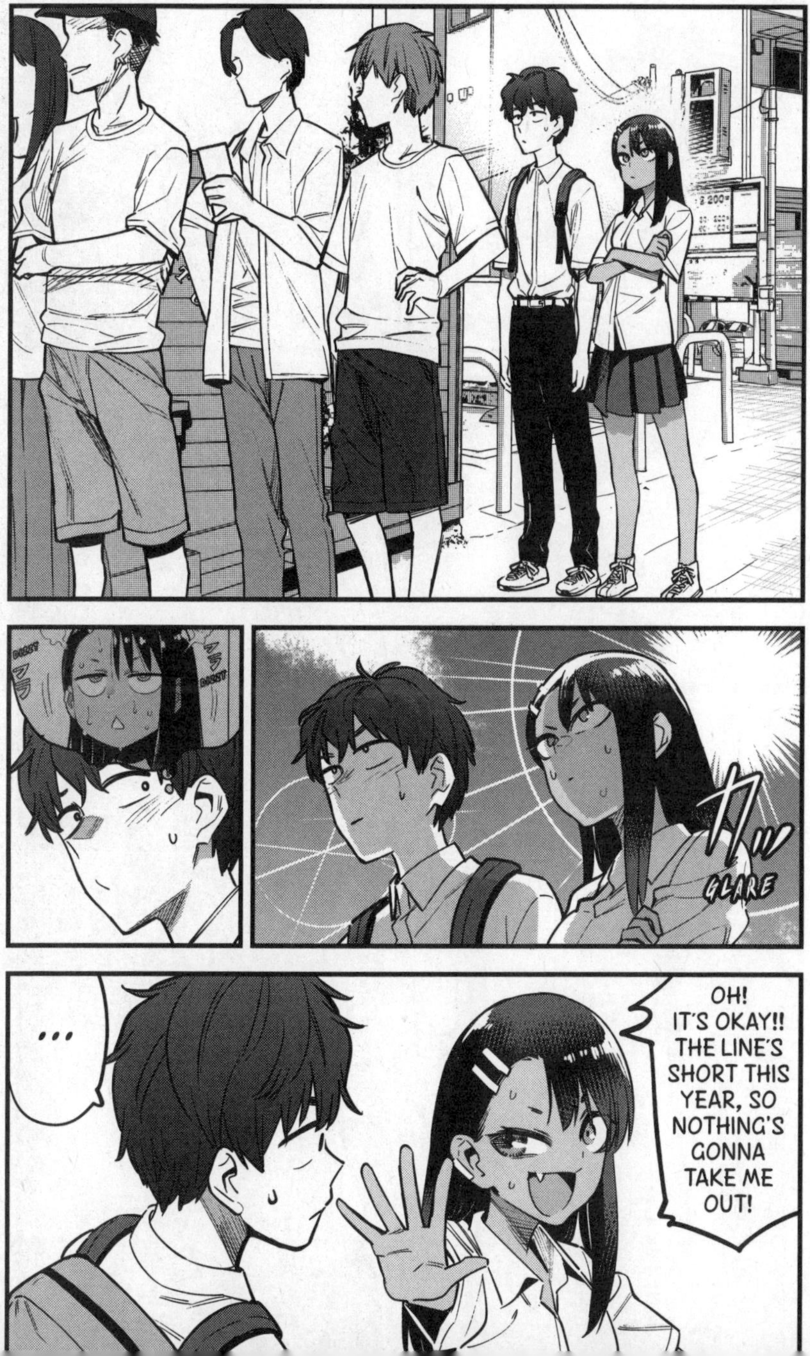
カッ
GLARE
フラ
DIZZY
フラ
DIZZY
OH! IT'S OKAY!! THE LINE'S SHORT THIS YEAR, SO NOTHING'S GONNA TAKE ME OUT!
...

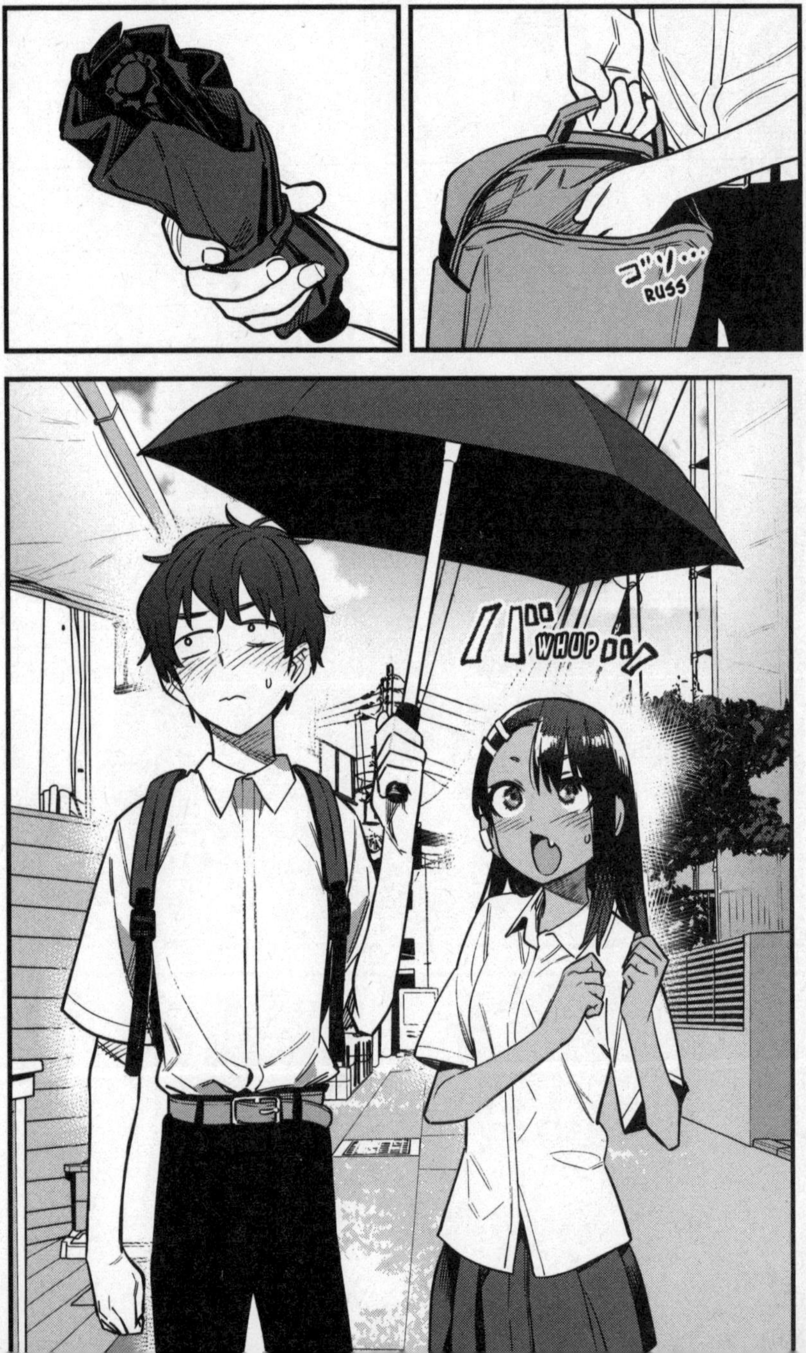
ゴソ…
RUSS
WHUP

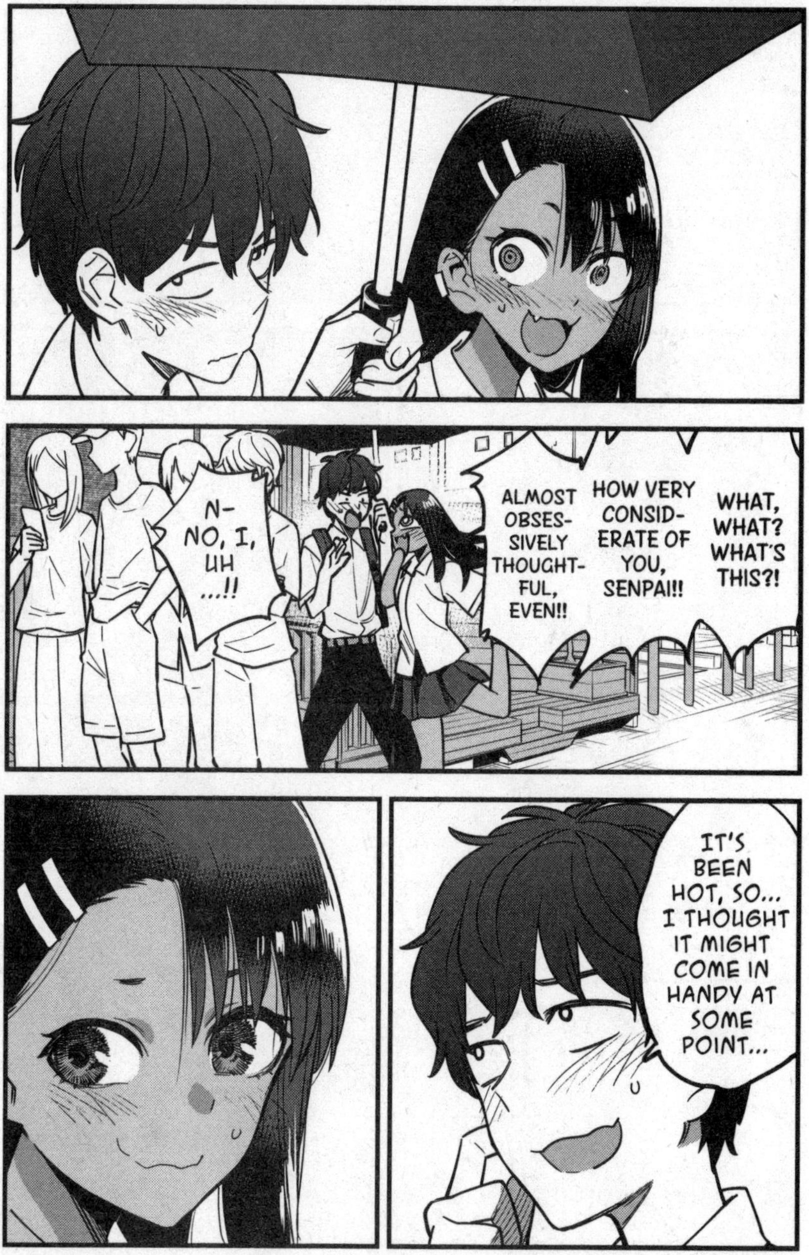
WHAT, WHAT? WHAT'S THIS?!
HOW VERY CONSIDERATE OF YOU, SENPAI!!
ALMOST OBSESSIVELY THOUGHTFUL, EVEN!!
N-NO, I, UH ...!!
IT'S BEEN HOT, SO... I THOUGHT IT MIGHT COME IN HANDY AT SOME POINT...

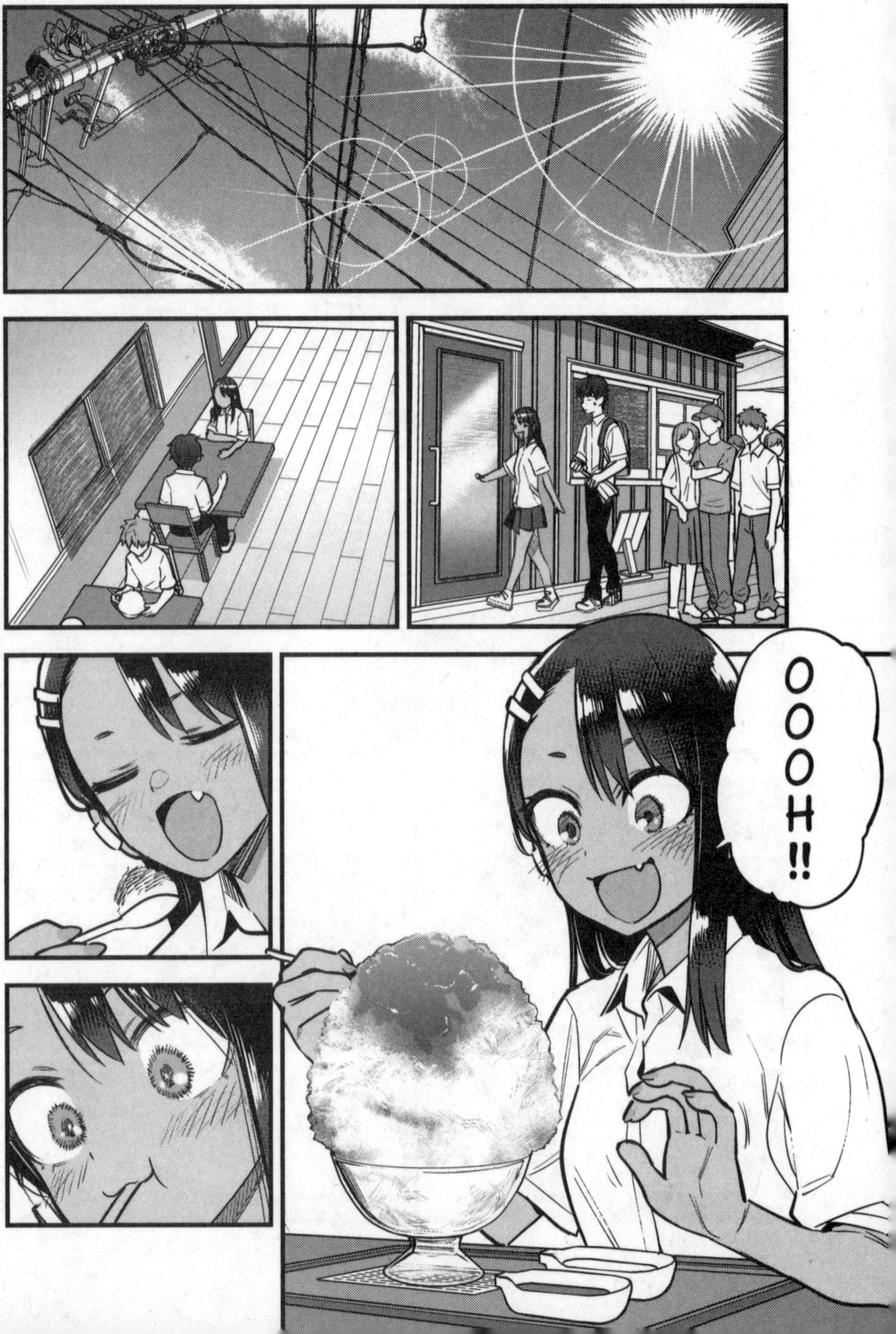
OOOH!!

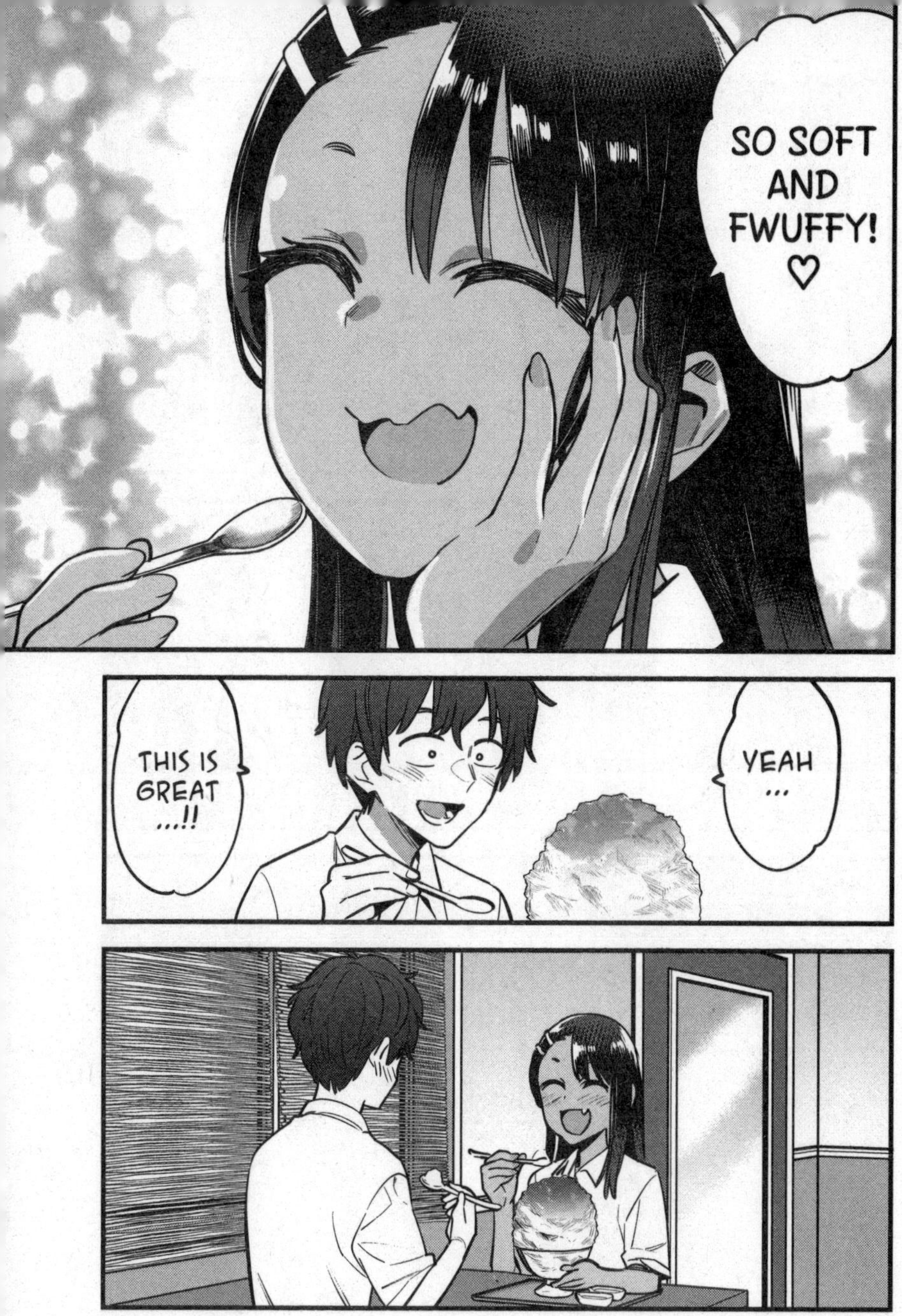
SO SOFT AND FWUFFY! ♡
YEAH ...
THIS IS GREAT ...!!

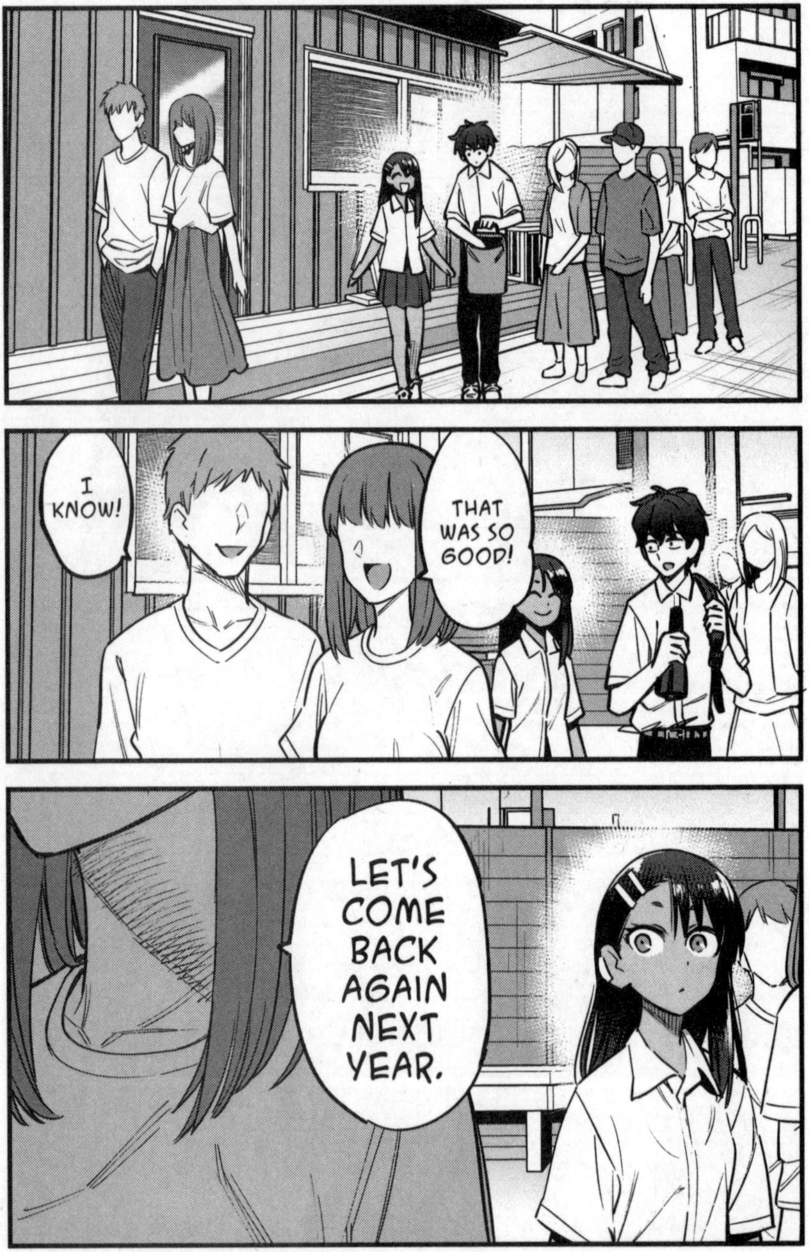
THAT WAS SO GOOD!
I KNOW!
LET'S COME BACK AGAIN NEXT YEAR.

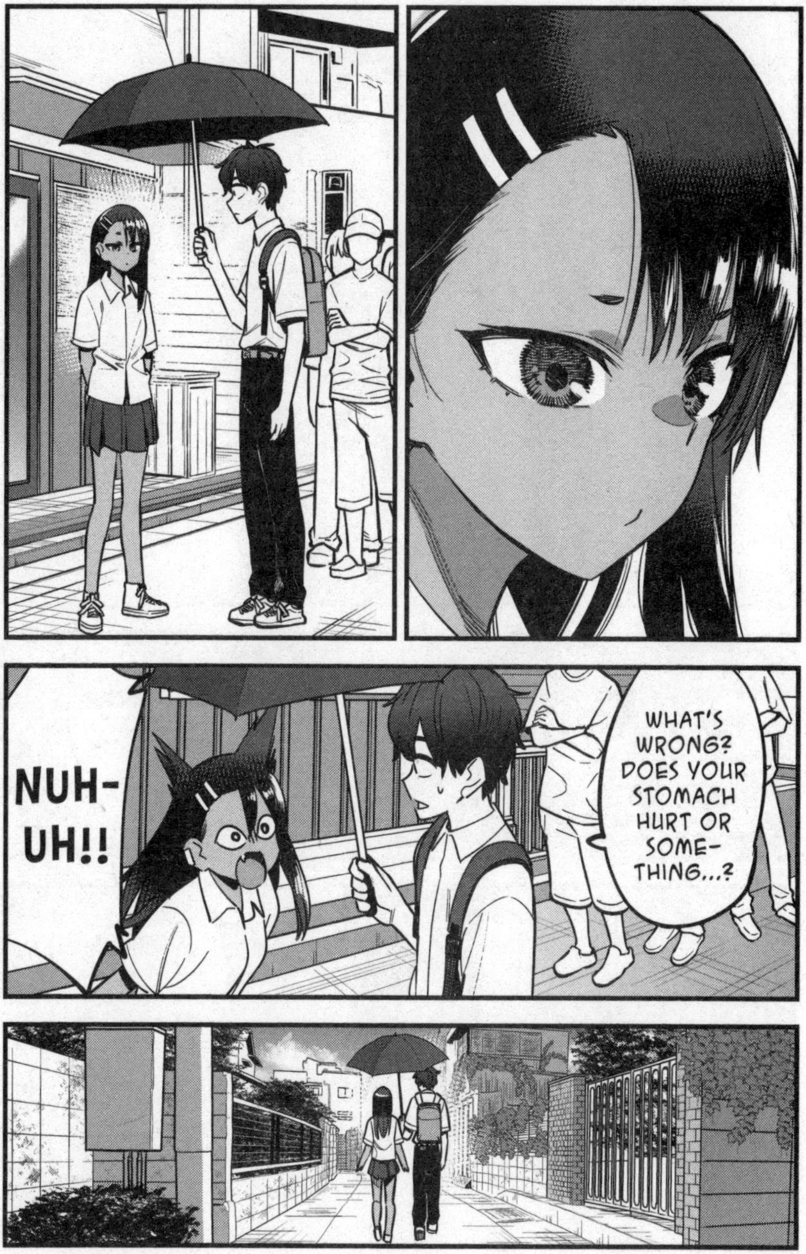
WHAT'S WRONG? DOES YOUR STOMACH HURT OR SOME- THING...?
NUH- UH!!

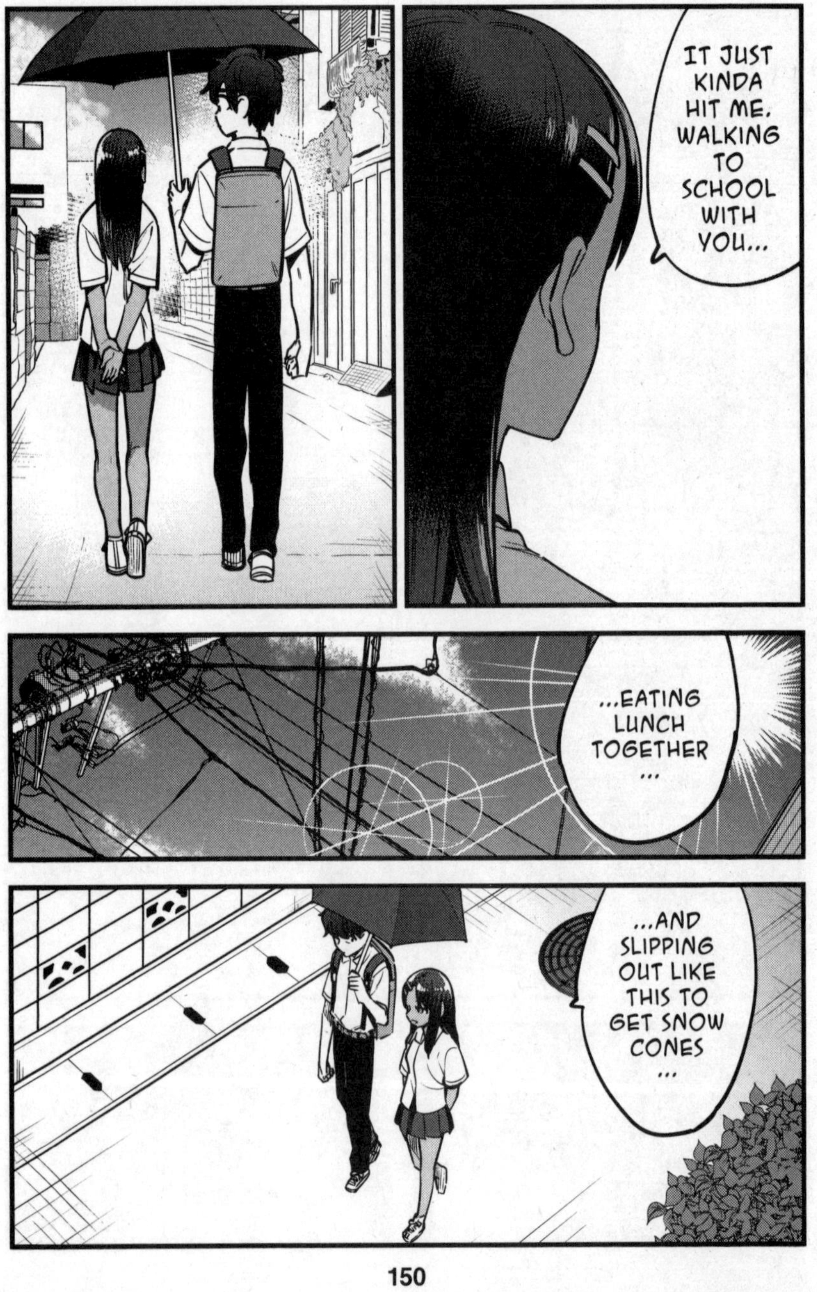
IT JUST KINDA HIT ME. WALKING TO SCHOOL WITH YOU...
...EATING LUNCH TOGETHER ...
...AND SLIPPING OUT LIKE THIS TO GET SNOW CONES ...

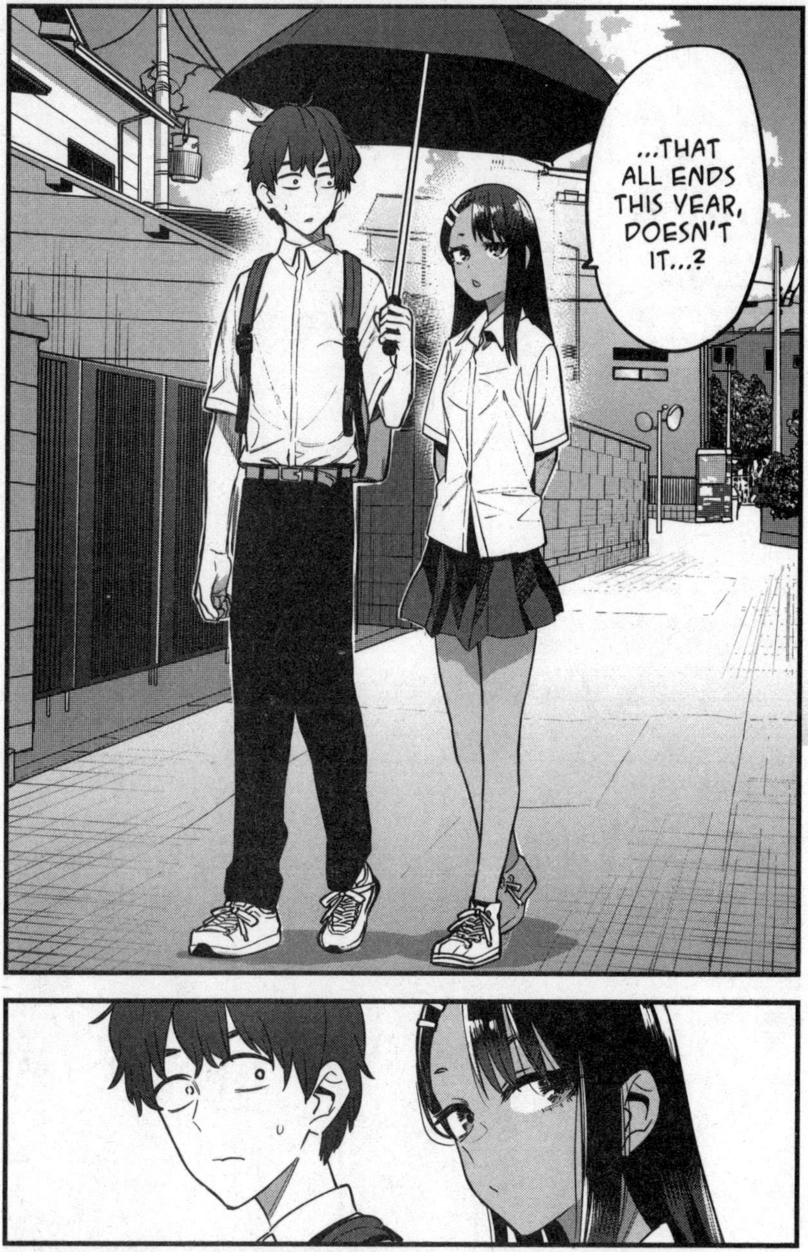
...THAT ALL ENDS THIS YEAR, DOESN'T IT...?

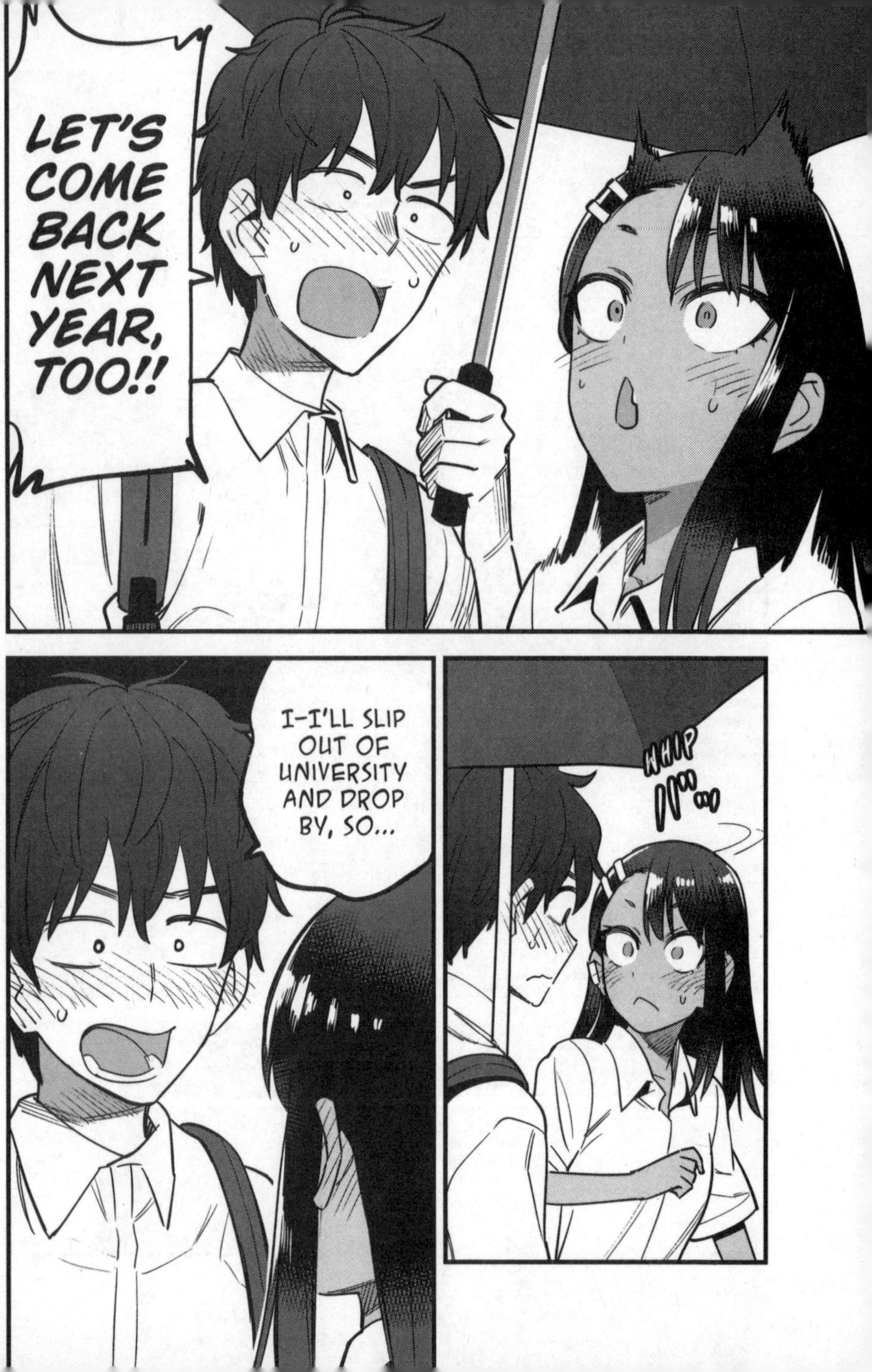
LET'S COME BACK NEXT YEAR, TOO!!
WHIP
I-I'LL SLIP OUT OF UNIVERSITY AND DROP BY, SO...

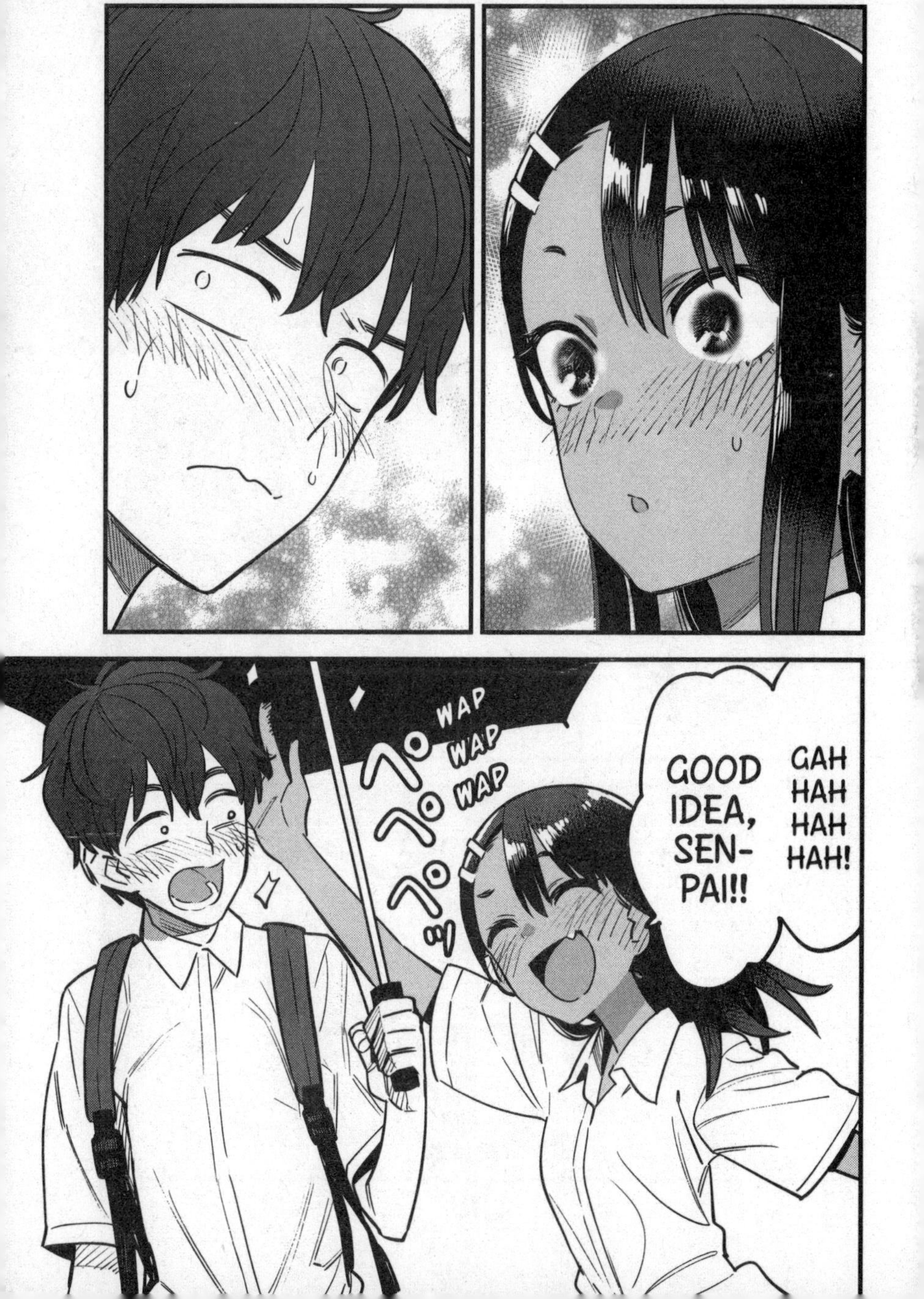
GAH HAH HAH HAH!
GOOD IDEA, SEN-PAI!!
WAP WAP WAP

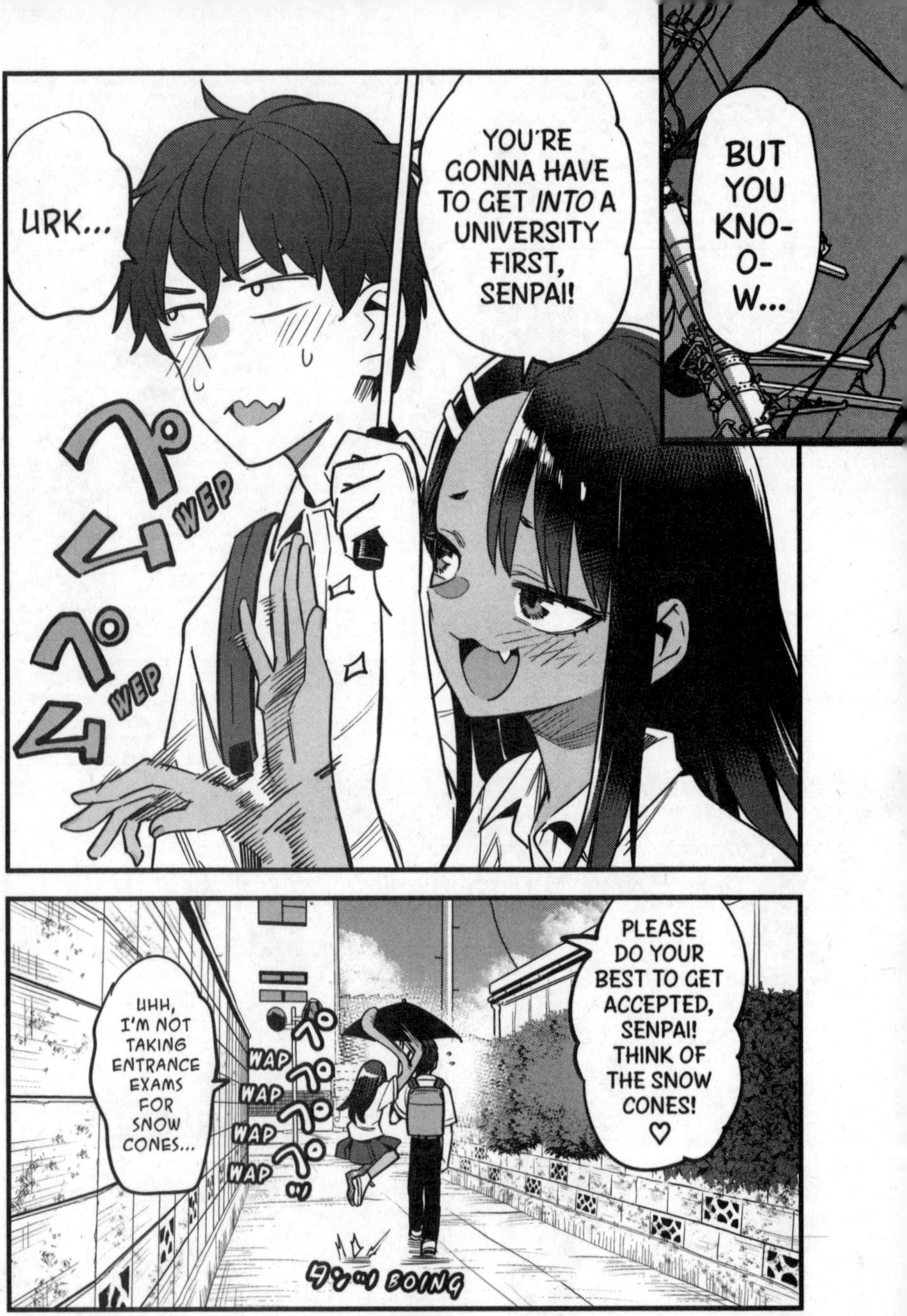
BUT YOU KNO-O-W...
YOU'RE GONNA HAVE TO GET *INTO* A UNIVERSITY FIRST, SENPAI!
URK...
WEP
WEP
PLEASE DO YOUR BEST TO GET ACCEPTED, SENPAI! THINK OF THE SNOW CONES! ♡
UHH, I'M NOT TAKING ENTRANCE EXAMS FOR SNOW CONES...
WAP
WAP
WAP
WAP
BOING

END

SENPAI, I'M TIRED. PLEASE PULL ME ALONG. ♡
HUH ...?!
I'M TIR-ED.
SO TIR-ED.
SO-O-O TIRED.
...

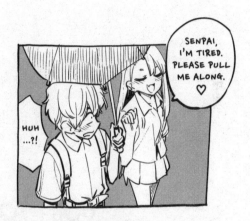

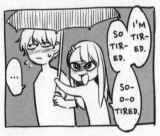

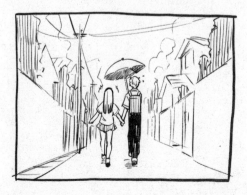

DON'T TOY WITH ME,
MISS NAGATORO

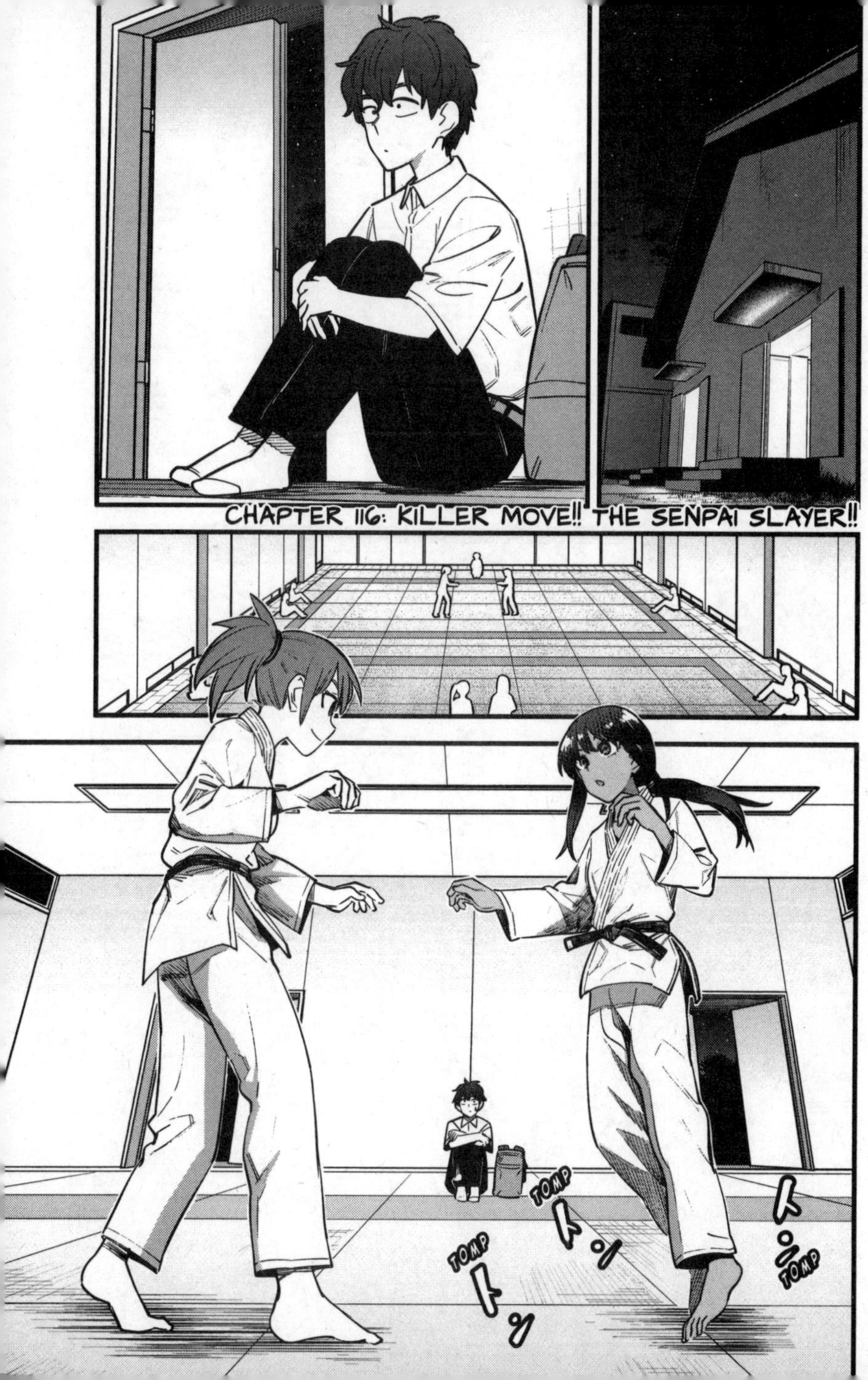
CHAPTER 116: KILLER MOVE!! THE SENPAI SLAYER!!
トッ
TOMP
トッ
TOMP
トッ
TOMP

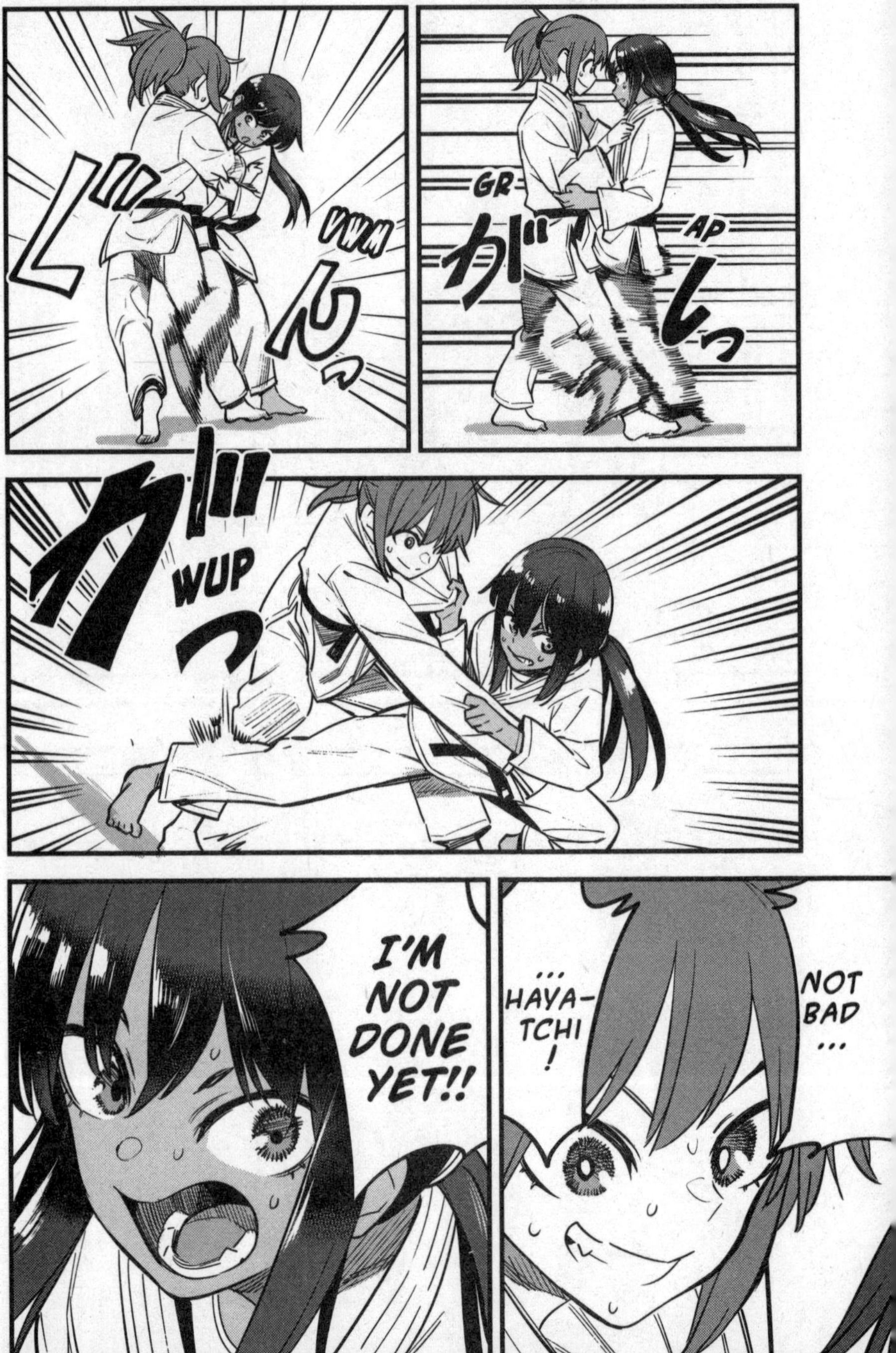

GR
が
AP
しっ
ぐい
VWM
んっ
がっ
WUP
NOT BAD ...
... HAYA-TCHI!
I'M NOT DONE YET!!

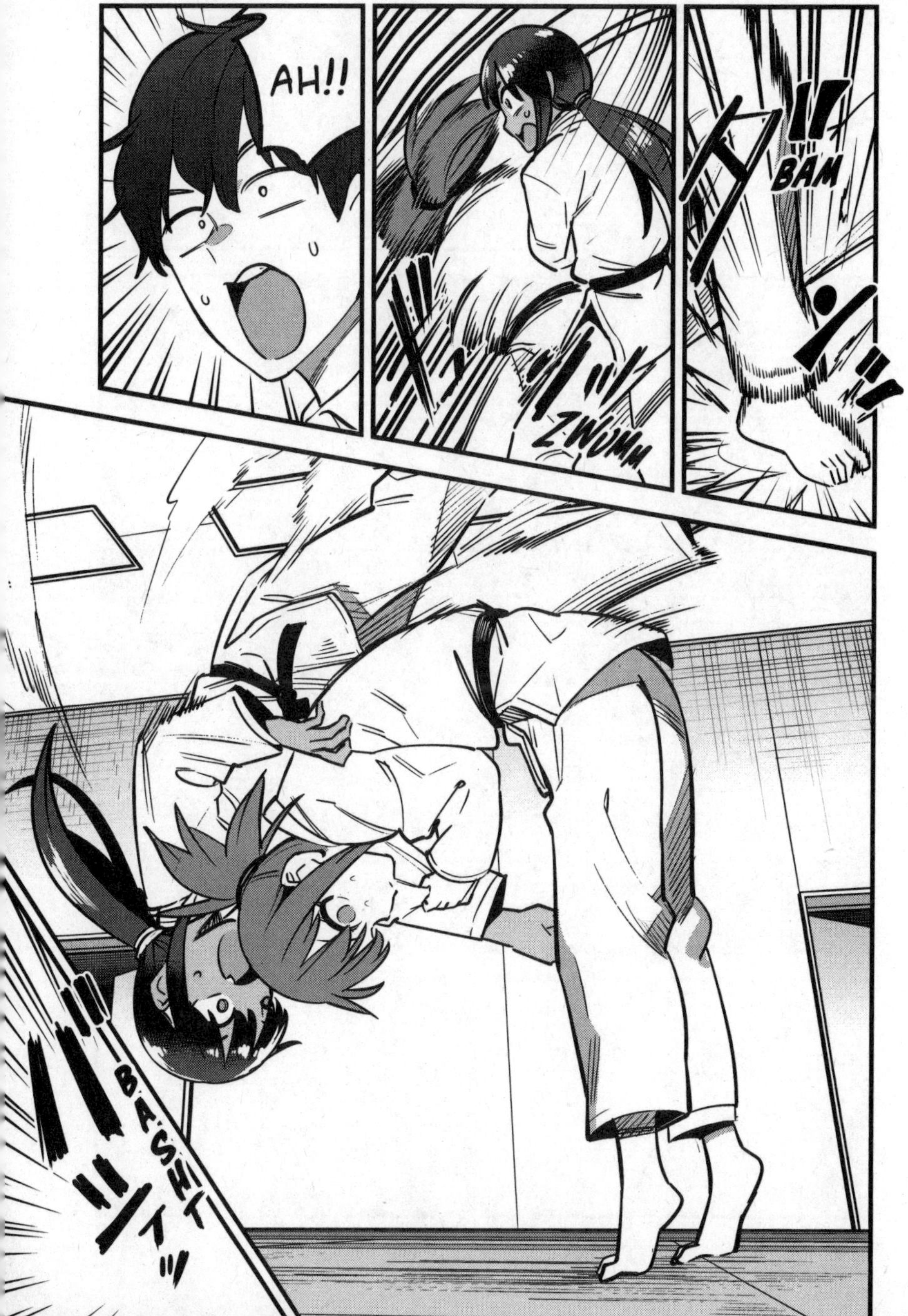
BAM
ZWUMM
AH!!
BASHT

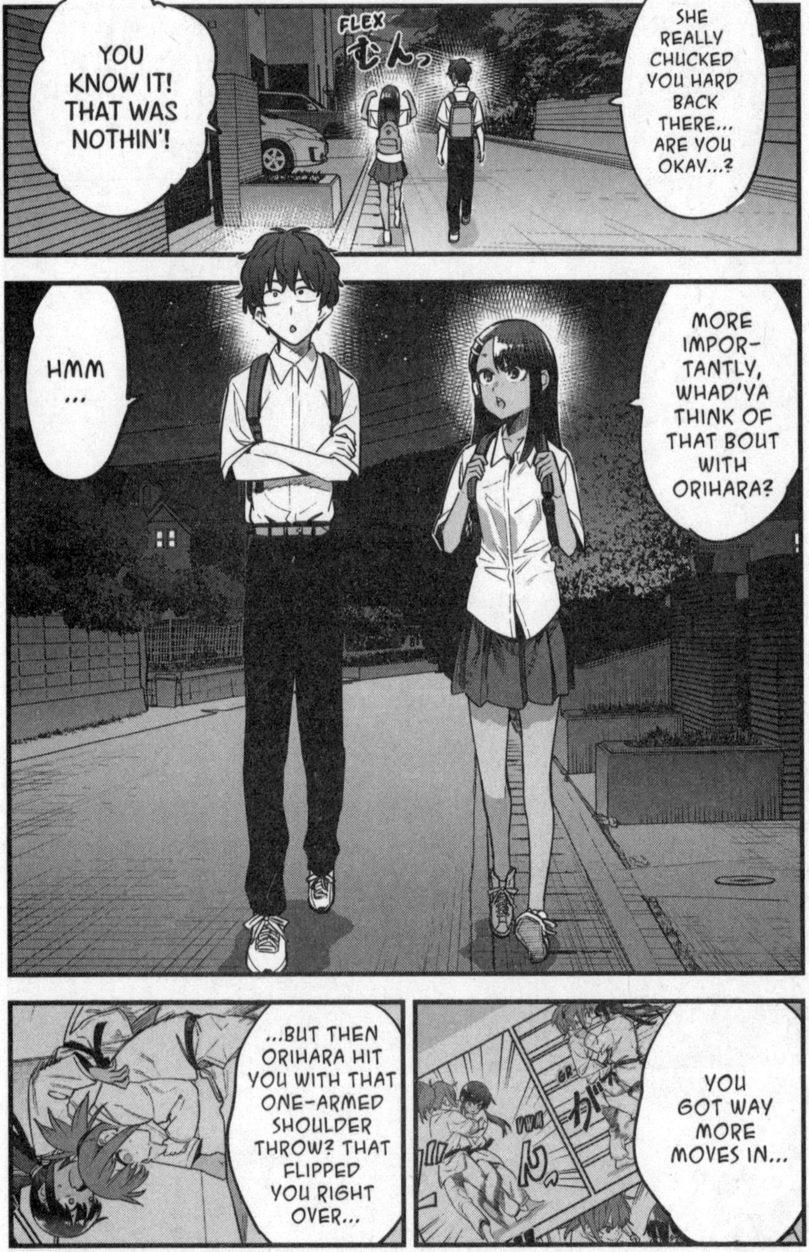
SHE REALLY CHUCKED YOU HARD BACK THERE... ARE YOU OKAY...?
FLEX
むんっ
YOU KNOW IT! THAT WAS NOTHIN'!
MORE IMPORTANTLY, WHAD'YA THINK OF THAT BOUT WITH ORIHARA?
HMM ...
YOU GOT WAY MORE MOVES IN...
GR
WHA
...BUT THEN ORIHARA HIT YOU WITH THAT ONE-ARMED SHOULDER THROW? THAT FLIPPED YOU RIGHT OVER...

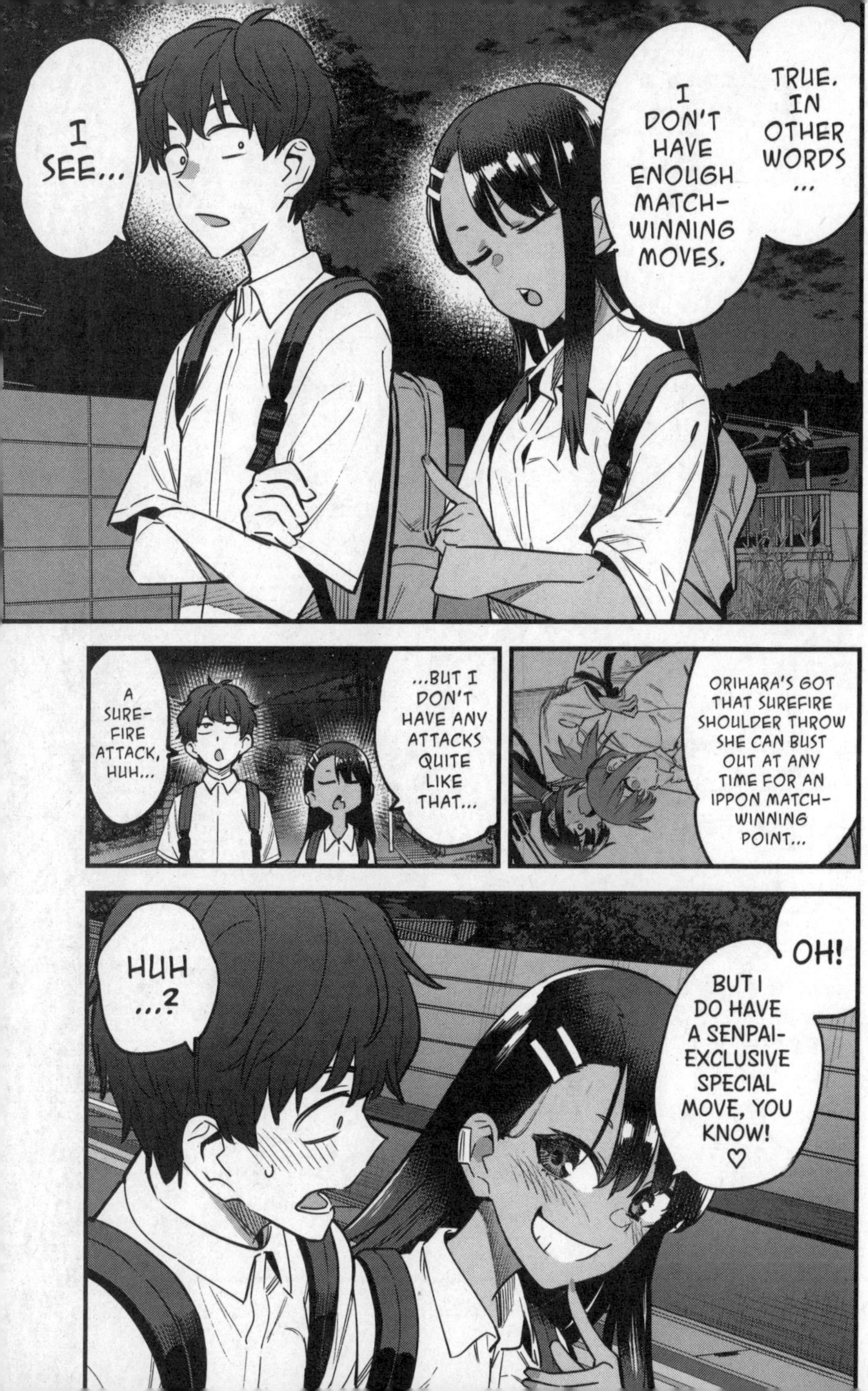
TRUE. IN OTHER WORDS...
I DON'T HAVE ENOUGH MATCH-WINNING MOVES.
I SEE...
ORIHARA'S GOT THAT SUREFIRE SHOULDER THROW SHE CAN BUST OUT AT ANY TIME FOR AN IPPON MATCH-WINNING POINT...
...BUT I DON'T HAVE ANY ATTACKS QUITE LIKE THAT...
A SURE-FIRE ATTACK, HUH...
OH!
BUT I DO HAVE A SENPAI-EXCLUSIVE SPECIAL MOVE, YOU KNOW! ♡
HUH...?

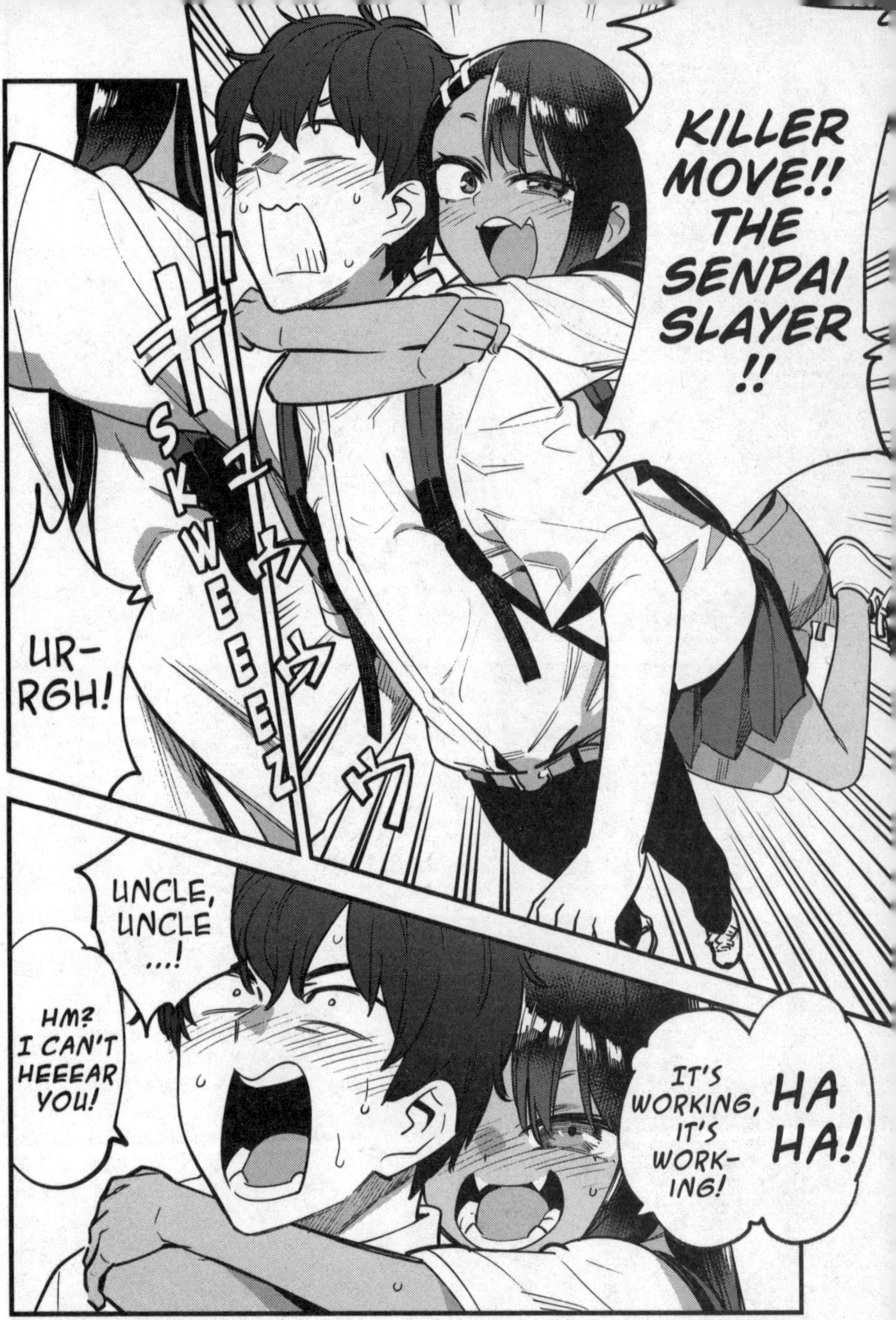
KILLER MOVE!! THE SENPAI SLAYER!!
SKWEEEEZ
UR-RGH!
UNCLE, UNCLE...!
HM? I CAN'T HEEEAR YOU!
IT'S WORKING, IT'S WORKING!
HA HA!

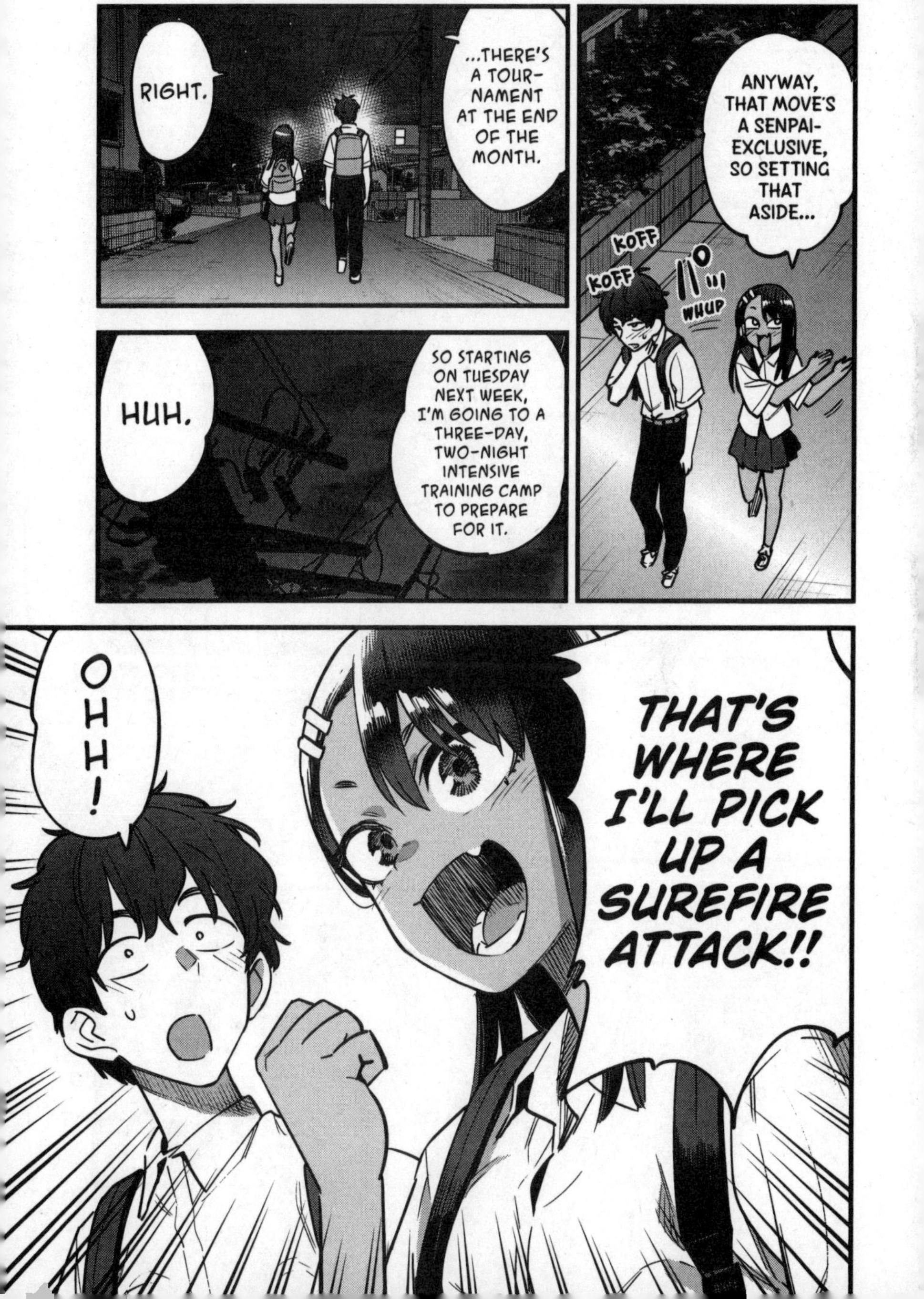
ANYWAY, THAT MOVE'S A SENPAI-EXCLUSIVE, SO SETTING THAT ASIDE...
KOFF
KOFF
WHUP
...THERE'S A TOUR-NAMENT AT THE END OF THE MONTH.
RIGHT.
SO STARTING ON TUESDAY NEXT WEEK, I'M GOING TO A THREE-DAY, TWO-NIGHT INTENSIVE TRAINING CAMP TO PREPARE FOR IT.
HUH.
THAT'S WHERE I'LL PICK UP A SUREFIRE ATTACK!!
OHH!

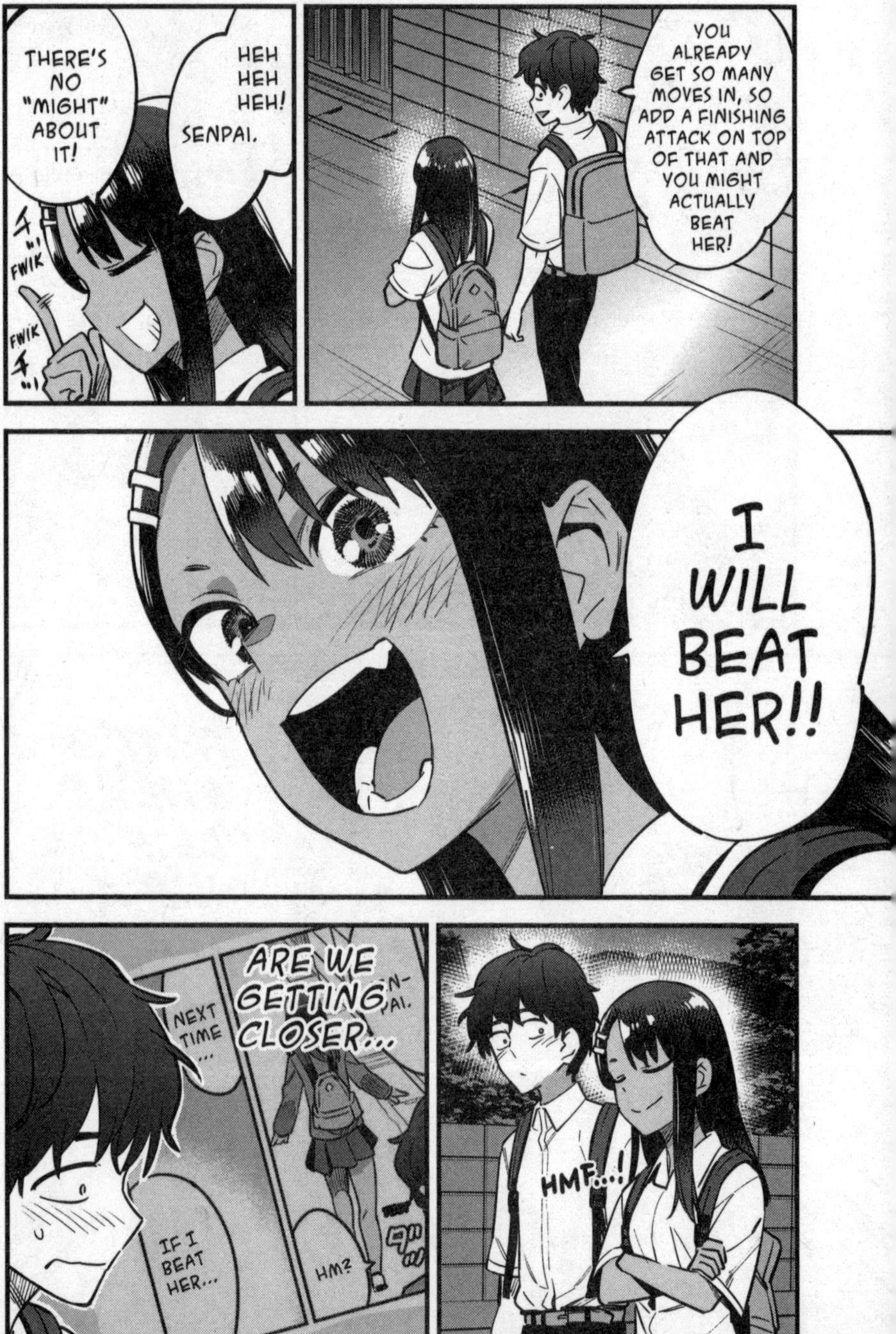
YOU ALREADY GET SO MANY MOVES IN, SO ADD A FINISHING ATTACK ON TOP OF THAT AND YOU MIGHT ACTUALLY BEAT HER!
HEH HEH HEH! SENPAI.
THERE'S NO "MIGHT" ABOUT IT!
FWIK
FWIK
I WILL BEAT HER!!
HMF...!
ARE WE GETTING CLOSER...
NEXT TIME...
HM?
IF I BEAT HER...

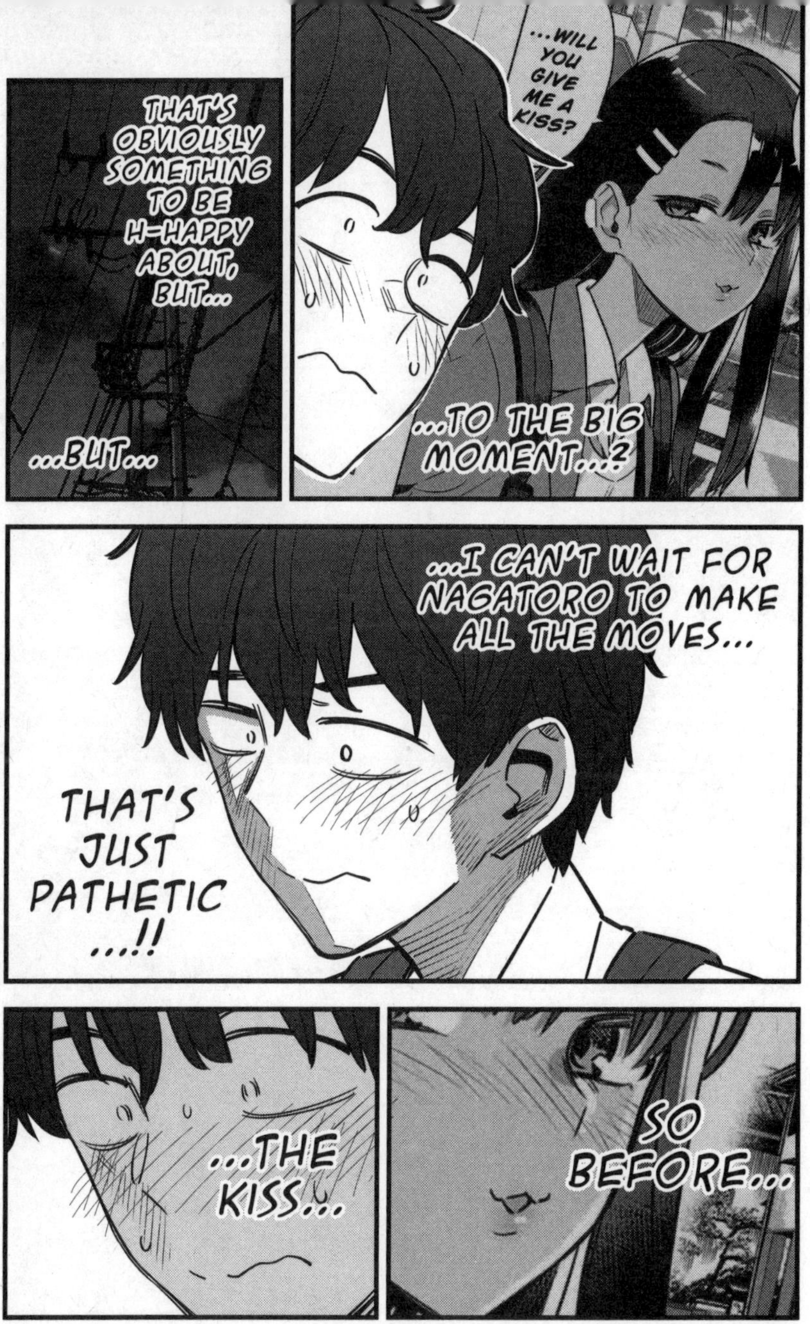
...WILL YOU GIVE ME A KISS?
...TO THE BIG MOMENT...?
THAT'S OBVIOUSLY SOMETHING TO BE H-HAPPY ABOUT, BUT...
...BUT...
...I CAN'T WAIT FOR NAGATORO TO MAKE ALL THE MOVES...
THAT'S JUST PATHETIC ...!!
SO BEFORE...
...THE KISS...

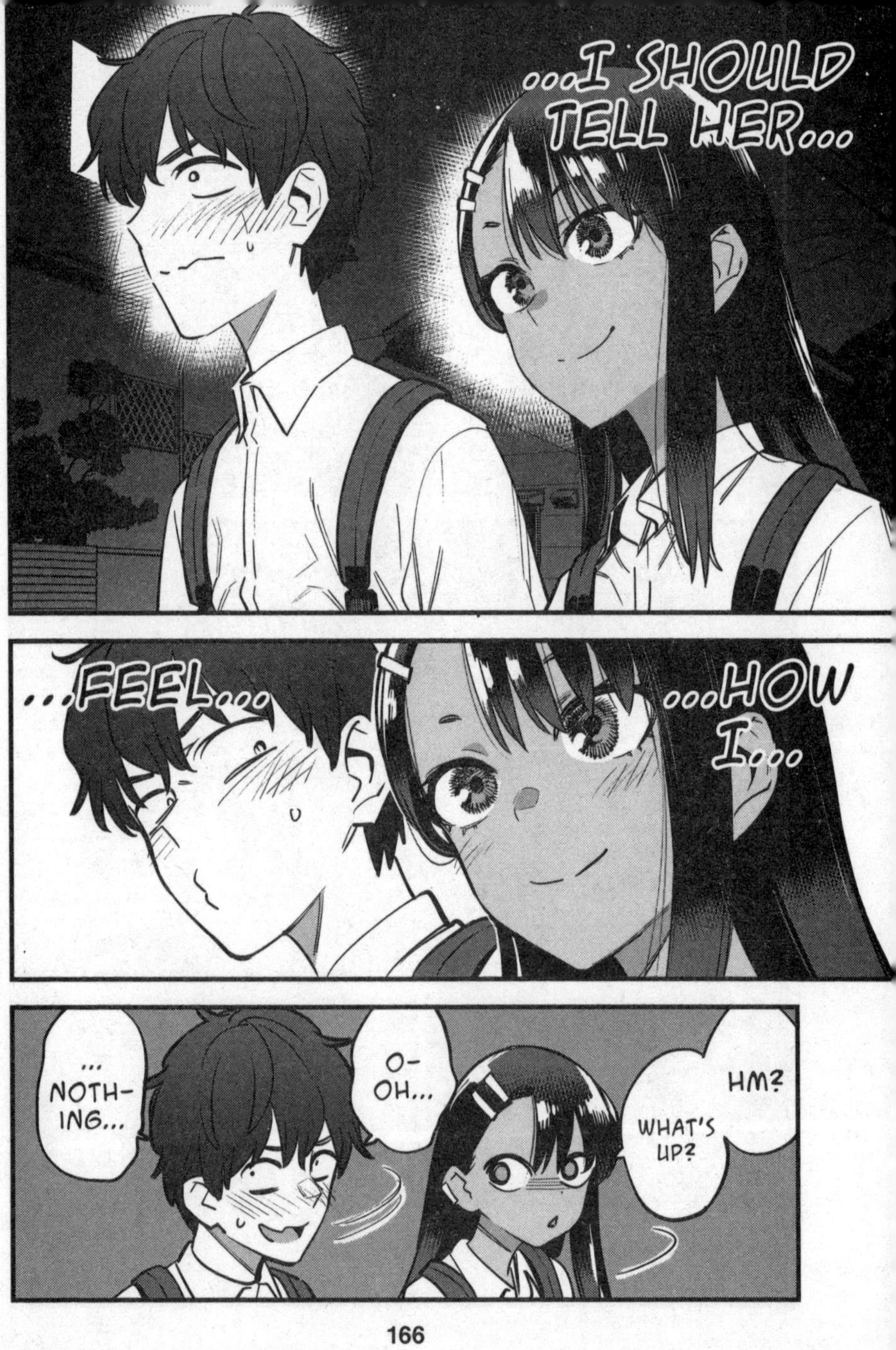
...I SHOULD TELL HER...
...HOW I...
...FEEL...
HM? WHAT'S UP?
O- OH...
... NOTH- ING...

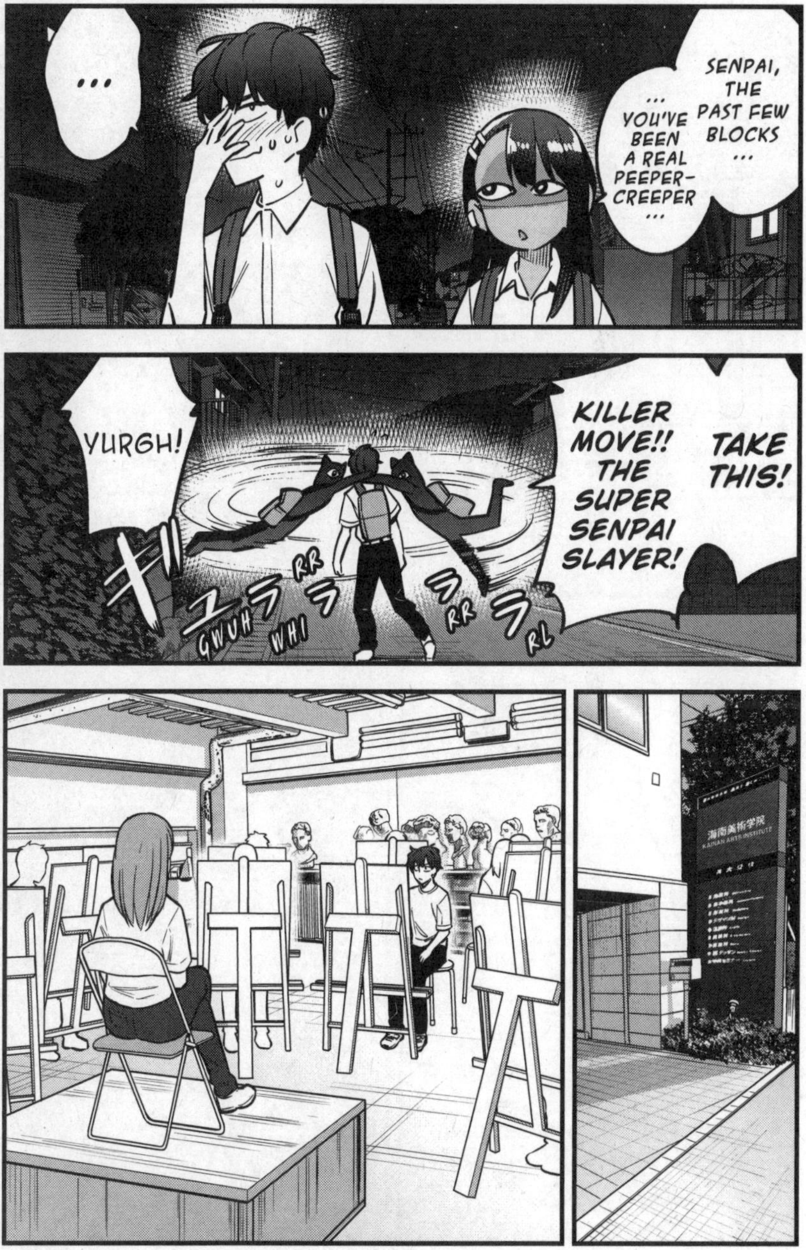
SENPAI, THE PAST FEW BLOCKS ...
... YOU'VE BEEN A REAL PEEPER-CREEPER ...
...
TAKE THIS!
KILLER MOVE!! THE SUPER SENPAI SLAYER!
YURGH!
RL
RR
WHI
RR
GWUH
海南美術学院
KAINAN ARTS INSTITUTE

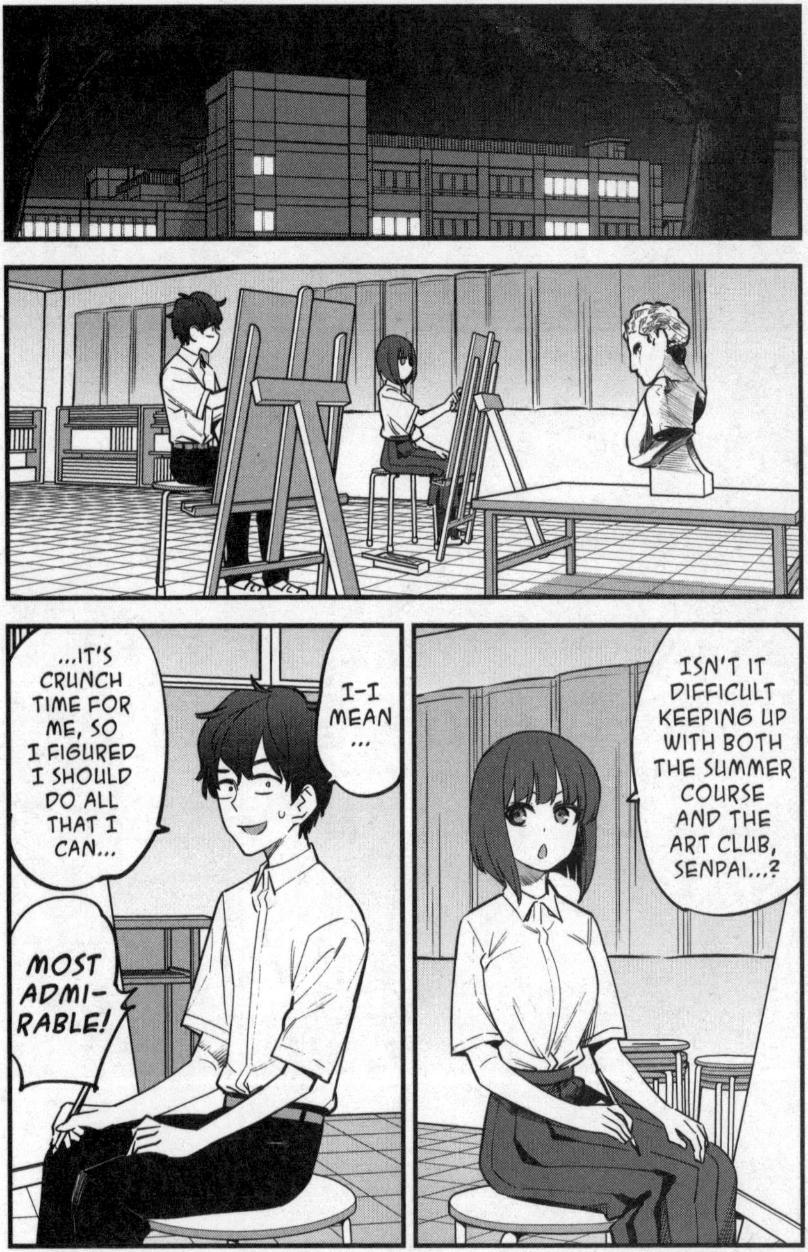
ISN'T IT DIFFICULT KEEPING UP WITH BOTH THE SUMMER COURSE AND THE ART CLUB, SENPAI...?
I-I MEAN ...
...IT'S CRUNCH TIME FOR ME, SO I FIGURED I SHOULD DO ALL THAT I CAN...
MOST ADMI-RABLE!

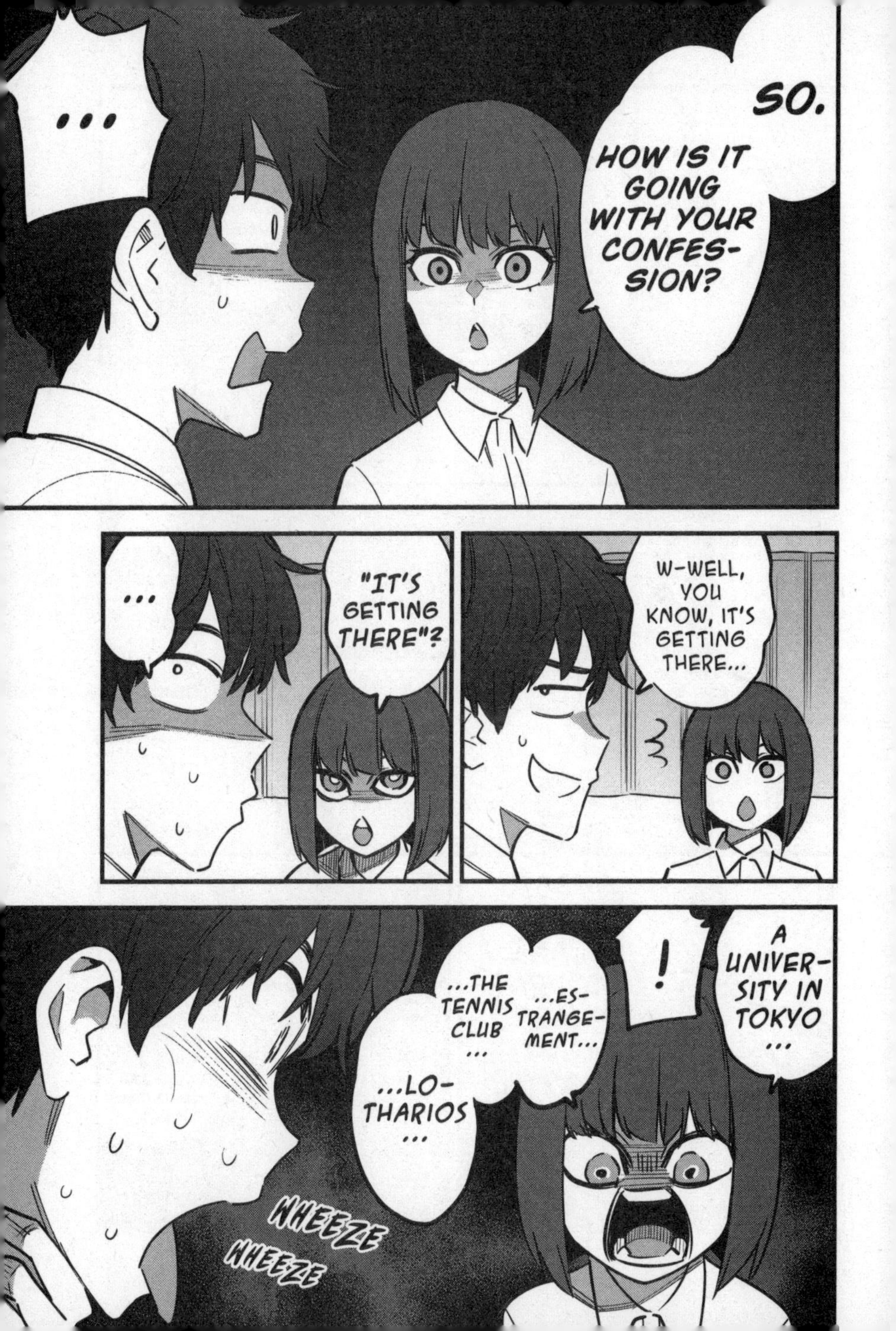
SO.
HOW IS IT GOING WITH YOUR CONFESSION?
...
W-WELL, YOU KNOW, IT'S GETTING THERE...
"IT'S GETTING THERE"?
...
A UNIVERSITY IN TOKYO ...
!
...ESTRANGEMENT...
...THE TENNIS CLUB ...
...LOTHARIOS ...
WHEEZE
WHEEZE

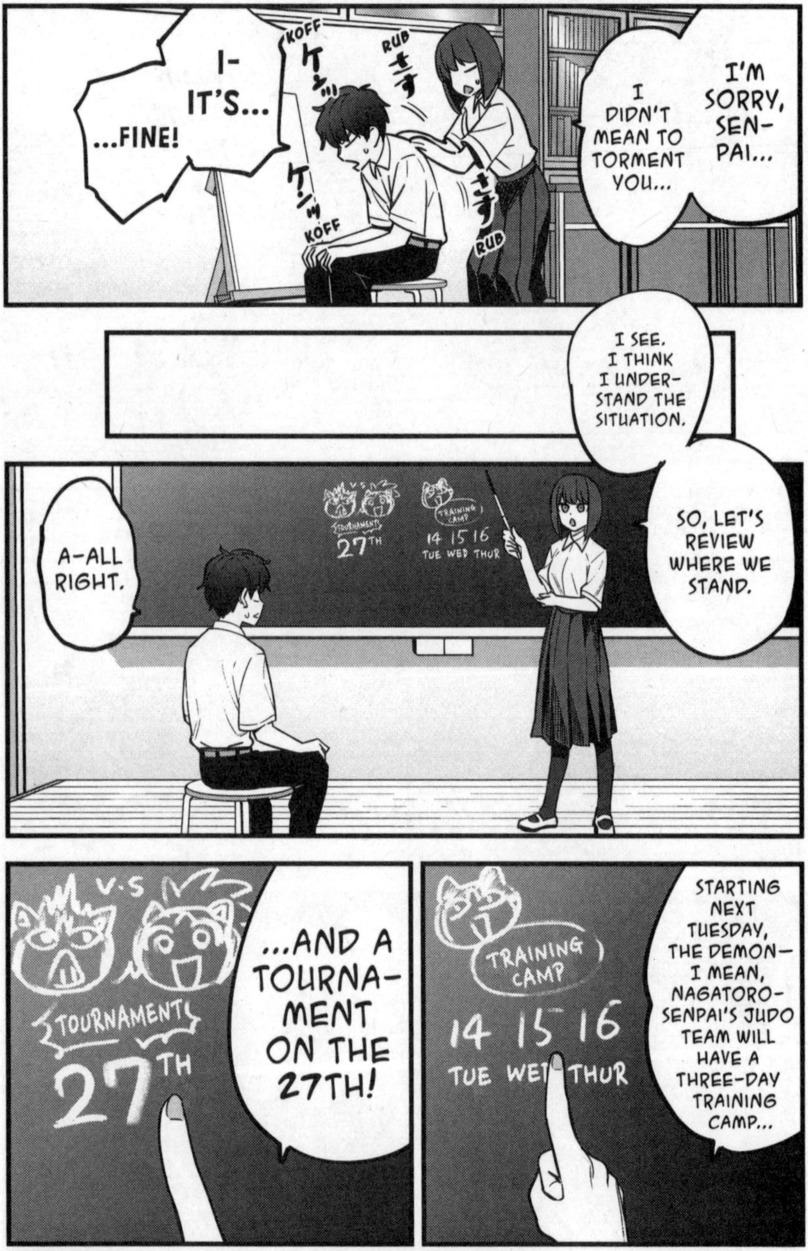
I'M SORRY, SEN-PAI...
I DIDN'T MEAN TO TORMENT YOU...
RUB
RUB
KOFF
KOFF
I- IT'S...
...FINE!
I SEE. I THINK I UNDER-STAND THE SITUATION.
SO, LET'S REVIEW WHERE WE STAND.
TRAINING CAMP
14 15 16
TUE WED THUR
V.S
TOURNAMENT
27TH
A-ALL RIGHT.
STARTING NEXT TUESDAY, THE DEMON- I MEAN, NAGATORO-SENPAI'S JUDO TEAM WILL HAVE A THREE-DAY TRAINING CAMP...
TRAINING CAMP
14 15 16
TUE WE THUR
...AND A TOURNA-MENT ON THE 27TH!
V.S
TOURNAMENT
27TH

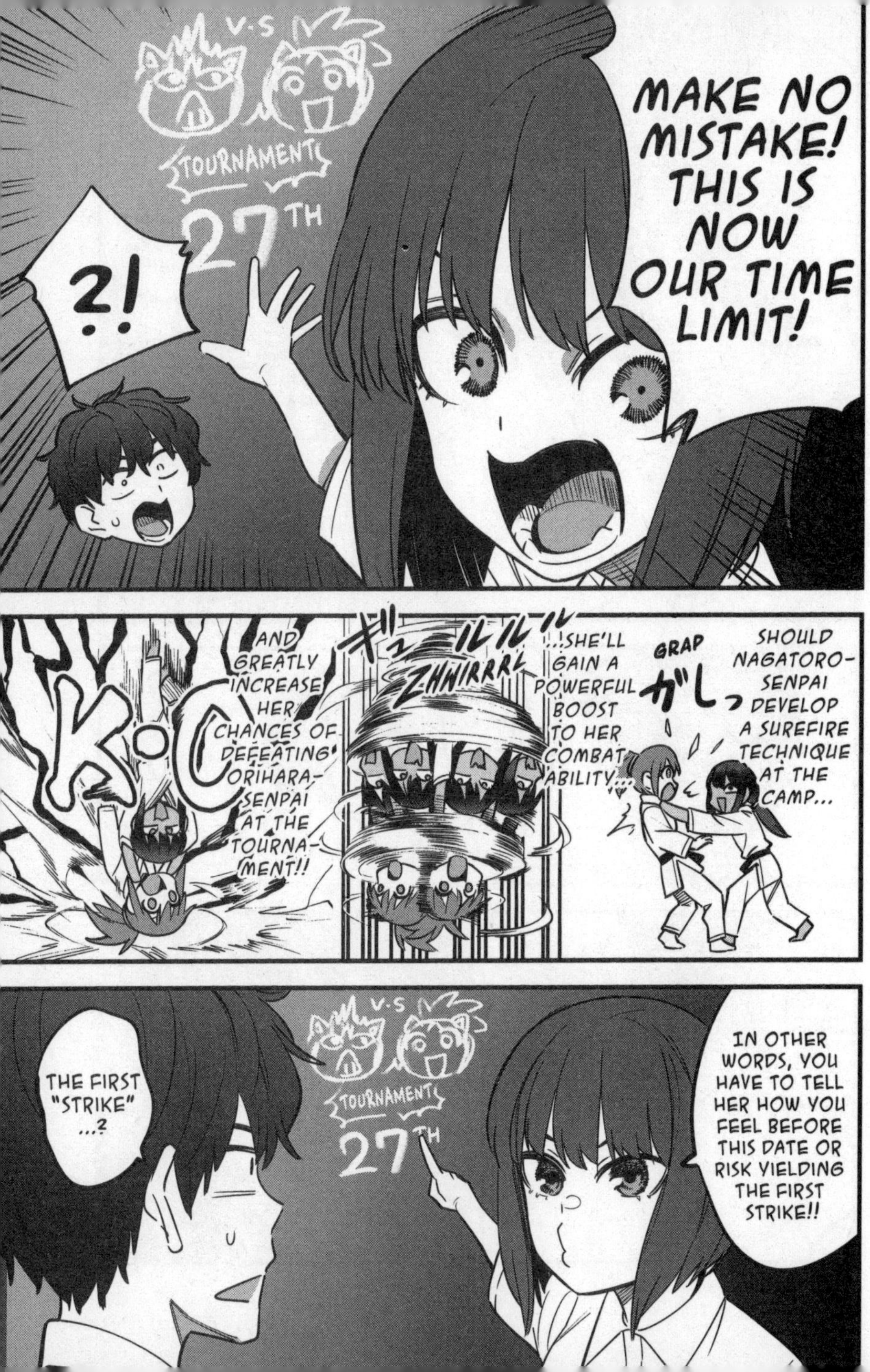
MAKE NO MISTAKE! THIS IS NOW OUR TIME LIMIT!
V.S TOURNAMENT 27TH
?!
SHOULD NAGATORO-SENPAI DEVELOP A SUREFIRE TECHNIQUE AT THE CAMP...
GRAP
がしっ
...SHE'LL GAIN A POWERFUL BOOST TO HER COMBAT ABILITY...
ギュルルル
ZHWIRRRL
AND GREATLY INCREASE HER CHANCES OF DEFEATING ORIHARA-SENPAI AT THE TOURNAMENT!!
K.O
IN OTHER WORDS, YOU HAVE TO TELL HER HOW YOU FEEL BEFORE THIS DATE OR RISK YIELDING THE FIRST STRIKE!!
V.S TOURNAMENT 27TH
THE FIRST "STRIKE" ...?

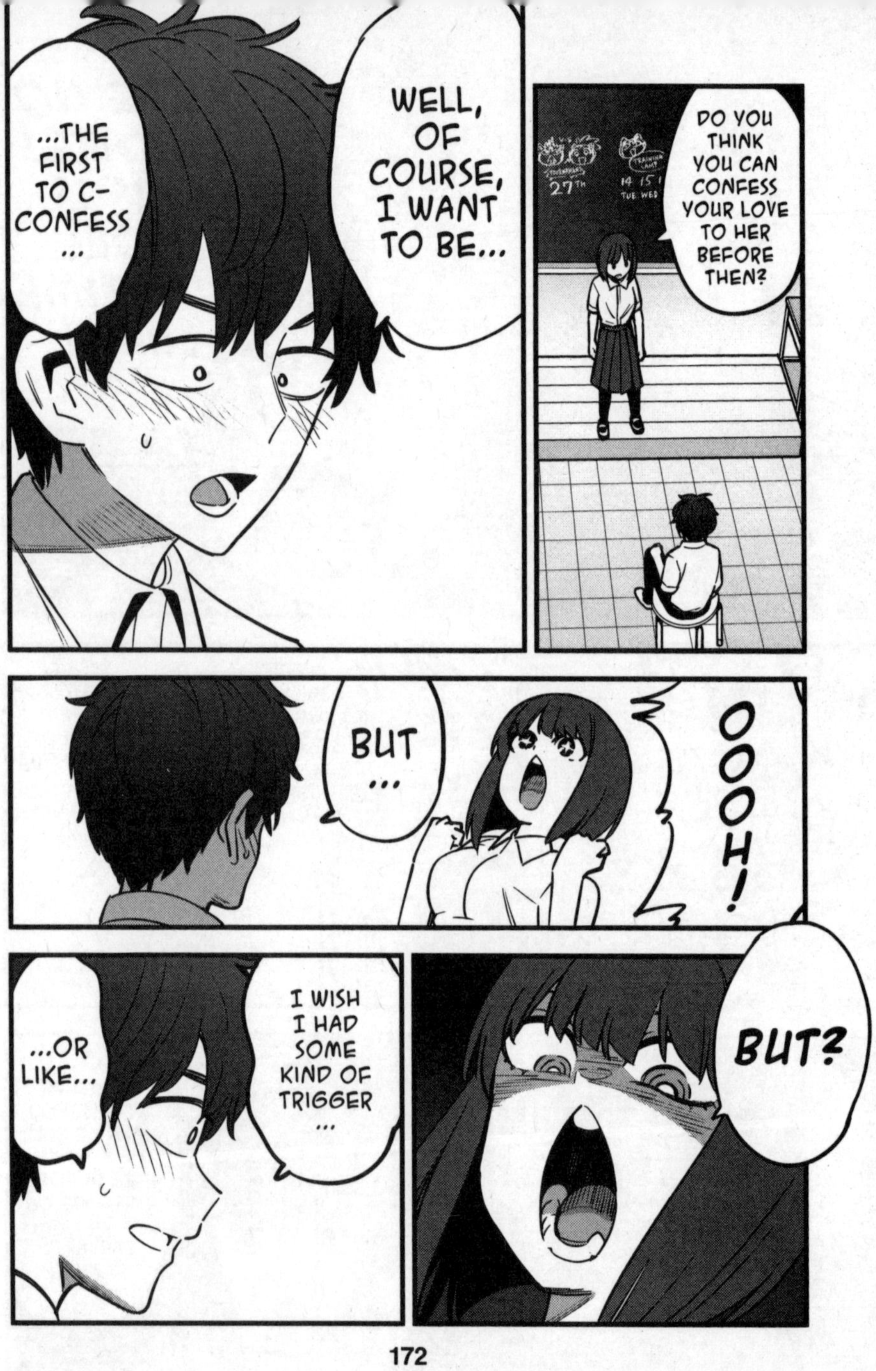
DO YOU THINK YOU CAN CONFESS YOUR LOVE TO HER BEFORE THEN?
WELL, OF COURSE, I WANT TO BE...
...THE FIRST TO C-CONFESS...
OOOOH!
BUT...
BUT?
I WISH I HAD SOME KIND OF TRIGGER...
...OR LIKE...

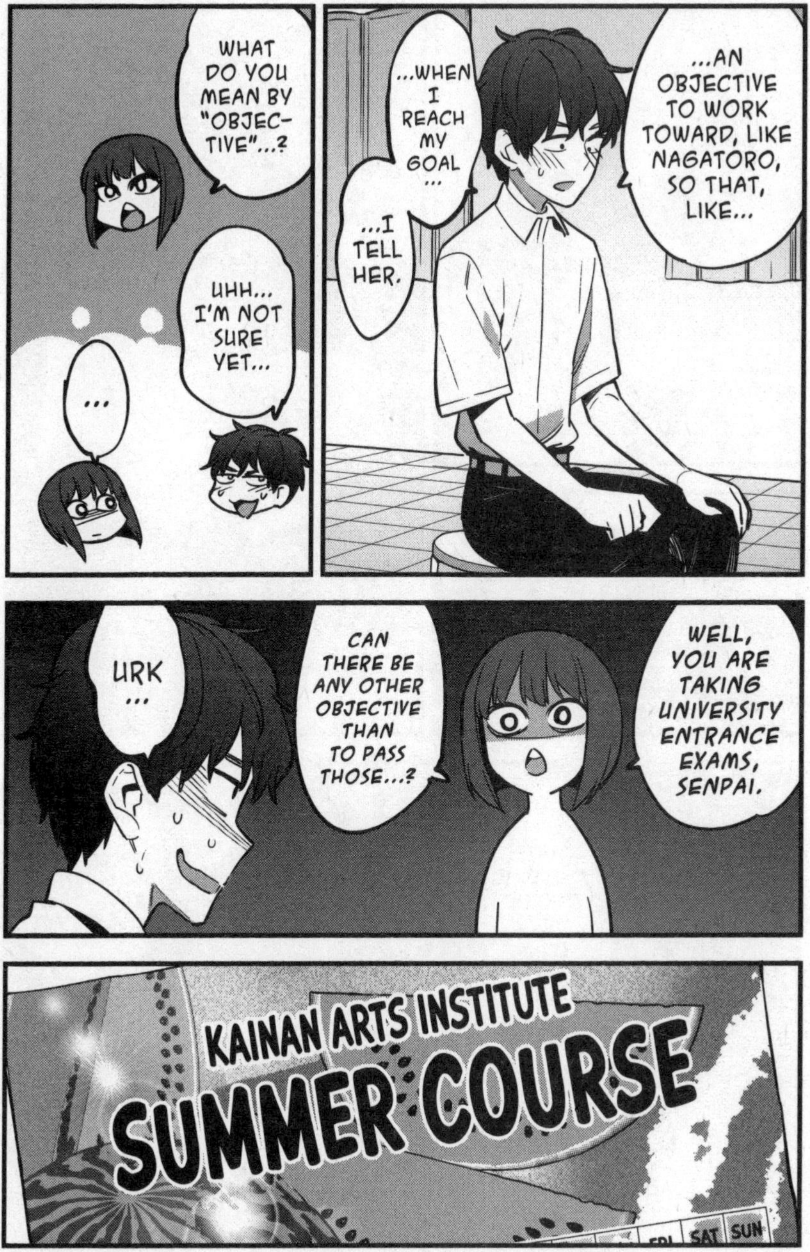
...AN OBJECTIVE TO WORK TOWARD, LIKE NAGATORO, SO THAT, LIKE...
...WHEN I REACH MY GOAL...
...I TELL HER.
WHAT DO YOU MEAN BY "OBJECTIVE"...?
UHH... I'M NOT SURE YET...
...
WELL, YOU ARE TAKING UNIVERSITY ENTRANCE EXAMS, SENPAI.
CAN THERE BE ANY OTHER OBJECTIVE THAN TO PASS THOSE...?
URK...
KAINAN ARTS INSTITUTE
SUMMER COURSE
FRI SAT SUN

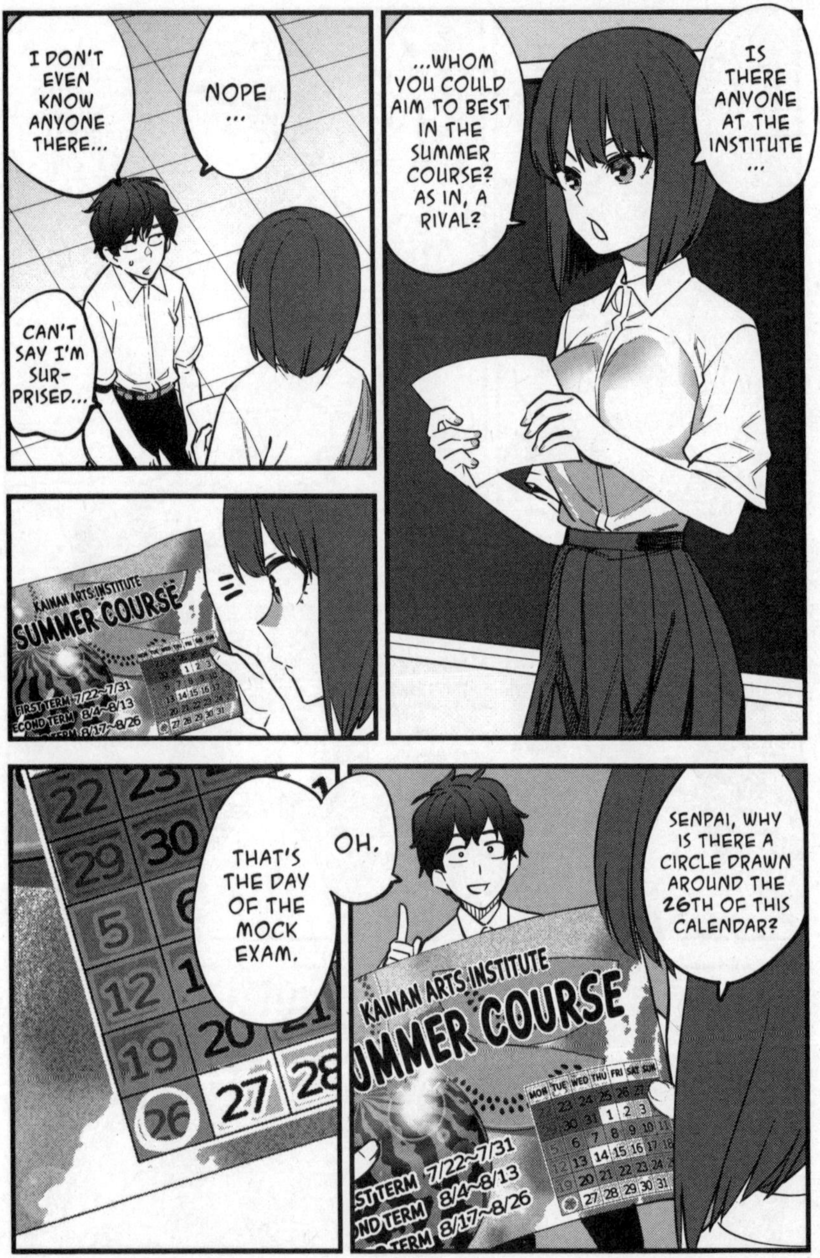
IS THERE ANYONE AT THE INSTITUTE...
...WHOM YOU COULD AIM TO BEST IN THE SUMMER COURSE? AS IN, A RIVAL?
NOPE...
I DON'T EVEN KNOW ANYONE THERE...
CAN'T SAY I'M SURPRISED...
KAINAN ARTS INSTITUTE
SUMMER COURSE
FIRST TERM 7/22~7/31
SENPAI, WHY IS THERE A CIRCLE DRAWN AROUND THE 26TH OF THIS CALENDAR?
OH.
THAT'S THE DAY OF THE MOCK EXAM.
KAINAN ARTS INSTITUTE

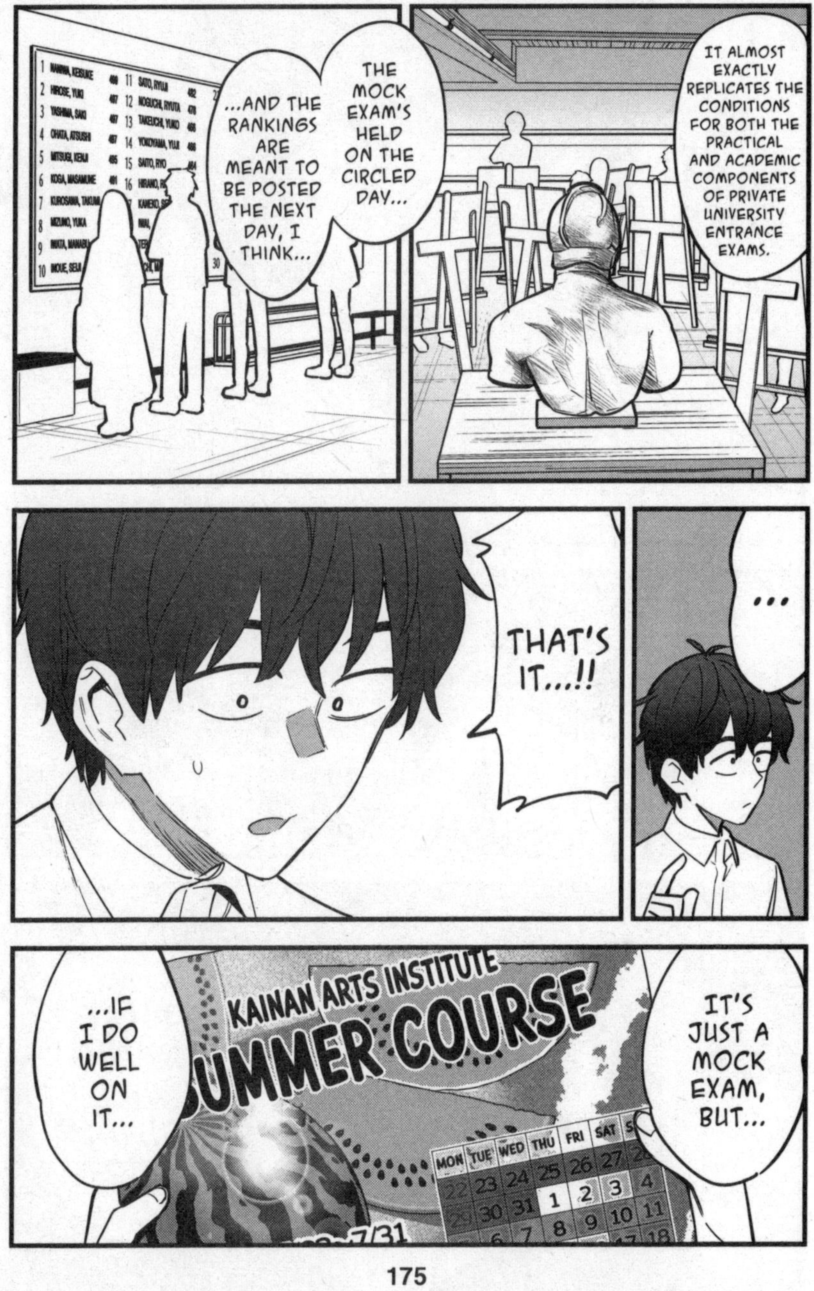
IT ALMOST EXACTLY REPLICATES THE CONDITIONS FOR BOTH THE PRACTICAL AND ACADEMIC COMPONENTS OF PRIVATE UNIVERSITY ENTRANCE EXAMS.
THE MOCK EXAM'S HELD ON THE CIRCLED DAY...
...AND THE RANKINGS ARE MEANT TO BE POSTED THE NEXT DAY, I THINK...
...
THAT'S IT...!!
IT'S JUST A MOCK EXAM, BUT...
KAINAN ARTS INSTITUTE
SUMMER COURSE
...IF I DO WELL ON IT...

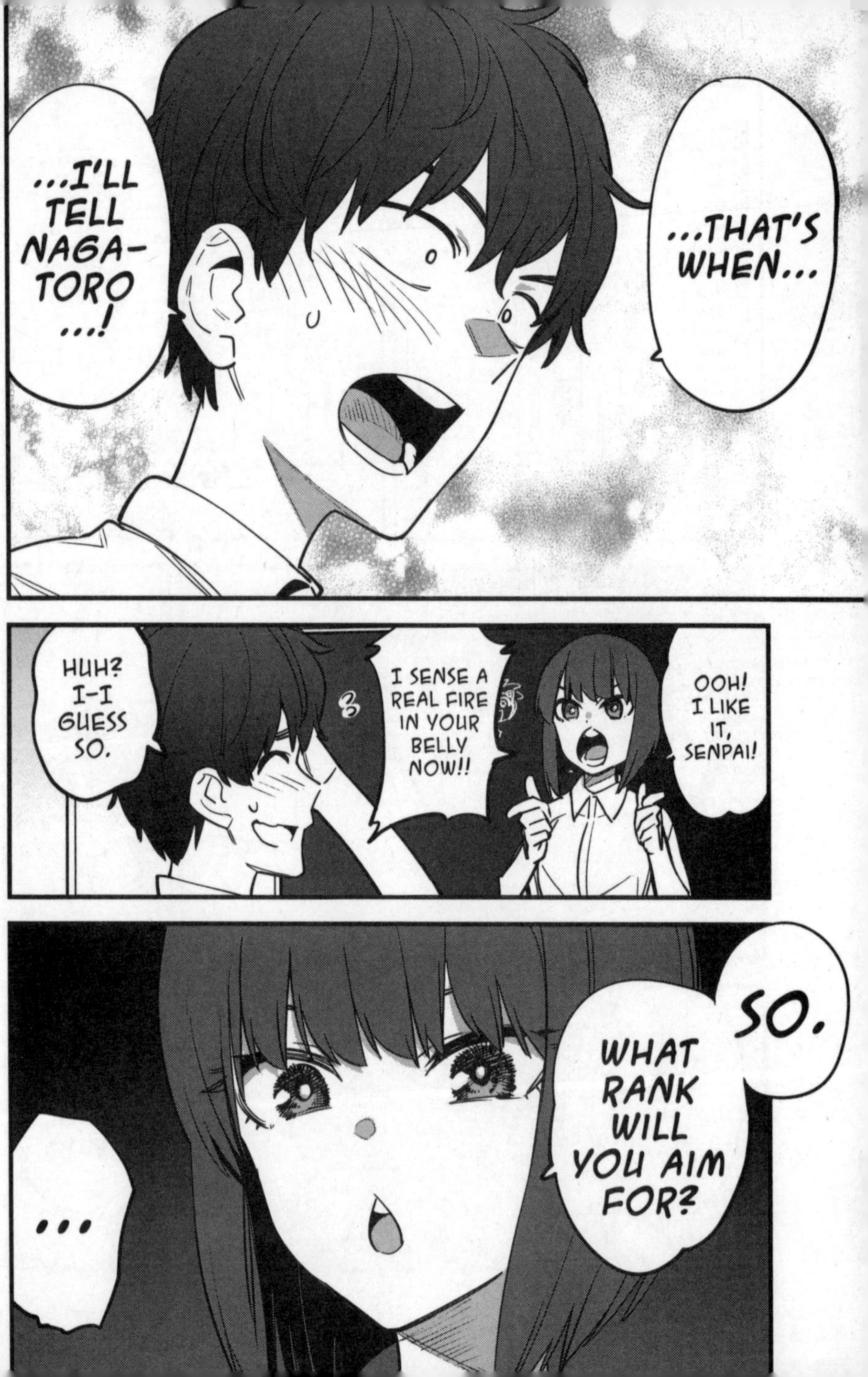
...THAT'S WHEN...
...I'LL TELL NAGA-TORO...!
OOH! I LIKE IT, SENPAI!
I SENSE A REAL FIRE IN YOUR BELLY NOW!!
HUH? I-I GUESS SO.
SO.
WHAT RANK WILL YOU AIM FOR?
...

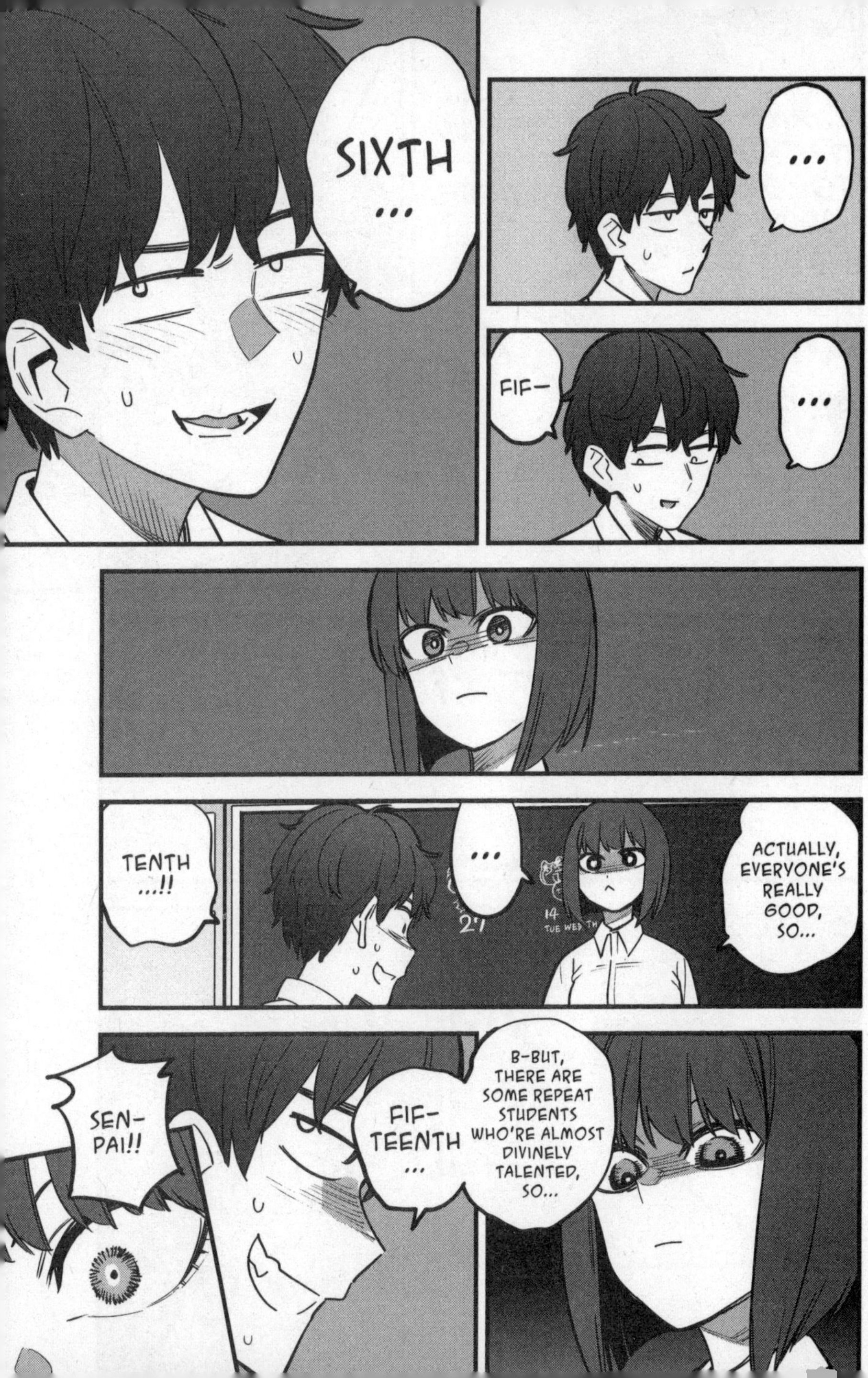
...
...
FIF—
SIXTH ...
ACTUALLY, EVERYONE'S REALLY GOOD, SO...
...
TENTH ...!!
B-BUT, THERE ARE SOME REPEAT STUDENTS WHO'RE ALMOST DIVINELY TALENTED, SO...
FIF-TEENTH ...
SEN-PAI!!

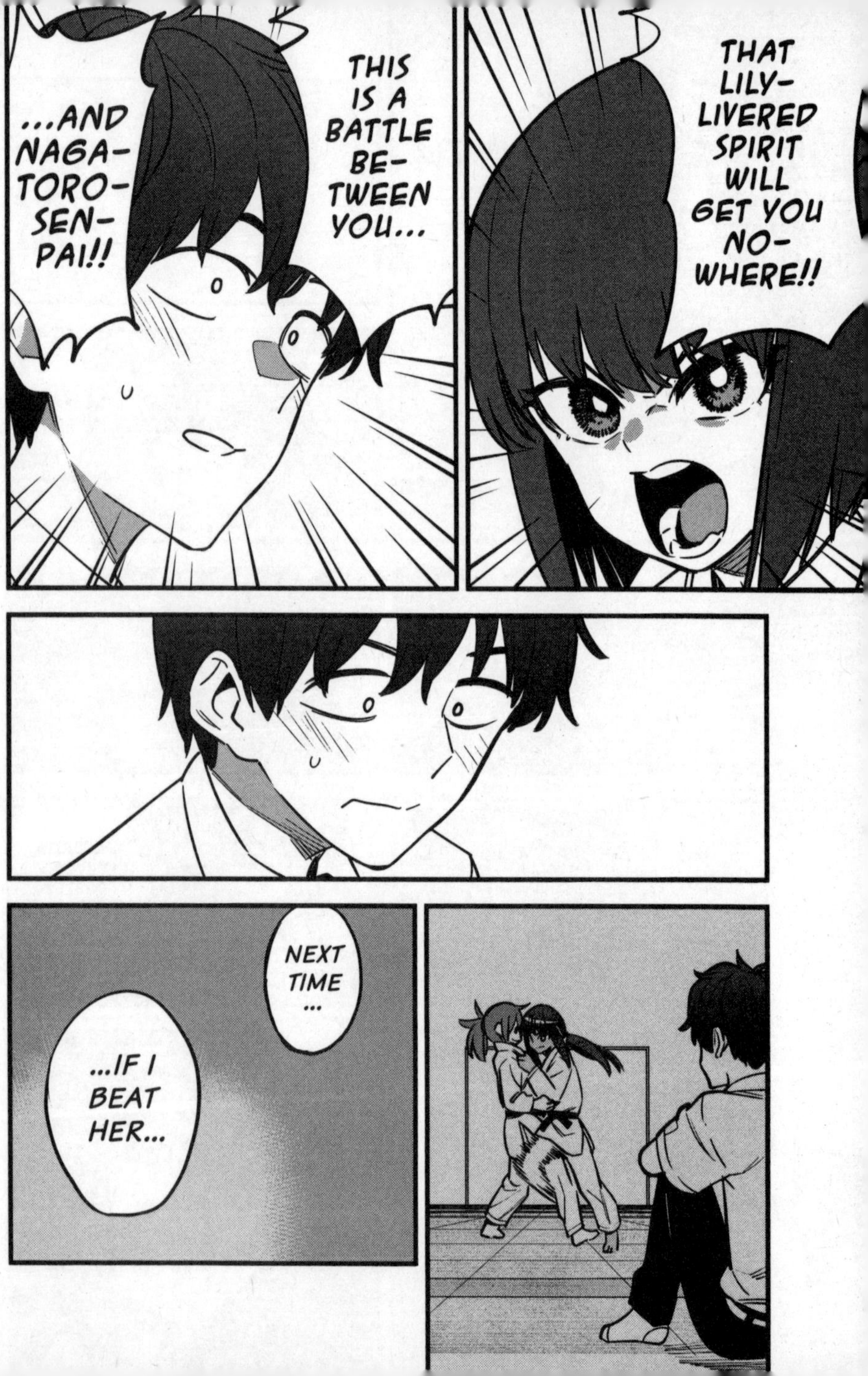
THAT LILY-LIVERED SPIRIT WILL GET YOU NOWHERE!!
THIS IS A BATTLE BETWEEN YOU...
...AND NAGATORO-SENPAI!!
NEXT TIME...
...IF I BEAT HER...

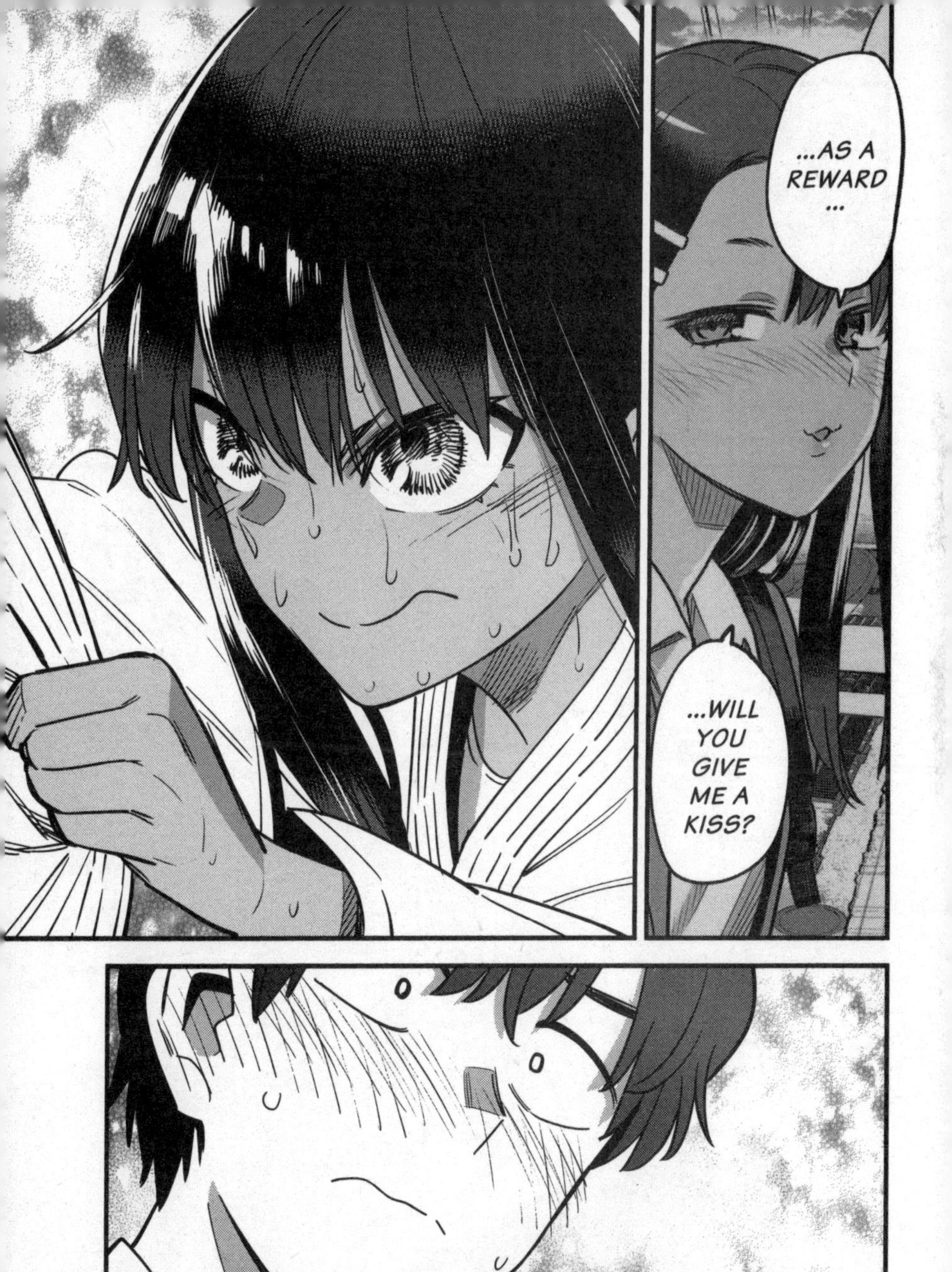
...AS A REWARD ...
...WILL YOU GIVE ME A KISS?

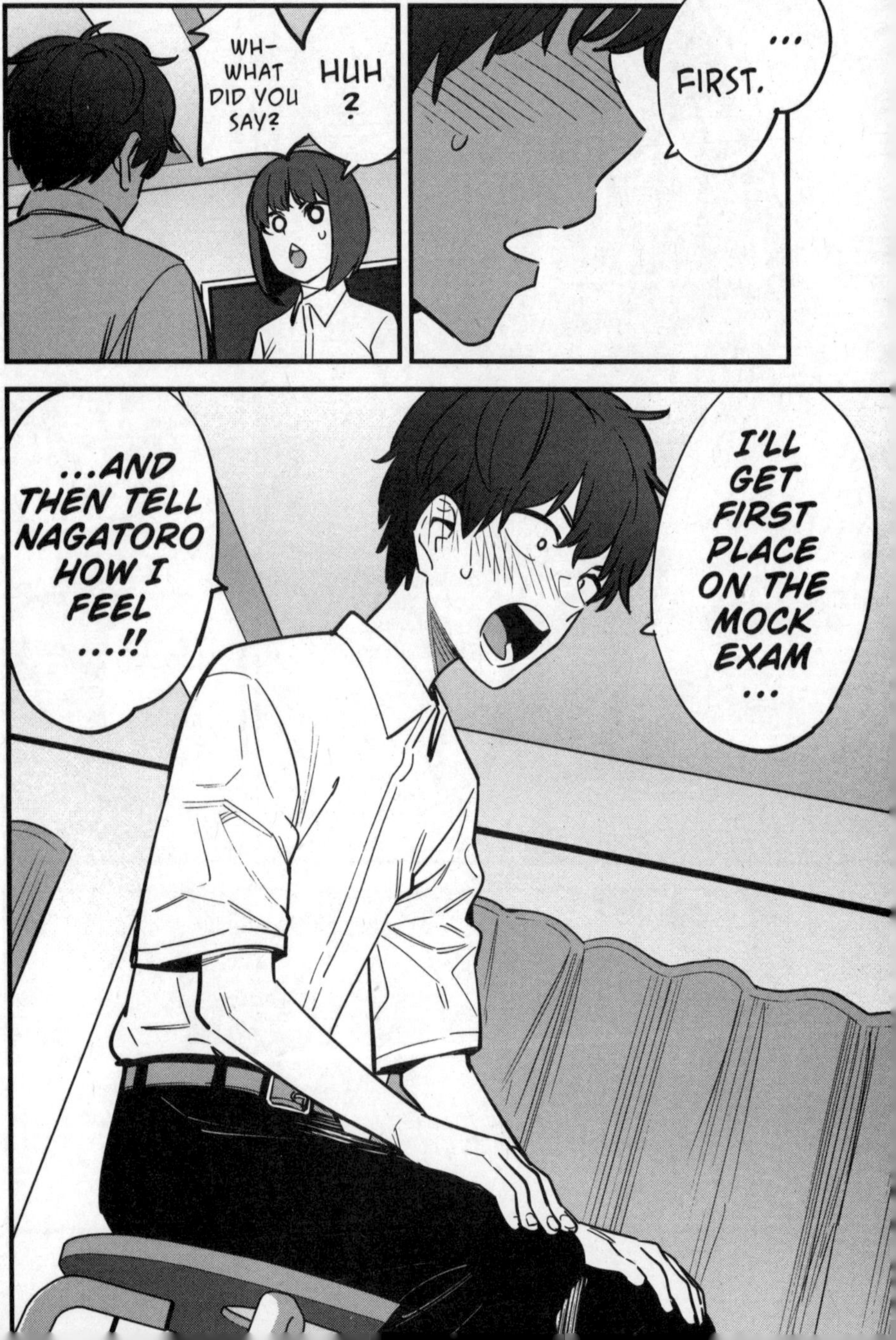
... FIRST.
HUH?
WH-WHAT DID YOU SAY?
I'LL GET FIRST PLACE ON THE MOCK EXAM...
...AND THEN TELL NAGATORO HOW I FEEL...!!

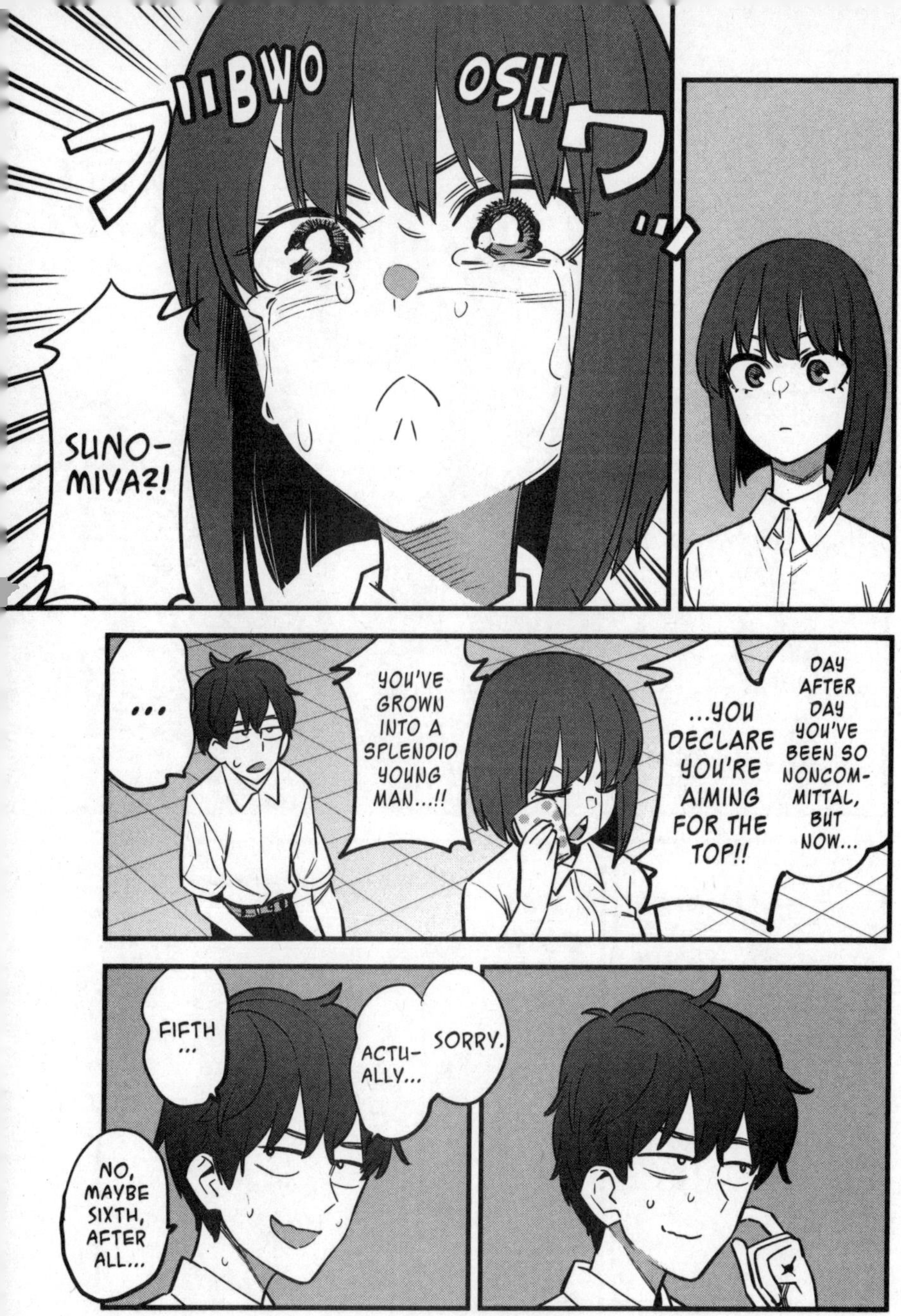
BWOOSH
SUNO-MIYA?!
DAY AFTER DAY YOU'VE BEEN SO NONCOM-MITTAL, BUT NOW...
...YOU DECLARE YOU'RE AIMING FOR THE TOP!!
YOU'VE GROWN INTO A SPLENDID YOUNG MAN...!!
...
SORRY.
ACTU-ALLY...
FIFTH...
NO, MAYBE SIXTH, AFTER ALL...

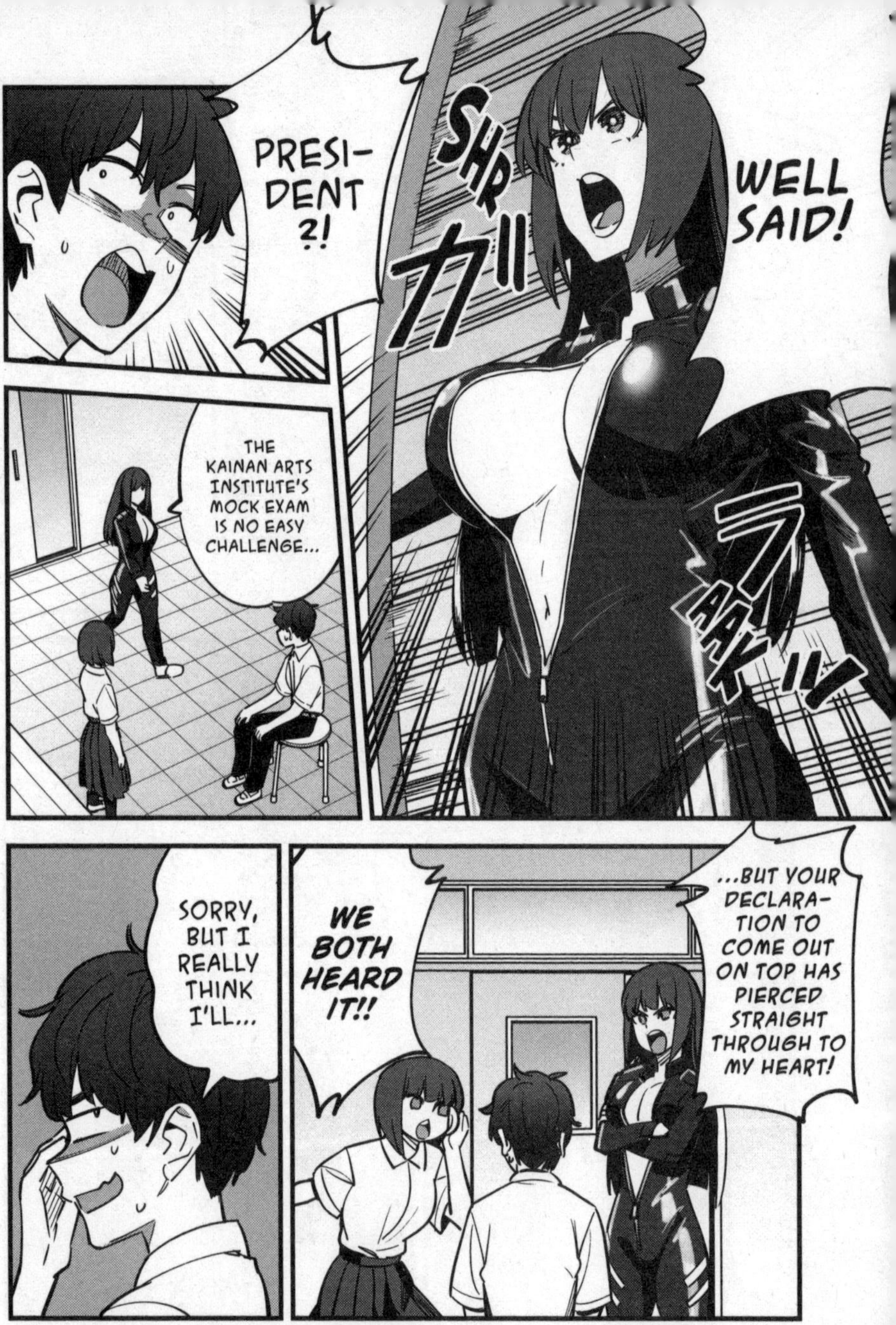
WELL SAID!
SHR
RAAK!!
PRESI-DENT?!
THE KAINAN ARTS INSTITUTE'S MOCK EXAM IS NO EASY CHALLENGE...
...BUT YOUR DECLARATION TO COME OUT ON TOP HAS PIERCED STRAIGHT THROUGH TO MY HEART!
WE BOTH HEARD IT!!
SORRY, BUT I REALLY THINK I'LL...

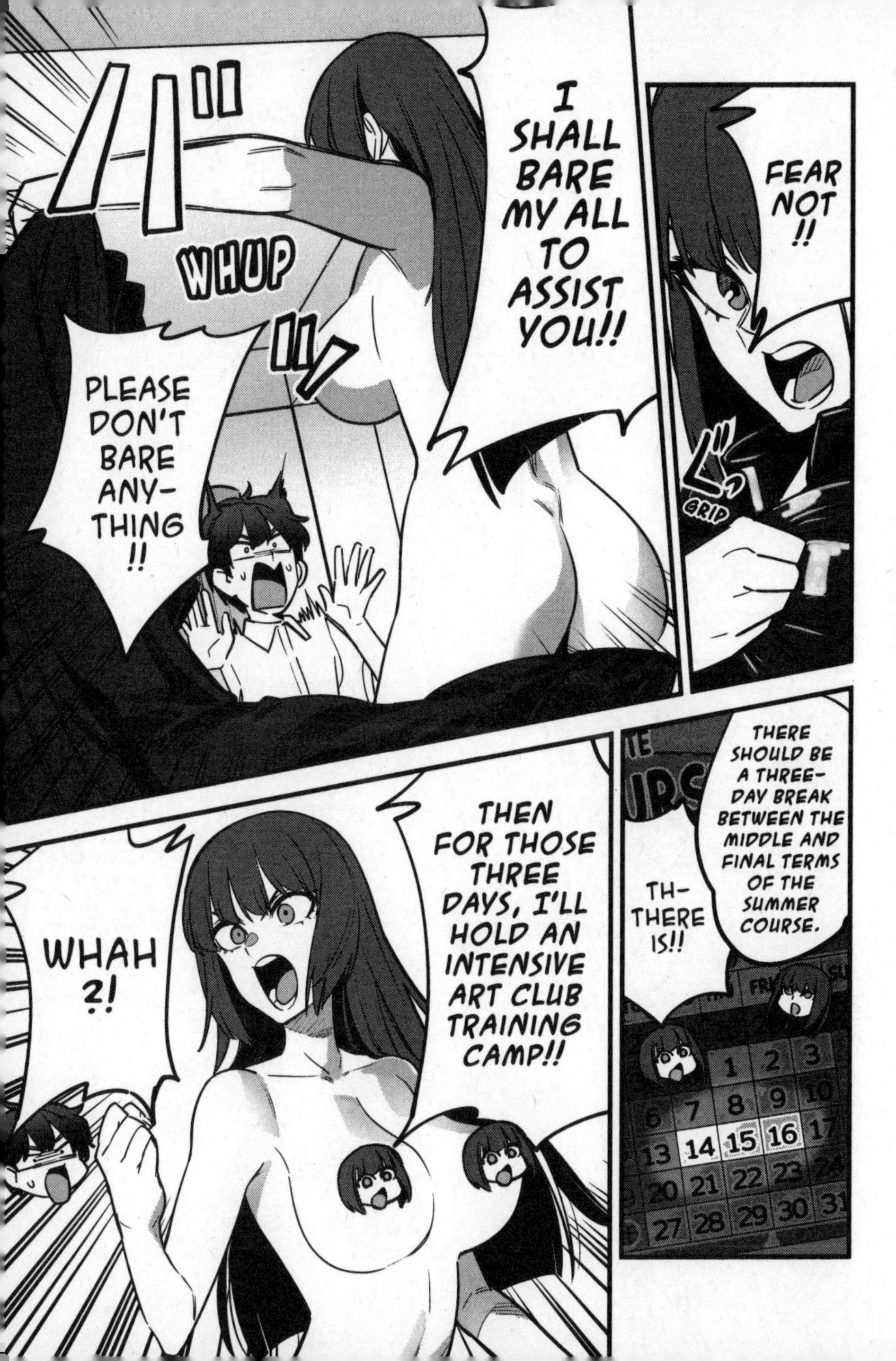
FEAR NOT!!
GRIP
I SHALL BARE MY ALL TO ASSIST YOU!!
WHUP
PLEASE DON'T BARE ANYTHING!!
THERE SHOULD BE A THREE-DAY BREAK BETWEEN THE MIDDLE AND FINAL TERMS OF THE SUMMER COURSE.
TH-THERE IS!!
THEN FOR THOSE THREE DAYS, I'LL HOLD AN INTENSIVE ART CLUB TRAINING CAMP!!
WHAH?!

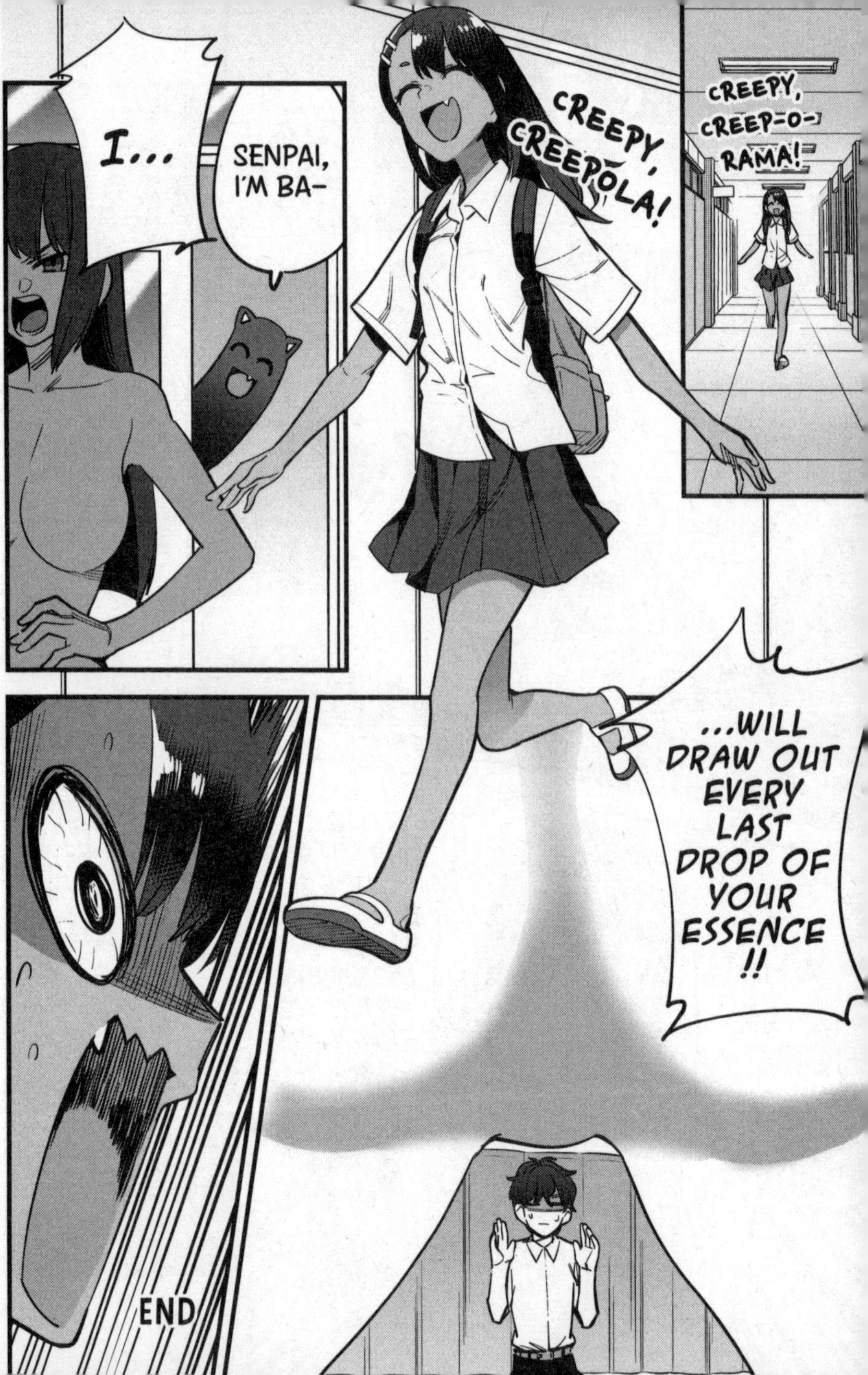
CREEPY, CREEP-O-RAMA!
CREEPY, CREEPOLA!
SENPAI, I'M BA-
I...
...WILL DRAW OUT EVERY LAST DROP OF YOUR ESSENCE!!
END

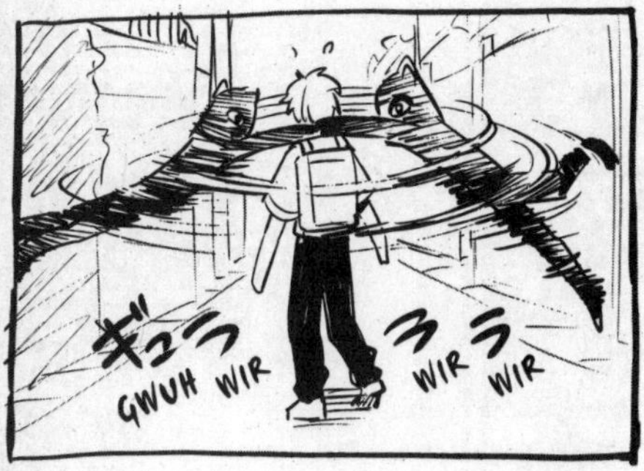
ラ
WIR
ラ
WIR
ギュラ
GWUH WIR

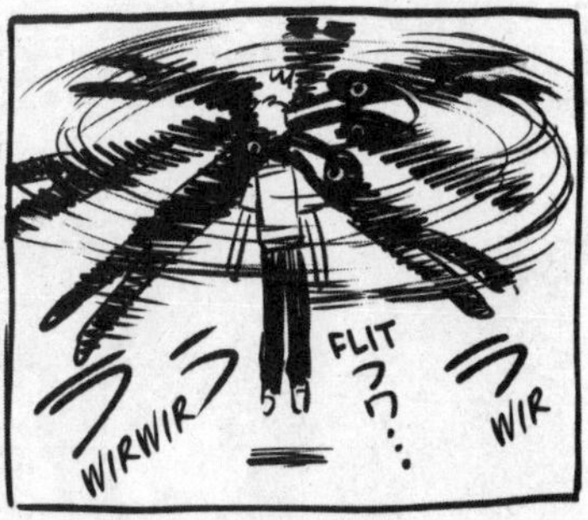
ラ
WIR
FLIT
フワ…
ララ
WIRWIR

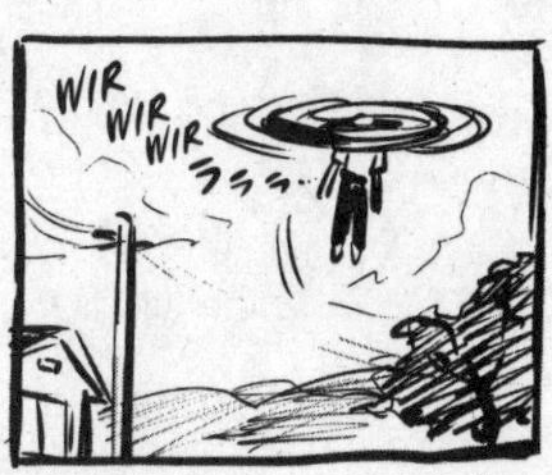
WIR
WIR
WIR
ララ…

BONUS: WOULD YOU...CARE TO STRIP FOR ME...?

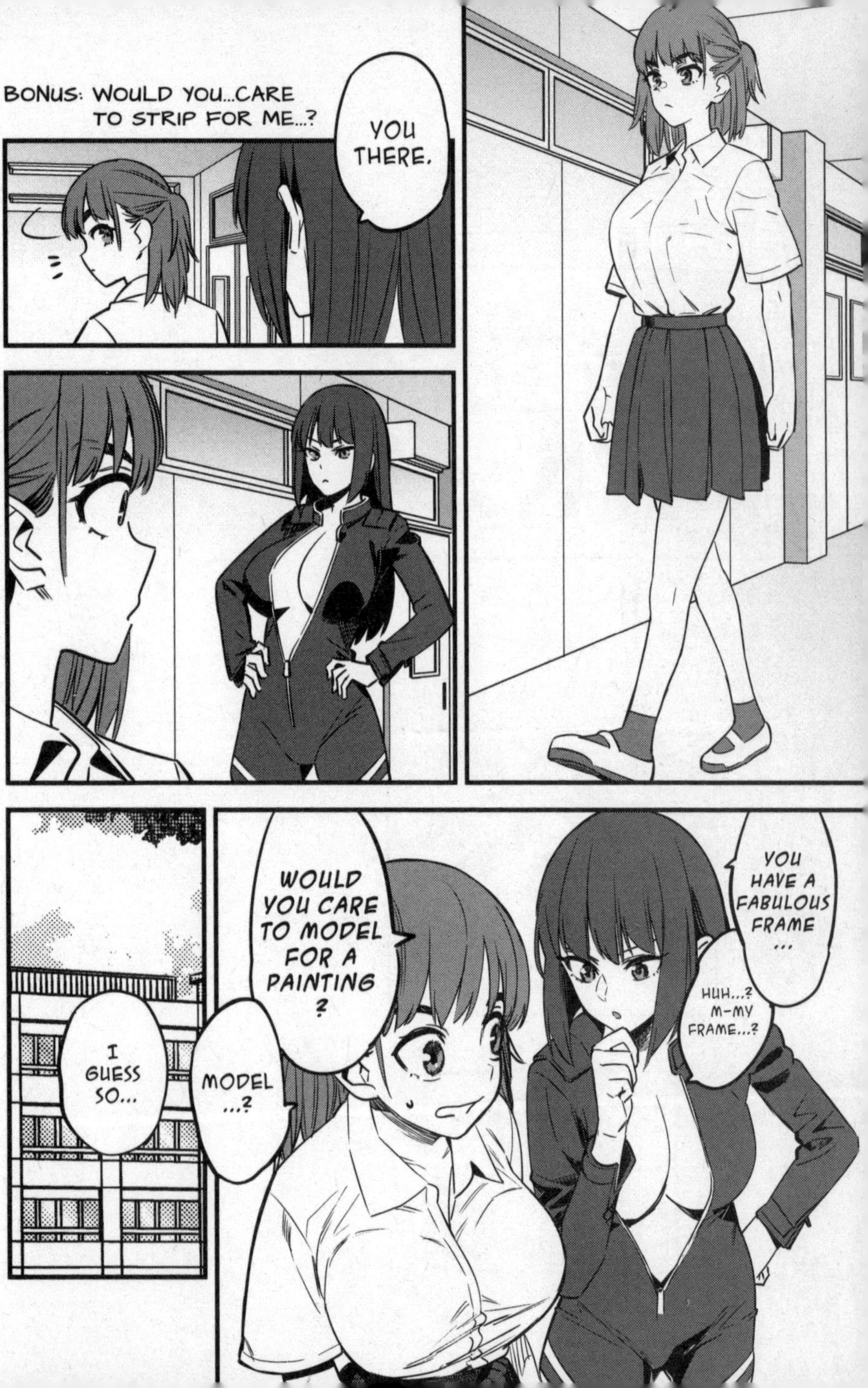

YOU THERE.
YOU HAVE A FABULOUS FRAME ...
HUH...? M-MY FRAME...?
WOULD YOU CARE TO MODEL FOR A PAINTING ?
MODEL ...?
I GUESS SO...

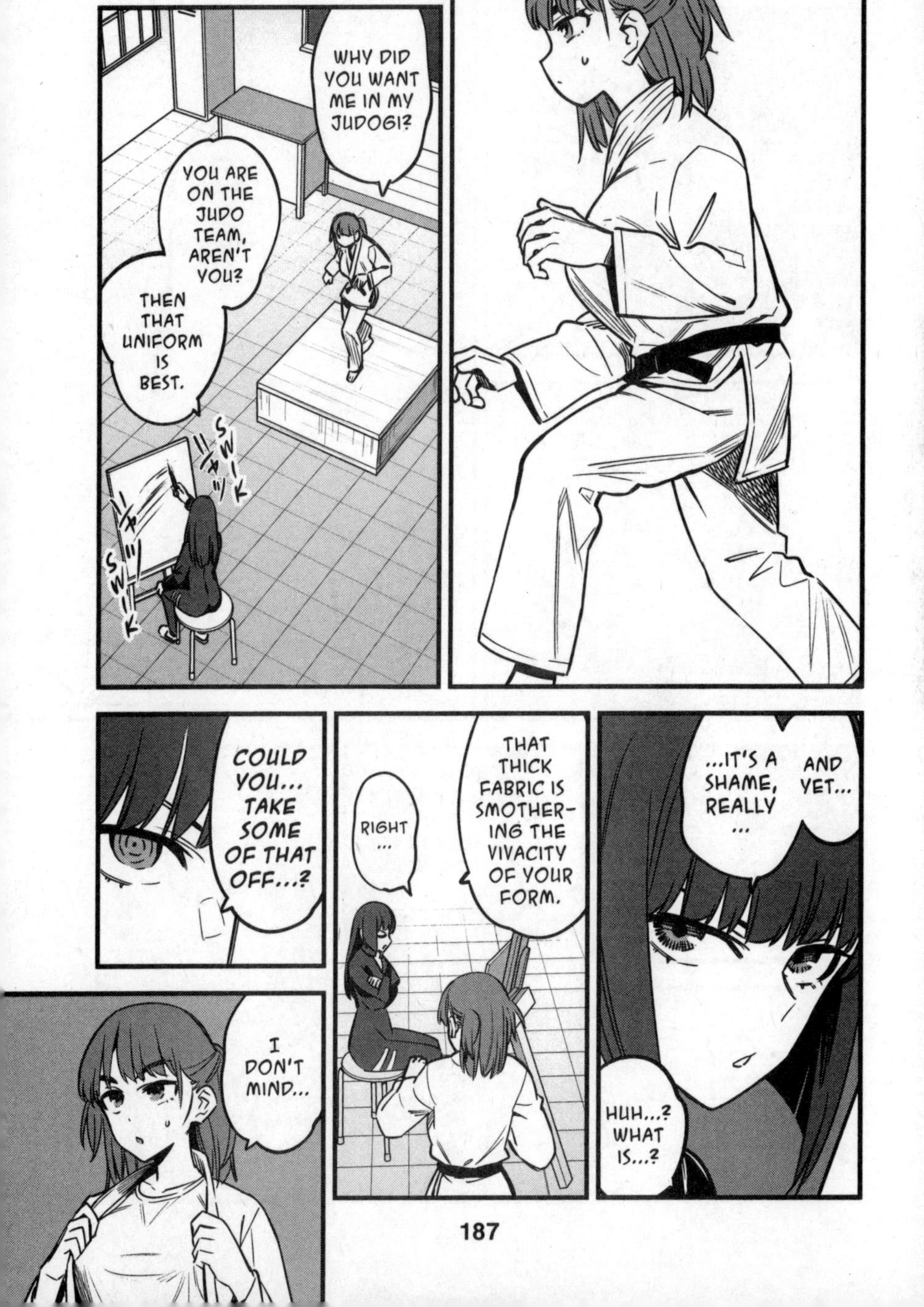
WHY DID YOU WANT ME IN MY JUDOGI?
YOU ARE ON THE JUDO TEAM, AREN'T YOU?
THEN THAT UNIFORM IS BEST.
SWIK
SWIK
AND YET...
...IT'S A SHAME, REALLY...
HUH...? WHAT IS...?
THAT THICK FABRIC IS SMOTHERING THE VIVACITY OF YOUR FORM.
RIGHT...
COULD YOU... TAKE SOME OF THAT OFF...?
I DON'T MIND...

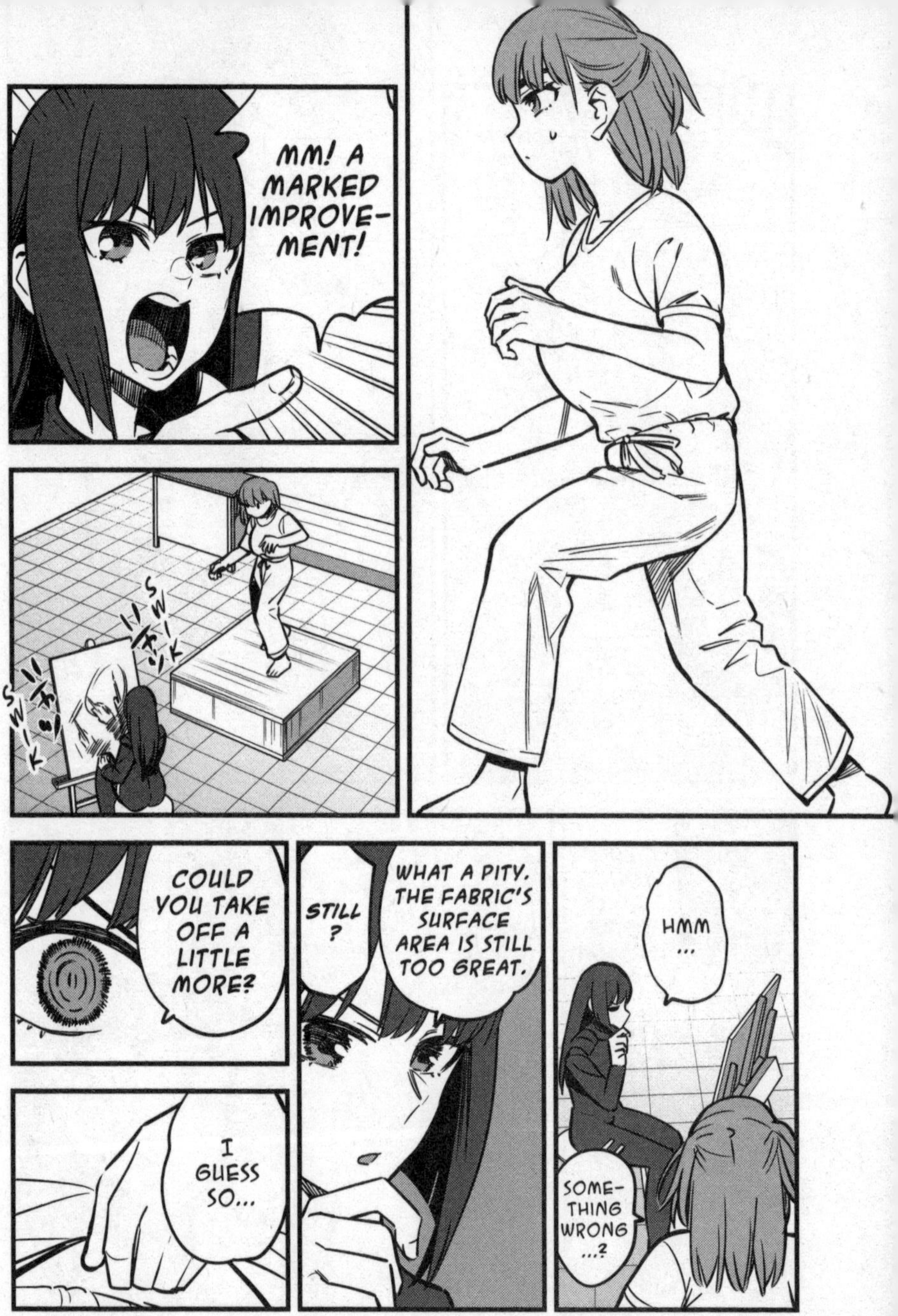
MM! A MARKED IMPROVE-MENT!
SWIK
SWIK
HMM...
SOME-THING WRONG...?
WHAT A PITY. THE FABRIC'S SURFACE AREA IS STILL TOO GREAT.
STILL?
COULD YOU TAKE OFF A LITTLE MORE?
I GUESS SO...

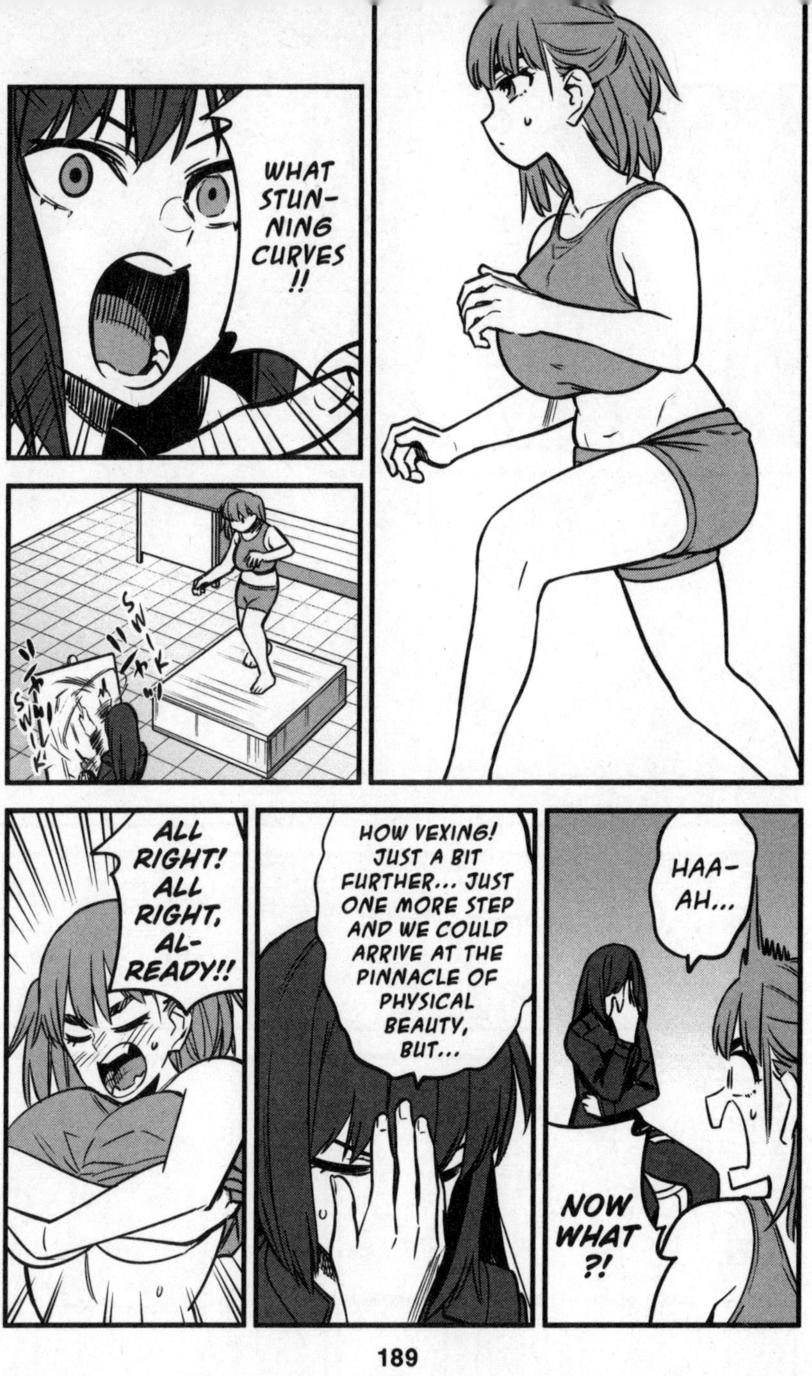
WHAT STUN-NING CURVES!!
SWIK
SWIK
HAA-AH...
NOW WHAT?!
HOW VEXING! JUST A BIT FURTHER... JUST ONE MORE STEP AND WE COULD ARRIVE AT THE PINNACLE OF PHYSICAL BEAUTY, BUT...
ALL RIGHT! ALL RIGHT, AL-READY!!

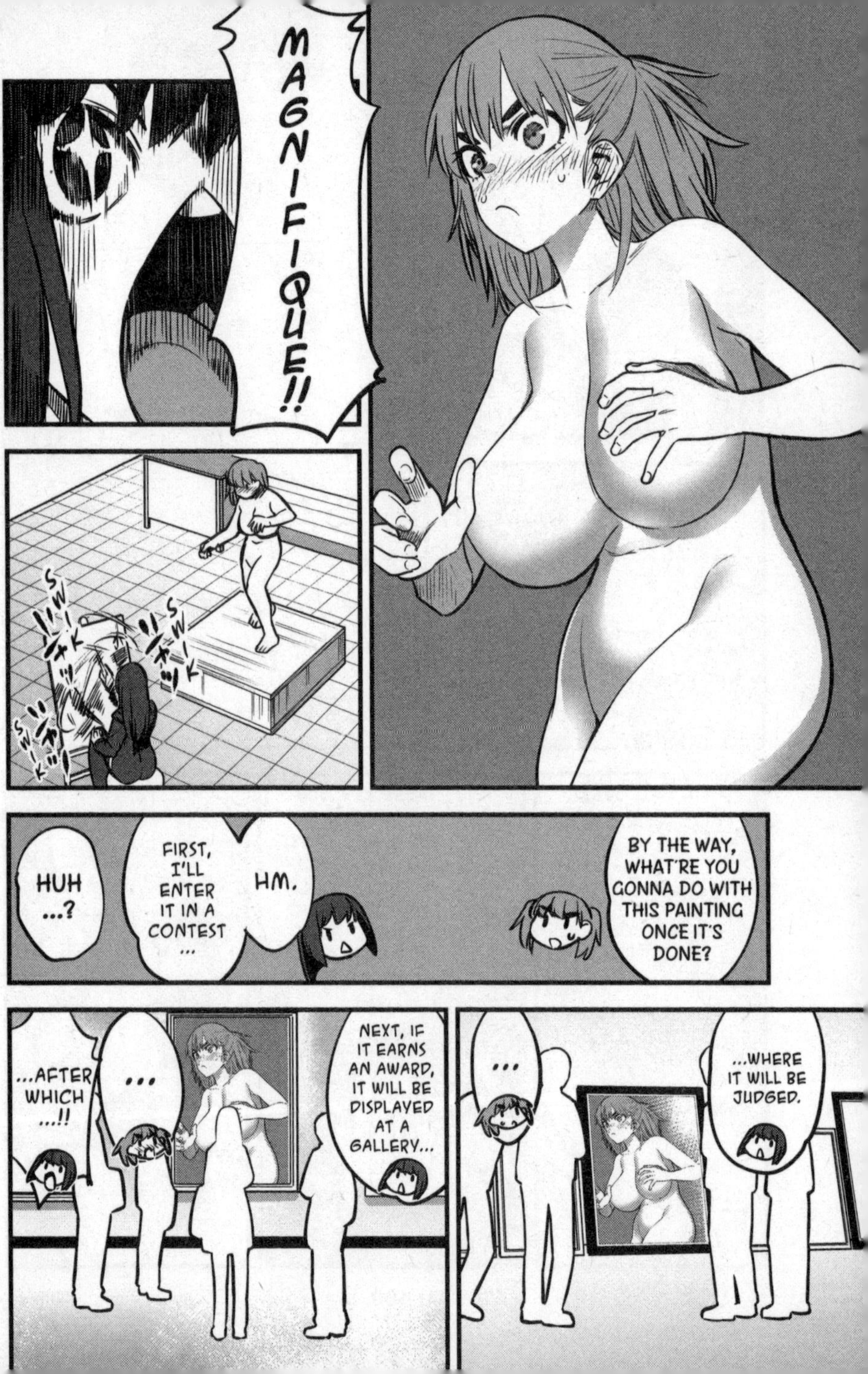
MAGNIFIQUE!!
SWIK
SWIK
SWIK
BY THE WAY, WHAT'RE YOU GONNA DO WITH THIS PAINTING ONCE IT'S DONE?
HM.
FIRST, I'LL ENTER IT IN A CONTEST...
HUH...?
...WHERE IT WILL BE JUDGED.
...
NEXT, IF IT EARNS AN AWARD, IT WILL BE DISPLAYED AT A GALLERY...
...
...AFTER WHICH...!!

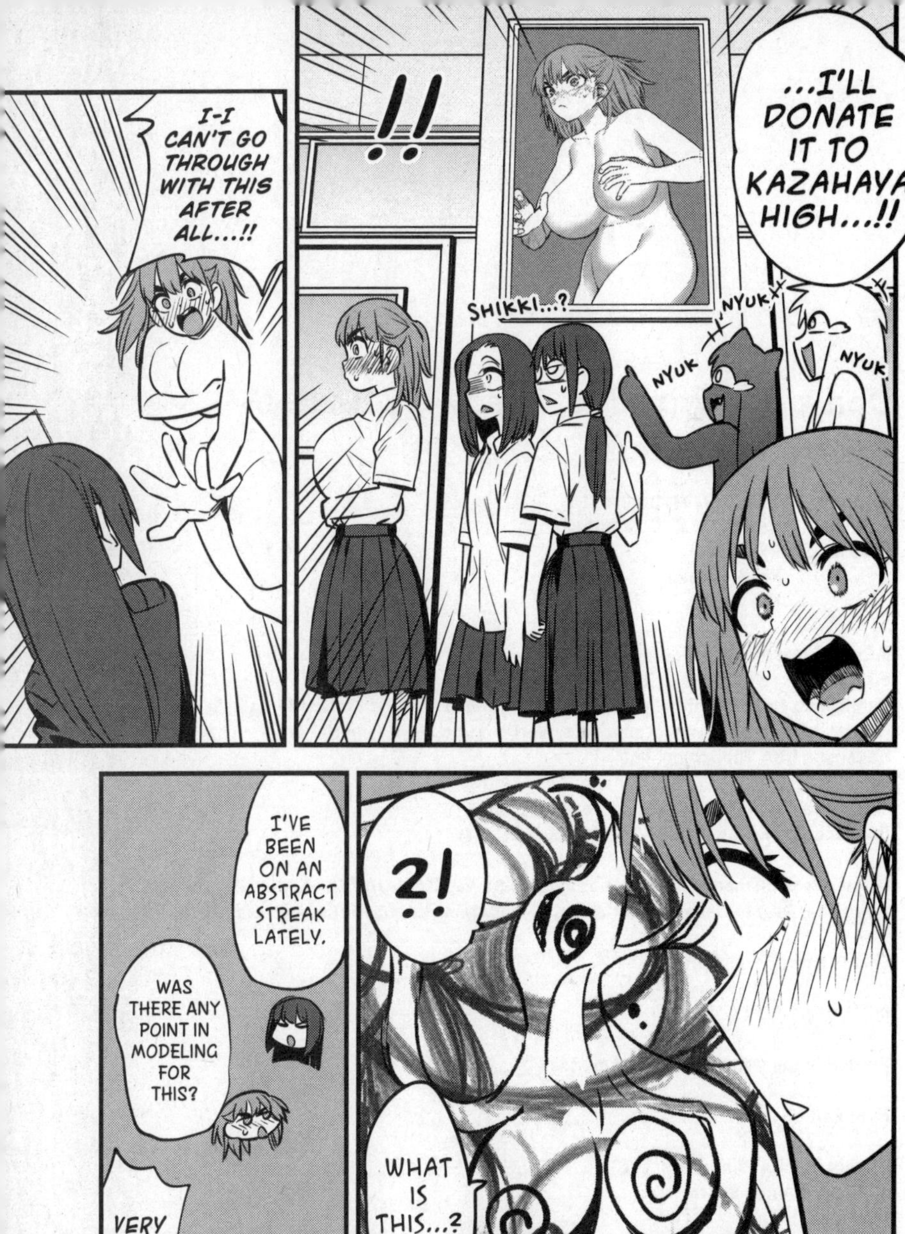
...I'LL DONATE IT TO KAZAHAYA HIGH...!!
NYUK
NYUK
NYUK
SHIKKI...?
!!
I-I CAN'T GO THROUGH WITH THIS AFTER ALL...!!
?!
WHAT IS THIS...?
I'VE BEEN ON AN ABSTRACT STREAK LATELY.
WAS THERE ANY POINT IN MODELING FOR THIS?
VERY MUCH SO!

END

Don't Toy With Me, Miss Nagatoro 15
A Vertical Comics Edition

Translation: Kumar Sivasubramanian
Editing: Alexandra McCullough-Garcia
Production: Risa Cho
            Pei Ann Yeap
            Eve Grandt

First published in Japan in 2023 by Kodansha, Ltd., Tokyo
Publication rights for this English edition arranged through Kodansha, Ltd., Tokyo
English language version produced by Vertical Comics, an imprint of
Kodansha USA Publishing, LLC

Translation provided by Vertical Comics, 2023
Published by Kodansha USA Publishing, LLC, New York

Originally published in Japanese as *Ijiranaide, Nagatorosan 15* by Kodansha, Ltd., 2023
Ijiranaide, Nagatorosan first serialized in *Magazine Poketto*, Kodansha, Ltd., 2017-

This is a work of fiction.

ISBN: 978-1-64729-226-3

Printed in the United States of America

First Edition

Kodansha USA Publishing, LLC
451 Park Avenue South
7th Floor
New York, NY 10016
www.kodansha.us

Vertical books are distributed through Penguin-Random House Publisher Services.